Monitoring Democracy

D1596722

Monitoring Democracy

WHEN INTERNATIONAL ELECTION OBSERVATION WORKS, AND WHY IT OFTEN FAILS

Judith G. Kelley

PRINCETON UNIVERSITY PRESS

PRINCETON AND OXFORD

Copyright © 2012 by Princeton University Press

Published by Princeton University Press, 41 William Street, Princeton, New Jersey 08540
In the United Kingdom: Princeton University Press, 6 Oxford Street, Woodstock, Oxfordshire OX20 1TW
press.princeton.edu

Cover photo: Haiti Elections, 2010. Taken by Ramon Espinosa, courtesy of AP Images.

All Rights Reserved

Library of Congress Cataloging-in-Publication Data
Kelley, Judith Green.
Monitoring democracy : when international election observation works, and why it often fails / Judith G. Kelley.
p.   cm.
Includes bibliographical references and index.
ISBN 978-0-691-15277-6 (cloth : alk. paper)—ISBN 978-0-691-15278-3 (pbk. : alk. paper)
1. Election monitoring.   2. Election monitoring—Case studies.   I. Title.
JF1001.K45   2012
324.6'5—dc23   2011026317

British Library Cataloging-in-Publication Data is available
Publication of this book has been aided by

This book has been composed in Minion Pro

Printed on acid-free paper. ∞

Printed in the United States of America

10 9 8 7 6 5 4 3 2 1

This work is based on work supported by the National Science Foundation under Grant No. 0550111. Any
opinions, findings, and conclusions or recommendations expressed in this material are those of the author and
do not necessarily reflect the views of the National Science Foundation.

To Liv Maria Kelley

Quis custodiet ipsos custodes?
[Who will guard the guardians?]
    —Juvenal, 1st/2nd century, *Satire IV, 346–348*

Contents

PART II

Illustrations

Tables

Preface

IN THE ARAB SPRING OF 2011, turmoil swept the Middle East and North Africa. After Tunisians toppled their dictator of thirty-four years, Ben Ali, historic protests spread to Algeria, Jordan, Yemen, the Palestinian Territories, Libya, and Syria. Protests in Egypt forced President Hosni Mubarak, in power for thirty years, from office. Elections did not spark these protests, but they will play a major role in the coming years as these countries attempt to transition to democracy. Most likely the international community will also play a strong role by sending monitors to these elections.

Elections are just one component of democracy, but a most essential one. As David Brooks wrote in his June 19 *New York Times* column in the wake of the June 2009 contested Iranian elections, "Recently, many people thought it was clever to say that elections on their own don't make democracies. But election campaigns stoke the mind and fraudulent elections outrage the soul. The Iranian elections have stirred a whirlwind that will lead, someday, to the regime's collapse. Hastening that day is now the central goal."

Whether elections spur protest or facilitate transitions, they are important. Without elections, there can be no democracy. Even after transitions, as countries settle into a democratic rhythm, elections remain a central accountability mechanism and the primary tool for citizens to express their preferences and choose their government.

Unfortunately, I do not have the right to vote. As a Dane living in the United States, I fail to fulfill the Danish residency requirement to vote in Denmark and the American citizenship requirement to vote in the United States. I am thus entirely disenfranchised. Perhaps this explains my fascination with elections. To me they represent that most fundamental exercise of a citizen: the right to express one's preference, to be counted, to be part of the conversation, to be considered worthy of persuading.

My interest in election monitoring was born in September 2004, when I went to Brussels to research a project on the European Neighborhood Policy. A scheduled interviewee was unavailable and instead I met with Michael Mayer-Resende, who worked with election monitoring and assistance in the Directorate-General for External Relations in the European Commission. This interview revealed several ambiguities and prompted a whole array of questions about the politics, efficacy, and norms of international election monitoring. How had international election monitoring evolved given that elections were traditionally such a stronghold of national sovereignty? Why were both intergovernmental and nongovernmental organizations involved, and why did there seem to be so little supranational structure to the ventures? Why did some countries invite monitors, yet clearly intend to cheat? And why did some organizations still bother to go to these countries? Did monitors influence the domestic politics? Most important, did they really improve the quality of elections? Why was there so much criticism of monitors by some commentators? Did monitors ever make mistakes, and if so, were these true errors or strategic maneuvers? Who were these monitors really, and what were they trying to accomplish?

I soon began to read all the scholarly work on election monitoring and found it contradictory and interesting. The literature was rich, but populated primarily by case studies. Systematic overviews were nearly absent, and there was little quantitative analysis. Most of the authors were practitioners, area specialists, or scholars focusing on the domestic situation and commenting only tangentially or casually on the practices and habits of international election observers. Furthermore, no analysis really used theories of international relations to examine the interaction between the international and the domestic levels.

This intrigued me, because I have always been interested in this interaction and in the influences of the international community on domestic politics and government behavior. I began to search for election monitoring reports and found that they were valuable primary documents with abundant descriptions, sometimes of book length. To my surprise, however, for some reason they had remained entirely unused by scholars. For example, given the many shelves that could be filled entirely with scholarship on the post-communist transitions, I was surprised to learn from staff at the Organization of Security and Co-operation in Europe that I was the first to request copies of their early 1990–95 election monitoring reports from these countries. The discovery of this fountain of information contained in the formal election monitoring reports led me to write a grant to the National Science Foundation to begin the Project on International Election Monitoring.

My debt to others for help on this project is enormous. Numerous Duke students have put in many hundreds of hours on this project. I thank Ashley Wallace, Anya Wingert, Dan Kselman, Elizabeth Bruns, Elizabeth Freeman, Emily Hanawalt, Erika Seeler, Hannah Kaye, Kian Ming Ong, Lenka Bustikova, Maria Cristina Capelo, Marin Magat, Nanette Antwi-Donkor, Rachel Bahman, Ren Yuan, Valentino Nikolova, Sophie Lehman, and Spencer Gilbert for their invaluable research assistance. I am especially grateful to Kiril Kolev, who worked for three years on the project and has been an invaluable assistant and friend, and to Mark Buntaine, who was an invaluable statistical expert and always a pleasure to work with.

I presented versions of this work at annual meetings of the International Studies Association and the American Political Science Association, and at a conference at Northwestern University, as well as at the University of Minnesota International Relations colloquium, the University of Chicago PIPES seminar, the Princeton International Relations colloquium, the Duke University Public Policy Fac-Doc Colloquium, and the CUIPS seminar at Columbia University, at seminars at both Lund University and the University of Stockholm, Sweden, and twice at the international politics seminar at Aarhus University, Denmark. I am grateful to all the participants who took the time to read the papers and offer their insights.

For comments on parts of the work and for encouragement on along the way I thank Karen Alter, Michael Barnett, Pablo Beramendi, Eric Bjornlund, Dawn Brancat, Valarie Bunce, Jeff Checkel, Gary Goertz, Ian Hurd, Susan Hyde, Bruce Jentleson, Peter Katzenstein, Bill Keech, Fritz Mayer, Jennifer McCoy, Layna Mosley, Halfdan Ottosen, Arturo Santa-Cruz, Andreas Schedler, Kathryn Sikkink, Duncan Snidal, Jack Snyder, and Felicity Vebulas. For reading the manuscript in its entirety and offering detailed feedback, I especially thank Jørgen Elklit, Goerg Sorensen, and Robert Keohane. Naturally, any errors remain my own. I thank Karen Kemp and Maria denBoer for valuable editorial assistance. I also thank the numerous anonymous reviewers, including those who have commented on the related articles that were published, and whose insights therefore have also found their way into the book.

I am also grateful to several interviewees at various monitoring organizations for their insights. My communication files contain hundreds of email exchanges with monitoring organizations, and I am grateful to the staff of these organizations took the time to respond and assist. For help in locating documents or for taking time for interviews, I thank especially Eric Bjornlund from Democracy International; Tynesha Green, Jennifer McCoy, and David Carroll from the Carter Center; Neil Nevitte from the University of Toronto; Anne Mullen, Georges Fauriol, and Lisa Gates from the International Republican Institute; Keith Douglas, an election observer; Pat Merloe and Julia Brothers from the National Democratic Institute; Yndira Marin and Betilde Muñoz-Pogossian from the Organization of American States; María Lourdes González from CAPEL; Anne Gloor, Anne Collignon, Nathalie Pire, and Rolf Timans from the European Commission, Milagros Pereyra from the Latin American Studies Association; Stina Larserud from the International Institute of Democracy and Electoral Assistance, Jackie Kalley from the Electoral Institute of South Africa;

Kathleen Layle and Bas Klein from the Council of Europe; Hanna Sobieraj and Urdur Gunnarsdottir from the Organization for Security and Co-operation in Europe; and several persons who have asked to remain anonymous.

I am particularly grateful to the National Science Foundation for its support and to Brian Humes, the political science director, who was supportive and understanding throughout the project, providing advice and extending further funding when the scope of the project broadened. Likewise, I was fortunate for a second time to work with Princeton University Press editor Chuck Myers and I appreciate his insight, support, and professionalism as well as the efforts of the production team at Princeton under the guidance of senior production editor Ellen Foos.

I am also grateful to Duke University, which offered support throughout the project and facilitated my sabbatical to write the book, and to the Department of Political Science at Aarhus University, Denmark, which provided me with a home during my sabbatical leave. My colleagues at Aarhus gave me valuable feedback and encouragement and inspired me to write more boldly.

I am most grateful to my family for their patience and support. It has indeed been a long time coming with this book. As I was putting the final touches on the manuscript my son asked, without pausing: "What are you doing, Mom? Writing a book? You've been working on it for five years! How long is it? What is it about? Politician science?" The book is about political science, but even more so, I hope it offers insights to improve political practice.

Judith G. Kelley, Durham, North Carolina, February 1, 2011

Abbreviations

ANFREL	Asian Network for Free Elections
ASEAN	Association of Southeast Asian Nations
AU	African Union (formerly the Organisation of African Unity)
CAPEL	Center for Electoral Promotion and Assistance
CC	Carter Center
CIS	Commonwealth of Independent States
COE	Council of Europe
CS	Commonwealth Secretariat
CSCE	Conference on Security and Co-operation in Europe
ECF	Electoral Commissions Forum of SADC
ECOWAS	Economic Community of West African States
EISA	Electoral Institute of Southern Africa
EP	European Parliament
EU	European Union
IDEA	Institute for Democracy and Electoral Assistance
IFES	International Foundation for Electoral Systems
IGO	intergovernmental organization
IHRLG	International Human Rights Law Group
IMF	International Monetary Fund
IRI	International Republican Institute
JIOG	Joint International Observation Group
NDI	National Democratic Institute
NED	National Endowment for Democracy
NGO	nongovernmental organization
NHC	Norwegian Helsinki Committee
OAS	Organization of American States
OAU	Organisation of African Unity
ODIHR	Office for Democratic Institutions and Human Rights
OIF	Organisation internationale de la Francophonie
OSCE	Organization for Security and Co-operation in Europe (formerly the Conference on Co-operation and Security in Europe)
SADC	South African Development Community
UN	United Nations
UNDP	United Nations Development Programme
USAID	United States Agency for International Development

PART I

CHAPTER 1

Introduction

> Look at these foreign observers. What they see is only the surface;
> they don't know anything about our country.
> —Nepalese voter outside a polling station, 2008[1]

DESPITE CONTENTIOUS DEBATE over the years about whether it is putting the cart before the horse,[2] the international community continues to push countries to hold elections as a way to promote freedom and democracy. Indeed, international election monitoring has become the primary tool of democracy promotion.[3] Today diverse organizations flock to observe elections all over the world and broadcast their findings to the domestic and international communities. These efforts have become a true growth industry, involving global and regional intergovernmental organizations as well as nongovernmental agencies and organizations (Figure 1.1). Given that countries have traditionally guarded elections as a strictly domestic affair and a sacred hallmark of sovereignty, the rapid expansion of monitoring is stunning.

International monitors often play central roles in election dramas. Consider Georgia, where in 2003 denouncement of election fraud by international and domestic monitors helped trigger the Rose Revolution.[4] Four years later, President Mikheil Saakashvili responded to sudden political riots by calling a presidential election for early 2008. To boost votes in the first round and prevent opposition voters from uniting against him in a runoff, he combined the implementation of social welfare programs with campaigning, stacked the central election commission (CEC) with partisan members, and occasionally used intimidation and pressure.[5] The international community feared further instability. The West was pulling for Saakashvili, Russia for the opposition, leaving the election observers in a difficult and prominent position. The *Financial Times* noted on the eve of the vote: "Pressure is mounting on more than 1,000 international observers who will play the key role in deciding the legitimacy of votes cast at some 3,400 ballot stations."[6]

Yet despite the sweeping prevalence of international monitors, global political developments are unsettling: After 2005, the democratic gains of the past two decades have stagnated, perhaps even begun to recede. In 2009, the year marking the twentieth anniversary of the fall of the Berlin Wall, freedom declined in

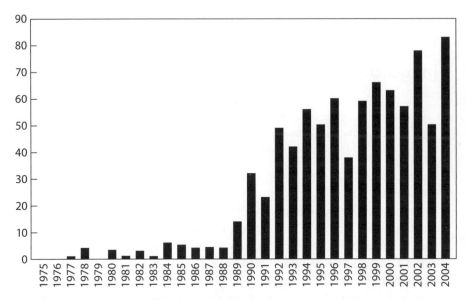

Figure 1.1: Number of national-level election missions per year, 1975–2004

no less than forty countries. This was the fourth consecutive year that declines trumped gains and the longest continuous period of deterioration in the forty years of reporting by Freedom House, the independent watchdog organization. The downward trend continued in 2010. With backsliding in Honduras, Madagascar, Mexico, Mozambique, Niger, Ukraine, and several others countries, by 2010 the number of what Freedom House calls "electoral democracies" dropped to 115—its lowest level since 1995.[7] It remains to be seen whether the Arab Spring will bring any relief at all to this downward slide. The elections in Kyrgyzstan in 2005, Pakistan in 2008, and Afghanistan in 2009 and 2010, among many others, were all monitored by international observers, yet these elections made it painfully obvious that elections cannot be equated with democracy and, furthermore, that simply holding an election does not ensure progress toward democracy, even if international actors invest heavily in monitoring it.

So is international election observation a good idea? Is it worth all the effort put into it? Does it actually promote democracy by strengthening elections? It would be naïve to expect all monitoring efforts to succeed or to infer from these broader developments that election monitoring itself is failing. Furthermore, regardless of the trends, elections remain a necessary component of a democratic society.[8] Yet, the signs of slippage in democracy and freedom around the world are clearly alarming. Given that measures of democracy rightly lean so heavily on the quality of elections, the declining scores suggest that in some countries the quality of elections is not improving or may even be worsening. This makes it more pressing to ask whether election monitoring is worthwhile. Furthermore, monitoring has become such a central tenet of democracy promotion that it is imperative to examine its role. Although monitors do not have as much prominence in every election as in the Georgia case, when they do, it is usually in the more critical and interesting cases. The domestic and international media listen to their statements, as do governments around the world. Thus, what international election monitors say and do is of great consequence.

Unfortunately, the answer to the question of whether international election monitoring is a good idea is: We do not really know. Despite the significance of international election monitors, their activities receive little real scrutiny. Critics were vocal in the early years of election monitoring, but they usually based their criticism on their unique experiences with particular elections.[9] Today, commentators occasionally question individual missions, as when the press accused the International Republican Institute (IRI) of withholding exit poll results after the 2007 election in Kenya,[10] but—by and large—few commentators question their credentials and most simply treat them as a force for good. This is true of scholars, who repeatedly point to international election monitors as an effective way to improve elections without providing any evidence.[11] It is also true of the media. For example, reporting on the downfall of a corrupt regime in Ukraine in 2004, *The New York Times* argued that the election monitors' report "lent credibility to Mr. Yushchenko's opposition movement and his supporters' mass demonstrations, provided a basis for an international outcry, and helped lead to a complaint to the Supreme Court, which nullified the voting."[12] Naturally, international monitoring organizations likewise promote their own brand, arguing that they strengthen democratic institutions, boost public confidence, and deter fraud, intimidation, and violence.

Yet, as early critics noted, international election monitoring organizations are highly complicated actors and monitoring is a complex undertaking. Despite the experience they have gained over the years, they face several serious challenges. Elections are much more than a polling exercise: They begin months before polling day, and they involve a legislative framework, extended campaigns, and complicated administrational and logistical issues. Assessing elections is difficult, organizations have limited capacity, and, on top of that, organizations have to juggle multiple political and practical concerns. Although they do not like to speak too openly about them, monitoring organizations are aware of the problems and many try to address them. However, the will to improve varies considerably among the motley profusion of organizations and solutions are rarely apparent and often difficult. On some issues, organizations are stuck between a rock and a hard place. For example, they gain their leverage from their ability to legitimate or invalidate elections, yet this very task of assessment can also lead to thorny political entanglement. Even when monitoring organizations can prescribe solutions, they often lack the capacity to follow up and are at the mercy of domestic politicians to implement them.

Thus, it is not as straight forward as proponents suggest to assert that international election monitoring is worthwhile. Given their intrusiveness into domestic affairs and the weight their opinions receive, a critical third-party perspective on their activity is necessary. As the Roman poet Juvenal asked in his *Satire IV* in which a man places male guards outside his wife's house to prevent her adultery: *"Quis custodiet ipsos custodes?"* [Who will guard the guardians?]. In a world that places so much emphasis on elections and on international election monitoring, this book assesses the guardians.

By injecting themselves into the domestic political process, monitoring organizations raise many interesting questions about their conduct and effects and, by extension, about the motivations of the international actors who sponsor them. For example: Do monitoring organizations actually reduce election violence by their presence or mediation?[13] Do monitors influence domestic politics in other ways, for example, by influencing the decision of opposition parties to boycott elections?[14] And what role do international monitors play in the training and effectiveness of domestic monitors?

This book touches on many of these questions, but it focuses exhaustively on two central and related questions: Do monitors assess elections accurately and objectively? Do monitors help improve the quality of elections? By focusing on the credibility of international institutions and the methods the international community uses to promote good domestic governance, these two questions focus the book on fundamental issues of global governance and democracy promotion.

Two questions

Do Monitors Assess Elections Accurately and Objectively?

The purported raison d'être of international monitors—their core mission—is to provide reliable and accurate information to the international community and to domestic actors.[15] This role is particularly important in countries without credible domestic watchdogs such as a free media, an independent judicial system, or domestic observer groups.[16] By taking on the role of producers of such information, however, monitoring organizations inevitably also become "legitimizers," because they assess whether the election conformed to recognized principles or accepted rules and standards and thereby determine the legitimacy of the elected officials.

Although some organizations claim that they do not make categorical or simplistic "free and fair" or "thumbs up/thumbs down" statements, most organization do just that—or at a minimum are *perceived* by domestic and international audiences to be doing just that. Indeed, the official commission created by Kofi Annan to review the contested 2007 election in Kenya notes that "one of the most common purposes of electoral observation is to assess the legitimacy of an electoral process."[17] Partly due to the international community's obsession with elections as the litmus test of democracy,[18] election monitoring is, by extension, often the primary tool the international community uses to assess the legitimacy of governments.[19] If international election monitors signal that elections were satisfactory, adequate, fair, legitimate—or whatever language they may employ—this has consequences for both international and domestic acceptance of the outcome. When Viktor Yanukovych claimed victory in the 2010 Ukraine presidential election, this did not prompt a second Orange Revolution, as it had in 2004, when international monitors disputed his claim. Instead, Prime Minister Yulia Tymoshenko, who had opposed him for the presidency, dropped her election challenge partly because this time international monitors had approved of the election, thus reducing her political ammunition.[20]

Yet, are monitoring organizations as impartial as they profess? Assessing elections is difficult. Monitors can only cover a fraction of polling stations and can only stay for a limited time at each station. Thus, choices are necessary. They may make pre-election assessment trips or have delegations in countries far in advance, but their resources are still limited, they lack local knowledge, and they may be up against politicians who work to deceive them. Thus, the efforts of international observers sometimes meet with cynicism, as expressed by the Nepalese voter in the chapter's opening quote.

In addition to these logistical challenges, sometimes the political pressures on monitoring organizations are considerable. In the 2008 election in Georgia, the problematic pre-election period was followed by a fairly organized and peaceful polling day, although some precincts were chaotic and had problems with the ink used to safeguard against multiple voting. The counting was also slow and had "procedural shortcomings."[21] When exit polls showed Saakashvili with 52 to 53 percent, barely enough to avoid a second round, the opposition cried foul. The observers did endorse the election, albeit hesitantly.[22] However, reactions were highly polarized as to the validity of that assessment; U.S. and Russian officials made contradictory statements and an Organization for Security and Co-operation in Europe (OSCE) observer openly criticized the mission.[23] Thus, assessing the quality of an election is frequently contentious, and when more than one organization monitors an election, the monitoring organizations sometimes generate controversy by disagreeing on their assessments.

It was perhaps with such complications in mind that, when monitoring began to spread in the early 1990s, the renowned legal scholar, Thomas Franck, noted the importance of considering "the legitimacy of the emerging international rules and processes by which the governance of nations is increasingly being monitored and validated."[24] In other words, what rights does the international community at large have to assess and judge elections around the world? And when organizations do so, do they really base their opinions on "the highest standards for accuracy of information and impartiality of analysis"?[25]

Because of the practical, ideological, normative, and political difficulties inherent in monitoring, the quality of the monitors' assessments cannot be taken for granted. This is an issue in global governance in general. Numerous monitoring bodies exist in global governance, but many of them are ineffective. This is particularly true in areas related to quality of government such as human rights, labor rights, gender equality, and similar issues on which governments have incentives to distort information about their less acceptable behaviors. Much of this monitoring occurs through self-reporting to various treaty organizations. Is the quality of election monitoring different from these processes? Do monitors provide more reliable information because they are present on the scene? Does the quality of the information vary between the different monitoring organizations or across different electoral contexts? If the quality of information varies, what does this mean for the legitimacy of international election monitoring itself and for the legitimacy that organizations bestow on governments? Thus, the question of quality of monitoring information has important normative implications as well as implications for the design of monitoring regimes more generally.

In addition, the quality of election monitoring assessments is important for the broader study of the nature of transnational actors. In the past this research has tended to assume that transnational actors are neutral and benign. Only recently have scholars begun to explore how the politics and preferences of transnational actors influence their behavior,[26] and subsequently their ability to advance democracy both domestically and in international governance. Studying what factors influence the quality of monitors' information encourages a deeper inquiry into the politics and norms of transnational actors in global governance.

To study the quality of information, this book asks a series of questions to help understand the motivations and methods of the actors involved: Why did election monitoring evolve in the first place? What sorts of organizations first became active, and what were their motivations? What countries invited monitors in the early days and why, and has the motivation to invite monitors since changed? How has the monitoring industry as a whole changed over time? When evaluating elections, what sort of considerations might monitoring organizations make? Is it possible to detect patterns in their assessments? Chapters 2–4 address these and other questions about the quality of election monitoring information.

Do Monitors Improve the Quality of Elections?

Most international election organizations seek not only to inform domestic and international actors about the legitimacy of elections, but also to improve the quality of elections. Indeed, the main thrust of election observation is to promote good elections as an essential building block to better democracy. Election monitoring has indeed become the central component of the democracy promotion efforts of many organizations and governments. A study of whether election monitoring improves elections therefore gets at the core of many prominent democracy promotion programs around the world.

Unsurprisingly, international monitoring organizations voice great confidence in their own effectiveness. The European Union (EU), for example, notes: "Election observation can contribute to strengthening democratic institutions, build public confidence in electoral processes and help deter fraud, intimidation and violence."[27] The claims of other organizations are similar, or even stronger.[28] The Asian Network for Free Elections (ANFREL) even argues that "the presence of international election observers has been proven effective in deterring and detecting violence and fraud as well as in providing greater confidence to candidates, political parties and the voting public."[29]

Unfortunately, however, in reality very little is known about the effects of election monitors. Some scholars claim that monitoring is effective, arguing, for example, that it "limits the capacity of incumbents to engage in large-scale fraud,"[30] that it has been "proven effective time and again in detecting and documenting deficiencies, manipulation, and fraud, thereby challenging the legitimacy of rulers who seek to stay in power through rigged elections,"[31] and that "election monitoring not only facilitates reasonably fair elections but the development of basic democratic institutions and habits as well . . . [and] has thus become the central element of a rapidly developing international regime to preserve and extend democracy."[32] However, these claims are mostly unproven assertions; like those of the international election monitoring organizations themselves, they have not been subjected to thorough examination.

Instead, the existing research consists primarily of a vast set of case studies that examine a variety of issues through the lens of a given election or a smaller set of regional elections.[33] Moreover, these case studies disagree about the effectiveness of international monitoring. Some case studies showcase benefits. For example, a study of the 2003 election in Armenia shows that although it was fraudulent, monitors lessened fraud in the polling stations they visited.[34] Several case studies also credit monitors with increasing the electorate's confidence in other elections. However, other studies strongly criticize international election monitors for being biased, unprepared, and under-resourced and question their ability to have any influence whatsoever on electoral struggles for political power.[35]

Together, these case studies present a valuable collection of research on international election monitoring, but given their disagreements they generate more questions than answers. Although practitioners and area specialists have paid attention to international election observers since the late 1980s, a comprehensive global study of whether international monitors improve elections across countries and over time is needed.[36]

Therefore, the second focus of this book is on whether international election monitors improve the quality of elections. Given the logistical and political challenges to their efforts to assess elections, as discussed above, skeptics would have plenty of reasons to question claims that monitoring organizations could actually influence the behavior of politicians in any way. Nevertheless, theoretically, monitors may be able to improve elections through several mechanisms.

First, monitors may be able to change the incentives facing the politicians. International monitors raise the cost of cheating by signaling increased international concern, calling greater attention to problems, and strengthening domestic critics. As the cost of cheating increases, politicians cheat less, or as one Carter Center (CC) observer expressed it, "they are more likely perhaps to play according to the rules."[37] International monitors may also raise the benefits of honesty by playing a verification role that makes it harder for opponents to dismiss honest victories as stolen. These changes in incentives may not always be sufficient to decrease cheating meaningfully. As this book explores, cheating is not an either/or choice, but a matter of degree. However, the rationalist expectation is that if an individual election is monitored, then the likelihood of cheating in that election decreases. The election is therefore more likely to be of higher quality.

Second, monitors may be able to change the conditions on the ground in various ways that facilitate improvements in the election process. Monitors make detailed recommendations that reinforce the message about what the international community expects. They can also help build capacity in several ways that can facilitate better implementation of electoral standards. Furthermore, over several elections the repeated interaction between external and national actors may socialize countries into norms and behaviors through persuasion and teaching.[38] These domestic activities may help national actors improve their conduct of elections.

These channels of influence are complementary and may work through both constructivist and rationalist logics, that is, they may work through a combination of norms and incentives. Indeed, often the actual mechanisms of influence will be difficult to distinguish. For example, some studies have found that governments respond to shaming,[39] a strategy whereby international actors strongly criticize governments publicly. It is hard to say whether governments react to such shaming because it alters their incentive structure or because they respond to the normative arguments. The same is true with international monitoring. Slow responses to the long-term engagement of monitors need not mean that the responses result only from socialization; domestic politicians may just as well be reacting to change in incentives over time. Regardless, both of these schools of thought provide theoretical reasons to expect that international monitors can improve the quality of elections through various mechanisms in both the immediate and the longer terms.

Yet many scholars remain skeptical that third-party actors ever really influence domestic politics or the behavior of governments. Realists have long dismissed international law and institutions as window dressing,[40] arguing that any apparent influence merely reflects the fact that countries self-select into various international activities and commitments that they are predisposed to keep. And even if the mechanisms discussed above theoretically can occur, realists would contend that they are but a drop in the bucket—far too weak to exert any meaningful influence. Thus, several studies on a variety of topics ranging from the environment to human rights have found international efforts to curb government behavior ineffective.[41] Following this line of thinking, international election monitors—who do not present a terribly formidable force—should have little influence. The harsh reality is that in politics power is everything: If incumbents risk losing power, they have no incentive to improve elections. They may even try to foil the efforts of international observers. This is perhaps why the skepticism about the effect of external actors is particularly pronounced among democratization scholars. Indeed, most accounts of democratic transitions remain decidedly domestic. Some scholars do acknowledge international influences,[42] but many consistently downplay their effect on democratization[43]—even when actors resort to direct intervention.[44]

Who is right? Is international election monitoring useless, or can it actually improve elections under some conditions? In Chapters 5–8, this book examines this question in depth by asking a series of questions: Can monitoring deter cheating? Do politicians outwit monitors by simply shifting the way they cheat? What happens when monitors repeatedly return to a country? Do their efforts pay off? Do governments implement their advice? Do improvements, if any, last?

Given the lack of systematic study to date and the disagreements about the ability of international actors to influence domestic politics in general, these questions are important for academic, practical, and normative reasons. They go to the heart of global efforts to promote democracy. They represent the core liberal belief that it is possible to spread norms to reluctant governments, to bring about change in recalcitrant states. Thus, they are the questions this book sets out to answer.

METHODS OF ANALYSIS

The lack of research on the quality of election monitoring and the accompanying lack of consensus about their influence is understandable; just as assessing the quality of elections is difficult, so is assessing the quality and effects of monitors.[45] Outcomes of democracy promotion efforts are particularly hard to measure,[46] and electoral fraud has, perhaps wisely, received only scant attention from scholars.[47]

One challenge is that neither an objective measure of fraud nor an authoritative definition of a competitive election exists. Many irregularities go unnoticed, and the electoral process and context differs in every country. This makes it difficult both to know the truth and to apply a consistent measure across elections in different countries and at different times. However, an effort to reach consensus on these questions is beginning to emerge. For example, the European Commission has compiled a compendium of international legal commitments that in various ways outlines the details of the responsibility of states to hold elections and of the necessary elements of a competitive election.[48] Experts from the CC are spearheading a similar and even more comprehensive effort.[49] The Organization of American States (OAS) has sought to develop a standardized method of assessment.[50] Likewise, scholarly work on the range and nature of election fraud is converging.[51] Most important for the execution of this study, monitoring reports of elections have long shared a basic structure. Most regard, as will this book, an election as a long and comprehensive process, starting months before polling day and including the completion of tabulation and handling of disputes. They all include a common list of areas of assessment such as the legal framework, the media, the conduct of the campaign, the administration of the election, and so forth. And while there may not yet be a consistent way to measure fraud, in practical terms, a shared definition of fraud exists. Although some organizations may choose to ignore these behaviors, no international monitoring organization, for example, ever argues that it is acceptable for the incumbent to control the media, that vote buying is an acceptable cultural idiosyncrasy, or that dead voters belong in the registry. Thus, while legal scholars, politicians, and practitioners from around the globe may continue to debate the finer points of what constitutes a proper competitive election, on an operational level the consensus is quite workable.

A bigger problem, however, is that, even for experts who have devised long checklists of essential elements of proper competitive elections, these cannot be weighted and aggregated into a unified measure that applies uniformly across contexts. Experts at international monitoring organizations continually express this frustration. Thus, even if a fairly wide theoretical consensus about what constitutes competitive and free elections is emerging among scholars and practitioners, assessing the quality and context of all the factors in a given election is inherently subjective and subject to measurement errors. Furthermore, monitored elections may suffer from a "reporting effect" similar to that on the issue of human rights: It may appear as if the problems are more pronounced in monitored elections simply because more information is available.

Another fundamental challenge is that monitoring efforts are never administered randomly. This makes it difficult to isolate the effects of monitors because whether an election is monitored may well be related to the expected conduct of the election. Exacerbating this problem, as Chapter 2 shows, the rise of international election monitoring has coincided with a global rise in democracy.

In response to these challenges, this book seeks to be as comprehensive and thorough as possible in understanding and evaluating the broader phenomenon of election monitoring. Extensive immersion in the topic for six years has made it possible to follow developments and engage in debates on a level that reduces the risk of making shallow and misguided inferences. The study takes a pragmatic approach to building knowledge by combining inductive and deductive approaches though the simultaneous consideration of both facts and theories.[52] As a result, the initial theories and ideas have been revised and refined through continued deepening of the inquiry. Furthermore, the focus is not exclusively on causal theorizing, but on deepening the understanding of international election monitoring and developing generalizations that can provide insights for policy.

To analyze the issues from as many angles as possible, the research relies on multiple methods of investigation. It combines historical inquiry, systematic comparative case studies, formal coding of the content of monitoring reports, and quantitative analysis, including descriptive statistics as well as more so-phisticated modeling. It draws on varied sources, such as primary documents, interviews, and secondary sources.

Each method serves a unique purpose. The historical analysis in the follow-ing chapter places the study within a broader context and lays the foundation for the analysis of factors that explain the rise of monitoring. The historical analysis also connects international election monitoring to broader world de-velopments such as the liberal efforts to promote freedom and democracy.

The comparative case studies investigate the role of monitors in countries over many elections. These case studies are updated through 2009. This long-term perspective provides understanding of conditions that influence the effec-tiveness of monitoring efforts over time and it also improves insights about the quality of the influence that monitors may have on a country. The case studies also help reduce spurious inferences by tracing whether the activities of moni-tors are plausibly connected with the development of policies and conduct of elections in each country. Situating the monitoring activities within richer nar-ratives highlights other factors that were also influencing the developments in the individual countries. This helps to identify possible alternative explanations and conditions that modify the effect of the monitoring activities.

The quantitative data have been generated specifically for the project. The data cover 1,324 national elections from 1975 to 2004 of which about one-third were monitored. The data, which are described further in Appendix A, are from the Project on International Election Monitoring, which coded more than forty thousand pages of election monitoring documents, such as reports, press releases, and interim statements from more than six hundred monitoring missions. These documents provide the formal record of the experiences and conclusions of election monitors, and their coding allows for statistical analysis of what would otherwise be insurmountable information. The resulting dataset has been titled DIEM, the Data on International Election Monitoring. This data-set was supplemented by coding of more than four thousand pages of reports from the U.S. State Department on Human Rights Practices, providing compa-rable data covering not only the elections that were monitored, but also many that were not monitored.

The data are used in several ways. First, descriptive analysis helps reduce the complexity that arises from a global study. The project uses simple aggregation of data to cast light on the patterns of monitoring and reveal trends and differ-ences between categories of data. The data are also used inferentially to analyze the questions of information quality and effect. Here a variety of different statis-tical models are used to examine the robustness of initial findings. In particular, the analysis of effects of monitoring takes advantage of some of the cutting-edge methods for addressing the selection problem discussed above.

Thus, although the empirical challenges make it tempting to set aside efforts to study election monitoring, this book argues that the topic is too important to justify ignorance. Monitoring has become the flagship of democracy promotion. It is costly, and, more important, the monitors' assessments can have serious consequences in both domestic and international politics. The study of election monitoring can also illuminate important debates in political science and law about the ability of international actors to influence domestic politics and the legitimacy of transnational actors in global politics. Examining the role of international election monitoring is therefore highly compelling, even if it must necessarily be done cautiously. That is what this book sets out to do.

The book's findings and arguments are complex, but the basic message is clear: International election monitoring is imperfect, but worth improving. The book refutes arguments that international efforts cannot curb government behavior and that democratization is entirely a domestic process. Yet it also boosts the critics who argue that democracy promotion efforts are deficient and that most outside actors are regrettably powerless. Although most monitoring information is credible, the book reveals flaws in the supposed objectivity of monitoring organizations and shows that these problems cannot be isolated to a few organizations. The book also shows that international monitoring works best as a reinforcement tool rather than a transformational tool. Monitors can promote progress, but only under certain conditions. Among these are constructive international incentives, domestic pressures for reform, less conflict-prone, zero-sum settings, and international monitoring organizations that are persistent, capable, and free of political baggage. The conclusion crystallizes several dilemmas that the international community faces regarding its use of international election monitoring to promote democracy. It also raises a host of questions to stimulate discussion about the quandaries the international community faces both regarding election monitoring specifically, but also about the legitimacy and value of the global promotion of democracy and liberal values more generally.

CHAPTER 2

The Rise of a New Norm

THE DISPUTE ABOUT THE UNIFICATION of Moldovia and Wallachia following the Crimean War led to a manipulated election,[1] which the Ottomans finally nullified under international pressure.[2] As a result, in 1857 a European Commission established by the Treaty of Paris observed the elections in the territories.[3] Since this first observer mission, international election monitoring developed in several ways. After its founding in 1945, the United Nations (UN) supervised many elections in "Trust and Non-Self-Governing Territories."[4] The Organization of American States (OAS) also started observing elections on a small scale in sovereign states in 1962, and starting in 1964, the Commonwealth Secretariat (CS) undertook several missions in territories controlled by Britain. The United States has likewise been active in Central America, the Caribbean, and Europe[5] and—spearheaded by the Carter Center (CC)—myriad U.S.-funded nongovernmental organizations (NGOs) began observing elections in the 1980s.[6]

Despite these activities, international election monitoring remained a rarity for a long time. Starting in the late 1980s, however, international election monitoring grew remarkably. As Figure 2.1 shows, monitoring in nonestablished democracies increased from an average below 10 percent of elections between 1975 and 1987 to a high of 85 percent of elections in 2004. The most drastic increase occurred between 1989 and 1991, when the rate rose from 30 to 46 percent.

Around this time international organizations also created new institutional capacity for monitoring elections and embedded the concept in their organizational agreements. In 1989, at the first meeting of the Conference on the Human Dimension of the Conference on Security and Co-operation in Europe (CSCE), member states began to discuss elections and monitors.[7] In October 1989, the commission recommended that it formally engage in election monitoring of member states,[8] and in November 1989, the OAS General Assembly officially recommended sending observation missions to member states that requested them.[9] In June 1990, the CSCE member states issued a standing invitation to election monitors, effectively obligating themselves to accept monitors in the future,[10] and the OAS called for the creation of the Unit for the Promotion of Democracy.[11] The CSCE likewise established an Office of Free Elections in

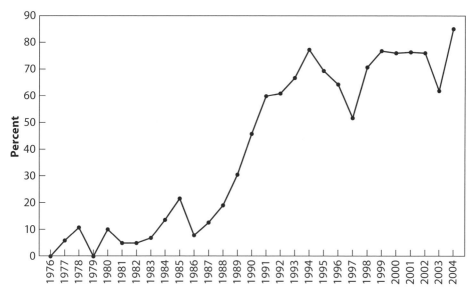

Figure 2.1: Percent of elections monitored in nonestablished democracies
Nonestablished democracies are defined as countries with a democracy score equal to or less than 7 in the year before the election. Democracy scores are based on the polity2 measure (see Appendix A). Monitoring is defined as described in the notes for Table 2.4.

November 1990,[12] soon after expanding to become the Organization for Security and Co-operation in Europe (OSCE). Along with this institutional growth, the quantity and the scope of monitoring activities also expanded. With some notable exceptions, early missions typically consisted of a short visit by a few people. Soon, however, organizations began to send pre-election assessment missions and long-term missions, and significantly increased the number of observers present on polling days.

The rapid rise of election monitoring is surprising. In the early 1990s, the expectation was that at best election monitoring might spread "through gradual, incremental steps," before possibly one day becoming a "universal habit."[13] But this was only expected to happen if established democracies showed the way by inviting monitors to their own elections. Without this, it was considered unlikely that states would volunteer, because this was "tantamount to a government's admission that it does not have credibility with its own people."[14] However, to this day established democracies are unlikely to invite full-scale monitoring missions. Only after the troubled 2000 U.S. presidential election has the OSCE begun to send missions to its most democratic member states, but most of these are not full-fledged traditional missions.[15] Accordingly, the rapid spread of election monitoring should not have occurred. Nonetheless, as the CC notes, "International election observation is now common around the world and is accepted as an international norm."[16]

The rise of election monitoring is a fascinating example of how global norms change and how world order evolves despite recalcitrant opposition.[17] Scholars generally argue that norms evolve through stages, each characterized by different actors, motives, and mechanisms.[18] New norms usually emerge despite considerable contestation. At some point so many states subscribe to the norm that its adaptation reaches a tipping point that then leads to a cascade of states joining, such that the norm becomes consolidated among a broader set of actors. This may then eventually lead to true internalization of the norm. This chapter discusses how the rise of international election monitoring exemplifies this pattern.

To begin the story of the evolution of election monitoring, however, it is important first to recall that election monitoring requires the consent of two parties: Governments must invite the monitors and the monitors must be willing to come. However, monitors need not simply await invitations; they often actively solicit them. As the CC described its 2002 mission in Mali, "It was initially unclear who was responsible for inviting international observers to Mali. Ultimately a letter indicating Carter Center interest in observing the election was sent to the government of Mali, and the Center received an invitation from Minister Ousmane Sy of MATCL [Ministere de l'administration territorial des collectivites locales] inviting the Center to observe the elections."[19] In other cases monitors may refuse to observe an election, as in 1993 when the CC and other international observers left Togo a few days before the polling, citing conditions too atrocious to permit a meaningful election. Because monitoring decisions derive from both governments and organizations, the motivations of both are important to consider. Why did the NGOs, the UN, and many regional organizations decide to engage in monitoring? Why did states permit these organizations to interfere in a highly sensitive and traditionally purely domestic matter such as elections? Perhaps most puzzling, why did even governments that were planning to cheat invite monitors?

The most obvious explanations for the rise of election monitoring are inadequate. For example, monitoring did not become popular simply because democratic transitions created a need for third-party verification. Earlier waves of democratic transitions had not required or prompted similar needs, so this does not explain why third-party verification was suddenly needed in the early 1990s. Indeed, the pace of democratic transitions between the mid-1970s and 1980s was similar to that of the 1990s,[20] so if a surge of transitions alone drove the rise of election monitoring, then election monitoring should have begun to spread during the late 1970s and risen rapidly during the 1980s.

The spread of monitoring was also not regional. As Figure 2.2 shows, international monitoring does vary considerably between regions. Between 1975 and 2004, the most heavily monitored regions were Eastern Europe and the former Soviet Union, followed by Africa and the Americas.[21] But despite these patterns, regional developments alone did also not spur monitoring; early cases of election monitoring occurred on most continents. Freedom House sent a mission to the 1979 election in then Rhodesia (now Zimbabwe). NGOs operated around the world without major difficulty in elections in Guyana in 1980,[22] Malaysia in 1982, Zimbabwe in 1985, the Philippines in 1986, South Korea in 1987, and the Soviet parliamentary election in 1989. It is true that the OAS pioneered monitoring in sovereign states,[23] but the early missions were mostly symbolic and had little resemblance to modern election monitoring. As the CC notes: "The OAS had sent observers to 19 elections in 15 countries from 1962 to 1982. . . . But the principal purpose of these missions was to legitimize an election, not to monitor or assess its fairness."[24] Indeed, Latin American countries opposed the push to expand UN monitoring facilities,[25] because they feared that election monitoring could lead to Panama-style unilateral military interventions and a new colonialism.[26] Thus, no one region drove the global rise of election monitoring.

The rise in election monitoring was also not simply a byproduct of the changes in the global normative environment about elections and human rights. New norms do not automatically change behaviors. Indeed, efforts to monitor many well-developed norms fail. The strong regime of human rights norms, for example, has not facilitated institutionalized monitoring of human rights practices to nearly the same degree as has occurred with election monitoring. Even though Article 40 of the Covenant on Civil, Political, and Social Rights obligates states to report on their domestic human rights, countries routinely fail to do so, and most human rights monitoring measures are low profile. Why has election monitoring flourished when monitoring of human rights has not?

A unique combination of normative and systemic changes created an environment in which it became rational for an increasingly broadening set of governments to invite monitors. This chapter explains the evolution of election monitoring based on analysis of hundreds of primary documents from the UN and regional organizations, historical analysis of legal standards, research on voting patterns in the UN, and data about election monitoring. The chapter also provides useful descriptive data on the practice of election monitoring. It concludes by discussing the variation in monitoring organizations and monitoring practices.

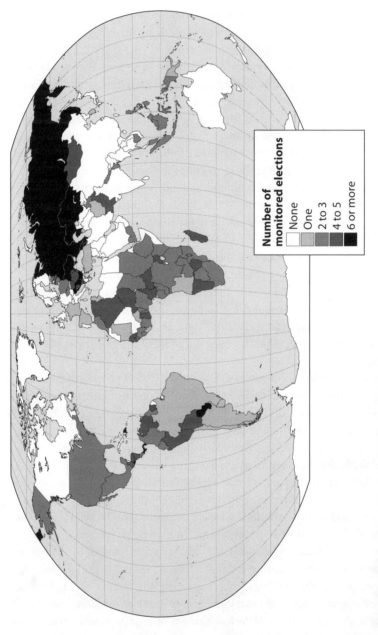

Figure 2.2: Geographic distribution of monitoring, 1975–2004
Frequency of monitoring is calculated based on the "Monitors" variable (see Appendix A).

THE CHANGING NORMATIVE ENVIRONMENT

The human rights and democratic entitlement norms that grew steadily after World War II were central in creating and shaping the concept of election monitoring. Three principles were particularly important: the principle of self-determination, the principle of free expression, and the principle of genuine and periodic elections.[27] Many different actors, or so-called norm entrepreneurs, connected election monitoring to these norms[28] by discussing and framing election monitoring in the context of human rights and democratic rights. Early proponents of election monitoring were essentially grafting ideas about election monitoring onto these recently developed principles.

The connections between these norms developed over a long time. Woodrow Wilson renewed the American commitment to self-determination during World War I. Self-determination then became associated with elections when many countries were first gaining independence.[29] During the process of decolonization, the UN developed the ability to observe and supervise elections, sometimes taking on "direct responsibility in order to ensure that the popular consultation is conducted in an atmosphere of complete freedom and impartiality."[30] This foreshadowed the growing role of the UN in electoral assistance, and as the Trusteeship Council promoted self-determination through supervision of elections in these non-self-governing territories, it also associated "monitoring" with the legitimacy of elections and governments. The principle of self-determination thus directly linked elections and the process of legitimation with some form of monitoring.

The principles of the freedom of expression and participatory rights, some of the core attributes of democracy as defined by Robert Dahl,[31] also enabled the emergence of international monitoring by institutionalizing election-related standards to which governments could be held accountable. In 1948, the American Declaration of the Rights and Duties of Man referred to voting rights and periodic popular elections held in a free and fair manner, and the UN Universal Declaration of Human Rights recognized the universal rights to freedom of opinion and expression and to peaceful assembly and association. In 1966, the Covenant on Civil and Political Rights specified the forms of expressions required to support freedom of expression and provided that all citizens should have the right to participate in public affairs either directly or through freely chosen representatives.[32] The covenant also declared rights to vote and be elected in genuine, periodic, and secret elections.[33] Regional developments such as the 1950 European Convention for the Protection of Human Rights and Fundamental Freedoms and the 1969 American Convention on Human Rights, as well as their respective courts, also bolstered the expectations of political rights and electoral competition. The CS's 1971 "Declaration of Commonwealth Principles"[34] and the 1975 Helsinki Final Act further supported these conventions by bolstering the norms of freedom of expression and participatory rights. These new declarations and conventions paved the way for the rise of external supervision of these new obligations.

These norms, however, could not in and of themselves propel the rise of monitoring. The longstanding norms of sovereignty and noninterference still hampered external engagement in elections.[35] Just as important for the emergence of election monitoring, therefore, were attacks on these normative prohibitions on external engagement in domestic affairs.

Global abhorrence of South African apartheid was particularly important in this respect. In 1954, the UN Commission on the Racial Situation in the Union of South Africa declared that South Africa's racial laws violated the UN Charter and the Universal Declaration of Human Rights. The UN Assembly followed up with successive resolutions rebuking South Africa and threatening expulsion. Throughout the following three decades the international community condemned South Africa and endorsed mandatory sanctions.[36] In the 1970s, states also began to claim more legitimate uses of external intervention.[37] The topic became a favorite in international law journals in the 1980s.[38] The UN Security Council passed Resolution 688 in 1991 insisting that the government of Iraq "allow immediate access by international humanitarian organizations to all those in need of assistance." The criteria for intervention were effectively broadened to include the promotion of human rights and democracy.[39]

Finally, as more states signed international human rights treaties, the notions of domestic jurisdiction and nonintervention became subject to these commitments.[40] In 1986, for example, the International Court of Justice ruled that a state is "sovereign for the purpose of accepting a limitation of its sovereignty in this field [of elections]."[41] A 1990 opinion by the Inter-American Commission on Human Rights refuted Mexico's contention that the commission lacked the right to address three claimants who alleged fraud in the recent local elections. The opinion stated that "the right of the state to develop its internal life freely has a counterpart in its obligation to respect the rights of individuals. . . . The correct interpretation of the principle of nonintervention is, therefore, one based on protection of the rights of states to self-determination provided that right is exercised in a manner consistent with respect for the rights of individuals."[42] Similarly, in 1991, the OSCE member states declared that "the commitments undertaken in the field of the human dimension of the OSCE are matters of direct and legitimate concern to all participating states and do not belong exclusively in the internal affairs of the state concerned."[43]

Thus, the permissive norms of self-determination, freedom of expression, and participatory rights gained strength while the prohibitive norms of sovereignty and noninterference weakened. This created an environment conducive to the emergence of election monitoring.

Contestation

New behaviors that violate existing norms are likely to meet with protest and efforts to derail the new behaviors,[44] and proponents of election monitoring had a difficult fight. States whose power balanced on these traditional noninterference norms fiercely opposed election monitoring. Entrenched regimes[45] such as East Timor and Ethiopia, which used the shield of sovereignty to abuse their populations without much scrutiny,[46] felt threatened and argued that elections should remain a purely domestic matter. Furthermore, the notion of "competitive" elections was still not part of international law, and consequently difficult to defend.

However, several elections fueled the debate. The UN observation of Nicaragua's election was embedded in a 1987 peace agreement, and therefore was legally justified on the basis of international peace and security. Nevertheless, it focused attention on monitoring because of its scale and because it was in a sovereign state. The debate truly escalated, however, with the 1990 election in Haiti, where even the UN secretary general expressed concern that the international dimension was less clear.[47]

The debate was most visible in the series of twin resolutions in the UN General Assembly. These resolutions, which recurred almost annually for fifteen years, began with the 1988 resolution on "The Principle of Periodic and Genuine Elections" (henceforth the "elections resolution") that was countered by a series of resolutions on "Sovereignty and Non-interference" (henceforth the "sovereignty resolution"). The UN secretary general commented: "This series of General Assembly resolutions, together with the respondent reports submitted by myself and other relevant UN entities, illustrates the ongoing process of dialogue, assessment, debate, and reform in the area of electoral assistance that has emerged in response to the rising tide of interest in democratization and requests for UN support."[48]

The language in the "elections resolutions" strongly connected competitive elections to human rights norms. They typically mentioned human rights in the first paragraph and then noted the provisions on elections in the Universal Declaration of Human Rights and similar provisions in the International

Covenant on Civil and Political Rights. Once again linking apartheid to human rights and then elections more broadly, the following paragraph condemned the system of apartheid and stated that "the right of everyone to take part in the government of his or her country is a crucial factor in the effective enjoyment by all of a wide range of other human rights and fundamental freedoms."[49] So in every way these resolutions linked elections and participatory rights to human rights, not to good governance, economic stability, or other general aims. Furthermore, the debate related directly to the role of external actors in elections, and specifically to election monitoring. The 1990 "elections resolution" praised UN support for elections in member states and authorized greater efforts for the UN secretary general to explore how to build that role. The 1991 resolution endorsed several steps for the UN secretary general to streamline UN election assistance. The link between human rights, the "elections resolutions," and external actors was very clear.

The language in the "sovereignty resolutions" was equally revealing. The early resolutions were entitled "Respect for the Principles of National Sovereignty and Non-Interference in the Internal Affairs of States in Their Electoral Processes"; they stressed Article 2, Paragraph 7 of the UN Charter[50] and argued that individual states have the right to determine their own destiny and system of government. After 1999, the language of the "sovereignty resolution" had become so muted that it no longer was the same resolution. The 2001 resolution even "reiterates that periodic, fair, and free elections are important elements for the promotion and protection of human rights."[51] By 2003, the term *noninterference* was dropped from the title and replaced with "respect for the principles of national sovereignty and diversity of democratic processes as an important element for the promotion and protection of human rights."[52]

In February 1991, UN Secretary General Perez de Cuellar asked member states to comment on the apparent conflict of the principles in the twin resolutions. In their replies many countries highlighted sovereignty, nonintervention, and noninterference. However, Western countries in particular portrayed these as compatible with external electoral assistance. They explicitly endorsed election monitoring and advocated a UN role in it. The European Union (EU) countries did not even mention sovereignty or noninterference. In contrast, countries such as the Soviet Union, Brazil, Ecuador, and Indonesia did not explicitly support monitoring and instead stressed sovereignty and nonintervention as well as the importance of a request. Most opposed were Cuba, China, Colombia, Mexico, Peru, and Uganda, which all criticized any increased role for the UN.[53]

The votes on the resolutions clearly reflected this battle of ideas. The first and second "elections resolutions" in 1988 and 1989 were adopted without a

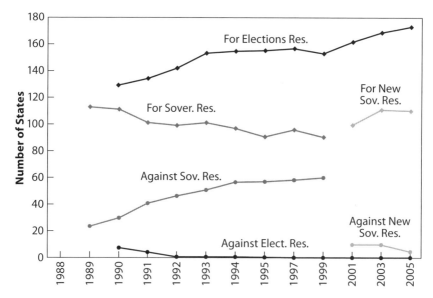

Figure 2.3: Voting for and against the twin resolutions
The 1988 and 1989 resolutions for elections were adopted without a vote and are therefore not recorded. There was no sovereignty resolution in 1988.
Source: UNBISnet.
Figure reproduced with permission based on Kelley 2008.

vote. The first counter-resolution on sovereignty was adopted in 1989. Figure 2.3 shows the number of states voting for and against each of the resolutions over time. There is a steady gain of support for the "elections resolution" and a steady decline of support for the "sovereignty resolution," until the latter softened its language.

The principles of self-determination, freedom of expression, and participatory rights thus promoted the emergence of election monitoring. Election monitoring emerged out of an intensive debate that specifically pitted democracy and human rights norms against traditional sovereignty norms. However, the rise in humanitarian interventions strengthened the link between democracy and human rights as entitlements[54] while whittling away at sovereignty objections to intrusions in domestic affairs.[55] The growth of election monitoring in turn ignited new debates that then further bolstered the norms of external action in domestic affairs. The process of "contestation," or debate of the prevailing norms, thus helped foster the new election monitoring norms.[56]

INCREASED SUPPLY AND DEMAND

The end of the Cold War provided a crucial opening for these emerging norms. Just as ideas associated with the losing side of war or with economic failure often get discredited[57] and winning coalitions get to construct a new order after political upheavals,[58] the end of the Cold War allowed the victors to change the rules. The collapse of the Soviet Union further strengthened the emerging election norms by revealing the failure of autocratic governments and communist doctrine in particular. Indeed, because the Cold War partly began with Joseph Stalin's prohibition of free elections in Eastern Europe, its end naturally led to a focus on elections there and boosted the emerging democracy and election norms.[59] Thus, at the 1990 CSCE conference, U.S. Secretary of State James Baker noted, "We are present at the creation of a new age of Europe" and "the free-elections proposal . . . has gathered strength from the dramatic events of last fall and the new elections of this spring."[60]

Furthermore, whereas the Cold War had forced Western countries to prioritize security concerns,[61] the war's end freed Western countries to push for democratic changes.[62] Indeed, democracy increasingly came to be seen as strengthening rather than undermining security interests. Western countries thus became increasingly willing to push for elections and spearheaded democracy promotion efforts in countries such as Namibia, Cambodia, Angola, and El Salvador.

Thus, Western actors led the advocacy, practice, and funding of election monitoring. Western countries spearheaded the movement to engage the UN in election monitoring and other election-related activities, to press for a set of international obligations establishing norms about elections and citizens' rights, and to normalize external engagement in elections more generally. For example, it was U.S. President George H. W. Bush who proposed the establishment of a UN special coordinator for electoral assistance and a UN electoral commission to monitor elections in emerging democracies,[63] and who spoke for the many General Assembly resolutions calling for an enhanced role for the UN in electoral matters. Western states also staffed and funded many of the observer missions in the post-communist states.[64] Most early NGO missions were trained, organized, and, although multinational, dominated by U.S. personnel and often included elected U.S. representatives.[65] Even the Center for Electoral Promotion and Assistance (CAPEL) based in Costa Rica operated principally on USAID and National Endowment for Democracy (NED) funds. Similarly, in 1984 when the Human Rights Law Group wrote "Guidelines for International Election Observing," the first standard in the field, that project was funded by the United States Agency for International Development (USAID).[66]

But the end of the Cold War did not just generate a supply of monitoring. The domestic turmoil generated by the war's end also boosted demand for election monitoring.[67] At times of transition, international monitors could help convince citizens that the domestic institutions were reliable and deserved respect,[68] so many governments invited monitors to help them refute accusations of fraud. Such need for legitimacy drove Mexico's invitation of monitors in 1994. The shocking level of irregularities in the 1988 presidential race,[69] the Chiapas uprising, and the assassination of the leading Institutional Revolutionary Party (PRI) presidential candidate all made outside observers essential to overcome the distrust and accusations of fraud.[70] Likewise, Mozambique also invited monitors to its 1994 election to strengthen domestic legitimacy. Without monitors, the Resistência Nacional Moçambicana (RENAMO) would have been more likely to reject the result.[71] As Canada observed in a UN debate, "Peoples around the world are demanding more responsible and representative governments and expecting from their representatives greater transparency in managing their resources and governing their countries."[72] Domestic monitoring groups multiplied and opposition parties such as those in Guyana and Zambia increasingly called for international observers.[73] The domestic turmoil generated by the end of the Cold War thus made many countries particularly receptive to monitors.

The data also show that many of the governments that invited monitors right after the end of the Cold War were honest and seeking legitimacy. Consequently, in these years, monitored countries demonstrated large democratic gains. As Figure 2.4 shows, in 1989 monitored countries averaged a gain of 6 on the Polity IV democracy scale, led by Chile and Panama (after an atrocious election led to the U.S. invasion). In 1990, monitored countries averaged a 5.5 gain led by mostly Eastern European countries; in 1991, monitored countries averaged a 3.75 gain; and in 1992, a 2.35 gain. After this, net gains decreased. Interestingly, as Chapter 7 discusses further, this is not because monitoring becomes less effective over time; indeed, some countries continue to make gains in the presence of monitors. However, the effect in Figure 2.4 is because more dishonest governments begin to invite monitors, as we will see later. The point here, however, is that the wave of governments that pushed monitoring past a trivial threshold in the early 1990s was led by honest governments that needed monitors to verify their conduct.

In sum, the breakthrough of election monitoring depended both on the pre-existing normative environment and on the systemic shift in power and priorities brought by the end of the Cold War. This is why the years 1989–92

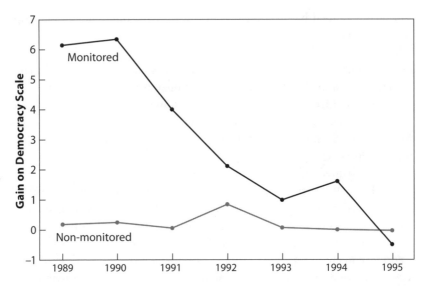

Figure 2.4: Average changes in democracy scores for nonmonitored versus monitored elections, 1989–95
Democracy scores are based on the Polity IV democracy scale ranging from –10 to 10.

demonstrated the sharpest rise in election monitoring and the greatest push toward institutionalization within the major regional organizations. The end of the Cold War presented both a normative and a practical "policy window,"[74] as it bolstered the emerging norms, spurred the development of institutional capacity, increased demand for legitimation, and supplied a new set of actors to promote these norms.

THE POPULARIZATION OF MONITORING

Still, why didn't monitoring recede after the initial Cold War transition? Instead, by 2004 monitoring had spread to nearly 85 percent of all nonestablished democracies. This expansion could not be driven purely by the countries in transition.

The spread of monitoring continued because a peculiar dynamic arose: Many dishonest governments began to invite monitors. As evidenced by the fact that deliberate cheating occurred in at least one-quarter of all the monitored elections in this study, it has become common for governments that fully intend to cheat to nevertheless invite scrutiny by monitors. As discussed more in the following chapter, they do so because the wave of invitations extended by honest governments made monitoring sufficiently prevalent to stigmatize governments that refused to invite monitors. Contrary to the expectation that governments would not invite monitors because it was tantamount to an admission of lack of domestic credibility,[75] the rising acceptance of monitoring by many honest governments reversed this logic. A cheating incumbent now had to consider that although rejecting monitors could allow a staged win it would also assure international criticism and jeopardize both domestic and international approval.

Such international criticism became important, because, as the Cold War ended, so did the patronage system whereby the superpowers doled out support conditional only on alliance stability. Governments could no longer survive just by "picking sides." Instead, democracy and good governance became more salient criteria for external political and financial support.[76] The international donor community such as the World Bank and the European Bank for Reconstruction and Development also began to link aid to democracy[77] and inviting international monitors became a prerequisite for "loosening the purse-strings" of donor governments.[78] For example, after Alberto Fujimori's 1992 coup, many countries, as well as the International Monetary Fund (IMF) and the World Bank, cut aid to Peru, forcing Fujimori to hold parliamentary elections and invite monitors. Elections in Indonesia in 1999, Kenya in 1992, Zimbabwe in 2002, and Uganda in 1996 are just a few other examples of donor countries pressuring governments to invite monitors. In a 1992 speech, Kenya's President Daniel arap Moi thus specifically welcomed foreign observers from the CS and the European Community as "our friends who have been helping us economically."[79]

The relationship between foreign aid and monitoring presence is evident. In the year before an election, the countries that were monitored received on average nearly U.S.$350 million, or about twice as much foreign aid as those countries that were not monitored.[80] As Table 2.1 shows, countries that had received *any* amount of foreign aid in the year before an election were monitored about 43 percent of the time, whereas countries that had not received any aid were monitored only about 6 percent of the time.[81]

Sanctions also became a more common tool for promoting democracy.[82] As Figure 2.5 shows, the number of sanctions with a core goal of promoting democracy spiked in 1991–92. Regional organizations, particularly the EU, linked democracy to institutional membership[83] and the OSCE made it a requisite for all members to welcome monitors for all their elections. In 1991, for example,

TABLE 2.1
Foreign aid and monitoring, 1975–2004

	Monitored	Not monitored	Total
Aid recipients	419 (43%)	547 (57%)	966
Others	23 (6%)	334 (94%)	337
Total	442	881	1,323

Notes: See Appendix A for data information. Pearson chi2(1) = 159.8146; *Pr* = 0.000.

the Council of Europe (COE) linked Albania's admission to the conduct of elections and sent its own team to monitor the election.

The data also demonstrate the relationship between sanctions and monitoring. As Table 2.2 shows, elections in countries that were subject to sanctions were monitored about twice as often as countries that were not subject to sanctions.

Finally, governments may have yet other reasons to seek external legitimacy. For example, Mexico's government decided to invite monitors to the 1994 election when negotiations for North American Free Trade Agreement negotiations were ongoing[84] and President Carlos Salinas was campaigning for the World Trade Organization presidency.[85]

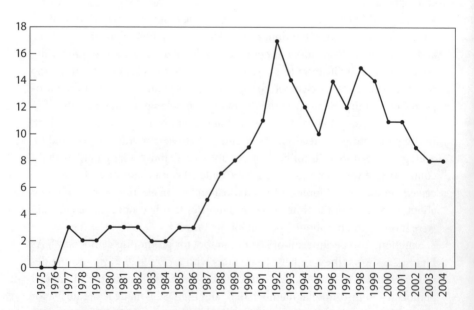

Figure 2.5: Number of democracy-related sanctions in a given year
For information in the measurement of sanctions, see Appendix A.

Because legitimacy was increasingly connected to so many different types of rewards or punishments in the international community, many incumbents calculated that inviting monitors was worth the risks, and might even have some domestic benefits as well. In the best-case scenario, monitors would not detect the cheating and the incumbent could then reap some reward for conducting a seemingly honest election. Even if monitors detected cheating, international criticism might not be much worse than if the incumbent had outright refused monitors. Indeed, given the imperfections, biases, and geopolitical constraints on monitors,[86] perhaps criticism would be muted or less harsh than if the government had refused monitors outright. If not, then governments could always try to spin the criticism in the media to minimize damages.[87]

The following two chapters explore these dynamics in greater depth and show how this demand for monitoring by dishonest governments led to the development of a shadow market, and how observing dishonest elections placed monitoring organizations in difficult dilemmas.

For now, however, the main point is that election monitoring continued to spread because external actors increased democratic conditionality and because the stigma associated with not inviting monitors motivated even cheating governments to invite monitors to avoid an automatic stamp of illegitimacy. Only strong pariah governments or governments whose geopolitical importance makes them immune to international criticism have nothing to lose by refusing monitors. These governments are therefore among the few that continue to refuse monitors and include Jordan, Kuwait, Cuba, Syria, and Uzbekistan, and—as least until the fall of President Hosni Mubarak—Egypt. Indeed, single-party states are practically never monitored.[88]

As a result of these demand and supply factors, monitors traditionally avoid both staunch autocracies and full democracies. Thus, elections in the middle of the democracy range are most likely to get monitored (Figure 2.6). Figure 2.6 is based on the Polity IV democracy score in the year before the elections, but an analysis using Freedom House data displays a similar pattern where countries Freedom House calls "partly free" are much more likely to be monitored.

Monitoring has also been sustained because domestic instability has continued to put pressure on governments to invite monitors. Data on corruption and government stability show that countries that invite monitors tend to be those that are less able to demonstrate their own credibility. Political Risk Group provides a measure of corruption that focuses on practices that can "lead to popular discontent," such as "excessive patronage, nepotism, job reservations, 'favor-for-favors,' secret party funding, and suspiciously close ties between politics and business."[89] This variable is 6 for the least corrupt country years, and 0 for the most corrupt. As Table 2.3 shows, the level of corruption

TABLE 2.2
Sanctions and monitoring, 1975–2004

	Monitored	Not monitored	Total
Sanctioned	31 (64%)	17 (36%)	48
Others	408 (33%)	837 (67%)	1,245
Total	439	854	1,293

Notes: An indicator of sanctions in the year before an election is used to avoid conflating the effect of hosting monitors on the enactment of the sanctions. See Appendix A for data information. Pearson chi2(1) = 20.8581; *Pr* = 0.000.

in the year before the election is higher in countries that are monitored than in those that are not.[90]

The Political Risk Group also provides a measure of stability, defined as "the government's ability to carry out its declared program(s), and its ability to stay in office."[91] The measure considers how unified the government is, its legislative strength, and measures of popular support, such as polls. The most stable

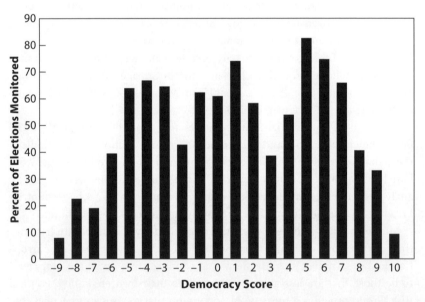

Figure 2.6: Percent of elections monitored, by democracy score in year before election, 1975–2004 Elections total: 1,171 (the number is lower than total number of elections in the study because of missing lags of polity variable). Democracy scores are based on the Polity IV democracy scale ranging from –10 to 10. Countries with a democracy score of 10 are considered fully democratic, those with a score of –10 are fully autocratic.

country-years are coded 12, while the least stable are coded 0. Table 2.3 shows that the level of stability in the year before the election is lower in countries that are monitored than in those that are not. The weaker credibility and greater instability increase the need of countries for external monitoring to gain domestic and international approval.

In addition, special elections, such as first multiparty elections or post-conflict or post-coup elections have continued to stimulate the demand for monitors. Nearly 10 percent of all the elections in the data, or 127 elections, are first multiparty elections. As Figure 2.7 shows, nearly 75 percent of these first multiparty elections have been monitored.

Monitors are also more likely to go to the first election after a conflict or a coup. Post-conflict elections may necessitate monitoring partly to assist with security matters. The UN engages in monitoring, particularly in such high-security settings. In post-conflict elections parties are also less likely to trust each other and demand some form of external validation of the election process. Classic cases include Nicaragua in 1990, Afghanistan in 2004, Angola in 1992, Serbia in 1997, and Cambodia in 1998. Because of these factors, two-thirds of all post-conflict elections have been monitored compared to only about one-third of non-post-conflict elections. Elections after a coup also signal a break with the past and sometimes a long period without elections, when external monitoring may be beneficial. Examples include Argentina in 1983, Bangladesh in 1986, the Ivory Coast in 2000, and Peru in 1992. Forty-six percent of post-coup elections were monitored compared to only 32 percent of non-post-coup elections.

These figures contrast with those for elections that are neither first multiparty elections, nor post-conflict elections, nor post-coup elections. Of these, only 27 percent have been monitored, but of course that figure includes both single-party elections and fully established democracies.

TABLE 2.3

Mean values of government stability and corruption in the year before the election

	Monitored elections	Not monitored elections	Difference in means
Corruption (0–8)	2.63	3.75	−1.12***
Government stability (0–8)	6.88	7.38	−0.5***

Note: See Appendix A for data information. T-test of the probability that the difference in means is equal to zero: ***$p < 0.01$.

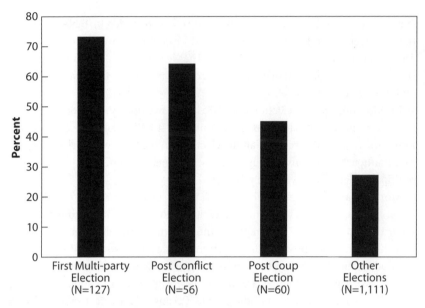

Figure 2.7: Percent of elections monitored, by type, 1975–2004
For more information on the variables, see Appendix A.

Monitoring Today: Organizational Variation

The acceptance of international monitoring still varies regionally, but monitoring has become an international standard. As the National Democratic Institute (NDI) president noted in 2000 when Zimbabwe rejected his organization, "The refusal to accredit certain observers violates international standards for democratic elections and is counter to the practice of Zimbabwe's neighbors and virtually all democratic countries."[92]

Today, monitoring organizations are extremely active and new organizations continue to emerge. However, monitoring organizations differ greatly.[93] Some of the major organizations that engage in monitoring are NGOs, or nonprofit institutes, while others are intergovernmental organizations (IGOs). Table 2.4 lists the number of missions to national legislative or presidential elections by the organizations included in this study, along with information about their scope, years of activity, and the number of reports that this study was able to locate.

Between 1991 and 2004, the most active organization was the OSCE, with a total of 124 missions. The OSCE has acted both through the Office for Democratic Institutions and Human Rights (ODIHR) and the OSCE parliamentary assembly, although in reality these have often coordinated their activities, if not cooperated. Both the OSCE and the COE have been particularly active because of the post-communist transitions in Eastern Europe and their strong democracy promotion focus. Both organizations have highly formalized standards on elections and human rights. The new member states or longstanding members emerging from Soviet dominance adopted these standards in the 1990s, and this has led to a high level of engagement by these organizations.

The EU has conducted monitoring by the European Commission and by the European Parliament (EP). The EP usually coordinates with the efforts of the commission, but if the commission is not sending a mission, the EP may still

TABLE 2.4

The activities of international monitoring organizations in national elections[a]

Acronym	Full Name	Years active in sovereign states	Reports available, 1975–2004	Number of missions, 1975–2004
OSCE	Organization for Security and Co-operation in Europe	1991 to present	121	124
COE	Council of Europe	1990 to present	75	77
OAS	Organization of American States	1962 to present	50	71
NDI	National Democratic Institute	1986 to present	47	58
IRI	International Republican Institute	1986 to present	47	63
OIF	Organisation internationale de la Francophonie	1992 to present	60[b]	60
EP	European Parliament	1994 to present	27	59
AU	African Union	1989 to present	0	47[c]
UN	United Nations	1990 to present	12	47
CS	Commonwealth Secretariat	1980,* 1989 to present	43	46
IFES	International Foundation for Electoral Systems	1988 to present	38	38
EU	European Union	1993 to present	34	34
CC	Carter Center	1989 to present	33	33
CIS	Commonwealth of Independent States	2001 to present	14	14
IHRLG	International Human Rights Law Group	1983 to 1990	10	13
NHC	Norwegian Helsinki Center	1995 to present	12	12

send its own delegation of parliamentarians. The EP also often cooperates with the OSCE or the COE. Monitoring by the European Commission was only really formalized in the late 1990s and prior missions were ad hoc.[94] However, since 2000 the EU has been on the forefront of election monitoring and has issued detailed guidelines and a thorough compendium on election standards globally.[95] The EU is unique in that it is a regional organization that specifically monitors only nonmember states, in complete contrast with other regional organizations, which monitor primarily their own member states.[96]

Although the European organizations have become more active since the 1990s, monitoring organizations have been active in Latin America much longer than in Europe. Indeed, with its 1962 observation mission to the Dominican

Table 2.4 (*continued*)

Acronym	Full Name	Years active in sovereign states	Reports available, 1975–2004	Number of missions, 1975–2004
ANFREL	Asian Network for Free Elections	1998 to present	12	12
ECOWAS	Economic Community of West African States	1997 to present	0	11
SADC	South African Development Community	1999 to present	10	10
ECF	Electoral Commissions Forum	1999 to present	6	8
EISA	Electoral Institute of Southern Africa	1998* & 2004*	8	7
Others	Other organizations	Varied	14	59
TOTAL			673	903

Notes: A monitoring mission is defined as the presence of a formal monitoring delegation from an international agency on the day(s) of the election. Smaller national delegations or local embassy activities are not counted, because they are ubiquitous and their observations usually remain internal. Missions of pure technical assistance (such as the OAS mission in Argentina in 2003) are also not considered monitoring events. Pre-election missions that leave before the day of the election and are not followed by another delegation present for the polling day itself are also not counted as missions. In many organizations, much of this information was originally in disarray. For more details on the process of gathering this information, see Appendix A.

*Active in just this year.

[a] Many organizations also attend local and regional elections, but these are not tallied here.

[b] The reports of La Francophonie were only coded for the "Main Assessment" variables. See Appendix A for more information.

[c] The AU claims to have conducted close to one hundred missions, but given the lack of documentation, this study was able to verify only forty-seven national-level elections. Some missions may have been to local or regional elections.

Republic, the OAS was the first regional organization to monitor an election in a sovereign country. However, the seventeen missions in the 1960s and 1970s were usually quite small and were more a form of electoral assistance than formal observation. The missions did not audit the elections in any way or make public statements on the quality of the elections.[97] It was not really until the creation of the Unit for the Promotion of Democracy in 1990 that the OAS began to perform more rigorous election monitoring.

The UN has conducted some election observation, but, as discussed, it has taken more of a backseat as regional organizations have developed capacity for routine monitoring of situations that do not require extensive security presence or logistical operations. The UN plays several different official functions in connections with elections,[98] and not all of them have a strong observer component. The United Nations Development Programme (UNDP) is also extensively involved in elections, but not directly as observer missions. The UN still undertakes observations in connection with peacekeeping missions, but today it is generally more active in providing logistical election assistance. Furthermore, the UN rarely publicizes standard observer assessments.

The Organisation of African Unity, now the African Union (AU), began monitoring in 1989 with a mission to Namibia together with the UN. However, although the AU claims to have sent more than one hundred missions by 2003,[99] the work has not been well documented and some of these missions may well have been pre-election visits or visits to local elections. Indeed, formal reports are impossible to find until the most recent years, although AU officials have often expressed their assessments in the media. A formal Democracy and Elections Assistance Unit was only adopted in 2006. The Economic Community of West African States (ECOWAS) has also become involved in election observation more recently, but most missions are ad hoc rather than conducted by an institutionalized branch within the ECOWAS with responsibility for election monitoring. Like those of the African Union, ECOWAS missions have been poorly documented.[100]

The CS, the main intergovernmental agency and central institution of the Commonwealth of Nations, was also a standard-bearer of election monitoring, as it began to monitor elections in the then British-controlled territories in the 1960s. However, its first foray into national monitoring came in 1980 in then-Rhodesia's transitional election, and in an election in Uganda. After this, the secretariat did not engage in monitoring until 1989, but its missions since then have been numerous and well documented. The Organisation Internationale de la Francophonie (OIF), the intergovernmental organization uniting countries with French culture and language, has also been highly active in international election observation since 1992. It has generally sent only small missions, although some recent missions have been larger. The latest regional intergovernmental organization to join in international election observation is the Commonwealth of Independent States (CIS), whose efforts sprung up in 2000 partly as a response to the work of the OSCE and the COE in the region, as discussed in the following chapter.

The two most active nongovernmental organizations are the U.S.-funded NDI and International Republican Institute (IRI). The other active NGO is the CC, which, led by former U.S. President Jimmy Carter, first observed elections as "The Council of Freely Elected Heads of Government," in the fateful election in Panama in 1989 and played a central role in promoting the practice of international election monitoring.[101] American NGOs often send multinational missions. It is not unusual for an IRI or NDI delegation to consist of observers with more than twenty different nationalities. The International Foundation for Electoral Systems (IFES) has also been active in monitoring, but today it is more involved in electoral assistance than in traditional monitoring. The International Human Rights Law Group (IHRLG), the NGO pioneer in election observation, sent missions as early as 1983 and formulated some of the first guidelines for international election observers. However, by the early 1990s it began to change focus and ceased its election observation activities.

Because of the high profile and experience of OSCE and COE, smaller European NGOs, such as the Norwegian Helsinki Council (NHC), have often joined the OSCE or COE missions, or worked as subcontractors to monitor specific aspects of an election such as the media. Thus, in contrast to U.S. NGOs, few European NGOs run completely independent missions. Toward the end of the 1990s, NGOs also began to spring up in other parts of the world. In Africa, the South African Development Community (SADC) and the associated Electoral Commission Forum of SADC (ECF)[102] both started sending missions in 1999. The Electoral Institute of Southern Africa (EISA), a South Africa–based NGO, began sending missions in 1998. In Asia the Asian Network for Free Elections (ANFREL) has been conducting monitoring since 1998 and has a strong record of documentation. New organizations continue to join the monitoring scene.

Mission Characteristics

The scope of activities varies widely between organizations and between elections (Table 2.5). On average, organizations have eighty observers present on election day and spend twenty-four days in the country. However, the variation around these averages is considerable and organizations that have been practicing longer may have lower averages because the activities in the earlier years were not as developed. This is particularly true of the OSCE, which initially issued very short reports, for example, and sent fairly small missions. The UN rarely sends actual formal monitoring missions, but when it does, they tend to be enormous because of the added security role. The length of the UN missions is difficult to estimate as the UN often has an ongoing security presence in countries when it monitors elections. The relatively new organization, the CIS, also tends to report large numbers of observers, but its reports are very short and lack much substance. Apart from these organizations, the organizations with the broadest scope are the OSCE, the EU, and the OAS, which send substantially sized missions and stay longer. The lower resources of the NGOs are reflected in their shorter and slimmer presence. Still, these organizations tend to work in countries where they have long-standing programs and contacts, so their monitoring missions may benefit from their other activities.

Finally, monitors engage in a wide variety of activities. For example, many monitoring organizations also send pre-election missions to study the legal framework and the administrative election infrastructure. As Figure 2.8 shows, roughly 40 percent of monitoring missions sent at least one pre-election visit. Of these, about one-quarter sent more than one pre-election mission. As will be discussed in Chapter 6, these pre-election missions may play important roles in pushing for changes.

Most missions interview members of political parties, election officials, and other election stakeholders. Sometimes they train domestic officials, conduct voter education, check voter registers and lists, observe election rallies, monitor the use of government resources and the ability of the candidates to run for office, and engage in general campaign activities. Many organizations systematically survey the media coverage of election issues. Most organizations also have legal experts who evaluate the electoral legislation and the legal framework for the elections. The organizations gather significant information about the pre-election environment and monitor the factors that contribute to the fairness of an electoral campaign. Some organizations issue press releases and reports prior to the election to report their activities and findings.

On election day organizations spend most of their time observing the voting. A severe limitation on observation efforts, however, is that even large organizations can only cover a small percentage of the voting stations, and even then each voting station may only be visited once during the day, leaving plenty of opportunities for fraud at other times. In addition to observing the actual voting, usually organizations try to monitor aspects of the vote processing such as

TABLE 2.5
Mission characteristics, 1975–2004

Organization	Number of observers (min/max)	Average number of days present (min/max)	Average number of pages of final report (min/max)
UN	523 (38/2,000)	N/A	18 (9/39)
CIS	225 (20/649)	N/A	5 (2/6)
OSCE	180 (1/900)	35 (6/74)	20 (2/46)
EU	113 (27/404)	69 (8/170)	53 (4/123)
OAS	62 (2/433)	43 (3/216)	46 (5/245)
ANFREL	37 (7/82)	21 (6/69)	49 (6/217)
CC	36 (1/80)	23 (2/166)	29 (16/143)
SADC	36 (11/70)	15 (5/30)	16 (19/66)
NDI	32 (3/100)	11 (4/98)	40 (7/136)
EP	28 (1/302)	6 (3/10)	14 (4/28)
EISA	26 (1/40)	10 (7/14)	20 (17/66)
IRI	26 (2/65)	9 (4/32)	62 (3/333)
CS	24 (5/104)	22 (5/45)	24 (29/144)
NHC	20 (1/165)	6 (2/9)	11 (8/17)
COE	14 (3/42)	6 (3/37)	13 (4/28)
IFES	12 (1/43)	20 (5/91)	44 (7/141)
IHRLG	6 (2/12)	11 (8/16)	66 (24/132)
ECF	4 (7/18)	14 (9/21)	66 (43/91)
OVERALL	80 (1/2,000)	24 (0/216)	39 (2/333)

Notes: The AU, the ECOWAS, and the OIF are not included, because this information was not available. For a list of acronyms, see page xix.

counting of votes, the transport of ballot boxes, the tabulation of results, and the announcements of results. They also observe the area around the polling stations and interview ordinary voters about their experiences, collecting reports of intimidation or deficiencies in the organization of the vote, and so on. In some cases organizations conduct or help organize parallel vote tabulations, which apply statistical sampling methods to predict the outcome of the vote, thus making tabulation fraud harder.

After the vote, nearly all organizations hold press conferences or make statements to the press about what they observed. They often issue a quick post-election statement in writing. They typically, though not always, end their observation by issuing an extensive public report containing specific recommendations. Indeed, many organizations have signed the Declaration of Principles for International Election Observation and Code of Conduct for International Election Observers,[103] which includes a commitment to trans-

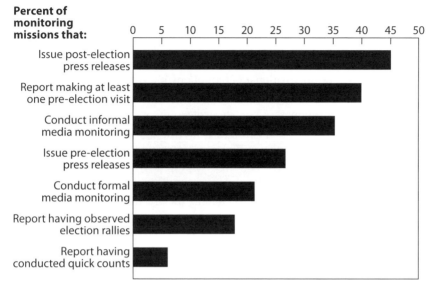

Percent of monitoring missions that:

Figure 2.8: Frequency of monitoring activities
Includes missions between 1975 and 2004. Does not include the AU/OAU, the ECOWAS, and the OIF for which this detailed information was not available.

parency and the publication of reports. However, sometimes organizations get so preoccupied with their next task that they fail to issue final reports, or, as will be discussed in Chapter 4, they may have concerns about their findings that lead them to purposefully avoid publicly issuing a final report. Figure 2.8 also shows the percent of monitoring organizations that engage in various activities. As evident, nearly two-thirds of missions conduct some form of media monitoring. However, only a few organizations conduct quick counts, or parallel vote tabulations, as checks on the tabulation process. This practice is quite effective, but because it is resource intensive and potentially highly intrusive, it is quite rare.[104]

Summary

A combination of several factors led to the rapid rise of monitoring. First, proponents were able to frame monitoring as a mechanism for upholding evolving political and civil rights at the same time as historical changes made relatively strong intrusions into domestic affairs more acceptable. Second, the end of the Cold War shifted the focus from security to democracy promotion and the domestic turmoil in many transition states created a demand for monitoring. Finally, donors and international organizations increased their use of political conditionality and, as the following chapter discusses further, this led even more governments—honest or not—to invite monitors.

Today monitoring is widespread and involves many different types of organizations, ranging from global and regional intergovernmental organizations to NGOs. These organizations take on a range of activities and vary greatly in their resources and activities. These factors as well as those driving the rise of monitoring are important for understanding the practice of election monitoring. They reveal the range of motivations involved in the practice of monitors as discussed further in the following chapters.

CHAPTER 3

The Shadow Market

> There were 33 teams of international observers, or 528 individual
> team members. Of the 33 teams [counting national delegations],
> 24 teams or 324 individual team members judged the elections to
> be generally free and fair while nine teams, or 204 individual team
> members, generally condemned the elections as neither free nor
> fair. . . . Taken together, the majority carried the day and so, the
> minority should submit to the verdict of the majority.
> —*The Herald*, a government-controlled newspaper, after the 2002
> Zimbabwe election[1]

THE RISE OF MONITORING had the paradoxical effect of encouraging numerous countries to invite international monitors and then cheat right in front
of them. The election in Panama in 1989 was a prime example, and although
the U.S. invasion that followed demonstrated the hazards of such behavior, it
nonetheless continues. In 2004, for example, monitors logged enough problems
to find about one-fifth of the elections they observed unacceptable. Even in
Afghanistan in 2009, when the eyes of the entire world were directed toward
the country, cheating was blatant. This chapter explores the challenges continued cheating has raised for international monitors and how it has changed the
market for monitoring, that is, the availability and use of different monitoring
organizations.

As Chapter 2 made clear, countries invite monitors for various reasons. Perhaps they receive foreign aid and are under some form of democracy-related
sanction, or are under pressure to demonstrate improved domestic governance
to continue or resume benefits from the international community. Or perhaps
they need international observers to obtain domestic approval because the government is unstable or the country is undergoing transition and needs to demonstrate that the election is not stolen. For a variety of reasons countries find
themselves in need of international approval of their elections.

For governments that are actually willing to hold honest elections inviting
monitors is unproblematic: The monitors will come and praise their progress,
and the country will obtain the desired approval. This was the situation facing several countries that underwent transitions in the early 1990s and whose

abundant invitations to international organizations helped bring about the rise in international election monitoring.

What is a government to do, however, if it needs the monitors' approval, but fears that the risk of losing an honest election is too high? A cartoon drawn right after Mexico's long-ruling Institutional Revolutionary Party (PRI) lost its legislative majority in the 1997 midterm election illustrates the dilemma of holding honest elections (Figure 3.1). So, what if a governing party is not willing to risk losing? Although international pressure can induce countries to permit monitors into their country and although in some countries opposition parties or electoral commissions are able to make independent decisions to invite monitors, the decisions to allow international monitors are ultimately made by government leaders—persons who aspire to hold power and have the ability to block monitors from being invited or from entering. This is especially true in countries where the governments tend to cheat in elections, because these are the governments that also are most resourceful about bending the rules to their advantage. From their perspective, the legitimacy that monitors can bestow on their country is a poor reward if making the required electoral improvements forces them out of office. What good is legitimacy to an ousted leader? In countries with a history of undemocratic politics, politicians and governments with low odds of winning without cheating are reluctant to run this risk.

On the other hand, for most governments simply refusing monitors is also a bad idea because it essentially amounts to a self-declaration of cheating. As a veteran observer and senior vice president of the International Republican Institute (IRI) has noted: "Those governments that oppose this kind of engagement from the international community have something to hide."[2] Such a characterization may be tolerable for countries that do not need or want to woo the international community or countries whose governments face little domestic opposition (such as Egypt under Mubarak or Cuba), but it is clearly undesirable for countries that may lose aid or other benefits or risk domestic unrest.

However, there is a third alternative to inviting monitors and running clean elections or simply refusing monitors. Governments can invite monitors but continue to cheat and hope monitors will not discover the cheating. That is, governments may count on the fact that monitoring activities are extremely difficult to implement, lack adequate resources, and are subject to many other constraints. To improve their odds, governments can actively seek to manipulate not only the elections, but also the monitors themselves: their access, their working conditions, and even the information they can access. For example, in 2005 Kazakhstan's government reportedly even conducted intelligence operations against the election monitors,[3] and in 2007 the Kazakh Embassy in Washington tried to stack the Organization for Security and Co-operation in

Figure 3.1: The dilemma of holding honest elections
Jeff Danziger / © 1997 *The Christian Science Monitor*. Reproduced with permission.

Europe (OSCE) mission in its favor by sending letters to its friends, encouraging them to enlist as OSCE observers.[4] Thus, governments may simply gamble on the chance that monitors do not discover their cheating. Such a gamble is, after all, an improvement in the odds over a certain denouncement for refusing monitors.

However, for many governments even this gamble is too risky; a safer option is needed, even if the legitimacy or approval it renders is compromised. To meet this need, a shadow market for election monitoring has developed: a supply of lenient monitoring organizations. Rather than taking a chance on the foibles of more critical monitors, governments may avail themselves of a supply of friendlier monitors supported by countries or organizations that realize the benefit of such alternatives. These organizations are akin to the phenomenon of government-organized nongovernmental organizations, or GONGOs, which some governments create to thwart actual nongovernmental organizations (NGOs).[5] Frequently these monitoring efforts are small parliamentary delegations from friendly countries, but they may also be delegations from formal organizations such as the Commonwealth of Independent States (CIS).[6] The assessments of these shadow organizations are less respected by the democratic countries of the world, but they may nonetheless be useful with some domestic audiences or with other autocratic governments, and, as the opening quote to this chapter shows, they may be useful in limiting the influence of more critical monitoring organizations.

The 2008 election in Belarus illustrates how international monitors can be used for show. A commentator notes the election was "orchestrated primarily for US and European consumption, with the primary purpose of improving Belarus' international image. The country's top election official has made it clear that the Central Election Commission's primary goal is to 'have the results be recognized by the international community.'"[7] Opinion polls showed the people of Belarus were very supportive of international monitoring, but the regime focused on its relationship with Europe and one-third of media coverage was about the international monitors rather than about domestic politics. Furthermore, the government "concentrated on the more friendly Commonwealth of Independent States observers. During the second week of August, the state news agency Belta devoted four times as much coverage to the CIS monitors as to their Western counterparts,"[8] and used "cosmetic changes in routine" to "produce good publicity" to impress the international community.[9]

By inviting friendlier monitors, either alone or together with the more credible organizations, dishonest governments can deflect or spin criticism while still claiming they are participating in the monitoring regime. In 2002, Zimbabwe's President Robert Mugabe officially prohibited the European Union (EU) from monitoring the election, but admitted other organizations. Sometimes rulers play a complicated game of veiled intentions. Russia, for example, increasingly vexed with the role of the OSCE in the region, formally invited the organization for the December 2007 Duma election and the March 2008 presidential election, technically fulfilling its OSCE obligations to accept monitors. In both cases, however, the OSCE eventually turned down the invitation, citing too many delays and restrictions that would hinder the organization from exercising its mandate. Sometimes the Organization of American States (OAS) also receives invitations rather late, making it difficult to mount proper missions, even if a mission is sent.[10] The OAS declined Venezuela's invitation to observe the October 21, 2004, election, after receiving an invitation only two weeks in advance. The director of the OAS Department for Democratic and Political Affairs, John Biehl del Río, said, "The proximity of the electoral process impedes us from having the necessary time to organize a mission able to meet all the technical, operational and financial requirements that an observation at this level demands." He urged Venezuela to allow greater lead time as had occurred in the past.[11]

The shadow market is not confined to specific monitoring organizations; all organizations may behave as shadow monitors at times. Even highly professional and well-equipped organizations face political and normative constraints that sometimes lead them to tone down their criticism of an election. Although monitoring organizations may attempt to avoid sensitive situations, these very situations are often high-profile events in which they may be compelled to participate for a variety of reasons. The 2009 election in Afghanistan, for example, was clearly going to be politically sensitive for the West—and for the United States in particular. Western countries, deeply embroiled in the North Atlantic Treaty Organization (NATO) engagement in the country, were keen to see a continuation of the regime to ensure maximum stability. Despite their vested interest in the outcome, simply skipping any monitoring of this election was not politically feasible. Similarly, Western governments, which are often the main supporters of international monitoring organizations, may have important state allies. They may push for monitoring organizations in these countries, because they need to be able to claim that the governments they deal with have some legitimacy, even if it is mostly artificial. As a result, some organizations have mixed records, acting critical at times and suspiciously lenient at other times.

The remainder of this chapter explores this pair of conundrums on the part of both monitoring organizations and the governments. It shows the pattern of invitations and the pattern of assessments by different organizations, which are consistent with the argument that a shadow market for monitoring has developed. Together with the following chapter, which statistically examines the factors correlated with endorsements of elections, it thus addresses one of the core questions in this book: Do monitoring organizations actually provide credible and quality information about elections?

DISAGREEMENTS ABOUT CONTESTED ELECTIONS

International monitors have long been criticized for endorsing flawed elections and failing to condemn flagrant fraud,[12] but the extent and nature of this problem has not been systematically evaluated. The fact that monitoring organizations sometimes provide questionable information is apparent in at least two different trends. First, sometimes the assessment of the monitoring organizations flagrantly differs from that of others in the domestic and international community. The Bosnia 1996 election discussed in the following chapter is a case in point. Here both the United Nations (UN) and the OSCE papered over severe problems, which others pointed out frankly. Second, sometimes, as in Chad in 1996,[13] monitoring organizations outright contradict each other.

A Few Examples

Zimbabwe's 2000 election exemplifies a case where all the organizations present were too lenient. The election occurred amid deepening economic and political crisis. Although the U.S. State Department criticized widespread voter intimidation, pre-election violence, vote rigging, and other irregularities,[14] the missions of the South African Development Community (SADC) and the African Union (AU) endorsed President Mugabe's victory. The AU observers said voters had been free to express their will and pronounced the election smooth and peaceful.[15] The SADC delegation also stressed the orderly polling day.[16] The Commonwealth Secretariat (CS) noted many problems that it said had impaired freedom of choice, but it too praised polling day.[17] The EU observers were the most critical, but although they noted that violence marred the election, they stopped short of questioning the final results and praised the orderly voting day.[18] EU Commissioner for External Relations Chris Patten said in a public speech to the European Parliament (EP) that "the report . . . concludes that [the election] was by and large satisfactory."[19] (Nevertheless, the EU was too critical for Mugabe's taste, and for the subsequent election in 2002 Mugabe refused several EU monitors access, prompting the EU to refuse to monitor altogether.[20]) In 2000, after the monitors left, Mugabe noted that "today the majority of them go away both humbled and educated, convinced and highly impressed by how we do things here."[21]

Disagreements among international monitoring organizations are quite common. In fact, when multiple organizations are present they disagree more than one-third of the time.[22] Sometimes disagreements occur simply because one organization remained ambiguous even if others disapproved of an election, or because some organizations endorsed an election although others chose to remain ambiguous. Particularly striking, however, are cases where organizations were diametrically opposed: One organization said the election was acceptable, while another found the election unacceptable. The elections in Cambodia in 1998 and Kenya in 1992 provide good examples.

The 1998 Cambodia election was held in a terribly violent pre-election environment. The security forces threatened, beat and killed opposition politicians. Brad Adams of Human Rights Watch argued that the brutal murder of opposition journalist Khim Sambo was "timed just before the election to have the maximum chilling effect on journalists, opposition party supporters, and human rights monitors."[23] A last-minute change of rules aided the incumbent's victory, but rendered the outcome highly questionable.[24] A joint memorandum by the National Democratic Institute (NDI) and the IRI called the pre-election environment "fundamentally flawed."[25] Although the NDI chair was criticized for hailing the election as the "Miracle of Mekong,"[26] the NDI issued a highly critical detailed report.[27] The IRI final report declared that the election "did not meet the standards of democratic elections" and noted that "the final vote count and post-election period were deliberately incomplete as the NEC [national election commission] and Constitutional Council dismissed complaints of vote fraud and irregularities without full and proper legal proceedings."[28] In contrast, the UN and the EU, cooperating under the Joint International Observation Group (JIOG), stated even before counting was complete that "in general the polling achieved democratic standards. . . . What could be observed by us on Polling Day and Counting Day was a process which was free and fair to an extent that enables it to reflect, in a credible way, the will of the Cambodian people."[29] After monitors left, violence erupted and there was an attempt on the life of the victorious incumbent.

Kenya provides another example of assessments that appear contrary to the facts. In the early 1990s, President Daniel arap Moi began to respond to international pressure. He released several political prisoners and reluctantly dismantled the one-party system. A critical opposition press began to flourish before the 1992 election.[30] But when it looked like Moi's political career was over,[31] he orchestrated interethnic violence to divide the opposition along ethnic lines.[32] The government refused to register millions of eligible voters in opposition strongholds, stacked the electoral commission with its supporters, and denied the opposition access to the media and permits for rallies.[33] Election day was fraught with problems, but voting was relatively calm.[34] With a fragmented opposition, Moi won the highest percentage of votes and was sworn in as president. After the polling, the IRI said the election was an important step for Kenya, but "the electoral environment was unfair and the electoral process seriously flawed."[35] The CS, however, announced even before the counting was over that "the evolution of the process to polling day and the subsequent count was increasingly positive to a degree that we believe that the results in many instances directly reflect, however, imperfectly, the expression of the will of the people."[36] When ethnic clashes nevertheless erupted, international actors tried to calm the violence and urged the opposition to take the seats in Parliament and seek redress through legal channels. Eventually Moi suspended the new parliament for about six weeks and gained the upper hand. By November 1993, the international donor group resumed aid to Kenya, citing the positive economic and political reforms. The 1997 election was essentially a repeat of this pattern.[37]

Disagreements between Organizations

Monitoring organizations do not disagree merely because they apply different standards. As the European Commission has shown in its compendium of legal texts, states around the world are committed, at least on paper, to quite similar standards.[38] Experts from the Carter Center (CC) have also compiled international commitments that underscore this.[39] Furthermore, election monitoring reports have long shared a basic structure. On some issues such as family voting there may be varying standards, but even this is generally discouraged. Therefore, disagreements cannot simply be dismissed as varying standards or cultural differences.

To understand how organizations vary in their propensity to criticize elections, it is useful to examine when they have disagreed with each other. Table 3.1 shows the assessments of different organizations in thirty-four elections where at least one monitoring organization assessed the election as unacceptable, but other organizations either were ambiguous or endorsed the election. Such cases are becoming more frequent with time and the more lenient organizations are often more recently established groups such as the Organisation Internationale de la Francophonie (OIF) or the CIS.

As the table shows, many organizations—even the most established—at times assess elections more leniently than others. However, before accusing organizations of excessive leniency, it is important to consider other possibilities. Perhaps organizations sometimes have incentives to portray an election as more fraudulent than it was. Evidence for this is scarce, however. Although a few instances have been brought to light where monitors may have been keener to criticize some elections, as in Venezuela,[40] there is very little evidence that monitors fabricate irregularities. Russia routinely accuses the OSCE of bias, but there is no evidence that the OSCE or the organizations that often support it are manufacturing reports of election irregularities.[41] It of course possible that some observer groups lack sufficient understanding of the local processes and misinterpret their own observations, thus leading to claims of fraud based on misunderstandings. The Independent Review Commission on the 2007 election in Kenya describes this possibility, although the commissioners disagreed whether this was the case.[42]

Table 3.1

Thirty-four disputed elections, 1990–2004

Country	Year	Election type	Critical organizations	Ambiguous organizations	Approving organizations
Albania	1991	Legislative	IRI, NDI		COE
Albania	1996	Legislative	OSCE	IRI	
Armenia	1999	Legislative	NDI	OSCE, COE, NHC	
Azerbaijan	1998	Executive	NDI, IRI, OSCE	COE, NHC	
Azerbaijan	2003	Executive	OSCE	IRI	CIS, COE
Belarus	2001	Executive	OSCE, EP, NHC	COE	CIS
Cambodia	1998	Legislative	IRI	NDI, ANFREL, IFES	UN, EU, OIF
Cambodia	2003	Legislative	IRI, ANFREL	EU	OIF
Dom. Rep.	1994	Concurrent	NDI		OAS
Georgia	2000	Executive	NHC	OSCE, COE	
Georgia	2003	Legislative	OSCE, EP, NDI, COE	IRI, CIS	
Haiti	1995	Legislative	IRI, CC	UN	OAS
Haiti	2000	Legislative	OAS		OIF
Kazakhstan	2004	Legislative	COE		OSCE, CIS
Kenya	1992	Concurrent	IRI		CS
Kyrgyzstan	2000	Executive	NDI	OSCE	
Malawi	2004	Concurrent	EU		CS, EISA
Mozambique	1999	Concurrent	CC		SADC, EU, CS, OAU
Niger	1996	Executive	NDI		AU
Nigeria	1999	Legislative	NDI/CC	IFES	CS
Nigeria	1999	Executive	NDI/CC	IFES	CS
Nigeria	2003	Concurrent	EU	NDI, CS	IRI
Pakistan	2002	Legislative	ANFREL	EU, EP	CS
Philippines	2004	Concurrent	IFES	NDI	
Rwanda	2003	Legislative	EU		OIF
Rwanda	2003	Executive	EU	EP	
Senegal	1993	Legislative	NDI	OIF	
Tanzania	1995	Concurrent	IFES, OAU	CS	
Togo	1998	Executive	EU		OIF
Ukraine	1999	Executive	OSCE	IRI, COE	
Ukraine	2002	Legislative	IRI	OSCE, EP, COE	CIS, NHC
Ukraine	2004	Executive	NDI, IRI, OSCE, EP	COE	CIS
Zambia	2001	Concurrent	CC, EU	SADC	
Zimbabwe	2002	Executive	CS, EISA	SADC	ECOWAS

Notes: Data on many OAU/AU and ECOWAS missions are missing. When available, assessments of these organizations were derived from news sources. Had all assessments been available, these organizations would probably figure more often among the approving organizations. Some organizations such as the SADC and the Electoral Institute of Southern Africa (EISA) have conducted relatively few missions and therefore are less likely to appear in the table. For a list of abbreviations, see page xix.

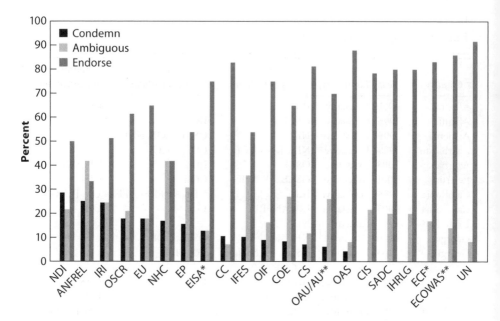

Figure 3.2: The distribution of all election assessments by different monitoring groups
Organizations are ordered from left to right by the percent of elections they criticized, with the
NDI being the most critical. The figure for the UN should be interpreted with caution, because it
rarely issues formal reports.
* Based on less than 10 observations. For a list of abbreviations, see page xix.
**The figures for the OAU/AU and the ECOWAS are estimated based on news reports, because
formal reports were seldom available.

Another way of looking at the individual organizations is to compare all their
assessments, as in Figure 3.2. This is interesting, but not very helpful in understanding differences between organizations, however, because some organizations may appear more critical simply because they systematically monitor
more problematic elections.

It is more useful to compare assessments of elections of similar quality by
instead asking: When an organization monitors a highly problematic election,
how often does it criticize that election? Figure 3.3 shows the results.[43] The CIS
is the least critical organization, criticizing only one of ten highly problematic
elections. Indeed, the CIS monitoring activity is widely discredited and regarded
as having been created merely to counter the criticisms of the OSCE in the former Soviet region.[44] The International Human Rights Law Group (IHRLG) also
appears rather uncritical. It "observed" the 1984 election in Nicaragua and the
1989 election in South Africa, and did not criticize either. However, the IHRLG

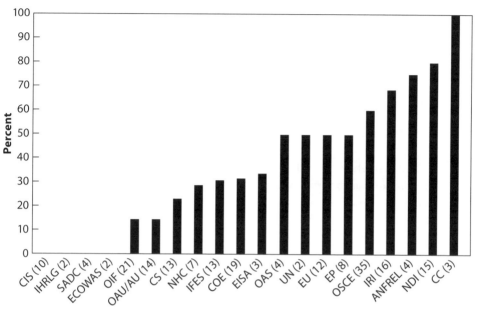

Figure 3.3: The percent of highly problematic elections criticized
Problematic elections are those rated unacceptable by other monitoring organizations or the U.S. State Department. For more information on coding, see Appendix A. For a list of abbreviations, see page xix. The numbers in parentheses are the number of highly problematic elections attended by each organization for which public post-election documents also exist.

was a pioneer in the field of election monitoring, before monitoring practices became standardized. It consisted of American lawyers who attended elections in the late 1980s and scrutinized domestic election laws, but it rarely issued critical statements and has ceased operating. The two UN missions included in this comparison are the 1995 election in Haiti and the 1998 election in Cambodia. In both cases other organizations denounced these elections, but the UN did not. Indeed, the UN is rarely critical, but this is partly because it often does not have a mandate to publically assess the election. OIF, one of the least critical organizations, has been described as "cautious" and rarely critical, and the AU as severely constrained.[45] The CS is also often criticized as too lenient.[46]

Perhaps surprisingly, the Council of Europe (COE) and the International Foundation for Electoral Systems (IFES), both of which have very good reputations, appear quite uncritical overall. This is because both organizations tend to remain ambiguous in their evaluations when elections are bad. (See Table 3.1 for several examples of this.) It is no wonder then that Russia has continued to cooperate with the COE, while being much less cooperative with the OSCE.[47] Overall, this comparison of assessments of problematic elections corroborates the conclusions of many of the case studies written by scholars and practitioners.

WHO INVITES WHOM?

The analysis above as well as in the previous chapter reveals that monitoring organizations are a very mixed group. They have different institutional origins, cultures, members or sponsors, ideological contexts, areas of operations, and so forth. Most notably, however, they have very different track records when it comes to criticizing elections.

The fact that some organizations are less critical than others does not by itself mean that countries use these organizations strategically nor does it prove the existence of a shadow market. However, examination of individual cases suggests that cheating governments do seek to invite those organizations they expect will be most friendly. This was the clear strategy of Zimbabwean President Mugabe, whom international donors pressured to invite monitors in 2000.[48] Although voter intimidation, violence, and reports of vote rigging and other irregularities were so widespread that the U.S. State Department denounced the election,[49] the organizations invited by Mugabe such as the SADC and the Organisation of African Unity (OAU) endorsed his victory.[50] Both organizations have strong ties to Zimbabwe and could be predicted to be mild in their criticism based on their records. The SADC delegation even went so far as to say that the election "set a good example" for other SADC countries.[51] The CS noted that "these elections marked a turning point in Zimbabwe's post-independence history."[52] The EU observers were the most critical,[53] so for the next election in 2002, Mugabe refused them access and even received OAU support for this.[54]

Similarly, when Russia released the list of certified international monitors for the March 2008 presidential election, the majority of the invitations were to groups and nondemocratic countries from which Russia could expect a friendly disposition. As Election Commission Chairman Vladimir Churov said of the invitations, "If you invite a guest, you invite someone you want to see, not just someone curious to see your house, right?"[55] The OSCE was nevertheless officially invited, because Russia is obliged to do so under its OSCE commitments, but as discussed earlier the restrictions on its work eventually forced the OSCE to cancel its mission.[56] Governments such as Zimbabwe's and Russia's have learned how to invite a mix of international observers to increase

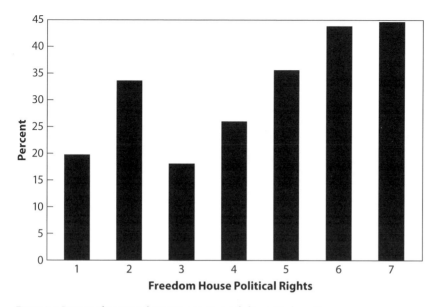

Figure 3.4: Percent of monitored countries inviting only less critical monitors
Number of observations = 438 monitored elections.
Less critical organizations are defined as the ones in Figure 3.2 that are less than 50 percent likely to criticize a highly problematic election. Regime types are measured by political rights as coded by Freedom House.

the likelihood of favorable assessments and to foster disagreements among observer groups.[57] At best these practices offer only pseudo-legitimacy in the international community, but they do allow dictators who control domestic media to spin the story to the domestic audience and to friendly governments in their regions.

These are of course only individual cases. Some governments reside in regions where the less critical organizations operate, so an invitation to one of these groups is not necessarily strategic. However, if the government invites only less critical organizations without inviting other more credible observer groups as well, this suggests the invitation may indeed be strategic. A systematic review of the practice of inviting friendly monitors shows a clear pattern. Less critical organizations are twice as likely as the other organizations to monitor elections alone. Furthermore, autocratic governments are most likely to rely on these organizations alone (Figure 3.4). About 45 percent of the time countries having the worst political rights scores invite only less critical observers. This contrasts with just about 20 percent of the time for regimes with the best political rights. There is a clear, statistically significant trend for more autocratic

TABLE 3.2

Strictest monitoring assessments when one organization is present versus when more are present

Number of organizations present	Percent endorsed	Percent ambiguous	Percent criticized	Total
One	90 (73%)	23 (19%)	10 (8%)	123 (100%)
More	105 (50 %)	56 (27%)	48 (23%)	209 (100%)

Notes: Pearson chi2(2) = 18.8210; Pr = 0.000.

regimes—those with higher Freedom House Political Rights scores—to host less critical monitors without inviting other monitoring groups.[58]

The data also suggest that organizations tend to be less critical when they monitor elections alone. When monitors are alone, they criticize elections only 8 percent of the time, but when more than one organization is present at least one organization criticizes the election 23 percent of the time. Thus the likelihood of criticism is about two-thirds lower for elections with solitary monitoring organizations (Table 3.2). For an incumbent government, a two-thirds drop in the likelihood of criticism may be very attractive indeed, even if the organizations will not bestow a whole lot of legitimacy.

Of course, it is possible that more organizations simply flock to worse elections, but additional statistical analysis (see Appendix B) confirms that the quality of the election is not likely to explain all the difference, and that solitary monitoring organizations are at least three times less likely to be critical.

DISCUSSION

Do monitoring organizations actually provide credible information about elections? The analysis suggests that not all organizations do and certainly not all of the time. This confirms longstanding criticisms. Furthermore, assessment problems cannot simply be attributed to the enormity of the task, or that the scarcity of resources sometimes lead organizations to misjudge. Rather, the data reveal distinct patterns. The evidence points to the existence of a shadow market in which organizations are sometimes intentionally too lenient, and in which some organizations are consistently more lenient than others. Thus, monitors sometimes endorse elections that do not meet common international standards. At other times they remain ambiguous despite convincing evidence of significant violations. In these situations the organizations tend to claim that they are simply following organizational policy to remain neutral. However, their willingness to critically assess other elections makes this look more like a convenient excuse. As Figure 3.2 shows, very few organizations *never* criticize any elections and can therefore claim that they are, as a matter of principle, refraining from judging an election. Only the UN is perhaps credible in this regard because its mandate is often restricted.

Thus, the track record of different organizations varies greatly. This variation stems not only from the fact that organizations monitor different elections. Rather, organizations have different propensities to criticize elections, with several of the more lenient organizations such as the CIS, SADC, and the Electoral Institute of Southern Africa (EISA) having entered the field of monitoring only in the end of the 1990s or later. Importantly, many more autocratic governments strategically invite less critical organizations. Furthermore, when organizations are invited without other organizations to provide a check on them, they are less likely to be critical. And even if governments cannot avoid inviting more critical observers, having less critical observers in the mix can serve their interest by making it easier to spin the statement of the various groups present.

A shadow market of monitoring thus exists, in which some organizations are created or at times willing to provide less critical assessments and bestow pseudo-legitimacy on the governments that are not willing to risk holding clean elections. As the following chapter discusses further, this is a precarious development for the broader election monitoring endeavor and for democracy promotion in general, because it undermines the credibility of the process and thus weakens its leverage.

This troublesome development is somewhat counteracted by efforts by international observers to raise their own standards and to appear as credible and systematic as possible. In the recent years many organizations, led by the EU, the OAS, and the OSCE, have published extensive manuals on election observation. Furthermore, under the UN aegis, several organizations have successfully crafted a declaration on principles of international election observation.[59] This is all well and good. However, political concerns can still override even systematic assessments, and any organization is free to sign the UN declaration. Many organizations, even the most experienced signatories, continue to violate its content.

The analysis thus casts some light on one of the central questions of this book: *Does international election monitoring improve the international community's information about the quality of elections?* Although monitor information is uncontroversial in many elections, the range of assessments and disagreements discussed above clearly shows that not all information from monitoring organizations is of high quality. Thus, monitoring organizations sometimes fall short in fulfilling their professed primary objective of providing reliable information on the election. Furthermore, the quality of information varies considerably among organizations, but also between elections. This raises the question of the extent to which these patterns are predictable. When are monitoring organizations likely to be less credible? What characteristics do the less credible organizations share? The following chapter examines these questions further.

CHAPTER 4

What Influences Monitors' Assessments?

> There is no future for election observation if it becomes politicized.
> —Ambassador Janez Lenarčič, 2008[1]

Two facts are by now quite obvious: Some organizations assess elections more leniently than others, and no organization has a perfect track record.[2] Observers sometimes recount political briefings before missions that reveal organizational biases.[3] As noted in a training document for European Commission election observers, sometimes observers are "allowing themselves to be swayed by the political interests of their home countries or the dispatching organization."[4] Biases were present in the earliest of missions,[5] but time has not erased them. One need only look at the 2008 presidential election in Armenia where both the European Parliament (EP) and the Organization for Security and Co-operation in Europe (OSCE) were criticized for their leniency.[6] Even their own delegation members were dismayed[7] when the organizations, after much handwringing, concluded that the election, in which a small margin of victory avoided a runoff election, "was conducted mostly in line with the country's international commitments."[8] The assessment did add that further improvements were necessary to address remaining challenges, but such phrases are so common as to have almost lost any meaning.

It is puzzling that organizations endorse bad elections, because this hurts their reputation and effectiveness. Like other transnational actors, their moral authority and influence depends on their veracity.[9] If politicians can easily dismiss the organizations' assessments as unreliable, then they need not worry about what the monitors say, and therefore they need not be concerned about whether the monitors witness any fraud. Monitoring organizations that lack credibility therefore lack influence. Furthermore, false endorsements may also legitimize undemocratic regimes, enable government manipulation,[10] and stifle viable opposition movements.[11] These effects only compound criticisms of the international community's narrow focus on elections.[12] Why, then, do international monitoring organizations nevertheless sometimes squander their precious moral authority?

Whereas the previous chapter described the rise of a shadow market in which governments strategically use more lenient organizations to avoid or spin criticism, this chapter examines some of the factors that may influence how organizations assess elections. Identifying such possible biases is necessary to assess the legitimacy of the monitoring process itself and identify when assessments may be questionable. It also advances the general study of transnational actors, who are playing increasingly consequential roles in global governance.[13] Scholars have long contended that transnational actors are both normative and strategic,[14] but only more recently have they begun to study how their politics and preferences influence their behavior.[15] Uncovering what influences the assessments of monitoring organizations therefore contributes to a richer understanding of the behavior of international nongovernmental organizations (NGOs) and intergovernmental organizations (IGOs).

To consider the quality of monitoring information and the legitimacy of monitoring more generally, this chapter systematically analyzes the determinants of monitors' assessments. The chapter will show that monitoring organizations are not as objective as they profess: International monitoring organizations sometimes endorse elections not only to protect the interests of their member states or donors, but also to accommodate other compelling but tangential organizational norms. Although I call these "biases," they are not inherently bad. At times these other factors align with the monitors' core objective to assess the election quality; at other times, however, the monitoring organizations face a dilemma between accommodating these factors and assessing the election honestly. Both norms and interests therefore can compromise the objectivity of the monitoring organizations. As noted by International Institute for Democracy and Electoral Assistance (IDEA), an organization specializing in elections around the world,

> The options open to observers on the ground when they detect serious deficiencies in an electoral process are frequently limited. Observers seldom operate in a political vacuum, and may face significant pressures constraining them from expressing their true convictions about the conduct of the electoral process if they are critical of it.[16]

ANALYZING SUMMARY MONITOR ASSESSMENTS

The analytical focus in this chapter is on the summary assessments that monitors provide immediately following an election. As discussed in Chapter 1, although some organizations claim to avoid making categorical or simplistic "free and fair" or "thumbs up/thumbs down" statements, most organizations do—or at minimum are *perceived* by domestic and international audiences as doing—

just that. For example, in the 1996 Bangladesh election, the National Democratic Institute (NDI) stated in a preliminary statement that "our purpose here has not been to supervise or certify the election . . . for it is the Bangladeshi electoral authorities, and ultimately the people of this nation, who must judge the quality and character of these elections."[17] Yet a week later, the NDI concluded: "We believe that the irregularities and problems that there were, although real and serious, were not of such a nature and scale, as to suggest that the result, taken as a whole across Bangladesh, fails to reflect the will of the Bangladeshi people. Once again, we found the electoral process . . . to be fundamentally transparent and honest."[18]

This is typical of the statements monitors issue immediately after an election, called post-election statements, preliminary statements, summary assessments, or simply press releases. These are followed by a longer report issued months later. The latter reports are quite detailed. The executive summary or conclusions of the final report typically repeat the summary assessments rendered immediately after the election, but the report's content often differs from the executive summary or conclusion by providing not only greater details, but often much more critical remarks. However, by the time the longer report comes out both the media and the world's attention have moved on, and details in the reports frequently escape attention. Thus, the world primarily hears the statements made shortly after the polling or the overall assessment that is usually repeated in the executive summary or conclusion of the final report. Therefore, the dependent variable is the overall summary assessment of an election by an individual monitoring organization. This summary assessment was used to create a three-level variable of whether the organization assessed the election as acceptable, ambiguous, or unacceptable. Appendix A describes this further.

Monitoring organizations themselves justify the analytical focus on the summary assessments. In its "Reporting Guidelines" the European Union (EU) stresses that in the early statements, "considerable care should be taken to drafting [the "headline conclusion"] so that it is [sic] clearly describes the overall view of the Mission. This is the phrase likely to be used by the media when reporting the findings of the Preliminary Statement."[19] Election experts elsewhere also support the analytical focus on the summary messages by the monitoring organizations. The commission created to inquire into the aftermath of the Kenya 2007 election wrote: "It must, however, be noted that the impact on legitimation is not always achieved by carefully thought-out reports, based on the information collected by observers and carefully analysed and chronicled by the media. Nor should it be assumed that the higher the quality and accuracy of the information on which the report is based, the greater the impact on public opinion.

Opinions are in many cases shaped by observer mission statements issued shortly after polls close and based rather more on overall political evaluation of the after-poll situation than on careful and detailed analysis of the information collected by the observer mission."[20] Reports rarely attract much attention after the initial statements.[21]

The fact that organizations often contradict their own summary endorsements by providing details of serious fraud and irregularities in the body of their reports is part of the puzzle of why monitors sometimes knowingly endorse problematic elections. The OSCE report from Russia's 1999 parliamentary election provides a typical example of such contradictions. According to the OSCE, polling day of the 1999 election went well.[22] The preliminary statement discussed various problems, but stressed up front that "the 19 December 1999 election of Deputies to the State Duma marked significant progress for the consolidation of democracy in the Russian Federation."[23] However, the final report documented major irregularities and contained many contradictions. The executive summary concluded that "the electoral laws . . . provided a sound basis for the conduct of orderly, pluralistic and accountable elections,"[24] but the body of report identified a "major flaw in the legislation"[25] and criticized it in numerous ways.[26] The executive summary also said that the election reflected a "political environment in which voters had a broad spectrum from which to choose,"[27] but the report documented abuses of government resources[28] and bias and restriction on the media.[29] In the press conference immediately following Russia's March 2000 presidential election the OSCE similarly gave the election an essentially clean bill of health, despite later issuing a harsh report full of violations of international election standards.[30] Thus, the OSCE was aware of the serious problems, yet chose to remain encouraging in the post-election press conference and ambiguous in its final report, even after describing the extent of the fraud.[31] The *Moscow Times* later reported that OSCE observers, speaking on condition of anonymity, "expressed disgust for the cheery tone of the day-after OSCE commentary, and dissatisfaction that the more thorough, official OSCE report on the elections—which was published two months later and was harsher and more informed—got no attention."[32]

Similar contradictions arose in the OSCE statements on the Bosnia and Herzegovina 1996 election. The OSCE prefaced its preliminary statement with considerable handwringing: "The CIM recognises the unique complexity of this election in a post-war environment, in which the election process is intertwined with a conflict resolution process. Therefore it is difficult to assess the election process in Bosnia and Herzegovina, after four years of war, in accordance with the term 'free and fair' as it is usually understood. The criteria as expressed in the OSCE Copenhagen Commitments (attached as Annex 2) and the Dayton

Peace Agreement remain the only relevant yardstick. Yet the election must also be considered in a conflict-solving capacity."[33] Both the preliminary and the second reports outlined numerous serious election irregularities. Nevertheless, the second report concluded that "the elections, although characterised by imperfections, took place in such a way that they provide a first and cautious step for the democratic functioning of the governing structures of Bosnia and Herzegovina," and that "these imperfections and irregularities are not of sufficient magnitude to affect the overall outcome of the elections."[34] The message for the world was that the OSCE and the UN accepted the outcome of Bosnia's 1996 election, leading some to accuse the OSCE of spin.[35] Other examples can easily be found in reports from other organizations, but since the OSCE is considered one of the most reputable organizations, these examples illustrate that the problem extends beyond a few "bad apples."

The focus of the analysis in this chapter therefore is to understand what factors influence whether monitoring organizations will issue favorable summary assessments of an election. How do the irregularities observed in the election explain the assessments of monitors, and do other factors also correlate with the monitors' assessments?

FIVE TYPES OF BIAS

Many factors likely weigh in as monitors draft their summary assessments. Indeed, given the highly individualized context of any election, there may be as many considerations as there are elections. This chapter, however, focuses on a few major types of biases that derive from the development of the shadow market, the electoral norms monitors strive to uphold, and the environments they operate in. At least five such major biases exist: the glasshouse bias, the progress bias, the special relationship bias, the subtlety bias, and the stability bias. These five biases are supported by the statistical analysis shown in Table C.1 in Appendix C. The analysis includes variables that seek to capture the different types of irregularities in an election as outlined in the full-length monitoring reports. It also includes other characteristics of the monitoring organization, the country, and the election that may influence the assessment of monitors.

The analysis demonstrates that several factors predict observer assessments. These are listed in Table 4.1, which shows how much the statistical analysis predicts that each factor will increase the likelihood that monitors endorse an election. The table illustrates the change in the likelihood of endorsement when a given variable changes from minimum to maximum value, or, in the case of

TABLE 4.1
Predicted probabilities of endorsement

	No	Yes	Min	Max	Percentage point change in likelihood of endorsement	Relative change in likelihood
Foreign aid			60	85	25	0.42
IGO	59	80			21	.36
Pre-election violence			60	78	18	0.30
Turnover	62	80			18	0.29
Transitional	67	84			17	0.25
Western NGO	59	57			-2	-0.03
Legal problems			78	58	-20	-0.26
IGO democratic			87	62	-25	-0.29
Pre-election cheating			85	49	-36	-0.42
Election day cheating			88	42	-46	-0.52

Notes: The table is based on simulations (using Clarify software) based on Model 2 in Table 4.1, for turnover and foreign aid on Model 3, and for IGO on Model 4, holding all other variables at their means, or, in the case of the organizational type, at 0. All figures are rounded to the nearest whole percent. Only significant variables are included in the simulation, but for viewing ease, standard errors are not displayed.

a binary variable, from no to yes. Thus, for example, row 4 shows that monitors endorse 62 percent of elections that do not produce a turnover in power, but they endorse 80 percent of elections that do produce a turnover. This is an absolute increase of 18 percent, or a 29 percent increase in the base likelihood of endorsement. The numbers are based on the underlying statistical model, but their primary purpose here is merely to give an impression of how important the analysis found each factor to be in relationship to the monitors' assessments. The rest of this chapter discusses these factors and the five major biases.

IGOs, NGOs, and the Glass House Bias

The previous chapter's discussion of the shadow market showed that less-democratic countries might try to constrain monitors who come to their country. Furthermore, not only may governments be concerned about monitors inside their own countries; they may not want critical organizations to operate freely in their region or neighborhood, because this may increase pressure on their own governments in the future. To protect their own regime from future criticisms or to prevent democratic transitions in their neighborhood, they may therefore seek to restrain critical organizations. For example, after the OSCE's active role in the "color revolutions" in Georgia and Ukraine, Russia has (unsuccessfully) pushed for institutional reforms to curtail the independence of OSCE observers.[36] Thus, organizations associated with many undemocratic countries may be more reluctant to criticize elections. One might call this the glass house bias. As the saying "those who live in glass houses shouldn't throw stones" suggests, undemocratic regimes may want to constrain criticisms directed at other states.

This raises the question of whether some of the differences observed in the previous chapter stem from the structure and membership of the organizations. Most notably, IGO member states have considerable influence and may prevent consistent application of standards. This has been seen, for example, within the International Monetary Fund (IMF).[37] Although some IGO staff has flexibility to implement their agendas,[38] most monitoring mission staff has little flexibility in drafting official assessments. Indeed, organizational documents and discussions with officials reveal that most IGOs have strict procedures for finalizing their official statements. Both the EU and Organization of American States (OAS) observer missions, for example, have strict supervisory mechanisms for the drafting of statements.[39] NGOs must also worry about their funding. The U.S. organizations in particular depend on grant or contract opportunities by the United States Agency for International Development (USAID) or other government agencies to monitor specific elections. Nevertheless, NGOs face fewer constraints than IGOs.[40] NGOs tend to have multiple and diverse stakeholders, which counters the dominance of donor preferences.[41] Furthermore, NGOs do not speak directly for any governments or donors, and this may give them greater freedom; certainly they do not face formal institutional procedures that allow governments to veto the wording of the election assessments.

Yet, even if IGOs can impose more constraints, not all IGOs are equally constrained. The statistical analysis shows that the degree of constraint that donors and member states impose on organizations depends as much on the level of democracy in the member states as on the organizations' formal structure. Although IGOs are almost twice as likely to endorse elections, this tendency declines the more democratic an IGO's members are.[42] This is quite consistent with the argument in the previous chapter about the shadow market, because it suggests that organizations experience political constraints. Simulations based on the statistical analysis show that the predicted probability that an IGO endorses an election is 80 percent, a sharp contrast with only 59 percent for Western NGOs (see Table 4.1). Whether an NGO is Western or not makes little difference. However, it does matter how democratic the membership of an IGO is. The predicted probability that "low democracy" IGOs endorse an election is 87 percent, but only about 62 percent for "high democracy" IGOs—much closer to that of NGOs.

The Subtlety Bias

The subtlety bias means that monitors are more likely to endorse elections with subtler types of irregularities. Although a broad set of conditions is necessary to ensure a free and fair election,[43] critics have long contended that monitors focus excessively on election day problems. This was apparent, for example, in Cambodia in 1998, when the Joint International Observation Group (JIOG) focused on the polling and counting days and in 2000 in Zimbabwe, where all the observers praised the calmness of election day itself. It was also evident in the election in Russia in 1999, described above, where election day ran smoothly and there were few signs of obvious breaches of the laws.

Election monitoring reports do stress obvious election day irregularities, but monitoring organizations also observe subtler types of fraud and evaluate the pre-election period. Thus, at least in the body of the election monitoring reports, just as much space is devoted to these issues as to others. The question, however, is whether, in making the overall assessment, monitoring organizations emphasize some types of irregularities more than others.

To explore this, the project analyzed the content of election monitoring reports in five major categories: legal problems, pre-election cheating, pre-election administration, election day cheating, and election day administration (Table 4.2), each of which were coded as having no, minor, moderate, or major problems, as discussed further in Appendix A.

The analysis suggested that when major problems were reported, endorsements were more likely to occur when those problems took place during the pre-election period (Figure 4.1). When organizations found major pre-election administrative problems, they nevertheless endorsed the election about 35 percent of the time. When they found major pre-election cheating, they endorsed elections about 23 percent of the time. Monitoring organizations endorsed elections with major legal problems least frequently, followed by elections with cheating on the day of election and administrative problems on the day of election.

Figure 4.1 is useful in that it simply shows how often monitoring organizations endorse elections when they themselves have observed certain types of irregularities. However, if organizations seek to render a mild overall assessment,

TABLE 4.2
Election irregularities

Variable	Description
Legal problems	Legal framework not up to standards, limits on the scope and jurisdiction of elective offices, unreasonable limits on who can run for office, etc.
Pre-election cheating	Improper use of public funds, lack of freedom to campaign, media restrictions, intimidation, etc.
Pre-election administration	Voter registration and information problems, complaints about electoral commission conduct, technical or procedural problems, etc.
Election day cheating	Vote padding, tampering with ballot box, voter impersonation, double voting, vote buying, intimidation, etc.
Election day administration	Insufficient informational about rules and polling locations, lax polling booth officials, long waits, faulty procedures or equipment, problems in voters' list, complaints about electoral commission conduct, etc.

Note: All categories are coded as none, minor, moderate, or major problems. See also Appendix A.

they may downplay details in their report. Thus Figure 4.1 may be misleading, because it is based only on the organizations' own reports. Figure 4.1 also does not make it possible to sort out the relative weight that organizations may put on different types of irregularities.

To rectify these problems, the statistical analysis (in Appendix C) took advantage of the fact that more than one organization was present in nearly three-quarters of the elections. For each election new variables were generated based on the *maximum level* of each type of irregularity reported in the body of the report by *any organization present*. Since no organizations can be everywhere, combining their observations improves the documentation and produces a more comprehensive measure of the breadth of what monitoring organizations have observed. This also goes some way toward ameliorating any intentional under-reporting.

Using these measures, the statistical analysis showed that monitors tend to pay more attention to obvious cheating on the day of election as well as in the pre-election period, and to legal problems. Only these categories are consistently significantly associated with whether monitors endorse an election, and the magnitude of their coefficients is also larger than that of the more administrative problems. Table 4.1 shows the results of using simulations to predict

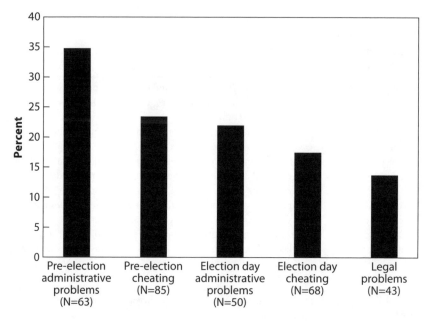

Figure 4.1: Percent of elections endorsed by international monitors despite major problems of a given type
Includes data on the organizations in Table 2.5, excluding the UN, the ECOWAS, the OAU/AU, and La Francophonie.

changes in outcomes when the values in the categories change from minimum to maximum. For example, if legal problems rise from none to the highest level, then the probability of endorsement will decrease about 20 percentage points. An increase in election day cheating shows the strongest effect with a 46 percentage point reduction in the probability of endorsement. It is interesting to note, however, that when there is a lot of cheating, monitors more often shift to an ambiguous assessment rather than to an outright denouncement. This is generally true for all the categories.

The focus on overt cheating and legal problems may be because monitoring organizations view these offenses as most damaging to the integrity of the election; administrative problems during the pre-election period may be easier to condone, because they can be construed as unintentional and if voters can act freely in the polling booth at least the possibility of choice remains. International election standards are also most direct in detailing the prominent elements of an election: the right to have votes counted equally and for voters to be able to exercise their political views free from intimidation and fear. No legal standard speaks directly to how the electoral commission should behave or how voter lists are compiled, although these factors clearly influence the ability of voters to choose freely. Similarly, monitors may focus on the legal framework for elections, because election monitoring originally began very much as an initiative of legal experts such as the International Human Rights Law Group (IHRLG). To this day, missions remain quite heavily staffed with legal experts.

The Special Relationship Bias

Monitoring organizations are usually cognizant of the risks of observing elections that are highly likely to be fraudulent.[44] Ironically, however, organizations such as the EU are also more likely to send missions to countries where they, or individual member states, have interests at stake, sometimes even if they expect the elections to have little chance of being acceptable. In some contexts, monitoring organizations may therefore experience particularly strong political pressure to be lenient toward countries with which they or their sponsors have a special relationship. Examples are plentiful. The Bosnia and Herzegovina elections in 1996 came at the end of the long engagement by the West in the conflict in the region and were important for the Western countries that had been engaged in the region for the first half of the decade. The OSCE was actually supervising the elections, not simply monitoring it. Furthermore, the election occurred just before presidential elections in the United States, which had staked much on acceptable elections in Bosnia and Herzegovina. Russia similarly benefited from some special concern in the mid- to late 1990s when the OSCE and the EU observers were hesitant to criticize the election although the obvious state dominance of the political space prevented true competition. In Zimbabwe in 2000, the election described in the previous chapter, the monitors from the South African Development Community (SADC) and what used to be the Organisation of African Unity had strong ties to Zimbabwe and this most likely contributed to their unwillingness to offer much substantial criticism. Another example of political pressure is the 1999 elections in Nigeria when important countries wanted to restore normal relations.[45] Both the Commonwealth Secretariat (CS) and the EU "sent their missions with strict warnings that their home governments wanted to endorse the elections and restore normal relations with Nigeria."[46] Thus, some organizations assign political importance to certain elections and criticize them less. Monitoring organizations may therefore display a special relationship bias toward geopolitically important states.

Although there are examples of elections where political pressure seemed prominent, these are idiosyncratic and therefore difficult to capture in statistical analysis. However, it is possible to see a pattern in foreign aid, which often connotes a political relationship.[47] As Chapter 2 discussed, foreign aid recipients already are more likely to be monitored, because donors often pressure aid recipients to accept monitors. Donors also have been keen for these countries to pass the election test so aid can continue or be resumed.[48] In Cambodia in 1998, for example, Japan, Association of Southeast Asian Nations (ASEAN), and Western governments wanted to resume aid and normal relations, and this constrained the IGOs monitoring the election.[49]

A review shows that monitors have indeed been more likely to endorse elections in nations receiving foreign aid.[50] Of the 70 missions to countries that received more than U.S.$1 billion in aid the year before the election, 54 endorsed the elections. That is a rate of 77 percent. In contrast, missions to countries with less or no aid endorsed elections 62 percent of the time. The difference could be because aid is given conditionally on good governance, in which case aid recipients would be inclined to hold cleaner elections. However, foreign aid does not seem to be a predictor of quality elections more generally. Indeed, one would expect foreign aid levels to correlate more with countries with poor domestic capacity and thus more problematic elections. The statistical analysis in Appendix C also suggests that monitoring organizations are more likely to endorse elections in countries that receive foreign aid, and the simulation results in Table 4.1 suggest that the effect is quite large, but in more extensive analysis the finding is not entirely robust. Thus, although there is some evidence that organizations are more lenient toward foreign aid recipients, generally the geopolitical pressures may be too difficult to capture in statistical analysis, as geopolitical relationships tend to be highly nuanced and idiosyncratic.

The Progress Bias

Many international monitoring missions are based within an agency that seeks to promote democracy. So when progress is partial but the election still falls short of meeting democratic standards, monitors may praise the progress, hoping their encouragement will help consolidate the gains. This bias makes monitors more likely to endorse elections in countries that display important progress. There are clear concerns that "to deny elections a passing grade would . . . risk provoking greater political closure."[51] This progress bias may lead monitoring organizations to endorse the results despite the still-flawed nature of the election.[52] Indeed, when monitors endorse highly problematic elections, words like *improvement* and *progress* often permeate their public statements. In the 1998 Cambodia case, for example, the JIOG stressed that the election was "a major achievement and a step forward."[53] In Kenya in 1992 the International Republican Institute (IRI) statement ended a critical report with a follow-up statement saying ,"but from our perspective we feel that this process is a significant step in Kenya's transition to genuine democracy."[54]

To assess the effects of the progress bias the statistical analysis used several different measures to examine the relationship between progress and endorsement. One indicator captured whether the organization itself described the election as "transitional" in its report. The analysis showed that international election monitors were more lenient toward countries transitioning toward democracy. The likelihood of an election being endorsed increased by 17 percentage points, from 67 percent for elections not characterized as "transitional" to 84 percent for those characterized as "transitional" (see Table 4.1).

Monitors also appeared more lenient with first multiparty elections. Monitors endorsed all the first multiparty[55] elections in the data with only minor problems while they condemned all the first multiparty elections with major problems such as those in Cameroon, Tanzania, Guinea, and Rwanda. However, when comparing elections that fell between these obvious cases, monitors more often endorsed first multiparty elections than not. However, in the statistical analysis this effect was never significant, and Table 4.1 therefore does not include predictions about first multiparty elections.

Finally, the analysis also showed that monitors were less likely to endorse the election if the incumbent kept power. Or, in other words, if the opposition won, the monitors were more likely to endorse the election. This is probably because, although the opposition sometimes also cheats, the incumbent is usually assumed to have the upper hand and a turnover of power is thus often seen as significant sign of progress. It is harder to claim that an election was fraudulent if the opposition managed to win. The simulation results in Table 4.1 show that that the probability that monitors will endorse an election jumps from 62 percent if the incumbent keeps power to 80 percent if the incumbent loses power.

Thus, monitoring organizations do show a progress bias. Measures of transition, first multiparty elections, and turnover all suggest that monitoring organizations are more lenient toward countries that appear to be making progress toward democratic ideals. The excitement of a transition or a change of power may lead to overly optimistic assessments of the quality of the election. This is indeed something the international community has observed time and again as the second elections after a supposed transition often will display what looks like backsliding.[56]

The Stability Bias

The stability bias means that monitoring organizations consider how their assessments may influence stability in the country. Although the prominent Cold War security-democracy dilemma eased with the rise of election monitoring in the early 1990s, violence during fragile democratization processes continues to concern the countries and organizations that work to promote democracy.[57] If international election monitors worry that their assessments may fuel violence, they may downplay their criticisms.[58] This is particularly worrisome, because strategic use of violence has even graver human rights implications than strategically omitting voters from the official registrar or restricting the media.

Monitors are more likely to worry about violent reactions to their assessments when pre-election violence has been widespread as in Zimbabwe, Cambodia, and Kenya. In such cases, the capacity for violence has already been demonstrated, and denouncing an election as flawed is more likely to provide a focal point for the opposition and fuel violence even further. As the elections in Zimbabwe in 2008 showed, incumbents who are unwilling to leave office may resort to violence to squash opposition supporters. Of course, it is also possible that opposition forces may revolt against what they perceive as a rubber stamp by election monitors. In the majority of cases, however, power lies with the incumbent and stability is best maintained by supporting the incumbent. If the incumbent is responsible for pre-election violence and then conducts a calm election day, monitors may downplay their criticisms in the interest of peace.

Examples abound. In Zimbabwe one commentator noted, "Perhaps it had become quite clear to all foreigners that if the opposition had won the elections, changing the government in Zimbabwe would not necessarily have been easy or peaceful."[59] Indeed, the EU mission took pride in having "contributed to reducing levels of violence."[60] In Kenya's 1992 election, fears of upheaval also tempered the criticism of outsiders.[61] The EU mission to Nigeria in 1999 likewise was caught in the dilemma between violence and truth. During the presidential election, "EU observation teams witnessed blatant examples of ballot box fraud in most of the 36 states of the Federation. The most celebrated instance was in the troubled oil-producing state of Bayelsa in the coastal Niger Delta region where, according to the Federal Election Commission's own figures, the turnout was 123%. Conflict within the EU delegation pitted a sizeable minority, which sought to make a formal condemnation of the election outcome, against a majority which favoured rapid stabilisation of a high-risk political situation."[62]

To examine the relationship between violence and endorsement, the analysis included measures of both pre-election violence and violence on the day of the election. The patterns in the data suggest that pre-election violence tempers criticism, but that a lot of violence on election day increases criticism. However, if a high level of pre-election violence is followed by a relatively calm election day, then monitors may hesitate to denounce the election because of the pre-election violence. Once election day turns violent, monitors realize that post-election stability is unlikely and that their statements cannot really change that. Furthermore, if election day is violent, a lenient assessment is likely to draw criticism. But if election day remains calm, then monitors may hope that the regime has the ability to maintain peace. As an example, the initially calm election day may be what led the EU to be quite positive at first about the election in Kenya in 2007. The chief of the mission told the press on election day that he had seen no evidence of fraud: "There are some technical problems but what is pleasing is that people are turning out to vote in large numbers and are doing so peacefully and patiently."[63] Yet, the EU observers themselves documented 190 cases of election-related violence, including murders, and noted that victims complained that both the police and courts ignored their complaints.[64] Thus it appeared that despite the horrendous pre-election violence, as long as election day was calm, the monitors were prepared to sound a positive note, the IRI even calling the election "successful" in the headline of its preliminary statement.[65] However, after violence spun out of control, the EU mission quickly changed tone and denounced the election.

In the statistical analysis in Appendix C, election day violence was not significant, but violence in the pre-election period was statistically associated with greater odds of endorsement. This relationship was highly robust across all the models. The simulation results in Table 4.1 show that when pre-election violence increases from the lowest to the highest level, the probability of endorsement increases from 60 to about 78 percent, or an absolute increase of about 18 percent. This is remarkable, because pre-election violence and irregularities are also highly positively correlated and it would therefore be logical if pre-election violence were associated with smaller—not greater—odds of endorsement.

Are the Supposed Biases Due to Resource Constraints?

The assessment of the quality of an election must often be accomplished with insufficient personnel, local expertise, and funds. Is the information failure because the election monitors face a resource constraint? On average, monitoring

missions have about eighty personnel present on the day of the election. However, a few outliers—missions that are able to send a far greater number of workers than most of their counterparts send—skew this figure. Thus, only about
half of missions deploy more than thirty personnel on the day of the election.
Because multiple missions frequently monitor the same elections, the average
number of observers from various missions in any given election nears 135 per
election. Again, however, outliers skew this, and only about half of all elections
have a total of fifty or more observers from the main organizations in this study.
Teams sent in advance, if any, are often smaller.

Meanwhile, the task is daunting: overseeing the integrity of the pre-election
conduct of media and politicians, law enforcement, and administrative election
preparation. In addition, on the day of the election, tasks include overseeing
the polling process at thousands of voting stations, some very remote, as well
as the handling of ballot boxes, the tabulation of the vote, the announcement
of results, and the formal complaint procedures. Although monitors typically
operate with a formal government invitation, full cooperation from the national
and local authorities may be lacking or misleading. Thus, the sheer task of as-
certaining the "truth" about the quality of the election is subject to numerous
practical constraints.

However, it does not seem that resource constraint plays a big role in whether
monitors endorse elections. Paradoxically, the amount of resources allocated to
a mission is a poor indicator of its credibility. Missions to elections that are fully
expected to be fraudulent are often small. Yet, because the fraud is so obvious,
such small missions will tend to issue highly critical and credible assessments.
Thus, smaller missions that criticize elections are not inherently less credible.
At the same time, the more resources an organization invests in an election, the
more likely it may be to spin its assessments positively. After all, when so many
resources are marshaled in an attempt to ensure free and fair elections, doesn't
a flawed election mean the mission somehow failed? Clearly the OSCE and the
United Nations (UN) faced this dilemma in the 1996 elections in Bosnia and
Herzegovina, which they not only monitored but also supervised. When organizations exert particularly large efforts, their sponsors may expect to see some
bang for their buck and elections should have benefited from the organizations'
presence.[66] Larger missions, therefore, are not inherently credible. A larger mission may allow monitors to collect better information, but this is no guarantee
that the assessments will be more honest. After the 2009 election in Afghanistan, for example, the UN mission in Afghanistan, which ran an election center
collecting data on turnout and fraud, only revealed evidence about the high
level of fraud after Peter Galbraith, the mission's deputy special representative,
publicly broke ranks.[67]

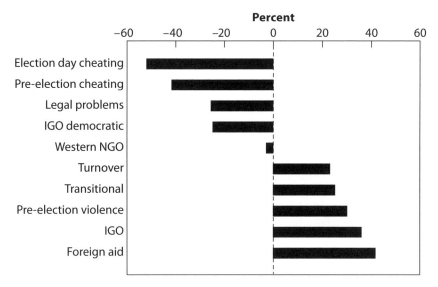

Figure 4.2: Relative changes in probability of endorsement based on changes from minimum to maximum values*
Based on Table 4.2. *In the case of indicators such turnover, it is the effect of moving from that indicator being equal to 0 (no turnover) to 1 (turnover).

DISCUSSION

What monitors say matters. Their endorsement can have important repercussions. In interstate relations it may affect future aid allocations,[68] the lifting of sanctions, and a country's standing in the community of nations. Even more important, it may matter domestically for the ability of a government to govern and to hold on to power and thus for the ability of the citizens to choose their government. As seen in Georgia in 2003 and in Ukraine in 2004, declarations of fraud can fuel revolutions or spur election reruns. Endorsements also can defuse tensions in elections that opposition parties otherwise might have challenged, as in Mexico in 1994, or facilitate the exit of the incumbent, as in Nicaragua in 1990.[69] The assessments of monitors thus shape the governance of countries and the lives of their citizens.

The neutrality of observer assessments is therefore very important. This is why the 2005 Code of Conduct on election observation states: "No one should be allowed to be a member of an international election observer mission unless that person is free from any political, economic, or other conflicts of interest that would interfere with conducting observations accurately and impartially and/or drawing conclusions about the character of the election process accurately and impartially."[70] Thus, neutrality is essential to the legitimacy of the monitoring process itself.[71]

However, the analysis in this chapter shows that monitors are not always neutral. Because of their various norms and politics, different organizations may assess elections differently, and even the same organization may evaluate elections of similar quality differently depending on their contexts. Specifically, the analysis identified five different factors that make monitors more likely to endorse elections: the nature of the sponsoring organization, the type of irregularities, the transitional nature of the election, any special relationships such as foreign aid, and, finally, the level of violence in the pre-election period. Figure 4.2 summarizes the findings by graphing the simulation results from Table 4.1 (column 4) as relative changes in probabilities. These are the effects of moving from the variables' minimum to maximum values. The findings establish more systematically than previous anecdotal evidence that certain biases are evident in the assessments and underscore that understanding the assessments requires attention to the monitors' politics and preferences beyond their formal mandates.

These biases may not themselves be good or bad, but they nonetheless compromise the neutrality of the assessments. This diminishes the credibility and authority of international organizations and transnational actors and detracts from the legitimacy of the monitoring process itself.[72]

The biases also alert both scholars and practitioners to when it may be more necessary to filter the information from monitors. For example, it may be wise to question assessments supplied from monitoring organizations when they are reporting from countries with high pre-election violence, or from countries that get a lot of foreign aid or otherwise have special relationships, or from countries considered to be in a volatile transitional stage.

Another concern is that if these factors lead monitors to inflate their confidence in the quality of the election, this may then also temper the efforts of the international community to address remaining problems.

CHAPTER 5

Do Politicians Change Tactics to Evade Criticism?

THE PREVIOUS CHAPTER SHOWED that whether monitors denounce an election depends partly on the types of irregularities committed. This raises an important issue: If politicians realize that they are less likely to be denounced for certain types of irregularities, do they or their accomplices stop cheating overtly and instead shrewdly shift their cheating to these less risky forms to evade criticism?[1] If they do, monitors may not only misjudge elections at times, but also distort how they are actually conducted. This is a serious concern.

But is it justified?

Politicians certainly do cheat quite creatively; some incumbents even try to manipulate the monitors as in the Kazakh example from Chapter 3. Despite these efforts, monitors were not fooled. Harassment and intimidation, restrictions on campaigning, media bias (even confiscation of entire newspapers), biased election administration, ballot box stuffing and failure to seal the ballot boxes, problems with the tabulation of the votes, and so on, were rampant. The Organization for Security and Co-operation in Europe (OSCE) report discussed an extensive mix of both overt and subtle forms of cheating and concluded that "the election did not meet a number of OSCE commitments and other international standards for democratic elections."[2] The use of subtler forms of fraud was part of a mix of forms of manipulation and did not appear chosen only to deceive monitors, nor was it successful at doing so.

In other cases, however, countries may be more successful. As Chapter 3 showed, some incumbents strategically invite less critical organizations. Therefore, the question is: Do politicians also shift into certain behaviors to evade criticism? If such shifts occur, how widespread is the problem and how much is it really driven by the presence of international monitors?

This question is not whether politicians shift to *clandestine* fraud. In theory, monitored countries could indeed deftly shift to clandestine forms of cheating, and if they do, then we will by definition never know. However, in practice, clandestine cheating is probably not that easy. Controlling the entire electoral apparatus is nearly impossible, and irregularities can occur at multiple levels. In heavy-handed regimes, fear may lead various decentralized actors to seek to please the regime by delivering the expected electoral outcomes through a variety of unsanctioned methods. And even if politicians skillfully conceal cheating at all levels, their repeated victories will raise suspicions and the world would witness a rise in countries that hold seemingly impeccable elections but never oust their governments despite various domestic problems. That said, some adept use of clandestine cheating may well occur on the margins, and no analysis can definitively rule out that politicians are using clandestine cheating to evade monitors.

However, it is more realistic to consider that fraud does not simply come in two forms: detectable and undetectable. Rather, all types of fraud are associated with a certain probability of detection, and, as explored in Chapter 4, a certain probability of criticism. And although politicians in monitored countries may have an even greater incentive to try to hide their cheating, with monitors present to scrutinize what is going on hiding malfeasance becomes harder.

Monitors are cognizant of the many possible weaknesses in the electoral process. They engage in a broad range of activities to uncover problems. In addition to direct observation, international monitors consult a wide array of sources, including incumbent parties, government officials, opposition parties, nongovernmental organizations (NGOs), and civil societies. Their often-extensive reports examine a vast array of behaviors, including manipulation of the media, voter rolls, election commissions, and so on. Thus, politicians may be creative in the ways they cheat,[3] but all cheating risks detection and monitors do report, though do not always denounce, a wide variety of irregularities. In the 1990s, for example, Kenya tried to institutionalize manipulation by using malapportionment and "nationality clauses" to discourage true political competition. And in 2000 both Russia and Peru used "borderline categories of targeted 'low-intensity' repression."[4] However, none of these behaviors went unnoticed by international monitors even if, as in the case of Russia in 2000, monitors still hesitantly accepted the election.

Thus all cheating risks detection and inviting international monitors does not make it easier to hide. Therefore, the question this chapter explores is not whether monitors cause politicians to shift into hidden forms of fraud. Rather it is: Knowing that monitors may tolerate some irregularities more than others, do politicians successfully change the way they cheat to evade outright denouncement?

WHAT CONSTITUTES EVIDENCE OF A MONITOR-INDUCED SHIFT?

If riskier irregularities are those that monitors are more likely to denounce, while safer forms of irregularities are those monitors are more hesitant to denounce, then if monitors cause politicians to successfully shift to safer forms of cheating, two patterns should hold.

The first pattern to expect pertains to the profile of any one given election. If monitors cause politicians to substitute successfully into safer forms of cheating to evade criticism, then in any one given election, when safer forms of cheating occur, riskier forms of cheating should be less common. However, this pattern should not hold in nonmonitored elections, where, if present, risky and safer forms of cheating should be complements.

The existence of this pattern does not in and of itself mean that monitors caused it. All dishonest politicians have incentives to vary how they cheat to evade attention and maximize their legitimacy.[5] As Andreas Schedler has argued, "The limits of the authoritarian imagination are not logical, but empirical. Rulers may choose a number of tactics to help them carve the democratic heart out of electoral contests."[6] Indeed, governments have long engaged in a variety of subtle methods of manipulation throughout the election period. Attempts at weakening the opposition were present during ancient Rome's strategy of *divide et impera*. Governments have long sought to prevent voters from acquiring true information about their choices. Singapore, Malaysia, and Thailand have all practiced such pseudo democracy since the mid-1960s, since the early 1970s, and during most of the 1980s, respectively.[7] Some of the redistricting battles in the United States attest to the continued forms of subtle manipulation even in established democracies, as did the longstanding attempts to bar black voters from registering to vote. Thus, the mere presence of safer forms of fraud is not unusual and does not prove that monitors caused the behaviors. However, if safer irregularities nearly always coexist with riskier irregularities, this undermines the argument that monitors cause politicians to switch to safer irregularities to avoid criticism.

The second pattern to expect pertains to changes in the mix of election irregularities over time. If monitors cause politicians to successfully switch to safer forms of cheating, then from one election to the next, increases in safer forms of cheating should correlate with decreases in riskier forms. However, this pattern should be less prevalent in nonmonitored countries.

Once again, however, even if monitors are associated with such a shift, this does not necessarily mean that they caused it. The conduct of elections may fluctuate for various reasons. For example, newly democratic countries often backslide.[8] Fraudulent elections may occur as a deviation from a better history, as in the 2000 election in Peru.[9] Indeed, a host of forces bring oscillation between democratic progress and setbacks,[10] producing a mixed quality of elections over time. In democratizing countries, some irregularities may take longer to address, because they require the passage of legislation and the creation of implementation mechanisms.[11] Overt fraud may be easier to eradicate, while subtler types may persist due to underdeveloped capacity and inexperience.

Thus, if international election observers are present, they may then be associated with a decrease in riskier fraud but persistence in subtler, safer types of irregularities. Because safer types of irregularities tend to be administrative, they may even increase during a period of democratization as more people are learning how to register to vote and as more parties compete. An apparent rise in safer irregularities could also be because some monitoring organizations have improved reporting practices over time. For example, the early OSCE reports were short and almost exclusively focused on election day. Since 1996, the reports have considered a variety of problems, but this does not necessarily mean that these problems have grown. Thus, a rise in safer irregularities does not prove that monitors brought this about. However, if countries where safer irregularities appear to increase over time do not also show a concomitant decline in riskier behaviors, then it makes little sense to accuse monitors of causing strategic substitution of safer behaviors.

Thus, neither the presence of a particular pattern of irregularities nor the presence of shift between types of irregularities necessarily means monitors are to blame. However, if safer forms of cheating are accompanied by continued or increased risky forms of cheating, then the use of the safer forms of cheating can hardly be characterized as strategic efforts to hide from monitors, and thus monitors can hardly be blamed for them. It would also be hard to blame monitors for a shift if the patterns in monitored elections really do not differ from those in nonmonitored elections. Thus, for it to be at least plausible that monitors cause politicians to change how they cheat, then safer and riskier forms of cheating should be *substitutes*, not complements. However, this pattern should not hold in nonmonitored elections, where, if present, risky and safer forms of cheating should be complements.

Even if we do see increases in safer forms of cheating accompanied by decreases in riskier forms, then it is necessary to investigate further whether the observed shift in a given country is possibly because of monitors, or whether it has alternative explanations.

What Are the Safer Forms of Cheating?

Safer forms of cheating are those that monitors are less likely to denounce. Thus, politicians may seek to shift the timing of their manipulation. As noted in the previous chapter, it is a standard criticism that monitors pay most attention to the events on election day and ignore events before the election.[12] Certainly international monitoring organizations have the largest delegation present on the day of the election and are more active on that day than in the pre-election period. Therefore, if politicians understand the biases of monitors and seek to exploit them, then the strategic response would be to shift manipulation from election day to the pre-election period. Instead of gross ballot box fraud, politicians would control the media, abuse incumbent resources, or manipulate the voting lists. Instead of buying votes and violating the secrecy of the vote, politicians would stack the electoral commission in their favor, make candidate registration difficult, and so on.

However, the previous chapter found that monitors' overall assessments depend less on the timing of the irregularities than on their nature. Monitors were more likely to criticize blatant forms of cheating both on election day and in the pre-election period. Thus, tabulation problems, voting fraud, intimidation, misuse of media or government resources, or restriction on freedom to campaign, and so on—those behaviors that are clearly intended to manipulate the outcome—were more likely to trigger negative assessments from the international monitors. Similarly, legal frameworks that enable biased electoral commissions, or restrict the scope of the office, or restrict who can vote or stand in elections and so forth, were also likely to draw criticisms. In contrast, monitors appeared willing to give countries the benefit of the doubt when the problems might stem from inexperience or lack of capacity. Administrative problems such as errors in voter lists, complaints about the conduct of the electoral commission, problems with voter information, logistical issues during voting, and so forth were not likely to trigger criticism by monitors. To exploit these tendencies, politicians would therefore shift away from the more overt irregularities to those that can be dismissed as administrative shortcomings.

Finally, violence and repression are common tactics for leaders to use to hold on to power.[13] Pre-election violence has been particularly prominent in countries such as Colombia, India, Iran, South Africa, and the Philippines. Violence during the pre-election period is relatively easy to observe and such violence is also generally associated with poor overall election quality. Monitoring organizations are therefore hard pressed to comment on it and they frequently do. Nevertheless, Chapter 4 found that monitors were less likely to denounce elections outright when pre-election violence was high. This hesitation to criticize could well be because monitoring organizations fear galvanizing further conflict after the election. If politicians realize this, then they may shift away from other types of fraud and instead increase their use of pre-election violence.

In sum, if politicians are seeking to reduce their risk of denouncement by international monitors, they might rely particularly on safer tactics such as (1) pre-election manipulation, (2) manipulation that could be construed as administrative, or (3) pre-election violence.

DATA: THE VARIETIES OF IRREGULARITIES

To examine the patterns of cheating, the analysis uses the data already discussed in Chapter 4, Table 4.2. For review, these larger categories are listed in Table 5.1. They are all ordered variables that rank problems as none, minor, moderate, or major.[14] Two datasets exist of these variables. One is based on election monitoring reports and therefore is only available for monitored elections. The other is based on U.S. Department of State Reports on Human Rights Practices, and is available for both monitored and nonmonitored elections. This chapter uses both sets of data. For more on these, see Appendix A.

The difference between administrative problems and outright cheating is not their probability of detection. If done cleverly, gross forms of cheating such as ballot stuffing or vote buying may be no more visible than misconduct by the electoral commission in the pre-election period. Indeed, problems with voter lists, for example, may be more visible than misuse of public funds. Rather, the difference between administrative problems and those categorized as cheating is the degree to which they can be assumed to be intentional and therefore be likely to draw strong criticism.

The behaviors classified as cheating are those where intent is reasonably certain. Politicians do not intimidate voters by accident. Vote buying is not a product of undeveloped logistical capacity. Reporting more votes for the incumbent than turnout justifies is not because the election officials cannot count. Similarly, incumbents do not restrict or dominate state media because no contrary voices exist, they do not ban campaign activities of opponents because there is nowhere to hold rallies, nor do they use government coffers to fund their campaigns because they forgot to open a separate bank account. Instead, the most likely intention of these behaviors is to manipulate the outcome of the election.

In contrast, for behaviors classified as administrative problems the intent is more ambiguous. Failure to inform voters of their polling station locations could be intentional, but it also could be because the information is difficult to get out. Voter list problems could be due to systematic manipulation to favor

TABLE 5.1
Main categories of irregularities

Legal problems
Pre-election administration
Election day administration
Pre-election cheating
Election day cheating
Pre-election violence
Election day violence

some parties and politicians, but they also could be caused by problems with processing paperwork. Lack of professionalism or neutrality on the electoral commission could be planned, but it could also be the result of a lack of proper training and experience. Not ensuring that voters have full secrecy or that campaign materials are kept at a proper distance from the polling station could be abusive, but such problems could also be oversights or lack of training for poll workers. So, in general, administrative problems could be intentional, or they could be blamed on lack of capacity or experience.

Legal problems are in a separate category. First, they do not occur at a specific time, so one cannot categorize them as pre-election or election day problems. Second, the degree to which their intent is discernable varies. Limiting the scope of an elected office is clearly part of a design to monopolize power, as is disenfranchising parts of the population, but other legal problems stem from inexperience with elections. Newly established democracies may take some time to develop proper campaign finance laws, to institute media regulations, to institutionalize the appointment of electoral officials, and so forth. In this analysis, then, only elections with overt restrictions on the scope of the office, voting rights, and so forth were classified as having a high level of legal problems that could be classified as overt cheating that therefore has a higher risk of drawing monitor denouncement.

As discussed earlier, riskier irregularities are those that monitors are more likely to denounce, while safer forms are those that monitors are more hesitant to denounce. Based on the discussion above, if the argument is that politicians change the *timing* of the manipulation, then safer tactics are all those that fall under pre-election administration and pre-election cheating, while riskier forms are election day administration and cheating. If the argument is that politicians change the *type* of their manipulation, the safer tactics are irregularities that pertain to the pre-election and election day administration, while riskier forms are pre-election and election day cheating as well as overt legal irregularities. In addition, pre-election violence may be considered a safer form of irregularity.

THE RECORD

It is now possible to examine whether the data on irregularities produce the patterns discussed earlier that would be expected if monitors were causing evasive behaviors. The first part of the investigation looks only at monitored elections. This makes it possible to take advantage of the higher density of the data in the election monitoring reports. Furthermore, multiple organizations are often present, which improves the reliability of the data. The second part of the investigation compares patterns in monitored and nonmonitored elections based on the U.S. State Department reports.

For overview, Figure 5.1 shows the distribution of the various types of irregularities reported by monitors. The most common type of irregularity is administrative problems, but overt cheating and legal problems are nearly as widespread. Aside from violence, which is least common, other irregularities appear with remarkably similar frequency.

Indeed, if one considers *type* of irregularities, then nearly one-third of monitored elections undertake the highest levels of at least one of the riskier manipulations, pre-election cheating, election day cheating, or legal problems.[15] If one instead considers *timing*, then nearly one-quarter of all elections had the highest levels of either election day cheating, or election day administrative problems, or both. These figures alone do not prove that some politicians are not changing tactics to evade criticisms, but they do show that, if politicians are trying to shift away from riskier types of irregularities or election day irregularities, then many are doing a poor job. Changing tactics may indeed be difficult.

Substitutes or Complements?

PATTERNS OF CHEATING

The first argument was that if monitors cause politicians to switch to safer forms of cheating, then when safer forms of cheating occur, riskier forms of cheating should be less common. In the data from the monitoring reports, however, safer and riskier forms of cheating correlate positively. Most elections

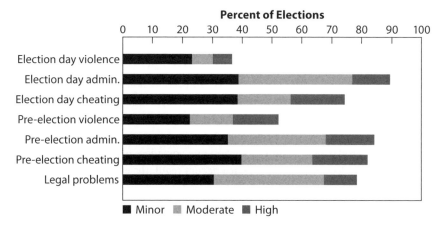

Figure 5.1: Incidence of various election irregularities in monitored elections as reported by monitoring reports
Number of observations for which data were available for these variables = 287 to 292 elections. Reports were commonly missing from the OAU/AU, the ECOWAS, and the UN. La Francophonie reports were also not coded on these detailed variables. Because these organizations operate in less democratic elections, Figure 5.1 may underestimate the incidences of different types of irregularities.

with many pre-election problems tend to also have many election day problems and those with few pre-election problems tend to hold better election days. The same relationship exists between administrative problems and more overt cheating. Elections with a lot of overt cheating and legal problems also have a lot of administrative problems and those with little overt cheating also have fewer administrative problems.

One way of looking at this more in depth is to consider only the elections where safer irregularities were high, because those are the elections where politicians may be using safer irregularities to evade criticism. Were riskier irregularities low in these elections, as a pattern of evasion would suggest? If one first considers types of irregularities, then sixty of the monitored elections, or about 21 percent, had the highest level of at least one of the two safer administrative forms of irregularities. That is, these elections can be labeled cases where safer forms of irregularities were particularly high. However, of these sixty elections, a full two-thirds also had the highest level of at least one type of risky irregularity. This is unexpected if the countries were strategically shifting from riskier to safer forms of fraud. Another 25 percent had a moderate level. Indeed, only four of the sixty elections, or less than 10 percent, had a low level of all the riskier forms of irregularities.

The patterns do not change much if instead one examines the timing of irregularities. Here, if one leaves out legal problems and violence and looks only at administrative and cheating problems that occur on the day of the election or in the pre-election period, it turns out that of the seventy-eight elections that have the highest level of at least one form of pre-election irregularity, only 14 percent have a low level of both of the election day irregularities. The concurrence of high levels of legal problems and high levels of obvious cheating is equally striking.

Finally, a similar picture emerges when one considers pre-election violence. Unfortunately election-related violence occurs regularly, even in societies that are not normally embroiled in conflict. Indeed, pre-election violence is much more common than election day violence or post-election conflict. About one-fifth of all the elections included in this study had high pre-election violence, which was often deadly. In terms of types of irregularities, of the forty-five monitored elections where pre-election violence was moderate or high, at least one of the forms of obvious cheating was also high in thirty-one elections, or nearly 70 percent of the time. In terms of timing, at least one form of pre-election irregularity was also high in half the elections. In just ten of the elections—or less than one-quarter—was high pre-election violence accompanied by only minor forms of other irregularities.

So, the available evidence suggests that monitored countries that use safer forms of manipulations tend to *also* use risky forms of manipulation. Only a few countries use high levels of safe manipulation combined with low levels of risky irregularities. Nevertheless, this is the combination of irregularities that would be most expected if indeed the presence of monitors were prompting politicians to switch from risky to safer forms of fraud. Rather, in monitored elections, the reality seems to be that *bad things tend to go together*. That is, safer and riskier forms of irregularities are complements, not substitutes, as would be expected if politicians were shifting into safer forms of manipulation to avoid criticism.

CORRELATION OF CHANGES

The second argument to consider was that if monitors cause politicians to switch into safer forms of cheating, then increases in safer forms of cheating should correlate with decreases in riskier forms of cheating. As opposed to the static comparison of levels of different irregularities above, this claim is about *changes* in levels from one election to another. The election data based on the U.S. State Department reports facilitate comparison of the correlations for both monitored and nonmonitored elections.

To focus on changes, my analysis ignored all the cases where nothing changed from one election to another, and instead focused on the elections where the patterns of irregularities varied. Although this substantially reduced the sample of elections, it illuminated whether at least a subsample of politicians shifted away from risky behaviors to safer ones, and if so, whether this was specific to monitored elections or occurred more generally.

Figures 5.2 and 5.3 show how shifts in one type of behavior correlated with shifts in another type for both monitored and nonmonitored elections.[16]

In terms of *types* of cheating, the likely scenario for a strategic shift would involve countries where overt types of cheating decrease on or before election day, or both.[17] Figure 5.2 examines this subset of cases. The darker of the central set of columns shows that when monitored countries decreased overt cheating, they most commonly did not increase safer administrative irregularities. On the contrary, nearly 50 percent committed the same level of administrative irregularities and nearly 40 percent actually reduced their administrative irregularities as well. Indeed, countries that decreased overt cheating were more likely to also decrease administrative irregularities than increase them, although in about 10 percent of elections increases did occur. Moreover, monitored countries were not more likely than nonmonitored countries to switch into administrative irregularities. If anything, countries that cut back their overt cheating also reduced their administrative problems more often when international monitors were present.

Because one might consider legal problems another type of overt cheating, Figure 5.3 inspects what happens when legal problems decrease. Figure 5.3 shows that when countries decreased their legal deficiencies, they did not typically shift to safer administrative problems.

Figure 5.4 examines timing: Did governments substitute election day cheating for pre-election cheating? Again, this was not the most common pattern. It did occur sometimes, but notably, politicians who decreased election day cheating increased their pre-election cheating more often when monitors were not present, suggesting that even if this pattern occurred sometimes, monitors were not to blame for the shift.

Finally, Figure 5.5 examines what happens to pre-election violence when overt cheating on election day decreases. Here the monitored and nonmonitored elections show nearly identical patterns, and pre-election violence is as likely to decrease as to increase when countries use less overt election day cheating.

One could continue to examine other shifts, but they tend to show similar patterns: Different types of problems tend to go together. Safer and riskier forms of irregularities are complements, not substitutes. Monitored countries do not behave markedly different from nonmonitored.

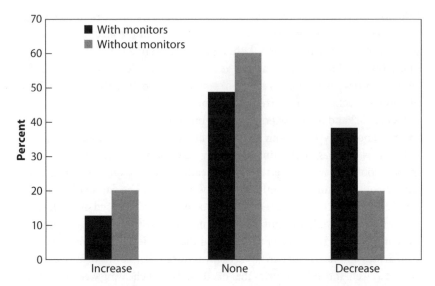

Figure 5.2: Changes in administrative irregularities when overt cheating decreases
Number of observations = 100.
Reproduced with permission from Kelley 2012.

Looking Briefly at Some Cases

To further determine whether there is great cause for concern that monitors prompt a switch toward safer forms of fraud, it is informative to look at a few cases. The short list of monitored elections that fit the profile of having the highest level of safer, administrative types of irregularities and a low level of risky overt cheating comprises Lesotho in 1993, El Salvador in 1994, Guyana in 1997, and Suriname in 2000.[18] Are these elections possible cases of monitor-induced shifts in patterns of cheating?

Lesotho's 1993 election was a first multiparty election in a country unaccustomed to running elections. Thus, the low level of risky fraud was likely due to goodwill to run a clean election, whereas the high level of safer irregularities very well could have been due to administrative inexperience.

In El Salvador the monitoring reports covered election problems extensively. However, the pattern was unsupportive of the notion that monitors induced a shift in type of irregularities. Appendix E discusses the case more extensively, but basically monitors reported low levels of risky cheating with moderate or high levels of safer irregularities throughout the 1990s. Improvements began with the gradual erosion of support for the Alianza Republicana Nacionalista (ARENA), domestically as well as by traditional supporters such as the United

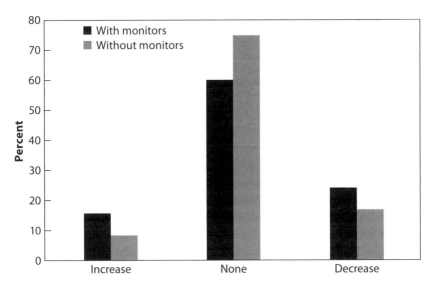

Figure 5.3: Changes in administrative irregularities if legal problems decrease
Number of observations = 74.
Reproduced with permission from Kelley 2012.

States. Thus, it does not seem that the 1994 election with its high level of safer irregularities was really a shift away from risky forms of cheating.

Guyana held two elections in the 1980s, one monitored (1980) and one not monitored (1985). A similar pattern of risky fraud and low levels of safer forms of fraud characterized both elections. The presence of monitors in one and not in the other thus did not appear to change the pattern of irregularities. It is possible that reporting at the time was not extensive enough to pick up on other types of problems or the problems were considered irrelevant given the high levels of obvious cheating. The elections in 1992 and 1997 were both monitored and were characterized by lower levels of risky problems while higher levels of safer problems persisted, so these elections could perhaps fit the profile. But then, in the monitored election in 2001, the risky problems in the pre-election period increased again. All these elections are characterized by violence, particularly on election day. The lack of a shift between the monitored and nonmonitored elections in the 1980s, combined with an increase in risky cheating in the monitored election in 2001, contradicts the idea that the patterns observed in the 1997 election resulted from a strategic shift due to the presence of monitors.

Suriname comes closer to a pattern of a strategic use of safer irregularities, because in the 1987, 1991, 1996, and 2000 elections the level of safer types of

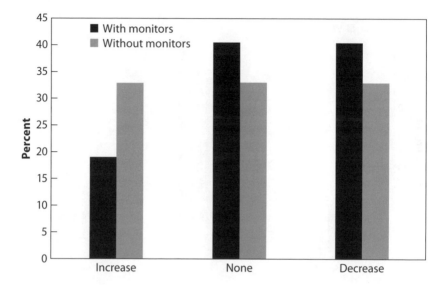

Figure 5.4: Changes in pre-election cheating if election day cheating decreases
Number of observations = 117.

fraud grows steadily in the presence of monitors. However, even here, this movement does not coincide with a clear shift *away* from more risky types of cheating, because, perhaps with the exception of the 1992 election, overt and risky cheating was never reported as being particularly prominent.

A similar examination can be done of the elections that displayed a pattern of low election day problems but high pre-election problems. The list of elections that fit this pattern includes Belarus in 1995, Colombia in 2002, Croatia in 1997, Guatemala in 1985 and 1990, Liberia in 1997, Paraguay in 1988, Russia in 1999, Uganda in 1996, and Zimbabwe in 1985. Do these elections suggest that these countries were reacting to the presence of monitors by shifting their manipulation to the period to the pre-election period when fewer monitors were present?

Not really. For most of these countries the combination of low election day irregularities and high pre-election irregularities look like an aberration from a trend where these problems either appear together or not at all. Gross levels of both election day and pre-election day problems, for example, have characterized the last three elections in Belarus, although they have all been monitored. Similarly in Guatemala: After elections in the 1980s, which were characterized by high pre-election problems, in the 1990s Guatemalan elections improved—even the 1994 election, which was not monitored, was decent. The

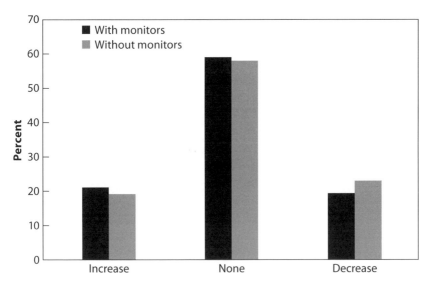

Figure 5.5: Changes in pre-election violence if election day cheating decreases
Number of observations = 97.

monitored election in 1995 worsened a bit, and then the monitored election in 1999 improved again. But then in 2003, election day problems were again quite high—despite the presence of monitors. Thus, there is no clear pattern that suggests the fraud was being shifted from one period to another in reaction to the presence of monitors. And although the problems in Zimbabwe's 1985 election were mostly confined to the pre-election period, this too appears to be an aberration. The widespread problems in 2000 and 2002 suggest that Zimbabwe has not learned to manipulate the observers by cheating only in the pre-election period.

Colombia held two elections in 2002, a legislative election in March and a presidential election in May. Both elections had high pre-election levels of intimidation. Both elections were monitored. The presidential election likely had a lower level of election day problems because of the outpouring of criticisms of the legislative election, rather than a strategic shift into pre-election irregularities. The Organization of American States (OAS) report talks about the attention paid to the parliamentary election by the media, which criticized officials for ignorance of the law, the lack of transparency in the selection of election judges, the lack of regulation of pre-count procedures, and so on. The OAS criticism of the legislative election may also have contributed to a better-run presidential election day, but that hardly means that the monitors caused a strategic shift from high election day problems into high pre-election irregularities, given that pre-election irregularities were high in both elections.

The 1999 election in Russia is the classic example of a smooth election day but heavily manipulated pre-election environment. Indeed, the Kremlin may have intentionally used and continued to rely on such hefty manipulations of the pre-election environment to minimize monitor criticisms. Russia has held seven monitored elections, and most of them have had problems in the pre-election period or on election day. However, it seems that the pre-election irregularities are simply the style of Russian "managed" elections that has earned Russia's the title of a "managed democracy," and that it serves primarily to manipulate the Russian voters rather than deceiving Western observers. Indeed, Russia's recent efforts to discourage OSCE participation altogether suggest that by now the Kremlin is not very interested in Western endorsements.[19]

Discussion

This chapter began by asking whether the expected presence of international monitors causes politicians to switch to forms of manipulation that monitors may be less likely to denounce. It argued that for this to at least be plausible risky and safer irregularities should be substitutes, not complements. However, the available data do not support this. In contrast, the exploration of the data suggests that risky forms of cheating are common in the presence of monitors; that safer and riskier irregularities are positively correlated; and that shifts away from risky irregularities do not coincide with shifts into safer forms. The examination of the individual countries where an election had displayed few risky but many safe forms of irregularities also suggested that these election patterns most likely were not the result of a shift in response to the presence of international monitors.

It is a concern that politicians may use violence in the pre-election period to unnerve the international monitors and the international community such that they are more likely to accept the election outcome. However, because a high level of other problems usually accompanies pre-election violence, politicians do not appear to be using pre-election violence *instead* of other forms of cheating. Pre-election violence is more common in monitored elections than in nonmonitored elections, but it is unclear whether monitors actually increase the use of pre-election violence. In a simple regression analysis, a history of pre-election violence is the main predictor of pre-election violence and the presence of monitors is not statistically significant. This suggests pre-election violence may simply be part of the political culture or of a larger historical pattern of gross irregularities intended to steal the election.

Overall, the data suggest that—whether elections are monitored or not—politicians who cheat are by and large neither subtle nor safe. The data in this analysis is naturally limited, and many irregularities likely go unobserved. However, it is unlikely that there is a form of clandestine cheating that is unique to monitored elections, because if such clandestine cheating were easy to do, then all politicians would have an incentive to use it to win elections and overt cheating should decrease. In reality, all forms of fraud carry risks of detection, and the high level of reported fraud suggests that the risks are quite large. In both monitored and nonmonitored elections a great deal of irregularities and problems continues to occur and be reported. Indeed, rampant cheating persists—a fact also bemoaned by the 2011 Freedom House reports, which even argues that it is getting worse: "To be sure, rigged elections, persecution of dissidents, and rule by executive fiat are not novel developments in these countries. But the violations were carried out with a striking degree of aggressiveness, self-assurance, and disregard for outside opinion."[20]

Thus, although Chapter 4 showed that monitors do sometimes falsely endorse problematic elections and that they are more likely to tolerate certain types of irregularities, politicians do not appear particularly adept at exploiting this weakness. Cheating is a difficult business and most cheaters need to avail themselves of a mix of strategies to manipulate the voters as well as the vote. Instead of shifting away from riskier forms of cheating, politicians appear to rely instead on the tactic in Chapter 3, which showed that some countries strategically invite friendly monitors. Why change the way you cheat to try to evade monitor criticism if it is possible to simply invite friendlier monitors? This does not mean that international monitors should not remain alert to efforts to cheat in new and creative ways. Indeed, their vigilance is necessary to prevent such strategies from becoming successful.

PART II

CHAPTER 6

International Monitors as Reinforcement

> International election observation has the potential to enhance the
> integrity of election processes, by deterring and exposing irregulari-
> ties and fraud.
> —Declaration of Principles for International Election Observation
> and Code of Conduct for International Election Observers, 2005[1]

> The most serious incident involved the chairperson of the local elec-
> tion committee reading out the wrong names when the ballot papers
> were to be put into different piles for the nine candidates. The chair-
> person was well aware of what she was doing. She was taking votes
> from Levon Ter-Petrosian and allocating them to the [then-] Prime
> Minister, Serzh Sarkisian. Election officials tried to hide what they
> were doing by holding their hands over the ballot papers or by plac-
> ing them in the middle of the piles so that I could not see them. . . .
> I noticed that all the election officials were well aware of what they
> were doing and they felt uneasy when I stood behind them watching
> the electoral fraud. But that did not prevent them from continuing
> to do what they had probably already planned, namely to ensure that
> the sitting prime minister got enough votes so that there would be no
> need for a second round.
> —Monitor in Armenian polling station, 2007[2]

ULTIMATELY INTERNATIONAL MONITORING GROUPS hope to do more than assess elections; they seek to improve them. The previous chapters have shown
that monitors do not always provide unbiased information and may sometimes
endorse fraudulent elections. This problem makes it even more imperative to
consider what benefits international monitors do provide. If there are draw-
backs to international monitors in terms of inaccuracy and bias, do they create
benefits in terms of improvements in elections? Elections may suffer from at
least two ailments. First, politicians may cheat. Second, countries may run elections poorly because they lack capacity and experience. By bearing witness and
by offering advice and assistance, monitoring organizations direct their efforts
at both problems. Indeed, most monitoring organizations are confident that
they deter fraud and improve elections. The Asian Network for Free Elections

(ANFREL) goes so far as to assert that election monitoring has been "proven effective" at deterring fraud.[3] But do international election observers actually improve election quality? That is the most elusive, yet also the absolutely central question about election monitoring.

Historically confidence in the ability of monitors to improve elections has been boosted by a series of extraordinary elections for which monitors have received considerable credit. These include the election in Chile 1988 that ended the rule of Augusto Pinochet,[4] the first multiparty election in Zambia 1991 that saw a peaceful transfer of power,[5] the 1990 election in Nicaragua, where President Daniel Ortega accepted defeat,[6] the path-breaking election in South Africa in 1994 that ended decades of apartheid, and the historic rerun of the 2004 election in the Ukraine.

Yet, just as many examples of ineffectiveness can be found in numerous countries where—despite repeated monitoring—elections have not improved. Prominent cases include Angola, Azerbaijan, Cambodia, Cameroon, Haiti, Kazakhstan, Kenya, Kyrgyzstan, Togo, Uganda, and Uzbekistan. These examples drive home that it is far from given that international election monitoring improves the quality of elections and that skepticism is warranted. Despite efforts to become more professional, monitors still do not present a terribly formidable force. Monitoring an election is an overwhelming task for which most international organizations remain woefully under-resourced. Monitoring a complete election campaign is challenging and requires many kinds of resources and local knowledge that many observer groups lack. Most groups visit only a fraction of polling stations and their patterns of visits are often fairly predictable due to logistics or security. Even for the stations that are visited, monitors cannot be present continuously. Polling officials may be able to give the appearance of propriety until monitors arrive and while monitors are present, only to cheat after they leave. In addition, as noted in previous chapters, international monitors come from many different types of organizations and are of highly varying quality. Several organizations are biased and weak, and may be even less likely to engender respect and motivate any sort of behavioral changes.

Furthermore, whereas it is hard for international actors to pressure countries to undertake any kind of reform, politicians are likely to be particularly reluctant to improve the conduct of elections, because this directly threatens their power. Indeed, for some politicians eliminating cheating may lead to a complete loss of power and rob them of the ability to reap any of the benefits that a stamp of legitimacy or other rewards linked to a clean election might provide.[7] These benefits will go to the victors of the elections. Such benefits will therefore mean little to incumbent decision makers who risk losing political power. Given that power is an enormous prize to lose, in extreme cases leading to prosecution or loss of life itself,[8] the efforts of international monitors to improve elections are really working against the odds. The notion that one could deploy monitors to just any election and expect improvements is probably misguided. So, it is unsurprising that numerous countries have been monitored several times, but their elections have not improved.

Despite the enormity of the challenge, monitors may be able to improve elections though several different, but complementary, mechanisms. First of all, according to traditional rationalist logic, politicians pursue their own interests in maintaining power; therefore, they respond to changes in their incentive structure. Monitors alter their incentive structure both by raising the cost of cheating and by increasing the benefits of honesty; politicians therefore cheat less because it is in their interests. The expectation of this argument is that if an individual election is monitored, then the likelihood of cheating in that election decreases and the election is therefore more likely to be of higher quality.

Second, according to constructivist logic, politicians behave according to their norms and beliefs; therefore, their behavior may change if their norms and beliefs change. Following this logic, through repeated interactions international monitors may socialize politicians and voters into a set of norms and expectations about elections through persuasion, teaching, and the like. Their advice and assistance may help countries build better institutions and combat entrenched acceptance of fraud as the best way to run elections. Improvements brought through socialization are most likely to materialize only over time as monitors attend a series of elections in a country and repeatedly interact and offer advice.

Drawing on both of these logics, this chapter discusses how international monitors may improve elections and when their efforts may be more likely to succeed or fail. The chapter argues that monitors can indeed improve elections, but their influence is conditioned by domestic and international factors. In reality, therefore, monitors play a reinforcement role by building on existing domestic potential and enhancing the effectiveness of other international leverage. The following chapters and appendixes explore these arguments empirically through both statistical analysis and country case studies.

ALTERING INCENTIVES TO CHEAT

The most basic rational choice argument is that monitoring improves performance because it changes the incentive structure of those being observed. International relations theory often stresses that the monitoring function of international institutions enhances cooperation by lowering member state incentives to renege on their commitments.[9] Similarly, when international monitors observe and report election irregularities they may alter the payoff structure, and thus the behavior, of domestic parties by exposing any fraud. In a quasi-experiment in Armenia, Susan Hyde has demonstrated that polling stations that had some contact with monitors during polling day reported lower votes for the incumbents.[10] District-level analysis of a field experiment in Ghana also found that the increase in voter registrations is lower in areas with election observers, indicating that less registration fraud may be occurring when monitors are present.[11]

Other scholars have argued that the presence of international observers "limits the capacity of incumbents to engage in large-scale fraud."[12] As discussed below, international monitors may increase the cost of cheating in several ways.

Increasing Risk of Exposure

One way monitors can increase the cost of cheating is to increase the risk of exposure. But is it harder to cheat when monitors are watching? Certainly the persistent reporting of gross fraud in nearly one-quarter of all election monitoring reports coded for this project shows that despite their limitations monitors are quite capable of discovering cheating. In many of these cases, however, the fraud might well have been exposed in any case. The fact that the Organization for Security and Co-operation in Europe (OSCE) was absent from the 2008 presidential election in Russia did not leave the organization in doubt about the quality of that election, for example. This was partly because other monitoring organizations such as the Council of Europe (COE) maintained a small presence, but it was also because there is a large diplomatic core in Russia, and a fairly open system of information so that the entire world was able to ascertain that Vladimir Putin's handpicked successor enjoyed unfair advantages of government resources in a variety of ways. Similarly, although international monitors are not present, Western commentators never gave elections in Mubarak's Egypt a clean bill of health. Some types of manipulations such as preferential media treatment are obvious, whether monitors are present or not. In subtler cases, international monitors may still increase the risk of detection. However, it is even more important that monitors may increase the risk of *exposure*, because they can call more attention to the fraud than domestic actors, and therefore the fraud becomes more visible.[13] For example, in Panama in 1989 the National Democratic Institute (NDI) and International Republican Institute (IRI) assisted the Catholic Church with a parallel vote tabulation, which revealed government manipulation. President Jimmy Carter, who was working with the NDI/IRI joint mission, drew vast attention by publicly denouncing the official voting results—a fact that helped trigger the subsequent U.S. invasion.[14] Similarly, in the wake of the Georgia 2008 election, monitors received extraordinary attention as others sought information about the quality of the election. Indeed, the Carter Center (CC) states that one of the main objectives of election observation is to "demonstrate the international community's interest and support for elections that meet international standards,"[15] and that "international observers can play a critically important supportive role by focusing both international and domestic attention on the process."[16]

Signaling Increased International Costs of Exposure

As the CC statement above suggests, the presence of monitors may not only expose cheating, it may also signal that the international community is placing greater weight on cheating in a given election. The United Nations (UN) declaration notes that "international election observation expresses the interest of the international community in the achievement of democratic elections."[17] Clearly in some cases, however, that "interest" does not translate into consequences. As prior discussions of monitoring in Kenya and Cambodia have revealed, international monitors may be unwilling to actually punish countries for bad elections. Despite such exceptions, monitors may signal that the international community is placing weight on the election and that negative consequences of cheating such as reduced aid or other forms of international pressure may be more likely. Indeed, research has found that regional organizations are more likely to punish electoral misconduct if monitors are present and criticize the elections.[18] This is important, because management research has traditionally found the strongest effects of monitoring on behavior occur not simply when cheating is exposed, but when monitoring connects behavior to consequences.[19] Monitoring can signal the international community's concern and underscore the international political will to punish cheating by shaming or ostracizing states or implementing other sanctions.

International monitors send this signal because most monitoring organizations are closely, if indirectly, tied to states. Many monitoring organizations are run by intergovernmental organizations (IGOs). As in other issue areas strong member states often direct the activities of these IGOs[20] and so these member states have a significant say in the organizations' international election monitoring activities. For example, European Union (EU) guidelines note that decisions about monitoring "must be balanced by an EU assessment of whether its global relations with the country concerned and EU general objectives make an EU electoral presence 'politically useful.'"[21] The other monitoring organizations are nongovernmental organizations (NGOs) that depend greatly on donors,[22] which often tend to have state ties. NGOs such as the IRI or the NDI, for example, rely heavily on government funding and may respond to the availability of U.S. government grants issued for monitoring specific countries. Thus, both nongovernmental and intergovernmental monitoring organizations represent international community interests and concerns and thereby increase the international cost of cheating. Not all monitoring missions send equally strong signals of international concern, but in general the presence of international monitors prompts governments to revise their estimate of the international costs upward, lowering their incentives to cheat.

Some states may be concerned about international reactions to their elections because they want to protect their reputations as credible partners in international cooperation.[23] As argued in earlier chapters, reputations matter because the international community has linked clean elections to other rewards such as trade and aid. That is, elections have become the subjects of classical conditionality, which of course has been much debated.[24] In 1989, the World Bank issued a report linking aid flows to "governance," defined as "the exercise of political power to manage a nation's affairs."[25] Good governance became more important to the international donor community, including the International Monetary Fund (IMF) and the European Bank for Reconstruction and Development, whose charter stated that it would only lend to pluralist democracies. For the EU, free and fair elections were a sine qua non entry requirement. After turmoil following elections in Romania and Bulgaria in the early 1990s, the European Parliament (EP) adopted a resolution reminding both countries that economic and technical aid and future relations with the European Community would be conditional on holding free and fair elections. In 1992, the Paris Club donors withdrew more than $70 million in nonhumanitarian aid to Malawi, citing concerns about human rights and democracy.[26] Furthermore, research has found that the presence of international election observers makes it more likely that IGOs will react to electoral misconduct and that negative reports by observers make punitive actions more likely.[27] Thus, the increased international cost of exposure is very real.

Increasing Domestic Costs

The exposure of cheating by international monitors may increase domestic costs. Research on the domestic factors that contribute to democratization highlights, inter alia, growth of political parties, civil society, education, and economic development.[28] These factors increase the societal demand for democratic governance and raise the capacity of citizens to challenge authority.[29] Subsequently, election cheating grows costlier. As opposition gains strength, manipulated elections become competitions not just over votes, but also struggles to undermine antidemocratic institutions.[30] When these domestic events build, monitors are not necessary to transition to free elections; many well-established democracies transitioned without the assistance of monitors. However, as discussed in Chapter 2, pressures on governments to allow international monitors often increase along with these other domestic factors.[31]

When international monitors are present, they can raise domestic costs of cheating by reinforcing domestic opposition in several ways. First, by holding press conferences and meeting with domestic actors, monitors increase citizen attention to cheating. Second, they can provide a third-party source of information on the election conduct, which may be more convincing for some citizens. Third, if domestic parties want to protest cheating but are uncertain of their success, criticism by international monitors can help overcome their coordination problem,[32] bolster their confidence in international support and thus boost their resolve. Thus, declaring elections fraudulent can be a powerful act. The recent regime changes in Georgia, Ukraine, and Serbia were all sparked by fraudulent national elections, which were followed by strong international criticism based on the assessment of election monitors. Earlier regime changes in Panama in 1989 and the Philippines in 1986 were also facilitated by denouncement by monitors, and in the case of the Philippines, by an extensive domestic network. As an important factor driving such changes Michael McFaul highlights, among others, "an ability quickly to drive home the point that voting results were falsified."[33] Whether these pressures are sufficient to make cheating too risky naturally depends on the complex domestic balance of power. Governments whose power is precarious and whose hold on the domestic apparatus for repression is slipping may find cheating a higher-risk strategy in the company of international monitors.

Increasing Incentives for Honesty

Decreasing incentives for cheating is the natural flipside of increasing the incentives for honesty. Nevertheless, it is worth pointing out that international monitors may also concretely increase the benefits of holding clean elections by playing a verification role. As Chapter 2 argued, many governments in the early 1990s intended to run clean elections and invited monitors to verify that they indeed did so. Although these countries already wished to run clean elections, international monitors may have increased their incentive to do so. It may be that without the ability to gain verification of a clean election, politicians would lose the incentive to behave honestly, because the honesty would be in any case questioned and therefore devalued. For example, in the pivotal plebiscite in Chile in 1988 the government would have preferred not to invite outside observers,[34] but General Fernando Matthei summed up the dilemma: "If the government's candidate wins, everyone will say it was fraud. If he loses everyone will say it was a fair election. So it is more in our interests than anyone else's, to be able to show that it was an absolutely fair election."[35] Thus, the availability of a validation scheme may change behavior. For example, if a system exists to certify organic foods, more growers who have wanted to grow organic foods may decide to do so. Similarly, the existence of monitoring may make governments willing to hold clean elections because a clean election backed by international monitors carries greater value. International monitors have played such a verification role in several elections where the polarized environment might otherwise not have allowed the victor a governing mandate.[36] Examples include South Korea in 1987, Bulgaria in 1990, Mozambique in 1994, and Mexico in 1994. Hamas's victory in the Palestinian Authority in 2006 would likely have been labeled fraudulent without several international observer groups acknowledging its validity. The IRI reports that in 2004 in Macedonia, the "IRI's observation mission and the publicity it received substantially contributed to the post-election acceptance of the results, despite vocal calls by the opposition for invalidation or annulment of the results."[37] Similarly, the EU observation report on Guatemala's 2003 election argued that the mission enhanced public confidence and deterred threats to the political process.[38] In a more concrete example, in its final report of the Guyana 1992 election, the CC argued that the violence at the election commission building had nearly caused the collapse of the entire election, but that it was averted partly because the international observers from the council and the Commonwealth Secretariat (CS) boosted the Guyanese people's confidence in the electoral process.[39] The validity that observers can bring to an election may thus give politicians an added incentive to compete fairly, and may broaden acceptance of the results. In sum, there are some reasons to accept the standard rational choice argument that international monitoring increases the cost of cheating and that in response politicians have an incentive to cheat less.

ALTERING DOMESTIC CONDITIONS

The wide range of activities of monitoring organizations described in Chapter 2 makes it clear that monitoring organizations seek to build capacity and improve administrative processes just as much as they seek to directly deter outright fraud.[40] This is point the UN declaration also drives home when it asserts that monitoring aims to build confidence and capacity "by providing recommendations for improving electoral processes."[41] Monitoring organizations also undertake a host of activities to build capacity and interact with politicians, officials, and citizens about elections.

Recommending Changes Both Before and After Elections

Most monitoring efforts aim not simply to deter overt cheating in a given election, but also to improve the structure of the electoral environment. This is why many organizations invest considerable time on the ground. Analyzing data until and including the year 2004, more than half of monitored elections had at least one pre-election visit by an organizational delegation. Furthermore, in about 40 percent of elections at least one organization arrived a month or more in advance. In these cases, monitors may suggest and even help implement very specific changes that make it harder to cheat or improve the quality of the election. For example, international monitors can expose (and thus enable election administrators to correct) administrative shortcomings that might otherwise lead to massive disenfranchisement or some other electoral ill. In this vein, international monitors provided information about the unintended, but problematic placement of voting centers to the Haitian electoral commission in the run-up to the 2006 election, and this allowed the electoral commission to make necessary adjustments.

Furthermore, international election monitors often include long lists of recommendations in their reports to call attention to problems in the legal and administrative framework for elections and make concrete suggestions for how to address them. For example, monitors may note that the current law inadequately addresses election finance issues and suggest a process of overview. Or they may recommend that a country adopt a particular form of voter identification, or revise the ballot counting or tabulation system. They may also make specific legal recommendations about the electoral system itself, for example, about the selection and composition of the electoral commission, or ways to eliminate systematic disenfranchisement of certain voters. Often they also make recommendations to improve the transparency of the election process or to achieve a smoother administration of the balloting. Such recommendations may influence domestic actors either because they learn new norms and behaviors, or because they underscore precisely what the international community expects from them if they want the international community to endorse their elections. Either way, the recommendations may provide impetus for behavioral change.

Building Capacity and Skills

Monitors may help improve election quality through a variety of mechanisms designed to build capacity and skills and demonstrate electoral norms and behaviors. For example, voter education and extensive discussion with politicians can help domestic actors improve the administration of elections. The training of domestic observers directly educates local actors about best monitoring practices and it also inculcates a set of norms about election administration. Many international monitoring organizations have a history of working closely with domestic observers and in some cases fostering their development. For example, in Mexico, international monitors facilitated domestic monitoring through intensive interaction and by exposing domestic actors to election monitoring techniques. Practical assistance on the day of election or during the formation of the voter registry or other practical elements of the election also demonstrates proper methods. The presence of observers at polling stations may alert voters to the problems of group voting, or impress upon them that political endorsements should not be present near or in the polling station.

These long-term activities may alter the domestic conditions for elections in several ways. As noted, theories of socialization and learning predict that long-term activities of international election monitors can help facilitate behavioral changes and socialize domestic actors to a number of important norms and practices surrounding the holding of regular elections.[42] The interaction provides opportunities for persuasion and for active demonstration of roles that domestic actors should play in proper elections. Indeed, the activities of monitors fit the three dominant mechanisms in Martha Finnemore and Kathryn Sikkink's explanation for the spread of emergent norms: socialization, institutionalization, and demonstration.[43] Election monitors certainly seek to socialize and demonstrate, in particular, and when making specific recommendations for legal changes or changes to the electoral commissions or administrative procedures, they also seek to institutionalize these changes in domestic law.

However, these activities can also influence the domestic environment in ways that alter the incentives of the domestic actors. Building capacity and educating voters empower citizens to stand up to fraud. The recommendations by monitors may influence domestic actors either because they learn new norms and behaviors, or because they underscore precisely what the international community expects from them if they want the international community to endorse their elections. Furthermore, some of these activities are less threatening to the incumbent partly because they are introduced gradually and may not immediately threaten the current power holders. In this setting, incumbents can earn praise and possible rewards for allowing some electoral reforms, while still hoping to hold on to office and enjoy the fruits of the increased legitimacy.

In sum, the point here is not to argue whether the long-term engagement of monitors changes the behavior of politicians by influencing their beliefs or by changing their incentives. The point is that the long-term engagement of international monitors may be able to improve the quality of elections in various ways as indeed some existing research suggests.[44] However, some of these mechanisms may take time to work, as monitors return for several elections and reinforce and follow up on their message.

If It Works, When Should It Work?

The above discussion developed several arguments for why monitored elections may be better than nonmonitored elections, and why countries with repeated engagement from monitors may improve their election quality over time. However, several factors are likely to affect whether monitors indeed have this effect.

First, given the discussion in Chapters 3 and 4 about the variance in the quality of election monitoring organizations, one might not expect all organizations to influence elections. Given the mechanisms discussed in this chapter, more credible organizations have several advantages. They should have a higher probability of exposing and criticizing fraud and they should therefore deter cheating more. When they validate an election outcome, high-quality monitors may be more credible and thus increase the incentive for honesty. Similarly, high-quality organizations should be expected to engage more in efforts to socialize domestic actors and therefore they should be expected to influence election processes more. Thus, high-quality organizations should be more likely to improve the quality of elections in a country.

Second, there are some basic conditions under which monitors should not be expected to have any effect at all, because the mechanisms outlined above have no grounds for operating. For example, because they lack competition and choice, single-party states cannot by definition run clean elections, whether monitors are present or not. Thus, international monitoring should not be expected to deter cheating in these countries. Furthermore, international monitoring organizations should not be expected to influence the quality of elections in highly democratic countries, since these countries already have a strong tradition of holding clean elections. This expectation is also consistent with the fact that other forms of restraint on regimes, such as human rights law, primarily influence transitional states.[45] As already discussed in Chapter 2, it is therefore also extremely rare for monitors even to attend elections in single-party states, and quite rare for them to attend elections in well-established democracies, although the OSCE and some other organizations have begun to send some lighter missions to democracies.[46] Thus, if international monitors improve elections, this effect should be expected only in multiparty states that are not well-established democracies.

Third, because international monitoring enters the domestic political environment, the domestic factors that influence democratization should also affect the opportunity structure monitors have to influence the quality of elections. Here, several chapters could be added to the book about the conditions for democratization, especially since many of these conditions remain debated.[47] However, most relevant for international monitoring is probably Thomas Carothers's "moving train" argument: Democracy promotion can speed up democratization only when the domestic train is already moving forward.[48] For example, the mechanism of increased domestic costs discussed above is more likely to operate in countries where political plurality and choice are gaining strength. External actors are unlikely to influence countries that are stagnated or regressing in their democratic transitions, or have never embarked on any transition. Furthermore, politicians in countries moving toward democracy are more likely to be open to learning and adopting new behaviors. Indeed, the literature on socialization suggests that countries in transition should be particularly amenable to the advice of external actors.[49] As Ambassador Christian Strohal, director of the OSCE Office for Democratic Institutions and Human Rights, said in an interview, the political will must exist for observers to be able to help.[50]

Fourth, if politicians are motivated by their self-interest in keeping power, progress is likely to suffer if parties cannot transcend winner-take-all politics, where those who do not win the elections completely lose influence in the political structures.[51] In polarized majoritarian political systems where losing even by a small margin means losing any and all representation, losing politicians have little hope that the winners will accommodate their preferences. Thus, it is harder for outsiders to influence domestic conditions when parties perceive politics as a game of all or nothing.[52] International monitors will therefore be less effective under conditions of such winner-take-all politics. This will be even more the case when the fight for power turns violent as, for example, in Kenya.[53] Thus, despite numerous visits by monitors, major election problems have persisted in countries such as Algeria, Burkina Faso, Fiji, Malawi, Sri Lanka, and others.

Fifth, as in other reform areas, democratic transitions also depend greatly on domestic capacity, not only on will. This is true in financial reforms promoted by international financial institutions,[54] and in the international influences on environmental compliance issues.[55] Thus, if international monitors can assist in the building of capacity, this may be a valuable contribution to improving the quality of elections. However, this may be a catch-22 situation: Initial low levels of capacity may also present barriers to monitor influence. Countries with little logistical and administrative capacity may find it more difficult to follow recommendations and monitors may find it harder to teach them new electoral norms if the domestic capacity to implement elementary processes is strained. Thus, in low-capacity countries, international monitors could be part of the means by which capacity grows, but in these countries changes should generally be slower and require more long-term engagement.

Sixth, because of the international signaling mechanism discussed above, international election monitors should enjoy greater influence when they have more leverage over a country. This is the classic conditionality argument.[56] The more the international monitors are connected to organizations that countries seek to join, or to countries that serve as important donors, the more eager domestic actors should be to make a favorable impression and the more receptive they therefore should be to international monitors and their advice.[57] Criticisms of conditionality have revealed several causes of its failure,[58] and therefore the presence of leverage need not always translate into concessions in election conduct. Several conditions may interfere. As argued earlier, incumbents who stand to lose power completely if they decrease cheating or reform the electoral framework in ways that diminish their control are less likely to cooperate. Furthermore, factors that compromise the will of external actors to actually punish a country for cheating will weaken the monitors' ability to increase the cost of cheating.[59] For example, even if monitors are critical, important donors are less likely to actually punish important countries.[60] In addition, other strong states may counter the influence of conditionality by acting as so-called black knights.[61] Yet, if these conditions do not interfere, then it still holds that the presence of leverage and conditionality such as EU membership, for example, or foreign aid will create conditions for influence that are more favorable than situations where the international community has little to offer. The other side of the coin, of course, is that the removal of such conditionality may produce backsliding.[62]

Summary

This chapter has drawn on both rationalist and constructivist theories to argue that international monitors can indeed improve elections, but that several

TABLE 6.1

Summary of mechanisms, observable implications, and modifying factors

Mechanisms	Observable implications	Modifying factors
Altering incentives to cheat	Monitored elections should be better than nonmonitored elections	Regime type
Increasing risks of exposure		The quality of monitors
		Stage of domestic transition
Altering incentives for honesty	Countries with repeated engagement from monitors improve their election quality over time	Violence and winner-take-all politics
Signaling increased international costs		Administrative capacity
Increasing domestic cost		Conditionality and political will to exert leverage
Altering domestic conditions		
Recommending institutional and legal changes		
Building new capacity and skills		

domestic and international factors affect their influence. In reality, therefore, monitors play a *reinforcement* role by building on existing domestic potential and enhancing the effectiveness of other international leverage.

Table 6.1 summarizes the argument. International election monitors can improve the quality of elections through two main mechanisms: Monitors can alter incentives by increasing the risk of exposure, signaling increasing international cost, increasing domestic cost, or increasing the incentives for honesty. Monitors can also alter the domestic conditions by recommending legal and institutional changes, and by teaching new norms and building capacity and skills that reinforce good electoral practices.

However, several conditions are likely to modify the influence of monitors: (1) High-quality monitors should be more effective than low quality monitors; (2) international monitors should only be effective in multiparty states that are not fully established democracies; (3) international monitors should be more effective in countries already moving toward democracy than in countries that are stagnated or regressing in their democratic transitions, or have never embarked on any transition; (4) international monitors should be less effective in violent winner-take-all politics; (5) the effect of international monitors should be rarer and slower when domestic capacity is very low; and (6) international election monitors should be more effective when they are connected with organizations or donor states that have something to offer a country *and* clearly make that offering conditional on electoral quality.

The following chapters examine the effect of monitors on the quality of elections as well as the conditions that may modify their influence. Chapter 7 examines whether there is a relationship between the presence of monitors and election quality in individual elections. Chapter 8 then looks at election quality in countries where monitors are present for several elections over time to explore whether monitors are able to gradually change conditions in these countries to improve their elections and whether monitoring has long-term and enduring effects.

CHAPTER 7

Are Monitored Elections Better?

THIS CHAPTER EXAMINES the influence of international monitors on the quality of individual elections. Using quantitative data to examine the quality of elections provides a far greater breadth of analysis than case studies alone can accomplish. However, using quantitative data to explore the effects of monitors on a given election is complicated. As discussed in Chapter 2, whether an election is monitored depends both on the organizations' interest in observing an election and on domestic willingness to host observers. Both of these factors are likely to be related to the expected quality of an election. This is the classic problem with analyzing data on any form of nonrandom intervention. If the anticipated quality of an election influences whether monitors are present, then monitors may not influence quality at all, but merely respond to it. That is, monitors may simply go to elections that are more likely to improve. Conversely, if elections do not improve, it may be because monitors go to particularly difficult countries that are less likely to improve.

This chapter begins with a discussion of the measures used to evaluate election quality. It then uses a mix of approaches to explore the data. First it presents some descriptive overviews. It then applies some of the most cutting-edge statistical techniques to reduce the bias introduced by the selection problem discussed above and identify the effect of monitors on election quality. The chapter ends by discussing the results in greater depth. Appendix D contains significant supplementary data and discussion about the statistical analysis.

MEASURES OF ELECTION QUALITY

Overall Election Quality

The analysis in Chapter 4 relied on the assessments of individual election observation missions. However, the present analysis cannot use this measure for several reasons. First, some elections have assessments from multiple organizations, making it unclear which assessment to use. Second, nonmonitored elections have no assessment at all. Third, as shown in Chapter 4, factors other than election quality may bias the monitors' assessment. The measure of election quality for this analysis should not consider how an organization chooses to represent its findings to the press or others in the immediate aftermath of the election. Rather, the goal is to find as accurate as possible a measure of how good the election actually was. For this analysis, an election quality measure was therefore derived from the annual U.S. State Department Reports of Human Rights Practices, which discuss the quality of elections as part of the consideration of the rights of citizens to choose their governments. This data is available for 1,204 elections.

The measure captures whether the State Department report, notwithstanding the level of problems, considered the election acceptable. Thus it is possible for an election to have a moderate level of problems that raise considerable concerns, yet for the State Department to conclude that overall the election was nonetheless acceptable, or, conversely, for the election itself to proceed with few problems, yet for the State Department to consider it unacceptable, perhaps because of major flaws in the legal framework. Appendix A has fuller description of the measure, and Table 7.1 shows the distribution of the variable.

Problems

The second measure uses the same source, but considers not only whether the State Department considered the election acceptable, but also the level of election problems discussed in the report. The variable is thus a combination of acceptability and level of problems. Table 7.2 shows the different levels and the distribution of the variable.

Biases in the Variables

Both the measure of overall election quality and the problems measure correlate well with other standard democracy measures to raise confidence in their reliability, yet they still differ enough to suggest they capture something other than broad democracy scores.[1]

Because these measures are based on reports produced by a U.S. agency, they may contain some political bias as discussed further in Appendix A. However, research has found that U.S. State Department reports have obtained considerable independence over the years and criticism of U.S. allies is quite common.[2] Thus, rather than political bias, a bigger concern is whether some cheating is systematically overlooked. However, this is more likely to occur when monitors

TABLE 7.1
Distribution of election quality

Level	Number of observations	Percent
Acceptable	792	66
Ambiguous	85	7
Unacceptable	327	27
	1,204	100

TABLE 7.2
Coding and distribution of the "Problems" variable

Election quality	Level of problems	Value	Number of observations	Percent
Acceptable	None	0	396	33
Acceptable	Minor	1	226	19
Acceptable	Moderate	2	169	14
Ambiguous	Moderate	3	55	4
Unacceptable	Moderate	4	142	12
Unacceptable	Major	5	183	15
		Missing*	34	3
			1,204	100

* Some elections were left as "missing" because their order in the ranking system was unclear.

are absent than when they are present. Thus monitored elections are likely to be perceived as more problematic, making it harder, not easier, to show a positive relationship between monitors and election quality.

Turnover

To provide an alternative check on the election quality measure, the study relied on the simple proposition that politicians who cheat less should keep power less often. Thus, a measure was created to capture whether the incumbent party keeps power in an election. The rules and sources for creating the variable are detailed in Appendix A.

Of the 1,324 elections in the data, the variable is missing in 41, or about 3 percent, of cases. Turnover occurs in 336, or about 25 percent of all elections, which means, of course, that incumbents retain power in nearly three-quarters of all elections.

Using turnover as a measure of election quality has the benefit of objectivity, but the drawback is that it may miss a great deal of reductions in fraud. Turnover is only a very indirect measure of fraud, and given that fraud can be reduced without power necessarily changing hands, it is a rather inexact way to examine whether monitors influence fraud, because decreases in fraud could well go undetected in this measure. In other words, whereas incumbents almost never lose power after a fraudulent election (the data contain only five such cases, including, for example, the Philippines in 1986), incumbents may well keep power in a clean election. Failure to find statistically significant effects related to turnover is therefore quite possible, even if monitors do succeed in reducing fraud. Conversely, finding a statistical relationship provides quite strong evidence that monitors reduce fraud.

AN OVERVIEW OF THE RECORD

Does a cursory examination of the data suggest that the presence of monitors deters cheating and leads to a better quality of elections? For simplicity, the following section focuses just on the overall election quality measure and turnover. Figures 7.1 and 7.2 display the data for five different samples that get progressively more restrictive.

The results from the full sample show the distribution in the overall election quality is very similar for both monitored and nonmonitored elections. About 67 percent of monitored elections were acceptable compared with about 65 percent of nonmonitored elections. For turnover the difference is more discernable, with incumbents in monitored elections about 10 percentage points less likely to keep power than incumbents in nonmonitored elections.

However, the full sample really compares apples and oranges. As noted in the previous chapter, monitors should not have any effect on elections in single-party states or in fully established democracies, nor do they tend to go to these elections. The second set of columns in each figure, which excludes single-party elections, shows that the elections that are not monitored do tend to be acceptable more often, although turnover rates are still lower due to the relatively high rates of incumbency in established democracies. The third set of columns also excludes democratic countries. In this sample, monitored elections are acceptable and produce turnover more often. Indeed, when formal single-party states

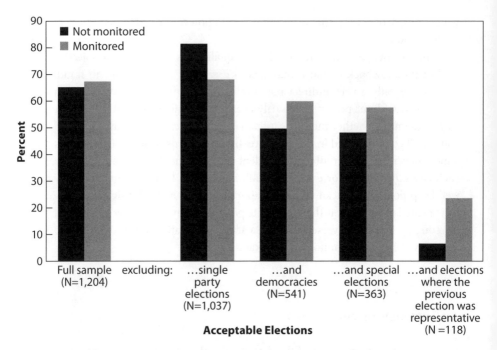

Figure 7.1: Percent of acceptable elections for monitored and nonmonitored subsamples
Note that although this figure displays only the percent of elections that are acceptable, the variable has three outcomes: acceptable, ambiguous, or unacceptable.

and fully established democracies are excluded, then incumbents in monitored elections lost power twice as often.

Still, the comparison groups may be hiding important factors. For example, the previous chapter also noted that monitors might be even more likely to influence the quality of elections in transition states. However, if the differences between monitored and nonmonitored elections are entirely because monitors attend special elections, then the argument that they improve elections is possibly fully explained by the nature of these special elections, rather than by the presence of monitors. Thus, it may be enlightening to narrow even further the subset of elections being compared. The fourth set of columns in Figures 7.1 and 7.2 excludes any special elections (that is, elections that occurred as the first election after a coup or after a conflict, or any first multiparty election[3]). By excluding all these special types of elections that monitors are more likely to attend and where changes in the conduct of election may be explained by numerous factors, the groups of monitored and nonmonitored elections become more comparable, and selection bias is reduced. The columns show that

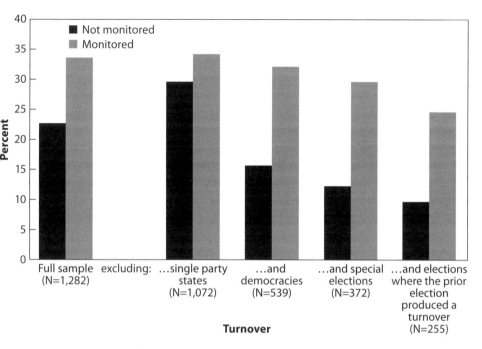

Figure 7.2: Turnover rates for monitored and nonmonitored subsamples

monitored elections still were acceptable more often, and politicians in monitored elections lost power more often.

The really interesting question, of course, is whether the presence of monitors increases turnover or improves election quality. Therefore, it may be useful only to look at elections in countries where the prior election was bad or there was no turnover. To do so, the last set of columns in Figures 7.1 and 7.2 excludes elections where the previous election was acceptable (7.1) or the previous election produced a turnover (7.2). This means that the columns show elections that *improved* in terms of quality or turnover. Again, the tables show more frequent improvements when monitors were present both in the acceptability of the elections and in the turnover.

Table 7.3 displays the underlying data for the 5th set of columns in Figure 7.1, showing not only the acceptable elections, but also the ambiguous and unacceptable elections.

Perhaps surprisingly, the differences between the third and fourth sets of columns in Figures 7.1 and 7. 2 are actually small. This suggests that discarding the special elections does not have much effect. Thus, whether an election is the

TABLE 7.3
Distribution of elections in terms of quality and monitoring*

	Acceptable	Ambiguous	Unacceptable	Total
Not Monitored	3 (6.12%) Maldives 1994L, Mauritania 2001L, Nepal 1986L**	5 (10.20%) Jordan 2003L, Malaysia 2004L, Mexico 1988B, Philippines 1984L, Singapore 1999P	42 (83.65%) Bangladesh 1988L, Cameroon 1997P, Chad 2002L, Djibouti 1997L, Egypt 1995L, Egypt 2000L, El Salvador 1978L, Eq. Guinea 2004L, Guatemala 1982B, Guinea 2002L, Guinea 2003P, Guyana 1985L, Haiti 1984L, Haiti 2000P, Indonesia 1992L, Lebanon 1996L, Lebanon 2000L, Lebanon 2002L, Mauritania 1997P, Morocco 1997L, Paraguay 1983B, Philippines 1981P, S. Africa 1984L, S. Africa 1987L, S. Africa 1989L, Serbia 1996L, Syria 1978P, Syria 1981L, Syria 1985P, Syria 1986L, Syria 1991P, Syria 1998L, Syria 2000P, Syria 2003L, Taiwan 1991L, Tajikistan 1999P, Tunisia 1986L, Tunisia 1994B, Tunisia 2004B, Uzbekistan 2000P, Zimbabwe 1996P	49 (100%)
Monitored	16 (23.19%) Albania 1997L, Algeria 2002L, Bangladesh 1991L, Burkina Faso 1992L, Croatia 2000L, Djibouti 1999P, Dom. Rep. 1996P, Gambia 2001P, Guyana 1992B, Indonesia 1999L, Niger 1999B, Panama 1991L,	6 (8.70%) Central African Rep. 1992P, Ethiopia 1995L, Georgia 2004P, Kenya 1997B, Morocco 2002L, Nigeria 1999P	47 (67.65%) Armenia 1996P, Armenia 1998P, Armenia 1999L, Armenia 2003P, Armenia 2003L, Azerbaijan 2000L, Azerbaijan 2003P, Belarus 1995L, Belarus 2000L, Belarus 2001P, Belarus 2004L, Cameroon 2002L, Cameroon 2004P, Chad 1997L, Chad 2001P, Cote d'Ivoire 1995L, Djibouti 1993P, Eq. Guinea 1999L, Eq. Guinea 2002P, Ethiopia 1994L, Gabon 1996L, Gabon 1998P, Gabon 2001L, Georgia 2003L, Guinea 1998P, Kazakhstan 1999P, Kazakhstan 1999L, Kazakhstan 2004L, Kyrgyzstan 2000P, Mauritania 1996L, Niger 1996L, Nigeria 1999L, Panama 1989B, Paraguay 1988B, Poland 1989L, Russia 2004P, Serbia 1992L, Tajikistan 2000L,	69 (100%)

TABLE 7.3 (*continued*)

	Acceptable	Ambiguous	Unacceptable	Total
Monitored	Peru 2001B, Philippines 1987L, Serbia 1998L, Ukraine 2004P		Togo 1998P, Togo 1999L, Togo 2002L, Togo 2003P, Ukraine 2004P, Uzbekistan 1999L, Uzbekistan 2004L, Zimbabwe 2000L, Zimbabwe 2002P	69 (100%)
Total	19	11	88	118

Note: L = Legislative, P = Presidential, B = Both.

˙Excluding single-party states and elections in countries rated "Free" by Freedom House in the year before the election, post-conflict elections, post-coup elections and first multiparty elections, and elections where the prior election was acceptable.

˙˙Note that although the U.S. State Department Reports noted them as acceptable, some elections, such as the Nepal 1986 legislative election, were not very competitive. See Appendix A for more discussion of the QED data.

first after a coup or conflict or whether it is a first multiparty election may not influence the quality of the election or the influence of monitors greatly.

This question deserves a little further exploration given that countries in transition were expected to be more susceptible to respond to the presence of monitors. Figure 7.3 compares turnover rates in four different types of elections: first multiparty elections, post-coup elections, post-conflict elections, and other elections. The second light-gray column from the left shows that monitored first multiparty elections produce a turnover 41 percent of the time, which is significantly higher than the 15 percent rate for nonmonitored first multiparty elections. This improvement in the turnover rate associated with monitors is also higher than in other elections, represented by the first set of columns. However, post-coup elections and post-conflict elections, although generally displaying higher turnover, do not seem to benefit as much from the presence of monitors—although one should be cautious about drawing conclusions based on the lower numbers in those categories. That said, the figure suggests that monitors may not really be more effective in post-conflict or post-coup elections than in other elections, but that they may actually be more effective in first multiparty elections. It is important to recall, however, that these simple correlations do not establish causality, so although turnover is higher when first multiparty elections are monitored, this suggests, but does not prove, that monitors are increasing the turnover rate.

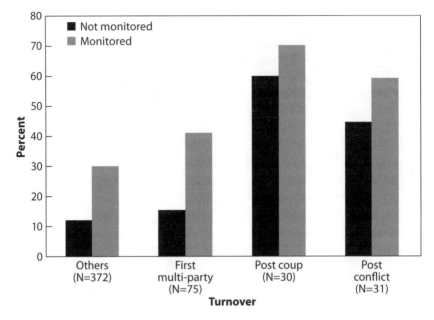

Figure 7.3: Turnover in different types of elections
Excluding post-conflict elections, and post-coup elections, as well as elections in single-party states or countries rated "Free" by Freedom House in the year before the election.

The previous chapter also argued that more credible monitoring organizations should be more effective at improving elections. A final way of looking at the data, therefore, is to consider differences between monitoring organizations. As Chapters 3 and 4 showed, some organizations are more likely to voice disapproval when there are problems. If monitoring deters cheating, then more critical monitors should have a greater deterrent effect. In Chapter 3, Figure 3.2 showed how often different organizations criticized elections that were highly problematic either in the view of other monitoring organizations, or in the view of the U.S. State Department. Based on this, an indicator of monitor quality was created for organizations that criticized highly problematic elections at least 50 percent of the time. This coding rule is arbitrary, but clear. These organizations were the Carter Center (CC), the National Democratic Institute (NDI), the Asian Network for Free Elections (ANFREL), the International Republican Institute (IRI), the Organization for Security and Co-operation in Europe (OSCE), the European Parliament (EP), the EU Commission, and the Organization of American States (OAS). Consistent with the claim that credible organizations

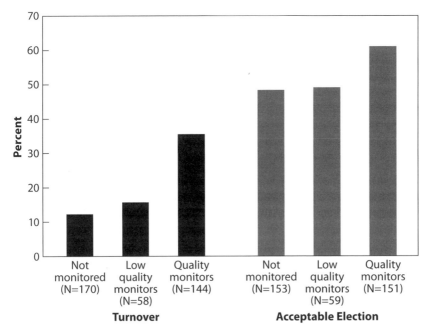

Figure 7.4: Monitor types, election quality,* and turnover
Excluding single-party states and countries rated "Free" by Freedom House in the year before the election, post-conflict elections, post-coup elections, and first multiparty elections.
*Note that although this figure displays only the percent of elections that are acceptable, the variable has three outcomes: acceptable, ambiguous, or unacceptable.

should be more effective, Figure 7.4 shows that elections monitored by the most credible organizations are indeed better and have greater turnover.

The discussions and data exploration above suggest that monitored elections are more likely to be acceptable and produce turnover more often, that first multiparty elections may be more likely to respond to monitors, and that the quality of the monitoring organizations matters. Incidentally, these patterns change little if the analysis is further restricted to elections after 1990.

STATISTICAL ANALYSIS

The above analysis is based purely on a descriptive examination of the data. That is useful because it shows the real frequencies of various events in the data and reflects actual experiences throughout the years. Narrowing the sample reduces some problems inherent in basic comparisons, but it still does not fully address the selection problem. Furthermore, descriptive analysis cannot take multiple factors into consideration simultaneously. Multivariate analysis provides a way to do this, and to examine the contribution made by an individual variable, such as monitoring, to an observed outcome conditional on the values of other variables. The rest of this chapter presents a multivariate analysis of international election monitoring and discusses the findings.

Chapter 2 discussed a series of factors that influence which elections are monitored. In general, monitors go to countries with more corruption and a history of problematic and fraudulent elections, but they rarely waste their resources on single-party states. Rather, monitors visit many first multiparty elections and go to countries with less stable governments. The fact that many of the factors that determine where monitors go also influence the quality of elections means that generalized linear models may produce biased estimates. Analysts sometimes attempt to correct this selection problem by including control variables, but this may actually increase bias in the coefficient estimate for the treatment effect in some cases,[4] and the results can be highly sensitive to model specification.[5] Another common solution is to use standard selection models. However, they may also not provide the ideal solution, because they add new distributional assumptions to the modeling effort about the covariance structure between the variables that select an observation into treatment and the effect of the variables on the outcome.[6] In reality these assumptions are very difficult to satisfy and verify. More recent methodological research has therefore focused on ways to reduce distributional assumptions when dealing with selection bias, rendering estimates less model dependent. This has led to a great deal of interest in matching techniques, which are employed for this analysis and discussed in greater detail in Appendix D.

The analysis in this chapter uses a genetic matching procedure to select treatment and control observations such that these two groups appear observationally similar in terms of control variable values.[7] Genetic matching has advantages over other commonly used matching techniques, such as nearest-neighbor matching based on propensity scores, because it automates the search for the best possible balance between the treatment and control groups. The matching was done using all of the available control variables that had an effect on election outcomes conditional on the treatment state.[8] This means that variables that were predictors of election monitoring only were included in the matching if those variables also were predictors of election quality or turnover.

Accordingly, the matched variables, which are discussed further in Appendix A,[9] were:

1. the level of corruption in the year before the election
2. the level of democracy in the year before the election
3. whether the country was under a democracy-related sanction in the year of the election
4. whether the election was a first multiparty election
5. the natural log of the level of foreign aid to the country in the year before the election
6. whether the election was the first after a coup
7. the government's stability the year before the election (for the analysis of turnover)
8. the quality of the previous election (for the analysis of election quality and problems)

In addition, year was used as a control variable to address time trends in the data, but it was not used for the matching itself, as this would be overly limiting. Several other variables that correlated with monitoring did not correlate with outcomes and they were therefore omitted to avoid biasing the estimates.

The matching was subjected to several tests as discussed in Appendix D. Furthermore, to decrease confirmation bias—the tendency of investigators to analyze data selectively to confirm of their hypotheses—an outside consultant assisted in the analysis.[10] The matching results were very good, meaning that the genetic matching procedure was able to produce samples of monitored and nonmonitored elections that were very similar. This is evident in the low standardized balance scores reported in the tables below . After matching, standard binary or ordered logistical regression analysis was used to make inferences about the effect of monitoring on election outcomes, as discussed above.

When estimating the effect of monitoring on election outcomes, it is advisable to first remove the cases where theory does not predict a monitoring effect.The analysis therefore excludes single-party states and countries considered "free" by Freedom House.[11] Relying on the Freedom House data permits inclusion of more countries, as the variable contains less missing data for smaller countries in particular.

The post-matching estimation method used is logistic regression analysis. In statistical analysis, logistic regression is used to predict probabilities that an event will occur. With binary outcome variables such as turnover, regular logit models are used. When the outcome variables are ordered, as are the variables capturing election quality and problems, ordered logit models are used.[12]

Findings

Table D.1 in Appendix D presents the results of the multivariate analysis performed after the matching. These results align well with the patterns revealed by the earlier descriptive analysis. The presence of monitors is positively associated with election quality, level of problems, and turnover. This means that when monitors are present, the models predict that it is more likely that the election will be considered acceptable, that it will have fewer problems, and that it will produce a turnover in power.

Although the matching process reduces the likelihood of biased estimators, the analysis still does not prove definitively that the presence of monitors causes elections to improve. However, this positive association across all the different measures of election quality does provide considerable support for the hypothesis that monitors improve election quality and increase turnover. Appendix D provides additional tests using different democracy variables and different ways to limit the subset of observations used in the analysis to examine how robust the results are. These additional tests show that the results are fairly consistent, but that there are some subset specifications where the monitoring variable is not significant. Appendix D discusses this further.

Only a few other variables in the models are statistically significant, and these make sense. As expected, the lagged dependent variables are significant. This simply means that the quality of the previous election is likely to play a role in the quality of an election. Furthermore, first multiparty elections are more likely to be acceptable and have fewer problems, but it is not clear that they produce a turnover in power more often. The significance of the Freedom House democracy variable shows that, as expected, elections in partly free countries are also better than those in countries that are not free.

The coefficients in logit models are difficult to interpret and therefore it is helpful to look at the effect that a change in monitoring has on the predicted probability of the outcome. For illustrative purposes, the predictions are based on the scenario of the values shown in the table below Figure 7.5. The figure shows the probability that an election will be acceptable, ambiguous, or unacceptable. Importantly, the estimates are based on elections where the last election was unacceptable, thus in essence showing the predicted probability of improvement depending on the presence of monitors. Given that these are all elections where the prior election was unacceptable, it is no surprise that the most likely outcome is an election that is once again unacceptable. However, monitored elections differ considerably. The set of columns on the left in Figure 7.5 shows that in countries that are not free the predicted probability of an acceptable election is only about 11 percent without monitoring, but it is about

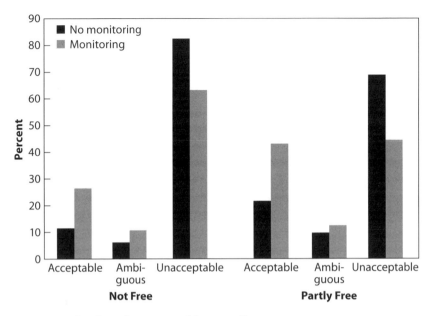

Figure 7.5: Predicted overall assessment of election quality

Value scenario for predicted probabilities

Variable	Value
Quality of last election	Unacceptable
Democracy-related sanctions	No
First multiparty election	No
Post-coup election	No
Foreign aid	Mean
Corruption	Mean
Year	Center value

Source: Based on Model 1 in Table D.1.

26 percent with monitoring. Similarly, the fourth set of columns shows that for partly free countries where the last election was bad, the predicted probability of an acceptable election is about 21 percent with no monitoring, but 43 percent with monitoring. In both cases monitored elections are then about twice as likely to be acceptable. Furthermore, the figure shows that most of the change is not due to change in the ambiguous category; that is, the improvement in the predicted probability mostly represents movement from the unacceptable to the acceptable category.

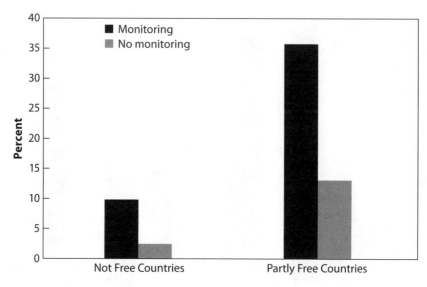

Figure 7.6: Predicted overall probability of turnover

Value scenario for predicted probabilities

Variable	Value
Turnover in last election	No
Democracy-related sanctions	No
First multiparty election	No
Post-coup election	No
Foreign aid	Mean
Corruption	Mean
Year	Center value

Source: Based on Model 3 in Table D.1.

The predicted probabilities for the "Problems" variable are more challenging to discuss, because the variable is unevenly distributed across categories. However, the take away message based on further investigation is that the presence of monitors is mostly associated with improvements for elections that are in the "middle" range of the level of problems. Elections that would be really terrible without monitors are likely to remain so with monitors, just as elections that would be great without monitors will remain so with monitors. It is those elections in the middle where monitors can make a difference. Table D.2 in

Appendix D displays predicted variables for a country whose last election was unacceptable and had moderate problems.

The dichotomous turnover variable is more straightforward to interpret. The predictions in Figure 7.6 are once again based on the scenario described in the table below the figure and are for the most recalcitrant cases: elections in countries where the incumbent kept power in the last election. For these elections, in countries that Freedom House rated "partly free" the year before the election, the predicted probability of turnover is only 13 percent when monitors are not present, but it is 36 percent when they are present. Thus the likelihood of turnover nearly triples when monitors are present. In countries that Freedom House rated not free the year before the election the predicted probability of turnover is only 2 percent without monitors, but 10 percent with them present.

These figures are of course not meant as predictions about future outcomes. They are based on historical data and they simply help put some perspective on the magnitude of the relationship in the data by illustrating it for the specified scenario. They indicate that the relationship between monitors and election quality is not only statistically significant, but that it has meaningful substantial size. That is, international election monitors are associated with sizable improvements in election quality and increases in turnover.

The above models assume that all monitoring is equal. However, as discussed earlier, high-quality monitoring should be more likely to improve election quality than low-quality monitoring. To test this proposition, high- and low-quality monitoring were coded as two separate treatment levels and compared to the control of no monitoring after matching. The coding of quality monitoring follows the discussion earlier in the chapter.

The analysis confirms the findings of the earlier descriptive analysis that the quality of monitors matters. Compared with no monitoring, high-quality monitoring is associated with improved election quality and turnover (see Table D.3 in Appendix D). High-quality monitoring is always statistically significant, whereas low-quality monitoring never is. The lack of significance could be due to the smaller sample size for some of the models, but it is also worth noting that the coefficients on high-quality monitors are always larger than the coefficients on low-quality monitoring, suggesting a stronger relationship between high-quality monitors and election quality than between low-quality monitors and election quality.[13]

Again, Appendix D provides several robustness checks that vary the democracy variable used to delimit the sample and used for matching. The findings are very similar to those discussed above.

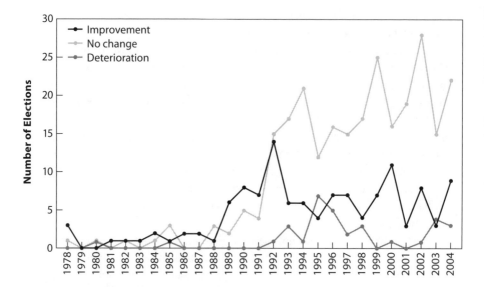

Figure 7.7: Direction of changes in democracy scores in monitored elections
Changes in democracy scores are based on the Polity IV democracy scale ranging from –10 to 10.

A Possible Objection

Is it possible that the findings are driven purely by the post–Cold War emergence of regimes whose leaders sought democracy legitimacy though monitoring? Chapter 2 argued that there was a surge of monitored elections in regimes seeking to demonstrate their honest transition to democracy at the end of the Cold War. Figure 2.4 showed that monitored elections around that time demonstrated strong average gains in their democracy scores, but that this effect declined by the mid-1990s. So is this surge of honest elections driving the findings above? Is election monitoring actually facing declining returns over time?

Closer examination shows that this does not appear to be happening. It has not become less common for election monitoring to be associated with progress. However, the mix of states that invite monitors has changed. More and more countries, with both better and worse regimes, invite monitors. This is illustrated by the rise in cases with no improvements or deterioration in their democracy score as shown in Figure 7.7.

The dishonest states that have joined the monitoring regime on false pretenses are having more of their cheating exposed, as illustrated by the line that shows the number of cases where the polity score deteriorates, and both they and the stable cases are therefore dragging down the average democracy gain as was seen in Figure 2.4. But if we look at the improvements, that is, the elections where the polity score was greater in the current election than in the previous election, then we see that the absolute number of states experiencing gains is actually continuing. The peak in 1992 is not that much of an outlier given the relatively small numbers, and therefore cannot drive the findings above. Thus it is not simply the case that monitors were effective at the end of the Cold War. They continue to be associated with progress. Only in the later years, the mix of monitored countries has changed. The cases of gains thus make up a smaller share of all monitored elections, but they persist.

Discussion

Are monitored elections better? Yes: Both the descriptive and the statistical analyses show that in multiparty elections in countries that are less than free by Freedom House standards the presence of monitors is associated with improved election quality and more frequent turnover. This is remarkable given that monitors have relatively few resources and tend to go to problematic elections where politicians have strong incentives to do everything they can to hold on to power.

The finding is fairly robust. The statistical analysis addressed the selection problem by using genetic matching techniques to generate a sample where the monitored and nonmonitored elections resemble each other on the most important variables that influence both monitoring and election quality.

Still, as noted earlier, even such careful matching cannot completely eliminate the problems of inference. Most important, as with all other statistical analysis, omitted variable bias remains an issue. For example, no variable measured whether a country has recently undertaken serious electoral reforms or whether the incumbent party had recently undergone an important leadership change. Both of these factors could improve elections, and perhaps monitoring organizations are able to gauge these as an election approaches and simply place themselves at the right elections to receive some credit for the improvements. Or maybe they attend such elections to help assure that the reforms are implemented correctly or to help facilitate a possible leadership change, which of course itself could be a way that monitors then end up making a difference. Yet, it is worthwhile to recall that monitoring organizations often need to make decisions about monitoring well in advance of the actual election dates. Due to logistics and funding such decisions are often made many months in advance, when it is harder for monitors to know whether an election is likely to present progress. And, as Chapter 2 noted, many of the factors that influence the decision to monitor make it hard for monitoring organizations to be opportunistic. For example, there may be donor pressure to monitor foreign aid recipients, or institutional precedent for monitoring new member states or for returning to previously monitored countries.

All in all, the evidence in this chapter supports the argument that the presence of international monitors is associated with improved election quality and increased turnover in countries in the middle of the democracy range—those countries that are no longer staunch single-party autocracies but are on the way to democracy. The positive relationship between monitoring and election quality does not prove causation, but it provides quite substantial evidence that a monitored election is more likely to be acceptable and to produce a turnover of power and resources. This positive finding suggests that, even if the previous chapters have criticized several weaknesses in monitoring operations, international election monitoring may have significant merit in improving the quality of elections and turnover. This is clearly important to the overall discussion about what the international community at large should do about international election monitoring—a discussion the conclusion revisits.

This chapter has also supported some of the propositions in the previous chapter about conditions that might modify the influence of monitors. Importantly, high-quality monitors do appear to have greater influence than low-quality monitors. As Figure 7.3 also showed, the monitor-related gains in quality or turnover may be slightly greater for first multiparty elections than for other elections. However, the limited number of observations and the observational nature of the data make it hard to use the data to pinpoint more precise conditions for when international election monitoring is effective and when it is a waste of time. Nor can the analysis of individual elections say anything about the lasting effects of international monitoring on elections. The following chapter seeks to address these weaknesses through studies of a series of elections in several countries over time.

CHAPTER 8

Long-Term Effects

> The business of elections should be seen as a marathon, not as a
> sprint race.
> —Dr. Kimmo Kiljunen, Special Envoy of the Organization of
> Security and Co-operation in Europe[1]

THE PREVIOUS CHAPTER found that good elections are more likely when monitors are present. However, this says nothing about whether improvements are
sustained. Nor does a focus on single elections make it possible to explore
whether, despite several persistently bad monitored elections, improvement
may occur in the long run. To examine this, it is necessary to research individual countries over longer periods of time. No study has ever systematically
compared how several countries respond to recommendations by monitors in
the long run, and whether the overall quality of elections improves throughout
multiple monitored elections. That is what this chapter does.

A long-term perspective is important for several reasons. First of all,
changes often take time. Second, international election monitoring is rarely
limited to a single election experience in a country. Most countries that invite monitors do so more than once; several do so repeatedly and over many
years. The Dominican Republic, for example, has one of the longest histories;
monitors first observed elections in 1978 and attended eight more elections
between 1990 and 2004. Figure 8.1 shows the number of countries that had
multiple elections monitored between 1975 and 2004. (Serbia is the outlier
country, with fifteen monitored elections.[2]) This repeated engagement makes
it compelling to also consider possible long-term outcomes over numerous
elections in a country.

Indeed, most monitoring efforts aim not simply to deter overt cheating in a
single round of elections, but to bring changes in the long run. This is one reason many organizations invest considerable time on the ground. More than half
of monitored elections have at least one pre-election visit by an organizational
delegation, and in about 40 percent of elections at least one organization arrived
a month or more in advance. Most important, international election monitors
usually include many recommendations in their reports. These recommendations call attention to current problems in the legal and administrative frame-

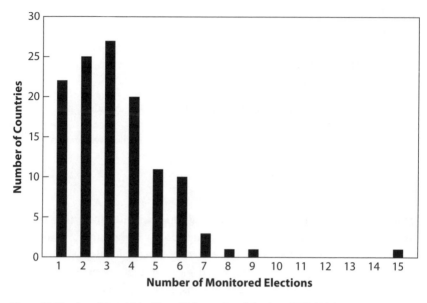

Figure 8.1: Number of countries with multiple monitored elections, 1975–2004

work for elections and often make concrete suggestions about how to address them. For example, monitors may note that the current law inadequately addresses election finance issues and suggest a process of overview. Or they may recommend that a country adopt a particular form of voter identification, or revise the ballot-counting system. They may also make specific legal recommendations about the electoral system itself, for example, about the selection and composition of the electoral commission, or about ways to eliminate systematic disenfranchisement of certain voters. Often they also make recommendations about how to improve the transparency of the election process or offer suggestions on how to achieve a smoother administration of the balloting.

As discussed in Chapter 6, the long-term activities of international election monitors may be able to improve elections by exposing domestic politicians to important norms and practices of competitive elections and by reinforcing the expectations of the international community. And although it is likely to be harder for monitors to facilitate change in countries with very low administrative capacity, they may be part of the solution to building new capacity and skills. This chapter considers whether there is any evidence that this actually works by examining the long-term engagement of monitors in several countries in depth. Does the long-term engagement of monitors show results in countries over time? What factors condition their effectiveness? What does a long-term focus on countries reveal about the ways that international election monitors may influence election conduct?

SELECTION OF COUNTRIES AND METHOD OF ANALYSIS

It is of course possible simply to look at the trajectory of the quality of elections in monitored countries over time. Such an overview suggests that about half the countries that have hosted monitors at some point in time have improved at least some since monitors first arrived, but that in about half of these countries huge problems persist. Overall, this says very little about whether monitors have helped these countries to improve their elections.

Rather than merely looking at trends, the goal of the country studies is to systematically examine the response of various countries to monitors' recommendations over time. Such analysis can show when monitors had no effect, and it can highlight instances when monitors may have had an effect. However, they cannot definitively prove that monitors caused any of the changes, because changes in election quality may have several causes that are difficult to disaggregate. However, studying the details of the recommendations and the actions countries take can make the causal role of monitors more or less plausible. Moreover, in some cases there is evidence of fairly direct connections. The substance of the changes may align quite specifically with the recommendations of monitors. There may also be testimony that the recommendations played an active role in the reforms. In Armenia, for example, the Organization for Security and Co-operation in Europe (OSCE) continued to work with officials on the recommendations in its 1996 final report. In follow-up meetings with the chairman of the Standing Committee for State and Legal Affairs, the chairman said he was leading a group to draft a new law and that International Foundation for Electoral Systems (IFES) personnel were present at all the meetings. He noted that each of the OSCE recommendations was being discussed during the drafting of the new law.[3] Similarly, after Russia's 1993 referendum, the vice chairman of Russia's central election commission (CEC) said that the International Republican Institute (IRI) report "served as the roadmap for the CEC in making improvements in the election law."[4] Eighteen of the twenty recommendations related directly to election law were adopted partially or substantially.[5]

The country case studies therefore provide context and continuity that improve inferences about the effects of monitors. Importantly, they can suggest factors that may condition the influence of monitors—something this chapter discusses extensively. The case studies can also highlight alternative factors that may be driving the changes within countries. For example, in the case of Bangladesh, a caretaker government installed after a domestic crisis in 2007 implemented an impressive round of reforms. Many of these aligned with prior recommendations of international monitors, but the monitors could hardly take all the credit. The practical situation had made the reforms painfully necessary and domestic groups also were pushing hard for them.

Because the country studies rely on information from multiple election visits and explore long-term effects, it is most useful to examine countries with well-documented long-term experience with monitors. If monitors only began to visit a country recently, for example, or if documentation was only available for one election, it is harder to learn anything from the case. Choosing countries with a long-term engagement with monitors does not by definition mean that the countries are more likely to have failed to respond to monitoring. Indeed, in the time span of the study, few countries ever "graduated" from monitoring, meaning monitors entirely stopped visiting their elections. Even some of the European countries have continued to receive monitors after their democratic credentials were well established. For example, the OSCE monitored Bulgaria in 2009. Thus, most countries continued to receive monitors even if their elections improved considerably. Therefore, repeated visits do not mean that the country by definition has not improved. Still, the selection of cases clearly is not random. This is not a big problem, however, because the purpose of the case studies is not to determine how often the presence of monitors and election improvements are associated, as in the previous chapter. Rather, the purpose is to identify the factors that may influence whether countries follow monitor recommendations in the long run and to examine how plausible it is that monitors are part of the reason changes occur.

About twenty countries had sufficient documentation and interest to be selected for in-depth study. Of these, fifteen were selected to create a sample that was regionally diverse and varied on several dimensions such as population size, income, geopolitical status, ethnic composition, and electoral systems. Table 8.1 shows the cases included, the number of monitoring missions, the elections attended by international observers, and the organizations involved in each country.

For each country, all the reports were read with special attention to recording the recommendations made and the performance in subsequent elections. Sometimes information on a given prior recommendation was missing in subsequent reports. Secondary sources were then consulted, but it was not possible to track down relevant information, and in such cases it was not possible to draw any conclusions on those particular issues. For each case, a table was created to keep track of recommendations over time. In most elections, the rec-

TABLE 8.1
Monitoring effort

Country	Number of missions	Organizations	Monitored elections/ (elections not monitored)
Georgia	23	OSCE, COE, NHC, ECOWAS, EP, NDI, IRI	1992, 1995, 1999, 2000, 2003, 2004, 2008
Russia	22	OSCE, NDI, IRI, COE, EU	1993, 1995, 1996, 1999, 2000, 2003, 2004, 2007, 2008
Albania	19	NDI, OSCE, NHC, COE, CIS, joint OSCE/UN mission	1991, 1992, 1996, 1997, 1998*, 2001, 2005, 2009
Armenia	17	NDI, OSCE, COE, CIS, EP, UN	1995, 1996, 1998, 1999, 2003, 2007, 2008
Nicaragua	15	IFES, IRI, CC, OAS, EU	1984, 1990, 1996, 2001, 2006
El Salvador	15	IRI, OAS, IFES, EU	1982, 1984, 1985, 1988, (1989), 1991, 1994, 1997, 1999, (2000), (2003) 2004, (2006), 2009
Bulgaria	14	COE, EP, IRI, OSCE, NDI	1990, 1991, 1994, 1997, 2001, 2005, 2006, 2009
S. Africa	14	IHRLG, EU, CS, UN, IRI, ECF, EISA, SADC, AU	1989, 1994, 1999, 2004, 2009
Bangladesh	13	NDI, IRI, EU, CS, UN, ANFREL, CC	1991, 1996, 2001, 2008
Guyana	12	CS, OAS, CC, EU	1992, 1997, 2001, 2006
Lesotho	12	UN, EISA, CS, SADC, ECF, NDI (pre mission only)	1993, 1998, 2002, 2007
Indonesia	12	NDI, IFES, EU, EP, AN-FREL, UNDP	1999, 2004, 2009
Mexico	12	IFES, CC, EU, EP, IRI/ NDI	1994, 1997, 2000, 2006
Panama	11	NDI, CC, OAS, IFES	1978,(1984), 1989, 1991, 1994, 1999, 2004, 2009
Kenya	10	IRI, NDI, CS, CC, EU, DDDG**, AU, EP	1992, 1997, 2002, 2007

Note: For abbreviations, see page xix.
  * Constitutional referendum.
  ** Donors Democratic Development Group.

ommendations were too numerous and extensive to be logged individually, and therefore larger categories were often used. Based on this research, detailed individual country case studies ranging from six thousand to ten thousand words were written. Country experts were asked to comment on the cases. Appendix E summarizes each of these case studies.

The cases are not complete accounts of the political developments in a country. Rather, they distill insights about electoral conduct and the role of international monitors in improving specific aspects of elections in a country. Including so many cases favors breadth over depth. This no doubt sometimes forfeits some detail and accuracy, but it offers a cross-national comparison that can yield more general insights.

Do International Monitors Improve Elections Over Time?

The case studies underscore that the engagement of international monitors in a country is very much a long-term project. Seldom are the recommendations of monitors implemented immediately, although it does occur. After Russia's 1993 referendum, for example, the IRI documented that "a number of IRI's suggested improvements were adopted by the time of the December 12, 1993 parliamentary elections."[6] In Panama, the Carter Center (CC) called for fairer regulation of access and use of printed media in 1994, and by the 1997 election this had been adopted. And sometimes monitors make recommendations after pre-election visits and are able to prompt changes in time for the election. More commonly, however, monitors point to weaknesses in the electoral process repeatedly before any changes occur. Often changes are only partial. In Albania, for example, the IRI and National Democratic Institute (NDI) recommended increased independence for the electoral commission in 1991. Partial improvements occurred by the 1995, 2001, and 2005 elections, but by 2009 the OSCE was still criticizing the institutional setup.

As Table 8.1 shows, in several cases monitors have been involved for multiple elections, sending numerous missions, yet the improvement in the quality of elections has been minimal. In Kenya and Russia, despite temporary improvements, elections continue to be highly problem-filled. Nicaragua's electoral administration has remained mired in political battles. As Table 8.2 shows, this does not mean that there have not been areas of success. Kenya, for example, altered regulations permitting electoral rallies and where to conduct the counting, and Russia did accomplish several legal reforms, just as Nicaragua made some administrative and logistical improvements. What is striking about these

TABLE 8.2

Least and most effective areas of improvement as of 2009

Country	Most effective areas of improvements	Least effective areas of improvement
Albania	Electoral system, many partial improvements to election laws, electoral commission permanence	General election administration,* firm electoral process timeline, campaign finance, abuse of government resources,* vote counting and tabulation, training of officials, complaint procedures*
Armenia	Voter lists, publication of electoral results, electoral system, electoral law reforms	General election administration/implementation of reforms, electoral commission independence, media bias and access,*corruption and vote buying, appeals process
Bangladesh	Electoral officials training, voter lists, ID cards, ink, constituency boundaries, electoral commission independence, campaign finance regulation, domestic observer access	Postal voting, publishing results, campaign finance enforcement, ballot secrecy, complaint procedures
Bulgaria	Electoral law (proportionality), ballot design, media regulations, redistricting, campaign finance law, equal access to public media	Voter lists, Central Election Commission (CEC) permanence and independence, vote buying, safeguards against multiple voting
El Salvador	General administration, voter lists, new ID card, timely polling station opening, timely tabulation	Electoral commission independence, campaign finance regulations, inadequate electoral legislation
Georgia	Allowing equal opportunity to run for office, election dispute resolution rules	Electoral commission independence, vote-counting and vote-tallying procedures
Guyana	Quick counts, mediation, CEC composition,** making CEC a permanent body, announcing polling station-level results in a timely manner	CEC independence, voter lists, comprehensive review of electoral legislation, campaign finance legislation, media regulation, state radio's monopoly, voter education

(*continued*)

TABLE 8.2 (*continued*)

Country	Most effective areas of improvements	Least effective areas of improvement
Indonesia	Allowing pens instead of nails to mark ballots, monitoring access and treatment.	Money politics. voter education, agent training, voter lists, voter education, electoral commission performance, experience and independence,* dispute resolution, transparency in vote count and tabulation, security of ballot boxes, polling center delays and delivery of materials
Kenya	System for granting rally permits, omitting voter card IDs on ballots	Electoral law (electoral commission), constituency size and structure, CEC appointment procedure and independence, campaign finance, establishment of an Electoral Dispute Resolution Court, opening polling stations on time, assisted voting, abuse of government resources, counting and tallying procedures
Lesotho	Training of commissioners, absentee voting, timely operation of polling stations, electoral system reform (but this has introduced new problems)	Abuse of government resources, regulation of campaign finance
Mexico	Public campaign financing, use of state resources in campaign, voter education, voter lists, electoral commission autonomy, electoral tribunal	Capacity of special polling centers, punctual opening of polling stations
Nicaragua	General administration, violence reduction, timely polling station opening, ballots and distribution, personnel training.	CEC composition and independence,* voter registries, campaign finances, voter ID regulation and distribution, abuse of government resources, complaints and appeals process.

TABLE 8.2 (*continued*)

Country	Most effective areas of improvements	Least effective areas of improvement
Panama	Voter list accuracy, media impartiality and regulation, electoral commission composition, ballot burning, vote counting and tallying, assisting in quick counts in 1989	Finance transparency requirements[#]
Russia[##]	Publication of results, removal of the "against all" option, campaign financing	Media freedom, abuse of incumbent resources, open and family voting, independence of the CEC,[*] voter lists,[*] clarity and feasibility of requirements for the registration of candidates, cooperation with international monitors
S. Africa	Election preparation and administration in general, counting and tallying procedures, voter list, electoral commission authority and operation	none

[*]Improvement, then deterioration.
[**]Some improvements occurred, although not independence.
[#]Some improvements.
[##] Russian election observation reports from 2008 and 2009 by the Council of Europe do not cover many of the issues of past reports, making it difficult to know the actual state of practice and legislation.

countries, however, is that, even after so many monitoring missions, progress has been quite limited and regression has occurred. As the CC noted about Nicaragua, "Repeated recourse to international election observation even after national organizations have developed a demonstrated capacity to fulfill their role should be a cause for concern."[7] Thus, a country such as Kenya may have held a marginally better election in 2002, but as the 2007 election demonstrated all too sadly, in the longer term such single-election gains do not necessarily translate into better elections in the long term.

In yet other countries, including Armenia, Guyana, El Salvador, Bangladesh, Lesotho, Indonesia, Albania, and, perhaps, Georgia, despite intermittent gains, the overall progress has been modest. Of course, one can quibble about categories such as "little" versus "modest," and indeed they hide considerable variation: Georgia has clearly made greater improvements than Armenia, for example. In these countries, however, monitoring organizations have on several occasions expressed satisfaction that the countries had addressed some important monitor recommendations. These often included important amendments to electoral laws, as in Albania and Armenia; improvements to voter lists, as in El Salvador and Bangladesh; de-politicization and independence of the electoral commission, as in Guyana and Bangladesh; or improvements in vote counting and tabulation procedures, as in El Salvador. Thus, some success has occurred.

However, in these countries the progress was often offset by evasive implementation or, even if meaningful, by failures to follow other equally consequential recommendations. The case studies in Appendix E thus show that many of these countries continued to exert influence over the electoral commissions, control the media, maintain poor voter lists, and repeat many other problems that clearly had the capacity to change the outcome of the election. Indeed, it is notable that such problems as electoral commission independence and voter lists seemed particularly resistant to monitor influence.

Although it is possible to point to several instances of specific reforms that monitors encouraged in various countries, only four of the fifteen countries made and maintained significant overall progress. These are South Africa, Mexico, Panama, and Bulgaria. In addition, Bangladesh also made significant progress in 2008, but this progress has not yet been tested in subsequent elections. Elections in these countries are by no means perfect now—Bulgaria being perhaps the most problematic with some backsliding after the nation joined the European Union (EU) and no longer had to be as careful to assure admission. Thus Bulgaria still struggles with faulty voter lists, lacks a permanent and independent central election commission, suffers from vote buying, and lacks safeguards against multiple voting. Yet these countries have all made major strides since the onset of international election monitoring, and have, perhaps with the caveat about Bulgaria, sustained their progress in the most recent election. Notably, South Africa, Panama, and Mexico have all tackled the sensitive—but central—issue of electoral commission independence and conduct. They have improved their voter lists, and Panama and South Africa have vastly improved their administrative procedures. Progress in these cases has thus been notable, but the case studies also suggest that international election monitors played only a supportive role in this progress. In South Africa, for example, the main international influence was through the independent electoral commission, not election observers. In Mexico, domestic actors clearly played the central role.

Table 8.2 summarizes some of the least and most effective areas of improvements in these countries over time. The table is illustrative, not exhaustive. It highlights instances where the information is reasonably clear and where improvements have been noticeably present or absent. In many other areas these countries have made partial changes that could be characterized as the cup being half full or half empty, depending on one's perspective.

In either case, as the above discussion suggests, countries sometimes do address monitor recommendations, but often the quality of elections nevertheless remains highly problematic because the countries still have not addressed many important concerns or new problems crop up. Furthermore, in some cases, even with as many as twenty-two monitoring missions, as in the case of Russia, there is little international monitors can actually do to improve the election in meaningful terms. In several cases, such as Armenia and Albania, international monitors may face a paper compliance problem: they may have extensive influence over the legislative framework, only to find problems in implementation.

Furthermore, the cases herein also demonstrate that changes often do take very long. Even in Mexico and Bulgaria this has been the case. Few countries show as rapid progress as Panama and South Africa, and when progress does occur, the main role of international monitors usually is to reinforce domestic actors.

The country variation discussed above and elaborated further in the case study summaries in Appendix E raises the question of which factors influence the effectiveness of international monitors. What factors facilitate their influence and what factors hinder it? The rest of this chapter turns to this discussion.

WHEN DO COUNTRIES FOLLOW THE RECOMMENDATIONS OF INTERNATIONAL MONITORS?

Chapter 6 discussed several factors that may diminish or strengthen the influence of international monitors. In the previous chapter we saw that there was indeed some support for the argument that high-quality monitors are more effective than low-quality monitors. The case studies make it possible to look more closely at some of the remaining conditions.

Negative Influences

VIOLENCE AND WINNER-TAKE-ALL POLITICS

Several countries that struggled to progress shared two characteristics: violence and a winner-take-all political system that leave little voice for election losers. Indeed, this combination is probably one of the biggest obstacles to progress. Kenya, Guyana, Bangladesh, and Georgia all fall in this category. With only a slight lull in 2002, ethnic violence has dominated the Kenyan democratization process, and incumbent leaders and their followers benefited economically and politically from continuing unrest and the dysfunctional institutional and political environment. The Kenya African National Union (KANU), representing the numerous Kikuyu and Luo ethnic groups, were long able to use majoritarian laws to exclude other ethnic groups from power.[8]

In Guyana the transition has similarly been hampered by deep, historic, ethnic divisions that solidified into the main cleavage between political parties, accompanied by violence as the primary tool for resolving differences. The People's Progressive Party (PPP), which represents the more sizable ethnic Indian population, has won all four elections in Guyana since the end of authoritarianism in 1992. Because the constitution gives the winning party the very powerful presidency, the losers fear exclusion from decision making and are therefore always prepared to challenge the outcome.[9] This has led to a series of disputed elections. Thus, Guyana has been stuck in a recurrent pattern of voting along ethnic lines, poor administration of elections, and violent electoral aftermath.

In Bangladesh, the bitter rivalry between the two major parties, the Awami League (AL) and the Bangladesh Nationalist Party (BNP), has been fueled mainly by the personal rivalry between their dynastic leaders. Politics has remained focused on political families, laudation of party history, and vague promises of economic growth and social stability. This has produced a pattern where the ruling party refuses a meaningful role for the opposition, the opposition walks out, and society is paralyzed by strikes and boycotts.[10] This constant rivalry long paralyzed Bangladesh's ability to improve the electoral process.

In these cases, violence and winner-take-all systems and mindsets have made it very difficult for international monitors to be heard, as following their recommendations would tend to open political competition further. As mentioned earlier, in Bangladesh international monitors were sometimes able to help persuade the opposition to accept defeat,[11] but only the crisis and caretaker government in 2007–8 was able to break the pattern somewhat and bring substantial reforms. As the Guyana case summary discusses, in Guyana only the most recent election has shown a reason for hope. Kenyan elections, unfortunately, have remained mired in ethnic conflict.

In Georgia a slightly different situation has played out, although it shares the characteristics of violence and political deadlock. The continuing tension in South Ossetia and Abkhazia has hampered Georgia's democratic transition. At the same time the tone between opposing parties has been excessively confrontational. According to the OSCE, the lack of political dialogue often resulted in complete inattention to any opposition demands, leaving the impression that there was a lack of political debate. This concern was most recently voiced following the 2008 constitutional reform plebiscite. In reality this meant that the political process came to a halt and no reforms were implemented.

An extreme winner-take-all system that frequently leads to massive riots has also hampered the effectiveness of international monitors in Lesotho. The contest has not been about ethnicity or ideology—Lesotho is ethnically homogenous—but about competition for jobs,[12] because of "the high premium placed on being in government."[13] However, a combination of a heavy-handed response from South Africa and extensive involvement by the South African Development Community (SADC), as well as the Commonwealth Secretariat (CS) and the United Nations Development Programme (UNDP), has been able to promote some administrative changes to the election process as well as important changes to the electoral system. Nevertheless, even the new proportional representation system has produced deadlock as the parties have found ways to evade its true intent by forming coalitions to evade the rules. The domestic battles over the electoral system have distracted from other reforms that monitors have suggested over the years. Thus, abuse of government resources continues, media still require regulation, and Lesotho has repeatedly ignored monitors' recommendations regarding campaign finance regulation.

These examples illustrate that it is extremely difficult for international monitors to influence election quality in winner-take-all systems, particularly when violence is common. The stakes are too high for the parties to adapt recommendations that may lessen their chance of holding on to power, the recurrence of violence distracts from political substance, and the political deadlock makes it difficult to pass reforms. In contrast, cessation of violence may give monitors, or other international actors, a window of opportunity, as in Nicaragua, El Salvador, and even South Africa.

LUKEWARM MONITORING

Another factor that can diminish the influence of monitors is their own unwillingness to push very hard or be explicit in their criticisms. As Chapter 5 discussed, international monitors may tone down their criticisms for several reasons, ranging from fear of conflict to political pressures. In some of the selected case studies the lack of effectiveness can be partly traced to halfhearted monitoring efforts. In particular, it is striking that it was apparent in two of the worst cases, Russia and Kenya.

The lackluster performance of Russia in terms of improving the quality of elections surely cannot be attributed solely to the weak efforts of international monitors. Far greater forces, such as increased centralization and concentration of power in the Kremlin likely controlled events. However, international monitors have been quite timid in their approach to Russian elections.[14] As a result, they were useful and welcomed by Russian politicians in the first years after transition when they brought legitimacy and were fairly hesitant to criticize officials. In these years there were even some signs of apparent success as Russia followed several recommendations to improve the election law, as discussed in the case summary in Appendix E.[15] In these years, international monitors were willing to give Russia the benefit of the doubt and to encourage the transition despite difficulties. For example, monitors were rather hesitant in their criticisms of the 1996 Russian election although Boris Yeltsin abused state resources, manipulated the media, and repressed the opposition.[16] The international monitors remained optimistic through the 2000 presidential election, arguing that "it marked the conclusion of a transitional period forged by President Yeltsin since 1991."[17] The more critical message that Vladimir Putin had consolidated his power fell on deaf ears. Even since then, after Russia made observation so difficult that the OSCE chose to stay away, remaining groups such as the Council of Europe (COE) have had a hard time articulating just how bad Russia's system is. Thus, after the 2008 election the COE noted that the election was "a reflection of the will of an electorate whose democratic potential was, unfortunately, not tapped."[18] The report is very critical, but such a statement reveals profound ambiguity.

In Kenya the dilemmas of international monitoring organizations and their subsequent ambiguity in assessing the elections has also circumscribed the leverage of international monitors. Chapter 3 already discussed how President Daniel arap Moi responded to international pressure in the early 1990s and began to dismantle the one-party system, and how he orchestrated interethnic violence to divide the opposition along ethnic lines[19] and used other fraudulent practices.[20] Criticism was nevertheless muted.[21] After ethnic clashes Moi suspended the new Parliament for about six weeks and gained the upper hand. However, just a year later the international donor group resumed aid to Kenya, citing the positive economic and political reforms. The lesson for Moi and other Kenyan politicians: Attending to the recommendations of international monitors is not really required. The 1997 election was essentially a repeat of this pattern.[22]

In Indonesia monitors have suffered from excessive optimism. The international monitors put in strong efforts in 1999 and 2004, only to drop the ball in 2009. After massive efforts in the early elections, international monitoring organizations such as the EU appeared eager to assume that the world's largest Muslim democracy was on track. Thus, in 2009, only the Asian Network for Free Elections (ANFREL) returned in full force. The CC sent a "limited observation mission."[23] Yet, many of the problems that monitors had pointed out in the 1999 election were still present ten years later. The lackluster showing of monitoring groups for the 2009 election suggests that international election monitoring organizations have been too quick to assume progress and ease their pressure on the authorities to reform.

INTERNATIONAL MEDDLING

In some elections the behavior of other countries has made it difficult for international monitors to address problems. In these case monitors may have appeared unsuccessful, but in reality powerful countries meddled in the politics and restricted their effectiveness. In Nicaragua, for example, the United States, due to its past support of the Contras, the counterinsurgency movement that opposed the Sandinistas, continued to actively support the Conservative Party of Labor (PCL) after 1990, while the Sandinista National Liberation Front (FSLN) drew support and funding primarily from Venezuela.[24] The foreign involvement persisted and reached a new high in 2006, prompting the CC to state, "Attempts by foreign countries to influence Nicaragua's election outcome reached a depth and visibility unmatched since 1990. While the U.S. government once again maneuvered to unify the Liberal forces to thwart a comeback by Daniel Ortega, Venezuelan leader Hugo Chávez came to Ortega's aid as a key ideological ally."[25] In practice, both parties resisted reforms to prevent other factions from competing. In Nicaragua, domestic struggles between political strongmen were the greatest hindrance to reforms. However, the larger-scale opposing support for different sides by external actors also made it harder for monitors to press for reforms.

A similar tale can be told about El Salvador. After the 1991 election, the United Nations (UN), USAID, and several other international actors were heavily involved in resolving issues in order to consolidate the peace. However, throughout the 1990s the incumbent Alianza Republicana Nacionalista (ARENA) was able to shrug off most of the monitors' criticisms and indeed their presence altogether, as the international community focused more on the success of the peace agreements and the continued holding of passable elections than on pushing hard for improvements. Improvements began with the

146 • Chapter 8

presidential election in 2004. These changes and the changes in 2009 were brought about by the gradual erosion of support for ARENA—domestically as well as internationally (by traditional supporters such as the United States). With 2009 bringing consecutive elections for Parliament and president, the attention of the international community refocused and the efforts to address longstanding criticisms made by the international monitors increased.

Russia has sometimes played a similarly interfering role. In Armenia, the conflict in Nagorno-Karabakh crippled the economy in the mid-1990s, wiping out 85 percent of the country's trade after Azerbaijani security forces blockaded its railroad system.[26] Importantly, the blockade also increased Armenia's dependence on Russian military assistance. Thus, while the incentives for democratization from the West were amorphous, Russian influence in the military and economy was tangible and strong, and diminished much of the impact of the legislative reforms that international monitoring organizations such as the OSCE had a clear hand in pushing through.

Thus, international monitors sometimes play second fiddle to other international actors intent on meddling in domestic affairs. If these meddlers favor reforms, then the monitors gain strong backing and leverage. If not, their efforts are curtailed.

CAPACITY PROBLEMS

Capacity is a catch-22 problem. If countries lack basic elements of election infrastructure and struggle simply to get ballots printed, to distribute materials, and so forth, it will also be harder for them to follow the recommendations of international monitors—especially those recommendations pertaining to capacity issues. Of course, nearly all of the countries in Table 8.2 have struggled with lack of capacity at some point, but some much less than others. For example, Panama's fast economic recovery and large service-based industry enabled the government to react to administrative recommendations and implement sophisticated computerized vote counting systems. Such resource availability facilitates the influence of international monitors by making it easier for governments to follow up with implementation.

In several other countries, such as Lesotho and El Salvador, lack of capacity was very debilitating in the early years, but showed some improvement. In some cases, however, a capacity deficit does present a significant barrier to effective reforms. In Guyana lack of capacity has several times contributed to actual postponements of the scheduled polling date. As discussed in the following chapter, Guyana has struggled with issuing voter ID cards on time and officials have struggled to cope with their duties. Elections have been disastrous in so many respects because the extremely low administrative capacity could not keep up with legislative reforms and requirements. This poor capacity has been one of the reasons monitors' effectiveness in improving the administration of elections in Guyana has been modest.

In Indonesia, capacity problems also loom large: With more than 171 million voters and half a million polling stations, the challenges in organizing single-day elections in such a vast and poor country are enormous. It is perhaps no wonder that it has been difficult to get accurate voter lists. Indonesia has also struggled to adequately train enough polling officials, to implement automated tallying systems, and to address other logistical issues. Voter education has been another continually lagging area of performance in an environment of low civil society capacity.[27] Despite massive international financial assistance, in such a vast, poor country, capacity is an enormous practical barrier to progress.

However, capacity problems cannot take all the blame. In Albania, for example, the inability to administer elections and enforce reforms has been closely related to lack of capacity, in terms of infrastructure, as well as logistical and institutional deficiencies. These problems were most evident in the early period, but persist due to underdevelopment of the country. In 1997, the collapse of a fraudulent investment scheme brought the country to the brink of economic collapse and prompted the UN Security Council to authorize humanitarian assistance. The monitors repeatedly note, however, that at the core, Albania's failure to meet international election standards is not foremost about capacity, but a matter of lack of political will. Thus, lack of administrative capacity does make it harder for monitors to get governments to implement reforms, but monitors could possibly also be part of the solution to rectifying capacity problems.

Positive Influences

DESIRES FOR EU/U.S. COOPERATION

Theory about political conditionality suggests that international election monitors should be able to assert greater influence when the country wants to cooperate with the West somehow. This was evident in several cases.

In Russia the greatest opening was between 1994 and 1999, when Russia received substantial International Monetary Fund (IMF) loans.[28] This period also saw the greatest improvements in the electoral framework and administration of elections. This period also coincided with Russia's efforts to join the COE. Indeed, the "generally positive" evaluation of the 1995 election led to the recommendation for Russia's admission.[29] Of course, the downside of this conditionality mechanism is that backsliding may occur, as indeed it did in Russia and in Bulgaria, another case where the desire to join the EU most surely allowed the international monitors greater influence.

Mexico's participation in the North American Free Trade Agreement and the Organization for Economic Cooperation and Development allowed greater international influence over that nation's democratization process, as Mexico needed to be perceived as stable to maintain vital international investment.[30] The improvements in Albania's 2009 election also came after repeated admonition of repercussions for Albania's relationship with European organizations. Before the 2009 election, the EU clearly stated that the election would be seen as a litmus test for Albania's democracy.[31] And of course, in South Africa the very decision to hold elections where all could participate in 1994 was predicated on intense international sanctions.

EU conditionality also played an important role in Bulgaria, where the EU used a bottom-up approach to democratization through election assistance.[32] Opposition parties used progress reports issued by organizations like the European Commission to discredit the government during the mid-1990s. The activities and approval of the OSCE and COE were important mechanisms for gaining entry to the EU. Thus, conditionality was a "benign yet effective tool of democracy promotion."[33] More problems resurfaced, however, when Bulgaria no longer faced the conditionality incentives derived from the pre-accession criteria put forward by the EU. It remains to be seen whether the robust backlash by Bulgarian media, which extensively covered vote buying practices, will manage to resolve the problems that surfaced in 2009.

In other cases the importance of conditionality is illustrated by its absence. Regarding Armenia, the COE was too concerned about security to use the leverage of admission to press for reforms. Instead, the COE hoped that admitting both Armenia and Azerbaijan would promote peace between them. But after admitting Armenia in 2000, the COE lost much leverage. Although the COE was still joining the OSCE in efforts to push for legal reforms, the list of changes that the COE had considered as a matter of urgency prior to admission in the organization focused primarily on legislation to improve human rights violations.[34]

DOMESTIC PRESSURES

As discussed in Chapter 6, the prevailing theme in the international democracy promotion literature is the pre-eminence of domestic factors.[35] Thus, domestic factors should also influence the effectiveness of international monitors. This is clearly the case. Several countries show that domestic pressures for reforms help international monitors promote better elections. This factor is not only important, but probably also necessary. In cases where the international community has pushed strongly for elections without domestic preparedness, such as in Kenya, efforts have backfired. Certainly the international community was no match for overcoming the strong antidemocratic pressures in Russia given Russia's low level of civil society development.[36] Lesotho's population has been among the least enthusiastic supporters of democracy in African opinion polls,[37] and the current deadlock is therefore not so surprising. Nicaragua's lack of progress is likewise mired in domestic troubles.

If the willingness to undertake meaningful reforms is absent, there is not much monitors can do. As the old saying goes, "You can lead a horse to water, but you cannot make it drink." Thus, even if Armenia has invited advice from international monitors and followed several of their legal recommendations, implementation has been lacking, and the reforms have had little real effect, prompting the OSCE to hint that the authorities are not taking the concerns seriously.[38] In Indonesia numerous unfavorable domestic conditions have hampered the ability of monitors to improve the administration of elections, such as political power struggles, endemic corruption, terrorism, poverty, the impeachment of the president in 2001, the insurgency in Aceh, and the tsunami in December 2004 that claimed 169,000 lives.

The importance of domestic pressures is clearest in the most successful cases such as Mexico and Panama. In Panama, the ability of monitors to work with the domestic opposition and the Catholic Church to organize a parallel vote count was highly influential in discrediting the 1989 election and bringing on the American invasion that brought the opposition to power. Starting in 1999, Panama's electoral process was deemed to be of very good quality.[39] Other important domestic conditions have been its fast economic recovery and large service-based industry, which have enabled the government to react to administrative recommendations and implement sophisticated computerized vote counting systems.

In Mexico, domestic factors also drove the political opening and transformation. The CC was particularly adroit at using the domestic political opening to gain access. Domestic observer groups and nongovernmental organizations (NGOs) deserve most of the credit for the tremendous transformation of Mexican elections since 1988, but international observers such as the CC were instrumental in building up this domestic capacity.[40] Not only did they help form these national groups and train them, but they also facilitated their visits to observe elections in the United States.[41] The CC sent missions, offered advice, and exposed central Mexican civil society activities to experiences overseas to bolster their capacities to build domestic observation.[42] However, it was because of domestic mistrust prior to the 1994 election that the government decided the election had little chance of being viewed as legitimate without international monitors. Furthermore, together with domestic actors, international observers placed campaign and party finances on the political agenda and encouraged the government to permit a televised debate between the main presidential candidates.[43]

Similarly, the marked decrease in post-election violence in Guyana after the 2006 election was driven not only by the presence of monitoring efforts, such as the violence reporting by IFES,[44] but by widespread efforts by domestic politicians to appeal for calm and peace and condemn violent methods. And in Georgia, any role that the monitoring organizations were able to play in the historic Rose Revolution rested on the dramatic domestic mobilization.[45]

Indeed, in some cases the domestic impetus for change has been so strong that monitors played only a small, complementary role. For example, the international community played a large role in bringing South Africa's 1994 election about, but already by the next national election in 1999 the government had addressed most of the weaknesses and international monitors faded from the scene. Thus these cases underscore that international monitors tend mostly to reinforce domestic pressures.

Even if domestic conditions play a large role in facilitating the influence of monitoring, the cases also show, however, that even in quite difficult situations such as Armenia, Guyana, and Lesotho international monitors have at least been able to claim some partial successes. In other cases international monitors play some role in helping to create conducive conditions. There is a long-standing debate about the extent to which external players can impose outright reforms on countries.[46] However, Panama illustrates that intervention can provide a window of opportunity for democratization. In 1989, monitors helped the NDI and the Catholic Church set up parallel vote counts and legitimize claims that the election had been stolen. This provided former U.S. President Jimmy Carter, who was working with the NDI/IRI joint mission, with enough support to publicly denounce the official voting results.[47] It was also at the core of official statements made by U.S. President George H. W. Bush and spurred the Organization of American States (OAS) to denounce the situation in Panama. Thus, it helped pave the way for the 1989 invasion, which permitted a more receptive political environment for monitors in years to come.

CONSISTENCY AND FOLLOW-UP

Chapter 6 argued that the long-term engagement of monitors might help improve elections by reinforcing the expectation of the international community, teaching and socializing actors, and building capacity and skills. Most of the cases studied did have rather consistent visits by the same monitoring organization(s). However, it is striking how some organizations invest heavily in a mission in a country, making long lists of recommendation, only to fail to show up for the next election. This is more understandable for NGOs that depend on varying funding opportunities. However, intergovernmental organizations(IGOs) also drop the ball at times. Thus, the EU went to Guyana in 2001, but did not return in 2006. The EU likewise went to Indonesia in 1999 and 2004, yet did not return in 2009. The IRI observed election in Nicaragua in 1984, 1990, 1996, and 2001, but did not go in 2006.

That said, the benefits of repeated and continued involvement were evident in cases like Armenia and Albania and even Russia, where the OSCE and the COE in particular were persistent in pushing for legal changes. However, these cases also show that the progress was still modest, so continued engagement was by no means a guarantee of success.

DISCUSSION

The statistical analysis in the previous chapter showed that internationally monitored elections are more likely to be representative, to be of better quality, and to produce a turnover in power. Isolating a statistical impact on some elections, however, may be possible without monitors really having any sustained influence on the quality of elections and the long-term development of the countries' electoral institutions. Such analysis may also overlook country-specific factors that do not generalize well across elections, but nevertheless contribute to the quality of elections. To complement this focus on individual elections, this chapter then asked: Is there any evidence that the long-term engagement of monitors improves the electoral process in countries over time? And what factors appear to affect the monitors' effectiveness?

Expectation of long-term persistent effects is of course a much higher bar to set for evaluating effectiveness. Even if some efforts improve only one election—that is still something. But in reality it is also true that temporary gains may not add up to much, so it is important to examine whether monitoring organizations are able to sustain improvements in the long run. The bottom line is again that the cases illustrate that monitors can indeed strengthen some reforms over time. There are many examples of international election monitoring organizations giving advice that has informed subsequent reforms. In at least four of the fifteen countries the overall quality of elections also improved after multiple rounds of monitoring.

But were the cases discussed in this chapter really representative of election monitoring results in general? It appears reasonably so. The rate of improvements in the case studies discussed in this chapter compares well with a more superficial analysis of all the countries that have been monitored. Such an analysis suggests that about half of the monitored countries displayed little to no improvement in aggregate measures of election quality.[48] It should be noted, however, that these aggregate measures often do not register smaller improvements in electoral procedures. In about another one-quarter of countries, improvements occurred since monitors arrived, but considerable problems persist. Importantly, however, about one-quarter of cases showed significant improvements—a rate not that different from the cases in this chapter and much higher than for countries without the presence of monitors.

The country case studies also illustrate many of the mechanisms that Chapter 6 argued monitors use to influence elections. Monitors play a variety of roles, from mediators to confidence builders to legal experts to capacity builders. Furthermore, the case studies confirm that several conditions modify the influence of international monitors. Monitors are more effective in countries that are already progressing toward democracy, and when international monitors are connected with organizations or donors that have something to offer the country. However, monitors are less effective in countries with violent, winner-take-all politics and where domestic capacity is greatly strained.

Thus, overall, the case studies support the central argument in Chapter 6 that international election monitors can play a *reinforcement* role by building on existing domestic potential and enhancing the effectiveness of other international leverage. Although monitors rarely have decisive influence, this does not mean monitors are inconsequential. That countries have potential for change in and of itself does not guarantee that improvements will happen. Monitoring organizations can increase the likelihood that reforms occur and are implemented.

Unfortunately, the case studies also show that there is ample room for pessimism. In the long term, more countries disappoint than succeed. Reforms often do not have a cumulative effect on progress over time. One good election is not necessarily followed by more of the same kind. This is partly the monitors' fault: Low credibility and lack of consistency reduce monitors' effectiveness. Lukewarm monitoring leaves openings for further electoral abuses. International meddling can overrule the efforts of international monitors. But countries also weaken the efforts: Often countries ignore the recommendations of monitors, follow them only partly, or regress. Some successes are very piecemeal: One can identify successful reforms that monitors helped promote, but somehow they do not add up to much better elections over time; the corrections are made

TABLE 8.3
Primary factors affecting long-term results

Country	Progress	Winner take all politics	Violence	Lukewarm monitoring	international meddling	Capacity problems	Consistent involvement	Desires for cooperation with the EU/US	Strong domestic pressure
Kenya	Very little	x	x	x					
Russia	Very little						x	x*	
Nicaragua	Little/modest	x		x	x	x	x		
Guyana	Modest	x	x			x	x		
Bangladesh	Modest	x	x						
Armenia	Modest		x		x		x		
Lesotho	Modest	x					x		
El Salvador	Modest				x		x		
Indonesia	Modest		x	x#		x			
Albania	Modest					x	x	x	
Georgia	Modest	x	x		x		x		x
Bulgaria	Modest/good						x	x	x
Panama	Good						x	x	x
Mexico	Good						x	x	x
S. Africa	Good							x	x

*During the mid-1990s.
#Easing monitoring efforts too early.

mechanically without the entirety of the democratic progress keeping up and problems simply arise in other areas.

The piecemeal progress in many countries is cause for concern. In several cases elections have passed the threshold where monitors say they are acceptable, but in reality the elections continue to suffer from many problems that add up to a messy and problematic process. These are not necessarily patently false endorsements, as discussed in Chapter 5, but in many cases the borderline is ill defined. In these situations, there is a danger that election monitors contribute to a false sense of security: As long as the elections squeeze by in terms of minimum standards, the country can maintain a reputation as democratic.

Still, many reforms, although slow, are significant. As today's well-established democracies testify, becoming a full-fledged democratic society takes time. Indeed, even the so-called established democracies today are far from perfect, and one need only recall the 2000 U.S. presidential election and the infamous "hanging chads" to see that even longstanding democracies can still have big problems running elections. It is important to recall that, as John F. Kennedy commented on the "gradual evolution of human institutions,"[49] change takes time. Countries with little experience in holding proper elections will not conduct perfect elections instantaneously. Thus, the case studies show that at least in some countries, under some conditions, improvements may be slow, but by reinforcing the domestic reform efforts, the activities of international monitoring organizations and their interaction have hastened some reforms as well as informed their substance.[50]

Conclusion: The Good, the Bad, and the Ugly

INTERNATIONAL ELECTION MONITORING has become the most prominent tool in the liberal effort to promote democracy and create a more stable and just world. After elections, media organizations everywhere hurry to the press conferences of the international monitoring organizations and headline their assessments. International leaders likewise rely on the monitors' information to justify their rejection or acceptance of newly elected governments around the world.

But several factors raise questions about the validity and effectiveness of international election monitoring. Monitoring organizations claim to provide objective assessments. But when more and more organizations join the practice without any uniform standards for assessing an election, and when different organizations sometimes disagree, how can outsiders know which organizations are reliable? When some politicians are able to use monitors' statements to legitimize manipulated elections, is election monitoring doing more harm than good? Monitoring organizations claim to deter cheating, boost voter confidence, and teach valuable new democratic norms. But when some countries continue to cheat blatantly in the presence of monitors, what are they really accomplishing? When some countries still require the presence of monitors after twenty years of repeatedly observed elections, are monitors really effective? When democracy is no longer progressing around the world, is it because the longstanding practice of election monitoring is actually failing? In short: Do we, the international community at large, which sponsors and relies on these international monitoring organizations, really know what we are doing?

This book has studied international election monitoring since its early rise. Its conclusion is well summarized by the title of classic the 1966 Italian western film, *The Good, the Bad, and the Ugly*: The good part is that monitors can improve election quality. The bad part is that most of the time they do not. The ugly part is that they are sometimes biased and contribute to the false legitimization of governments.

Election monitors can be a force for good. Although they generally cannot bring about change singlehandedly, they can reinforce existing pressures on a country.[1] They can help improve elections and increase turnover, and politicians sometimes do follow their advice and make real changes to the electoral process. This is both important and remarkable. Such success of international election monitoring validates longstanding theories that domestic politicians do respond to incentives or engagement from and by the international community even on such central issues as elections. In practical terms, it also implies that although election monitoring may be broken in many ways, it is worth fixing.

However—and that is a big however—it is clear that international election monitoring suffers from significant weaknesses that make it vulnerable to criticism and diminish its effectiveness. International monitors can only improve elections under certain conditions, and in many situations even repeated efforts in a country are futile. Progress is often piecemeal. Furthermore—and this is the biggest problem—international organizations, whether intergovernmental or nongovernmental, have political entanglements, practical constraints, and normative concerns that compromise not only their effectiveness, but also, more important, their long-assumed neutrality.

The findings of this book thus crystallize several dilemmas that the international community faces regarding its use of international election monitoring to promote democracy. This chapter begins by revisiting the two fundamental questions raised in the book: Do international election monitors assess elections accurately and objectively? Do they improve the quality of elections? While there is no shortage of opinions about these questions, this book has assessed them systematically and comprehensively. After summarizing the findings and discussing their main implications practically, normatively, and theoretically, the chapter returns to consider the dilemmas they raise and suggest ways to address them.

Do Monitors Assess Elections Accurately and Objectively?

As Chapter 1 discussed, one of the main purposes of international election monitoring is to provide an objective assessment of the quality of the election. A grand coalition of international monitoring organizations confirmed this in their joint United Nations (UN) declaration about election observation. The rush of most monitoring organizations to hold press conferences as soon as possible after the polling ends likewise shows their eagerness to share their opinions. Yet, assessing elections is very complicated. How good a job do international observer organizations do?

Although the truth of an election's quality is by nature elusive, it is possible to say that most of the time the assessments of international election monitors are fairly uncontroversial, and align well with a version of reality that most other commentators are willing to accept. Monitors do, by and large, provide fairly good information. However, most of the elections where the monitors' assessments are broadly accepted also tend to be the cases where the quality of the election was not much in question to begin with, because it was expected to be either quite decent or quite poor. For example, although monitors may have given greater force to the facts, it did not require monitors to know that the 2010 election in southern Sudan would be manipulated. As *The New York Times* headline read: "With outcome foretold, Sudanese elections begin."[2] That these elections were the first supposed multiparty elections in more than twenty years did not lead anyone to expect that they would be clean. Thus, in many cases international monitors provide reliable, albeit not particularly revealing, information. As discussed later, the micro-level recommendations that monitors make about how to improve the election may be valuable for domestic actors even in these cases, so even if monitors do not greatly improve information in terms of the big picture of the election quality, their micro-level data may still add significant value.

Although monitors provide fairly good information in most cases, in plenty of others monitors also disagree with each other, or other credible actors dispute the analysis of international monitors and question their assessments. In these cases, the limitations and biases of some international monitoring missions may color their information.

As Chapters 2 and 3 discussed, the nature of their biases derives partly from their historical context. The rise of international election monitoring represented a remarkable change in global norms. But the factors driving this change also led to conditions that created some of the problems identified in this book. To recap, both supply and demand factors drove the market for international monitors. On the supply side, after the security imperatives of the Cold War receded liberal states were eager to spread democratic values and pushed for internationally monitored elections. Many states and international organizations linked aid and other political favors to improved elections. On the demand side, these changes stimulated requests for international monitors by political actors in transition states and state leaders who were eager to demonstrate their new democratic credentials to the world, yet still lacked sufficient domestic institutions.

Meanwhile, recalcitrant states, fearful of intrusions into one of the most sacrosanct areas of domestic political affairs, elections, jealously guarded their sovereignty and strongly opposed the rise of a centralized regime for international election monitoring. This struggle had several implications: Instead of being centralized within one agency such as the UN, international election monitoring became a "free for all" activity. This prevented strong veto players or institutional demands for consensus from blocking international election monitoring. However, it also undermined any notion of common professionalized procedures for monitoring elections and opened up the field to a plethora of actors with a wide range of experience and motivations.

In addition, the linkage between aid and monitored elections and the increasing acceptance of monitoring as a standard practice made it difficult for reluctant governments to continue to hide behind claims of sovereignty. Refusing monitors became equivalent to a self-declaration of cheating for nonestablished democracies. Thus, the rise of monitoring had the paradoxical effect of encouraging politicians to invite international monitors—even if they still intended to cheat. These conditions in turn prepared the way for the rise of a shadow market of monitoring in which some organizations were created or at times were willing to provide less critical assessments in order to bestow pseudo-legitimacy on highly problematic elections.

Thus, these historical developments influenced the quality of information that monitors provide, because they led monitors to sometimes endorse elections that do not meet international standards or remain ambiguous despite significant evidence of strong violations.

The Nature of the Biases

But are the problems isolated to a few bad apples in the barrel? Is it is possible to identify just a few organizations that consistently mislead? If so, then the shadow market is less problematic. Unfortunately, it is not that simple. Some organizations clearly are more credible than others, but the analysis shows that no organization is 100 percent credible all the time. It is a matter of degree.

It is the case, however, that intergovernmental organizations (IGOs), particularly those with less democratic membership, are less critical of elections than nongovernmental organizations (NGOs). This is because the Commonwealth of Independent States (CIS), the African Union (AU), and the Commonwealth Secretariat (CS), and others are concerned about approval by their member states that do not want to establish precedents that could lead the organizations to next turn criticism toward them. This makes it much harder for these organizations to openly condemn fraudulent practices.

However, whether they are embedded in large, regional IGOs or housed in smaller NGOs, all international election monitoring missions face practical, normative, and political constraints that limit their ability to be forthright at all times. The analysis in Chapter 4 identified several other factors that may lead international monitoring organizations to compromise on the truth.

One such factor is political relationships between the monitored country and the countries that sponsor a monitoring organization. Organizations or their donor states may have a multitude of political concerns regarding a country. Sometimes they are concerned about the continuity and stability of conditions in countries that are aid recipients or military partners. Donors may be keen to resume aid, as in Cambodia in 1998, or reluctant to reduce it, as in Kenya. They may be concerned about introducing uncertainty, as in Afghanistan in 2009 when future military cooperation with the West seemed best assured by President Hamid Karzai's continued hold on power. Thus, international monitors may know that their member or sponsor states may not want them to make highly critical statements that would undermine the claim that aid or political relations are conditional on clean elections. For example, Chapter 4 described how, for the 1999 elections in Nigeria, both the CS and the European Union (EU) warned their missions to endorse the elections so that their home governments could restore normal relations. To survive, monitoring organizations may therefore be willing to moderate their criticisms to please their sponsors.

Another bias arises because international election monitoring organizations seek to advance democracy more generally. This leads them to focus not only on the quality of the election itself, but also on the progress the country has demonstrated. So in the process of assessing elections, the quality of an election becomes relative rather than absolute; the behavior of a country is seen in the context of its trajectory. In practice this means monitoring organizations are more likely to be positive when they consider elections to be transitional, or when there is a turnover of power. The statistical analysis confirms this. In addition, the language of monitors often reveals this bias. For example, after the 1998 election in Cambodia, the Joint International Observation Group (JIOG) stressed that the election was "a major achievement and a step forward."[3] This is not necessarily a bad thing. Organizations do it to encourage further progress rather than throw cold water on the efforts made because they are still only partial. Still, it is worth keeping in mind that the assessments of elections in transitional elections may be more lenient than the actual facts on the ground might warrant.

In the same vein, international monitoring organizations are also more willing to tolerate administrative problems than outright manipulation of the voting process or election laws that compromise the very integrity of the meaning of competitive and inclusive elections. Thus, monitoring organizations may admonish countries repeatedly for administrative failures, but as long as the problems can be construed as not intentionally directed at thwarting the election outcome, monitoring organizations are more likely to express their support for the elections and to concede that the elections express the will of the people.

Lastly, monitors are more hesitant to condemn elections in countries that have been plagued by high levels of pre-election violence. Violence costs lives and imperils fragile democratization processes and thus it greatly concerns the countries and organizations that work to promote democracy. They may fear that they face a choice between optimizing stability by endorsing fraudulent elections, or risk contributing to post-election violence by supporting claims that the election was rigged. This is especially true if the incumbent party has shown its capacity to wreck havoc in the pre-election period, but then to pull off a calm election day. For example, Chapter 4 discussed the leniency of monitors after Zimbabwe's election in 2000 because they likely realized that a government change would have been neither easy nor peaceful. Indeed, the EU mission took pride in having "contributed to reducing levels of violence."[4] Again, however, this bias is not necessarily bad. Clearly at times important tradeoffs exist; protecting lives cannot be weighed easily on a scale against frankness in election evaluation. What is important, however, is to be aware that the bias exists and interpret statements accordingly.

Chapter 4 therefore revealed some problems with the quality of the information that election monitors provide. Most of the time international monitoring organizations are good about letting the conditions on the ground dictate their conclusions, thus offering as accurate and neutral assessments as is possible given the available information. However, there are identifiable patterns that show when monitoring assessments are less likely to be credible.

Implications

The major implication of the existence of biases is that international monitoring organizations may at times endorse fraudulent elections. This, in turn, carries several risks. This book has not explored these risks systematically, but they are at least worth stating. First, it may have important implications for the contestation of domestic politics in the given country. Citizens could be disillusioned with international standards of democracy or with international organizations, or they could be misled and accept the legitimacy of an election on false grounds. The implications of this for domestic governance are possibly vast and highly complex, but clearly grave. Furthermore, international scholars and practitioners relying on the assessments of monitoring organizations may misjudge the quality of an election and overestimate the progress made in a given country. Such overestimates could lead to faulty analysis by scholars working with democracy data that are partly composed of information on election quality, as are all the major existing measures of democracy. Scholars could assert misleading theories based on such data, and practitioners and policy makers could be similarly misled into thinking that their strategies have been fruitful, when in fact they have not, and thus leading them to continue practices that are not working as they think.

The implication of this in turn is that consumers of election monitoring information—media, governments, academics, and voters—need to be wiser about the information international election monitoring organizations provide. Specifically, they should be more skeptical of assessments by IGOs dominated by nondemocratic member states—something that may be particularly hard for citizens of states where the government dominates available information. Similarly, if the organizations have a politically important relationship with a country in the form of aid, for example, or even military relations, then the assessments may also be less frank. Furthermore, they should be aware that monitors may be more positive when there is considerable progress in an election, or when there are significant risks of post-election conflict that monitors may be seeking to avoid.

Another practical implication is that monitoring organizations need to consider and be more frank about their own biases when deciding to monitor a given election. It is a shame that some IGOs are more likely to face the political entanglements discussed above, because they are more likely to have the resources and connections to conduct more professional monitoring missions. The EU, for example, has become very well equipped over the years and is in an enviable position compared to many of the smaller NGOs. Yet the EU tends to visit countries in which it deems it can have an influence on the process, but also in which it has a political interest. EU guidelines note that decisions about monitoring "must be balanced by an EU assessment of whether its global relations with the country concerned and EU general objectives make an EU electoral presence 'politically useful.'"[5] Such a selection criterion sets up organizations for conflicts of interest.

The biases thus raise a very poignant question for election monitoring organizations, their sponsors, and those who rely on their information: When monitors assess elections they act as legitimizers. But how legitimate are the monitors themselves? Many of the election standards that organizations seek to uphold are embedded in international laws and declarations, but this legal footing does not necessarily mean that the processes used to uphold them are flawless or appropriate. When countries such as Russia lambast the Organization for Security and Co-operation in Europe (OSCE) and criticize it for being biased and seek to weaken the organization, citizens of democratic countries cannot simply use the fact that Russia itself is sliding into authoritarianism to dismiss its criticisms. Instead, they must acknowledge that such accusations may contain some truth and that even organizations founded on solid international principles are never entirely free of political and practical constraints or normative dilemmas that may lead them to shroud their observations.

The biases also raise concerns about the extent to which domestic politicians are able to exploit them. If politicians understand that administrative problems are less likely to draw fierce criticism and turn to these methods to evade criticism, then international election monitors may distort elections considerably. The analysis in Chapter 5, however, found no evidence of that. Some countries clearly do rely heavily on administrative forms of irregularities that buy them success at the ballot box. Russia is a prime example. However, there is no evidence that monitors are causing politicians to shift away from overt cheating to more subtle administrative irregularities. Indeed, it seems that bad things tend to go together—meaning that high levels of administrative problems coexist with high levels of overt cheating and legal problems. Manipulating elections is a fairly gruff business.

Even if politicians so far appear inept at exploiting the biases, the other concerns discussed above remain valid and serious. Their existence endangers the broader endeavor to monitor elections and promote democracy, because it undermines its credibility and thus weakens its leverage. Continual efforts by international observers to improve their own standards and appear more credible and systematic underscore the urgency of the problem, but appear to be rather ineffective at addressing it. Thus many organizations, led by the EU, the Organization of American States (OAS), and the OSCE, have begun to publish extensive manuals on election observation, and under the UN aegis, several organizations have successfully crafted a declaration on principles of international election observation.[6] This is all well and good. However, political concerns can still over-ride even systematic assessments, and any organization is free to sign documents such as the UN Declaration of Principles for International Election Observation and Code of Conduct for International Election Observers. Subsequently many of the signatory organizations, even the most experienced, continue to fail to live up to the commitments it contains.

It is also important to consider that the biases may be symptomatic of the dysfunction of democracy promotion in general and not just isolated problems of election monitoring. The biases may therefore signal even greater problems that liberal democracy-promoting states need to face up to. The duplicity in aims and morals leads to damaging claims of hypocrisy that undermine democracy promotion efforts. It is of course a complex question how upfront liberal states should be about their own duplicity and whether it is better to be forthright about the priorities that motivate values such as democracy. Nevertheless, it is an important debate to have if countries that claim to support democracy around the world want to maintain some integrity.

On a related note, monitoring organizations need to accept responsibility for their assessments. The EU, for example, typically offers a disclaimer on the front of reports. Thus the 2001 Nicaragua report notes that "this report was produced by the EU Election Observation Mission and presents the EUEOM's findings on the Presidential and Parliamentary election in Nicaragua. These views have not been adopted or in any way approved by the Commission and should not be relied upon as a statement of the Commission's. The European Union does not guarantee the accuracy of the data included in this report, nor does it accept responsibility for any use made thereof."[7] Although standard, such disclaimers are remiss and should be removed. If an organization of the stature of the EU is going to publish reports in its name, by personnel it trained and missions it funded, such reports have consequences and require accountability.

In a similar vein, monitoring organizations must acknowledge that they make assessments and indeed that this is their business. As stated quite clearly in the UN declaration: "Election monitoring is . . . the drawing of conclusions about the character of the electoral process."[8] Some organizations claim that they do not judge, condemn, or approve elections. However, their repeated statements about whether an election met international standards and so forth send a different message, even if the organization chooses to call this a "balanced assessment," and not an approval or condemnation.[9] Monitoring organizations are widely perceived to make assessments, whether they like it or not. It is true that organizations are increasingly moving away from the use of the phrase "free and fair." For example, the International Republican Institute (IRI) 1994 report on South Africa notes that "the IRI did not and will not make a statement as to the freeness and fairness of this election. IRI is increasingly moving away from 'free and fair' as assessment adjectives in election evaluation. Although notwithstanding the importance of procedural efficiency and ethical standards in elections, IRI believes it is most important that a majority of voters and parties are satisfied with the election and feel comfortable that the result accurately represents the will of the majority of the voters."[10] However, the efforts to shift language away from the terminology of "free and fair" to instead assess whether an election "represented the will of the people" does not change the fact that the observers are rendering an opinion. Such vacillations serve no one; clarity and consistency would be much more valuable.

Nor are claims to neutrality very credible. In most cases this ambiguity is strategic and the claim to neutrality is betrayed by the same organization's willingness to render frank statements in other elections. (If a teacher gives A's to all the good students but no grades to the poor students, has she refrained from grading the poor students?) In some cases organizations even contradict themselves within the same election, at one point saying that they are not there to judge, the next, doing just that. A typical example is the aforementioned National Democratic Institute (NDI) statements in the 1996 Bangladeshi election.[11] Such behavior is not limited to any one organization, nor has it changed substantially over time.[12] As Chapter 3 showed, very few organizations *never* criticize any elections and can therefore claim that they are, as a matter of principle, neutral regarding the overall quality of the election. When organizations are ambiguous, this too sends an important signal that organizations must use with care. Some organizations, such as International Foundation for Electoral Systems (IFES), for example, have been moving toward an increasingly descriptive assessment that refrains from overall assessments. However, such a complete change in strategy, while attractive in many ways, also robs organizations of much of their leverage.

In addition to the problems of the biases, another implication of the rise of the shadow market is that the existence of such a wide array of monitoring organizations may essentially allow incumbent governments to "forum shop"—that is, to pick and choose organizations to their liking. This turns out to be a more prevalent practice than shifting strategically toward more subtle forms of irregularities as discussed earlier. It is simpler to just choose friendlier organizations. Prominent examples include Kenya in 1992, Zimbabwe in 2000 and 2002, and Russia in 2008.[13] The whole notion of the shadow market is that governments do indeed understand that some monitoring organizations may treat them more leniently than others. Chapter 3 found that less democratic governments do invite less critical monitors more often. The field of international monitoring organizations can get very crowded. For example, in Georgia's 2008 parliamentary election, the central electoral commission registered thirty-seven domestic and forty-three international organizations, and sixteen embassies to observe the election.[14] If so many organizations agree, then their consensus can bolster their individual legitimacy and the norms they stress; if they disagree, politicians can play them against each other, as Zimbabwe did after the 2002 election, when, after tallying the members of various observer groups and finding that the membership of the approving organizations exceeded that of the critical organizations, the government-run newspaper concluded that "the minority should submit to the verdict of the majority."[15]

On the more positive side, organizations can strengthen each other's work, as is common among the European organizations.[16] In Kenya in 2002, organizations even agreed to use the same observation forms, pooled their information, and coordinated their deployment and press relations.[17] However, cooperation between very different organizations, especially joint operations, can lead to lowest common denominator problems.[18] Furthermore, to sustain their mandate, organizations are all seeking to get credit for their work and a crowded field makes this harder. As the Council of Europe (COE) complained after having to essentially work under the OSCE for the Russia 1999 parliamentary election, the cooperation "prevented the other delegations from getting full credit for their involvement and their investments in the observation of the elections."[19] Thus, the crowded election monitoring field also spurs competition among organizations that can, as in Cambodia in 1998, lead to lack of information sharing and waste of resources.[20] Organizations may also make contradictory recommendations about specifics of the election. For example, in Russia, international monitors initially criticized the "against all" voting option, a remnant of the Soviet period. Ironically, after this option was removed in 2006, the COE pre-election mission expressed concern that the option was no longer available.[21] International monitoring organizations need to focus more on cooperation between organizations. They also need to consider whether they are willing to operate alongside all other organizations, whether it is important that they are there to provide an alternative voice,[22] or whether they are better off declining invitations to countries they anticipate will spin their statements.

What can be done about the biases and proliferation of international observer organizations? One attempt is to streamline election observation methods and standards. Thus, organizations are increasingly looking for "standardized, systematized, and professionalized parameters, methods, and techniques for ensuring the objectivity, efficiency, and relevance of missions."[23] Unfortunately, it is unclear how to weigh and aggregate different observations in any meaningful way that can then be used across diverse electoral contexts to draw uniform conclusions.[24] So far, international observer groups have not solved this problem.[25]

Finally, one might consider whether increased resources can mitigate the biases. Resources are, of course, usually helpful, and in many cases monitors are indeed spread very thin. As much weight as the international community puts on election observation, it is remarkable how underfunded most missions still are. However, it is not clear that resources are the problem or that they would reduce biases. Resource allocation decisions are themselves fraught with problems. Missions to elections that organizations expect will be fraudulent are often small, but highly critical and credible. But the more resources an organization invests in an election, the more incentive it also has to spin its assessments positively. After all, when so many resources are used, doesn't a flawed election mean the mission somehow failed? The OSCE and the UN faced this dilemma in the elections they supervised in Bosnia and Herzegovina in 1996. Thus, larger missions are not inherently credible. In sum, there is little reason to think that the size of the mission itself reduces bias. It may allow monitors to collect better information, but this is no guarantee that the assessments will be more honest. As

Chapter 4 notes, international involvement in the 2009 election in Afghanistan was exorbitantly high and the UN had access to the best information available. Yet, the UN only acknowledged the high level of fraud after some personnel publicly broke ranks. An increase in resources may therefore mitigate information deficits, but it will not alleviate the normative or political constraints, and may even exacerbate some organizational pressure on monitoring organizations to demonstrate their usefulness. As will be discussed later, to decrease their resource deficits, monitoring organizations may instead want to reexamine their methods and their allocation of existing resources. Next, however, this chapter turns to the second of this book's central questions.

Do Monitors Improve the Quality of Elections?

Chapter 1 argued that the current stagnation of global democratic progress, which may or may not be broken by the Arab Spring, begs the question whether democracy promotion efforts such as the longstanding practice of election monitoring are failing. Most international organizations that monitor elections claim that they deter fraud, boost participation, increase confidence in the results, teach democratic norms, and much more.[26] But does international election monitoring actually improve the quality of elections? If not, then it might be wiser to simply abandon the practice than worry about how to address its problems. The question of whether monitors improve elections is also central to the more general and longstanding scholarly debate about whether international actors can have any influence at all on domestic politics—a debate that democratization scholars in particular tend to dismiss and that the topic of election monitoring therefore has particular leverage to inform.

This book has relied on a comprehensive survey of monitored and nonmonitored elections globally over thirty years to analyze individual elections as well as the effect of monitors in countries over time. The findings are both encouraging and discouraging.

The encouraging part is that monitors can improve elections by altering incentives to cheat and by engaging with domestic actors. Monitors alter the incentives to cheat because they make fraud more visible to international actors and signal that the international community is placing greater weight on cheating in a given election. This is a special concern for states that need to protect their reputations to attract trade and aid.

International election monitors also increase the domestic costs of cheating. As growth of political parties, civil society, education, and economic development increase pressures for democratization, domestic actors grow more capable of challenging authority and begin to demand clean elections. The pressures on governments to invite international monitors often increase. In these contexts, international monitors can increase citizen attention to cheating and boost domestic resolve by providing a convincing third-party source of information and signaling international support. International monitors thus reinforce domestic criticisms and increase the risk of protest—a scenario played out in, for example, Georgia in 2003, Ukraine in 2004, and Panama in 1989.

International monitors can also increase the benefits of holding clean elections by playing a verification role. Without monitors, a clean election might go unrewarded if politicians cannot demonstrate that the election in fact was clean. However, if monitors verify the process this makes clean elections more valuable and therefore more attractive. In several elections such as South Korea in 1987, Bulgaria in 1990, Mozambique in 1994, and Mexico in 1994, the environment was so polarized that without international monitors the victor might not have been able to establish a governing mandate. Certainly many countries would have labeled Hamas's 2006 victory in the Palestinian Authority as fraudulent if it were not for several international observer groups stressing its validity. Thus, endorsement by international monitors makes victory more valuable. As *The New York Times* reported after the Ukraine 2010 election, "Ms. Tymoshenko had charged that Mr. Yanukovych had again relied on dirty tricks this year. But analysts said she had little chance in court, given the margin of Mr. Yanukovych's victory and the election monitors' assessment."[27]

In addition to altering the incentives to cheat—and it is important to stress that this is not an alternative but a complementary function—international monitors can alter conditions on the ground. The conduct of elections is not only about overt cheating, but also about capacity, experience, norms, and institutions. Through repeated election missions, interviews, and consultations with government and opposition officials, extensive written recommendations, and practical assistance, international monitors can help teach domestic actors how to run democratic elections and reinforce the expectations of the international community about political competition. When in a country, monitors can both demonstrate and persuade. They have opportunities to meet with and discuss electoral norms with officials, and they can also showcase proper methods by giving practical assistance on the day of election or, for example, providing advice on the formation of the voter registry.

Both the statistical and qualitative analyses support these arguments. The statistical analysis showed that in multiparty states that are not yet fully established democracies, monitored elections are both likelier to be seen as representative and to produce a turnover in power. The descriptive analysis of the data in

Chapter 7 showed that, depending on the subsample, monitored elections have been acceptable about 10 to 20 percent more often in absolute terms. If one only examines elections in countries where the previous election was considered unacceptable, the rate nearly quadruples. Furthermore, in many subgroups of elections, monitored elections produced a turnover nearly twice as often as nonmonitored elections.

These relationships do not exist simply because monitors favor first multiparty elections or less stable countries. The matching analysis accounted for this by comparing monitored and nonmonitored elections that were nearly similar on these and several other important characteristics that might lead to better elections and turnover. Chapter 7 discussed several caveats in interpreting the findings, but it is important to note that the statistical analysis, which is the most comprehensive and systematic attempt to date to examine the relationship, does provide considerable support for the existence of such a relationship.

Qualitative analysis bolstered the statistical findings. About half the countries that have hosted monitors have improved at least some since monitors first arrived. The case studies summarized in Chapter 8 provided several examples of cases where countries have followed the specific recommendations of monitors regarding laws, or improved administrative processes in ways monitoring organizations suggested. Some of these improvements may be coincidental, but there are some fairly clear cases where the engagement of the monitors has been so direct and visible that their influence is highly plausible—indeed, seems quite evident. For example, in Mexico, international monitors facilitated domestic monitoring for the 1994 election through direct interaction and by exposing domestic actors to election monitoring techniques in other countries. Monitors also played this constructive role in Kenya leading up to the 1992 election.

International election monitoring therefore provides new evidence that external players are able to influence the behavior of domestic governments. The findings also add further support for the argument that domestic political actors respond to a combination of incentives and various forms of more direct engagement, or, as some scholars might argue, that rationalist and constructivist mechanisms complement each other.

Despite the good news, the findings are also partly discouraging. Improvements can take extremely long to achieve, flagrant cheating continues in many cases, backsliding is common, improvements are often minor, and governments often fail to act on the recommendations of monitors. For example, the case studies show that although countries may have a better election in one year, such as Kenya in 2002 or Albania in 1997 where incumbents lost power, such improvements may be short lived. Monitors may thus "win battles, but lose the war." In Kenya, for example, elections have not improved significantly despite the presence of monitors over four elections since 1992 and the optimism following the 2002 election. Thus, although the statistical analysis suggested that monitored elections are better than nonmonitored elections, Chapter 5 also showed that even when monitored, at least one-quarter of the time politicians cheat extensively on election day (including the post-vote processing), and just as much in the pre-election period.

Thus, studies of countries over time paint a more discouraging picture than the positive statistical finding about individual elections. Of course, this is partly a matter of whether one looks at the glass as half full or half empty. It is true that most of the countries studied did not show remarkable and robust progress, and for those that did several factors contributed to this outcome and international monitors played but a partial role.

But this is not surprising. Election monitoring alone can hardly be expected to miraculously set a country on course for permanent consolidation of democracy. Prima facie, the odds are against election monitors, who do not present a terribly formidable force. After all, power is precious and costly to lose, especially in societies where corruption and cheating line the pockets of the power-holders or where losing power may carry criminal and potentially life-threatening risks. Furthermore, if incumbents lose power, the rewards for honesty go not to them, but to their successors. Thus, monitors face quite strong challenges, and one could argue that it is remarkable they are able to exert some influence at least some of the time.

The great variation in the effectiveness of monitors therefore raises the all-important question: Why do monitors so often fail, and when can they be effective? The following section turns to this question.

What Factors Influence the Effectiveness of Monitors?

Although the evidence suggests that monitors can improve elections, it is important to stress that they would be ineffective without the presence of several domestic and international factors discussed in the previous chapter. It is therefore more appropriate to think of international monitors as playing a *reinforcement* role by building on existing domestic potential and enhancing the effectiveness of other international leverage.

International incentives can be crucial. International election monitors are able to assert greater influence when the country wants to cooperate with the West somehow. When authorities realize there may be important repercussions, they become more open toward international monitors and make greater efforts to meet some of their demands. Examples include Nicaragua in 1990, Russia in the mid-1990s, and EU enlargement incentives for Albania and Bulgaria. Indeed, underscoring the importance of incentives, Bulgaria has regressed on a number of issues after joining the EU, just as in the absence of strong conditionality, it has responded halfheartedly to the recommendations of monitors. These findings are very consistent with the rationalist argument that monitors increase the international cost of cheating and with the existing research on conditionality.

A favorable domestic environment is essential. It matters where an election is in the democratization process. Monitoring organizations may be particularly well suited to help ensure that first multiparty elections represent more than a symbolic leap forward, and they have played important roles in several high-profile elections where the country signaled that it was prepared to break with the past. Similarly, domestic pressure for reforms helps international monitors promote better elections. In Panama, monitors were able to help discredit the 1989 election, because they could work with the domestic opposition and the Catholic Church to organize a parallel vote count. In Mexico, the Carter Center (CC) needed the domestic political opening to gain influence and help build domestic capacity, and international observers worked with domestic actors to draw attention to election finances and push for a televised debate between presidential candidates. Similarly, the IFES and other monitors likely contributed to the relative calm after Guyana's 2006 election, but the appeal for calm and peace by domestic politicians was fundamental. In contrast, in cases where the international community has pushed strongly for elections without domestic preparedness, such as in Kenya, efforts have backfired. Certainly the international community was no match for the strong antidemocratic pressures in Russia and Russia's low level of civil society development. Thus, if domestic willingness and mobilization to undertake meaningful reforms are absent, monitors may not be able to do much. On the other hand, if domestic pressures for reform are active and strong, the efforts of international monitors are more likely to succeed, even if they are also less likely to be highly noticeable. This emphasis on the domestic environment is very consistent with other research on international democracy promotion.[28]

Certain domestic factors present particularly formidable hurdles for international election monitors. Countries riled by violence and winner-take-all politics are particularly unlikely to respond to their presence and advice. For example, an extreme winner-take-all system that led to massive riots in 1998 has hampered the effectiveness of international monitors in Lesotho. Even after reforms, parties have produced deadlock by forming alliances to circumvent the new seat distribution rules. Deep historic ethnic divisions have also hampered Guyana's transition. After a series of disputed elections, Guyana has been stuck in the same recurrent pattern of voting along ethnic lines, and violence has been the primary tool for resolving differences. It is extremely difficult for international monitors to influence the election quality in such winner-take-all systems, particularly those that are violent. The stakes are too high for the parties to adopt recommendations that may lessen their chance of holding on to power, recurring violence distracts from political substance, and the political deadlock makes it difficult to pass reforms.

Domestic capacity problems present a catch-22 problem. Monitors may be able to improve domestic capacity, but lack of domestic administrative and logistical capacity can also dampen the effectiveness of international monitors. In several countries, low administrative capacity has several times contributed to actual postponements of the scheduled polling date. Countries with extremely low capacity tend to struggle to implement legislative reforms and requirements. It is no wonder that international monitors have not been very effective at improving elections in countries like these, such as Guyana. In the vast and poor Indonesia, insufficient capacity has likewise been an enormous barrier to progress, despite massive international assistance.

Not surprisingly, monitors also achieve little progress when they are timid. As Chapter 5 discussed, international monitors restrain their criticisms for several reasons, ranging from fear of conflict to political pressures. This seriously undermines monitors' ability to exert any leverage. For example, although a more aggressive approach probably would not have been able to counter the antidemocratic forces in Russia, international monitors did not help themselves by being quite timid in their approach to Russian elections during the mid- to late 1990s. When they finally became more vocal after the ascent of Vladimir Putin, their window of opportunity had closed.

Sometimes monitors also weaken their own influence by failing to follow up. The benefits of repeated and continued involvement were evident in several reforms in Albania, although Armenia also shows that such engagement is by no means a guarantee of success. Still, it is striking how some organizations invest heavily in a mission in a country and make long lists of recommendations, but then fail to show up for the next election. In Indonesia, for example, monitors hampered their own influence by being overly optimistic. International monitors put in strong efforts in 1999 and 2004, but they dropped the ball in 2009, when only the Asian Network for Free Elections (ANFREL) returned in full force and the CC only sent a "limited" observation mission. Yet, as the elections showed, many of the prior problems persisted. International election monitoring organizations forfeited an opportunity for influence by too quickly assuming progress and easing their pressure on the authorities to reform.

Finally, sometimes other international actors thwart the efforts of international monitors. Thus, in some cases monitors were useless partly because powerful countries curtailed their effectiveness. In El Salvador, for example, maintaining peace and keeping the Alianza Republicana Nacionalista (ARENA) out of government was an overriding concern for the United States. In Afghanistan the United States has also been torn between pressuring for clean elections and maintaining stability. Russia helps Belarus withstand pressure. The agendas of strong states can thus weaken sincere efforts by monitoring organizations by decreasing the incentives of domestic stakeholders to heed the organizations or entrenching domestic political stakeholders.

Implications

Because the effectiveness of monitors depends extensively on both the domestic environment and the international environment, it makes sense for monitoring organizations to seek out the most conducive conditions. International monitors should continue to focus on first multiparty elections, many of which fail to meet international standards, but nevertheless present greater opportunities for monitoring organizations to be heard and play an important role. Monitors can maximize their influence by seeking out countries with significant domestic pressure for reform and where international actors also are prepared to offer support and boost the leverage of international monitors. True, these are cases where some progress might occur without monitors. But the case studies suggest that when countries are in transition they often lack knowledge and experience, and monitors can provide valuable guidance to improve processes that affect election quality. A willingness to change may not always translate into actual changes, and even greater progress may be achievable when monitors are present.

In general, monitoring organizations are taking advantage of these underlying conditions conducive to reform by being present in force in these favorable situations. As Chapter 2 showed, monitors are more likely to focus on countries in transition or on countries facing international sanctions. However, monitoring organizations also invest time and resources on a lot of other countries and elections where their efforts are more likely to fail, such as countries with poor administrative capacity, violence, and winner-take-all politics.

The international community should not ignore these problematic elections. However, it may be wiser to assist countries that struggle with basic administrative capacity in addressing that problem first, rather than send teams whose central mission is to assess the quality of an election publicly.[29] Evaluating the election in such settings can be productive to the extent that it helps identify necessary areas of improvement, but it may be premature to assess the extent to which the election truly meets the full set of international election standards. Countries must learn to crawl before they can walk. Just as the OSCE began around 2002 to develop so-called assessment missions to visit fully established democracies—clearly signaling that these are not regular election observation missions—organizations could create other forms of missions to countries that are severely challenged in administrative capacity. Some organizations, such as IFES, the United States Agency for International Development (USAID), and the United Nations Development Programme (UNDP), already do this.

Similarly, as the South African Development Community (SADC) and the CS discovered in Lesotho, and as other European organizations have discovered in the post-communist states, sometimes it is necessary to address electoral systems that perpetuate deadlock and hinder political reforms. The more that winner-take-all politics enlarge the value of political power, the less likely monitors are able to reduce cheating and encourage reforms that limit control over political outcomes. Spending a lot of resources on assessing election fairness and making procedural recommendations in this context may be futile. It may be necessary to focus first on ways to encourage greater fairness in the electoral system.

High-profile international election monitoring may also be unwise in highly violent electoral contexts such as Kenya, Guyana, Pakistan, and Afghanistan. This is for two reasons. First, countries bogged down in violence are not prepared to focus on implementing the reforms of monitors after an election. Monitors come and go, but in between elections chaos reigns and the country cannot address the many recommendations of the international monitors. Second, as discussed earlier, when monitoring organizations hesitate to be direct and critical—in essence, easing the pressures on the country—they potentially help extend the legitimacy of the regime. In such contexts, international election monitors may need to be embedded in peacekeeping operations. As noted, the problem, however, is that when IGOs take a strong organizing role in an election, as the UN did in Afghanistan in 2009 or the OSCE did in Bosnia in 1996, they have a difficult time admitting failure as it reflects poorly on the contributions of their own organizations. This book cannot solve the complicated and much studied question of elections in the context of conflicts and war termination and so forth. This area of research must be studied in depth,[30] not as a tangential issue, as in this book. In some cases it may be undesirable for the international community to even push for the holding of elections in violent societies.[31] However, the findings in this book at least suggest that *if* elections are to be held in a violent setting, traditional international election monitors are unlikely to accomplish their goals, and extra caution is necessary in deciding whether it is useful to have international monitors take a public stand on the quality of the election.

This finding also brings up more generally the points already raised by the earlier discussion of monitor biases. When the efforts of monitors are only half-hearted and their assessments too lenient and cautious, they undermine their own effectiveness. If monitoring organizations are not prepared to criticize elections, either because they are weary of regime change, or worried about relations with the country in general, then their missions are also less likely to be effective at promoting electoral reforms and deterring intentional irregularities. It is imperative for monitoring organizations to examine their own political and normative constraints before deciding to monitor an election. That said, the very factors that sometimes lead to bias also make it harder for organizations to stand on the sidelines, so such self-restraint may be very unlikely.

Similarly, scattered efforts in a country do not provide the same level of consistency and guidance as an intensive ongoing relationship. Consistency and follow-up is no guarantee of success, as Russia demonstrates, but several other cases also show that when progress occurs it is often through repeated long-term engagement. Thus, individual monitoring organizations should make an effort to return to the countries where they have previously monitored elections and made extensive recommendations. When they do so, they should read their previous reports carefully and report on the actions taken in response to their previous recommendations—something few organizations currently do consistently. In cases such as Indonesia, it seems counterproductive for the EU to issue elaborate recommendations in 1999 and 2004, only to fail to follow up in later elections.

If their resources are limited, monitoring organizations may boost their effectiveness by focusing consistently on fewer countries rather than spreading themselves thin across different countries from one year to the next. Admittedly, funding opportunities constrain the choices of many organizations, but IGOs at least should be able to muster greater consistency in returning to countries, as organizations such as the OSCE and the COE have indeed demonstrated. First multiparty elections may present special opportunities for influence, but the second and third elections can be just as vital for democratic progress.[32] It is therefore important to bring as many resources as possible to bear on these. On the other hand, in a world of shrinking democracy-promotion funding, if some countries repeatedly ignore the recommendations of monitors, perhaps monitors can have greater influence by denying them the legitimacy that comes with international observers until they begin to address past recommendations. Of course, this may give dubious organizations free play to endorse the elections, so the international community will need to be vigilant in questioning their claims.

The subject of follow-up brings up a related point, namely, that despite their commitment in the Declaration of Principles for International Election Observation and Code of Conduct for International Election Observers to issue reports after their missions are complete,[33] organizations sometimes even fail to wrap up their mission properly by issuing final reports and making them publicly available. For example, the NDI never publicly issued more than a brief statement for Mexico in 2000 although the first statement explicitly promised a full report.[34] In some cases the failure to issue public reports may be strategic. For example, despite numerous requests, the IRI never publicly released several reports, including the 2004 report for Macedonia. The IRI even denied the report existed although inside sources (insisting on anonymity) admitted this was not true.[35] Sometimes, however, organizations simply drop the ball because they get too caught up in organizing their next big mission. This problem of missing final reports is important, however. What is the point of going to an election such as Mexico's in 2000, sending more than forty people, and then not taking the time to write and distribute a timely report? In doing so, monitors forgo important opportunities for systematic and thorough follow-up. Thus organizations should place greater priority on issuing a final report in a timely fashion.

Another issue is that international monitors sometimes play second fiddle to the other international actors intent on meddling in domestic affairs. If these meddlers favor reforms, then the monitors gain strong backing and leverage. If not, however, their efforts are hampered. The implication of this is that monitoring organizations need to question where the real blockage to reforms lies. In the case of strong meddling by countries such as the United States in El Salvador, for example, there may not be much the monitors can do. But are they willing to criticize this meddling? Often, the geopolitical interests involved may affect their own funding, and this may make them reluctant to speak out. But ultimately it is in their best interest to at least document such meddling clearly in their reports.

Lastly, the piecemeal progress in many countries is cause for concern. Elections may have passed the threshold where the monitors call them acceptable, but in reality the elections continue to suffer from numerous problems that add up to a messy and problematic process. Failures to denounce these elections are not necessarily equivalent to false endorsements, as discussed in Chapter 5, but in many cases the borderline is ill defined. These countries may very well fall into a pattern of "thin" democracy, characterized by some form of elections but few other aspects of democracy.[36] In these situations there is a danger that election monitors contribute to a false sense of security: As long as the elections squeeze by in terms of minimum standards, the country can maintain a reputation as democratic. It is therefore important for monitors to not only make statements about the current election, but also to comment more broadly on concerns about stagnation, as the CC has done in Nicaragua, for example.

That said, it is worth recalling that elections in many of the so-called established democracies today are neither perfect, nor did they arrive in their current advanced state overnight.[37] The United States, one of the foremost nations behind the efforts to promote democracy around the world and encourage elections and the use of election monitors, left a large portion of the population disenfranchised for decades, went through long spells of dubious election practices, and still gerrymanders districts. International monitors would still have plenty to criticize in American elections, and indeed, after the 2000 debacle, OSCE monitors have started to visit the United States.[38] The development of democracy and elections takes time and requires constant vigilance. Perhaps what monitors therefore can engender is what John F. Kennedy called "a gradual evolution of human institutions."[39]

CLOSING THOUGHTS

International election monitors embody the liberal belief that it is possible for external actors to promote democracy. This book has shown that they can be a force for good. But although they have operated for years and accumulated much experience, they still face serious problems. This book has pointed out many issues that monitoring organizations may know, but seek to avoid discussing openly. These can be crystallized into several dilemmas that the international community faces regarding its use of international election monitoring to promote democracy.

- The autonomy dilemma: The organizations with the greatest resources and leverage to conduct effective and professional election monitoring are also those with the greatest political baggage and least autonomy. No organization is entirely free of constraints, but smaller NGOs are freer than large IGOs. Yet, the large IGOs are better equipped and also have greater opportunities to exert political and economic leverage.
- The targeting dilemma: The countries that are most receptive to the advice of international monitors are also those that need international monitoring the least. Countries in which citizens demand reform are keener to follow the advice of international monitors. Yet, these countries could possibly get

by without monitors. In contrast, countries without any domestic demand for reforms are those that need external help the most. But in these cases monitors are usually powerless. Despite low odds of success, international monitoring organizations frequently expend resources in these countries.

- The attention deficit dilemma: Monitoring organizations must focus on upcoming elections, but this tends to occur at the expense of lessening their attention on the elections they recently monitored. As a result, pressure on countries eases between elections and recommendations are often forgotten by the time the next mission comes around. Thus, in the rush to prepare for new missions, organizations lose valuable leverage that could have been derived from past work.
- The election fixation dilemma: Elections are central to democracy, but they are not sufficient. By focusing so much on elections, the international community cannot avoid defining democracy as foremost about elections, yet this deemphasizes other democratic institutions that are essential to supporting good elections.
- The resource dilemma: More resources and engagement in a country improves monitoring capacity, but it can also lead to biases because the monitors become too invested in the process. In addition, a high level of external resources and engagement can neutralize local political actors who are essential to the eventual withdrawal of resources.
- The assessment dilemma: The mandate to assess elections frankly and the power to validate them are necessary to motivate progress, but this mandate is also what leads to entanglements and biases. Neutrality, the only true solution to the problem, is unrealistic, and while attractive in many ways, would also rob organizations of much of their leverage.
- The proliferation dilemma: More organizations mean greater coverage, more engagement in monitoring, and better distribution of findings. Yet it also invites manipulation, conflicting recommendations, spin, forum shopping, and competition for resources and credit.

These dilemmas are important to address. Ineffective monitoring may disenchant voters about the international community and democracy more broadly, devalue international election monitors, and further decrease their leverage. Thus reforms are necessary if international election monitoring is to play a constructive role in democracy promotion.

As new handbooks, training manuals, and guidelines attest, monitoring organizations are trying to improve. Most organizations are sticking with the traditional model of monitoring, but new models are emerging. For example, when the CC realized that it lacked resources to monitor the 2000 Mexican election in the traditional way, it posted an observer at the offices of each of the main political parties to monitor the complaints that flowed through their offices. It also sent personnel to follow the domestic observers and the UN operations, and posted an observer at the headquarters of the Mexican election authorities. Observers also accompanied the quick-response units in Mexico City to see how they resolved problems. The idea was that "by monitoring the communications networks used to report problems, the Center could cross-reference concerns and keep its leadership team apprised of developments without mounting a massive monitoring effort."[40] This innovative model worked well, but although the CC seeks to replicate parts of this model, a similar mission has not been implemented since, because it is very difficult to obtain such a high level of access.[41]

Another positive development is that some organizations such as the OSCE have begun to send more missions to established democracies. This signals equal treatment for all countries and can also help address remaining weaknesses of elections in these democracies. Staffing such missions partly with observers from countries with less experience also facilitates learning. It is important, of course, that such efforts do detract from more needed missions, but to the extent that they actually facilitate training, this need not be.

Despite these innovations, international monitoring organizations need to be open to criticisms and to continue to seek new ways to improve their operations. This will be hard. Even if organizations know how to fix the problems, not all the actors involved will listen and governments will continue to pick and choose to their liking, while journalists and politicians try to sort out the mixed messages. This book does not have all the solutions to the dilemmas posed above. That said, several recommendations flow directly from the discussion in this chapter:

1. Consumers of election monitoring information—media, governments, academics, and voters—need to ask more questions about the information international election monitoring organizations provide.

2. Monitoring organizations should disclose their own conflicts of interests and biases, especially if they invest vast resources in an election. Monitoring organizations should document geopolitical meddling that may hinder domestic progress and interfere with their work.

3. Monitoring organizations need to accept responsibility for their assessments. Formal disclaimers are remiss, claims of neutrality are specious, and vacillations serve no one. Clarity and consistency are more valuable.

4. In contentious situations, monitoring organizations should consider setting higher thresholds for formal cooperation and access at all levels as

a condition for their work. After all, if governments are not willing to cooperate fully with the observers about the process of observation, this may also signal their unwillingness to follow their advice.

5. It may be wiser to assist countries that struggle with basic administrative capacity with addressing that problem first, rather than send teams whose central mission is to publicly assess the election's quality.

6. In countries where electoral systems perpetuate deadlock and hinder political reforms, assessing election fairness and making procedural recommendations may be futile. It may be better to focus first on how to encourage equity in the electoral system.

7. In violent electoral contexts, more subdued forms of electoral assistance may be better than high-profile international election monitoring whose public assessments can increase tensions.

8. International monitors should continue to focus on first multiparty elections, but—although they may be less glamorous—second and third elections may require as much or more attention. Furthermore, when organizations return to countries they have previously monitored, they should review their previous recommendations and systematically recount the actions—or lack thereof—taken in response.

9. Because competition for attention can breed hasty announcements by monitoring organizations, a common moratorium on their statements for a fixed number of hours after polls close might be useful.

10. Organizations should place greater priority on issuing a final and public report in a timely fashion, preferably posting these permanently online.

More research is needed. This book has made some advances, but it is by no means the final word on the matter. Many questions remain for future research. For example, this book has barely touched on the relationship between elections, monitoring, and violence. Does the presence of monitors contribute to calmer elections? Or do they exacerbate conflict? Is it possible to draw any general conclusions about the repercussions of false endorsements of elections on the stability of a country or its regime, or perhaps even on its democratic trajectory? Another issue that deserves more attention is the relationship between international and domestic monitors. Their work is often intertwined, and international monitors have sometimes played important roles in supporting the development of domestic organizations.[42] More focused study of the use of parallel vote tabulations or quick counts will also be useful, as this practice is often associated with both international and domestic monitors and such counts have sometimes played a central role in assessing the validity of an election.[43] Yet another question is: Does the presence of international monitors influence the tactics of different political actors during the election campaign? Some monitoring organizations try to use election missions to teach team members. For example, the NDI claims that several individuals who participated in the 1987 mission to the Philippines later introduced important changes in their home countries.[44] Do such experiences help diffuse electoral norms between countries? These, and many other questions on other forms of electoral assistance, require future research.

Meanwhile, this book has shown that under certain conditions international election monitors can help improve elections and promote domestic reforms, thus refuting arguments that international efforts cannot change government behavior and that democratization is entirely a domestic process. This is cause for some optimism. However, the book has also revealed serious limitations and biases of international election observers. Therefore, both those who sponsor monitoring efforts and those who rely on them must raise their expectations and scrutinize their strategies more closely.

Appendix A: Data Description

Two Datasets

Data on International Election Monitoring (DIEM)

The data used for this book have been developed as part of the Data on International Election Monitoring (DIEM) Project.[1] The project began as an effort to study international election monitoring by gathering and quantifying the content of official documents from election monitoring organizations around the world for as far back as possible. All in all, the project coded more than forty thousand pages of election monitoring documents, such as reports, press releases, and interim statements from monitoring missions. These documents provide the formal record of the experiences and conclusions of election monitors and their coding allows for statistical analysis of what would otherwise be an insurmountable amount of information.

The documents produced by international election observers often provide detailed firsthand records of observation during elections, yet most scholars had ignored these documents and organizations themselves had often had found little purpose for them as time passed. Therefore many organizations had not retained their documents, and had not even kept a record of past missions. When the project started, information on organizational websites was often very spotty and often inconsistent. Some organizations, such as the Commonwealth Secretariat (CS), had kept impeccable records and even published their reports with full ISBN numbers so that they could be retrieved through any library system. Other organizations such as the European Union (EU) had not centralized their information at all, and records of many election monitoring missions from the 1990s were difficult or impossible to locate, as no central agency had at that time housed the election observation function. The Organization of American States (OAS) had likewise been conducting missions since the early 1970s, but many of the reports were often impossible to locate, even if it was possible to find the document ID numbers. Eventually the OAS library assisted in assembling a portion of the documents. Locating reports by the Council of Europe (COE) required extensive searching as there was no list of the document titles or number to be found anywhere, and the searches were therefore mostly long hit or miss efforts. Contact with the Organization for Security and Co-operation in Europe (OSCE) office revealed that nobody had ever requested most of the reports issued before 1995, but that they were indeed sitting in a file cabinet somewhere, and were subsequently digitized. After extensive digging, the project was able to identify 903 monitoring missions[2] and locate a final post-election statement or report for 673 of these missions, that is, for about three-quarters of all missions. However, the missing reports tended to be from a few organizations such as the African Union (AU)/Organisation of African Unity (OAU), the United Nations (UN), and the Economic Community of West African States (ECOWAS). For example, the AU/OAU maintained no accessible records and it is not clear whether reports were ever issued for most of the older missions.

Quality of Elections Data (QED)

QED, the Quality of Elections Data, was developed to make it possible to compare the quality of monitored and nonmonitored elections. To maximize the comparability of the datasets, the data cover a subset of the same variables as DIEM. QED is based on coding of more than four thousand pages of reports from the U.S. State Department on Human Rights Practices, paying particular attention to the section on the rights of citizens to choose their government, which discusses the quality of elections. Other parts of the reports were also read for additional information. The information in the U.S. State Department reports was in most instances less detailed than in the election monitoring reports. Because the State Department reports do not go back all the way to 1975 and in the early years did not cover all countries, the data cover 1,206 elections.

Coding Process

To code each individual report, graduate and undergraduate students worked in pairs, such that two people coded all reports, at least one of which was a doctoral student. The coders were trained extensively through the coding and discussion of numerous test-documents and their instructions are posted on the project website.[3] Most of the coding occurred in a full-time work setting where coders were working in the same room. After each coder independently coded all materials for a set of elections, any differences were reconciled, if necessary with the help of the principal investigator. To get an impression of how consistent the coders were *before* reconciling, each dataset contains measures

TABLE A.1
Average intercoder reliability scores

	Overall assessments	Main categories
	Election quality	Legal problems
	Level of problems	Pre-election administration
		Pre-election cheating
		Pre-election violence
		Election day cheating
		Election day administration
		Election day violence
DIEM	86.5 %	83.0 %
QED	88.5 %	89.3 %

of intercoder reliability prior to reconciliation. As Table A.1 shows, agreement ranged from 83.0 to 89.3 percent.

For discussion of the main categories, see the section on variables, below. The scores calculate the average agreement for each level of election quality variable. For example, if, for a given report, the two coders had identical codings for five of the seven main categories, the value of the intercoder reliability score for that election for the main categories would be 5/7 = 71.4 percent.

Biases

Chapter 4 discussed the possible biases of the election monitoring reports extensively. However, because the QED is based on reports produced by a U.S. agency, it may also contain some bias. Bias is important for analysis mostly when it coincides with the claims being analyzed and therefore could distort the conclusions. The U.S. State Department reports are clearly not entirely objective sources, but they are consistent and replicable, and the bias can be understood. Importantly, there is no reason to think the bias systematically aligns with the inquiry so as to cause spurious findings. Thus, in the case of the QED data, election monitors would have to be more likely to go to countries toward which the U.S. State Department reports are also likely to be less critical and the monitors would then also have to cater to the United States in dampening their criticisms. This is theoretically conceivable, but not likely to be a trend that is so prevalent as to influence the analysis heavily. This is particularly so, because, as discussed below, several of the possible biases are actually more likely to make it harder to establish a positive effect of monitoring on election quality.

The U.S. State Department reports were first issued in the mid-1970s for a limited number of countries. However, already by 1980 they were quite extensive and reliable. Criticisms of U.S. allies are quite common even in early reports.[4] The U.S. reports also quickly grew more detailed. The latest reports are on average about four times longer than the very earliest reports. Because longer reports also correlate with harsher assessments and the time trend also correlates with the rise of international election monitoring, monitored elections could have longer reports and therefore harsher assessments. Similarly, State Department reports also often incorporate information from monitoring missions, and may therefore have greater details about monitored missions, which again may make these appear more problematic. Another concern is that some cheating is overlooked, not necessarily because it is by definition undetectable, but rather because the resources applied to its discovery are limited. Although some cheating is surely overlooked, it is just as likely or perhaps even more likely to occur when monitors are absent than when they are present. All of these possible biases, if anything, make it harder to find a positive relationship between monitors and election quality.

Scope of Analysis for This Book

The year 1975 was chosen as a start year for the data to include several years before election monitoring became common. Given the many other forms of data that would be needed for the project, going back even farther would only introduce a lot of missing data. As the project coding and data collection process began in 2004, this was chosen as the end year for the quantitative data. Thus, the data covers thirty years of national elections, from 1975 to 2004.

One of the first tasks of the project was to compile a list of national-level legislative and executive elections since 1975 as it turned out existing data were very incomplete. During this study's span the 182 countries included in the data held 1,324 elections, of which 442 were monitored by at least one of the organizations included in this study.

VARIABLES

The variables in the data fall into four categories: (1) election quality, (2) election attributes other than quality, (3) mission attributes, and (4) country attributes. These are organized in the four tables below. Most variables are described briefly in the tables, but a discussion of select variables follows.

Conceptualization of the Election Quality Variables

It is crucial to stress that the assessments of election quality are not objective and true measures of election quality. Rather, they are quantifications of the opinions stated by the sources. That is, in DIEM, the variables quantify the assessment of the individual international observer group. In QED, the variables quantify the assessment of the U.S. State Department. These measures are proxies for actual election quality.

There is an extensive debate about how to measure election quality. This project does not resolve that debate, but simply provides details on a number of subcomponents of elections as reported by the sources. However, some decisions were nevertheless necessary to create the categories and rules for coding. Indeed, hundreds of categories could easily have been created and would have made coding simpler in some ways, but use of the data too unruly. Thus, simplifying rules was a necessary evil. To establish the categories for coding, this project drew on several detailed and careful academic works about the nature of election irregularities.[5] In addition the project also drew on organizational documents about electoral standards,[6] and treaty standards, many of which are elaborated in an extensive compendium compiled by the EU.[7]

The coding of the QED variables and the DIEM variables follows the same conceptualization, but there are differences. The overall assessment variables have different analytical goals, and they therefore use their sources differently, as discussed below.

DIEM OVERALL ASSESSMENT AND LEVEL OF PROBLEMS

These measures are used in the analysis in Chapter 4. The purpose of these variables is to capture the opinion of the organization as it chooses to express it immediately after the election. Usually right after an election, each organization issues a summary statement, called a post-election statement, a preliminary statement, or simply a press release. These are followed by a longer and much more detailed reports issued months later. The executive summary or conclusion of the final report typically repeats the summary assessments rendered immediately after the election, but the report's content differs from the executive summary or conclusion by providing not only greater details, but often more critical remarks. However, by the time the longer report comes out attention to the election has faded, and the details in the reports usually escape attention. Thus, the world primarily hears the statements made shortly after the polling or the overall assessment that is usually repeated in the executive summary or conclusion of the final report. Therefore, the dependent variable is the overall summary assessment of an election by an individual monitoring organization. The DIEM overall summary of the election quality variable as well as the DIEM level of problems variables is based exclusively on press statements, preliminary statements, the introduction/executive summary, or conclusion of the report only, and not on the content of the body of the report. Coders were not allowed to read the body of the report until they had already coded the summary assessment.

QED OVERALL ASSESSMENT AND LEVEL OF PROBLEMS

These measures are used in the analysis in Chapter 7. The measure of election quality in the QED is not intended to capture how an organization may spin its opinion immediately after an election. The reports are all written at the conclusion of the calendar year. The purpose of these measures is instead to find as accurate as possible a measure of how good the election actually was. This measure is therefore based on the entire content of the State Department Report on Human Rights Practices, paying particular attention to the introduction, the section on political freedoms, and the section on the rights of citizens to choose their government. The overall assessment measure captures whether the State Department report, notwithstanding the level of problems, considered the election acceptable. Thus it is possible for an election to have a lot of problems, yet for the State Department to conclude that it was nonetheless acceptable, or, conversely, for the election itself to proceed with fewer problems, yet for the State Department to consider it unacceptable, perhaps because of major flaws in the legal framework. The level of problems is coded separately, ranging from none to major.

MAIN CATEGORIES

These main categories were used in Chapter 5, and to create the MAX variables discussed below. Types of irregularity are based on a number of subcategories as shown in Table A.2. In the DIEM dataset, these subcomponents were actually created, but in QED the information was usually too scarce to allow coding of these. The subcomponents coded for DIEM were not used in the analysis in this book. However, their coding was an important part of ensuring that the main

TABLE A.2
Main categories of variables

Main categories	Subcomponents
Pre-election administration	Problems in voter lists/registration
	Complaints about electoral commission conduct
	Voter information and procedural problems
	Technical/procedural difficulties
Election day administration	Informational insufficiencies and confusion
	Administrative insufficiencies
	Problems in voter lists
	Complaints about electoral commission on election day
Legal problems	Deficiencies in legal framework
	Limits to scope and jurisdiction of elective offices
	Unreasonable limits of who can run for office
Pre-election cheating	Improper use of public funds
	Restrictions on freedom to campaign
	Restrictions on media
	Intimidation
Election day cheating	Vote processing and tabulation tampering
	Voter fraud
	Intimidation on election day
Pre-election violence	Physical violence and unrest before election day
Election day violence	Physical violence and unrest on election day

categories were systematically assessed. More information on the subcategories can be found on the project webpage. The main categories were not in any way an index created based on the subcomponents, as these cannot simply be aggregated or weighted in a consistent way. Therefore the subcategories informed the coders as they coded the main categories, but the coders were asked to make an assessment of the level of the main categories as a separate judgment. In DIEM, the subcomponents were used to flag data entry errors.

THE MAX VARIABLES

This measure is used in the analysis in Chapter 4. The MAX variables take advantage of the fact that more than one organization was present in nearly three-quarters of the elections. For each election new variables were generated

TABLE A.3
Election quality variables

Variable	Description	Values (all variables are ordered)
Overall assessment of election quality (DIEM)	The organization's statement about whether the election represents the will of the voters, is free and fair, or in other ways frankly endorses the outcome, based exclusively on the information in the monitoring organization's summary assessment or press releases*	1 = Acceptable 0.5 = Ambiguous 0 = Unacceptable *Note:* Depending on the context of the discussion, sometimes this variable is inversed so that 0 = Acceptable and 1 = Unacceptable.
Election quality (QED)	The State Department's assessment of whether the election represents the will of the voters, is free and fair, or in other ways frankly endorses the outcome, based on the entire content of the State Department report	
Problems (QED)	This is a composite variable, derived from a combination of the QED "Election Quality," and the QED "Level of Problems" variables as shown.	0 = Acceptable, no problems 1 = Acceptable, minor problems 2 = Acceptable, moderate problems 3 = Ambiguous, moderate problems 4 = Unacceptable, moderate problems 5 = Unacceptable, major problems
Level of problems (QED)	The level of problems based on the entire content of the State Department report	0 = No problems 1 = Minor 2 = Moderate 3 = Gross/major
Level of problems (DIEM)	The level of problems based exclusively on the information in the monitoring organization's summary assessment or press releases	

Legal problems (DIEM)　Legal framework not up to standards, limits on the scope and
Legal problems (QED)　jurisdiction of elective offices, and unreasonably limits of who
can run for office, etc.

Pre-election cheating (DIEM)　Improper use of public funds, lack of freedom to campaign,
Pre-election cheating (QED)　media restrictions, intimidation, etc.
Pre-election administration (DIEM)　Voter registration and information problems, complaints about
Pre-election administration (QED)　electoral commission conduct, and technical or procedural
problems, etc.

Pre-election violence (DIEM)　Violence and unrest before election day
Pre-election violence (QED)

Election day cheating (DIEM)　Vote padding, tampering with ballot box, voter impersonation,
Election day cheating (QED)　double voting, vote buying, intimidation, etc.
Election day administration (DIEM)　Informational insufficiencies about rules and polling locations,
Election day administration (QED)　lax polling booth officials, long waits, faulty procedures or
equipment, problems in voters' list, or complaints about elec-
toral commission conduct, etc.

Election day violence (DIEM)　Violence and unrest on election day
Election day violence (QED)

Legal problems (MAX)　The maximum level of each type of irregularity reported in the
Pre-election administration (MAX)　body of the report by *any* organization present.
Pre-election cheating (MAX)
Pre-election violence (MAX)
Election day cheating (MAX)
Election day administration (MAX)
Election day violence (MAX)

Sources: QED, U.S. State Department data; DIEM, the election monitoring report; MAX, see discussion above.
* For an extensive discussion of the reasoning behind this coding, see the introduction to Chapter 4.

Table A.4
Election attributes other than quality

Variable name	Description	
Election	Indicator of whether an election occurred in a given year. An election can be for executive or legislative office, but it must be a direct, national-level election.	0/1
First multi-party election	The first multiparty general election, the first multiparty legislative election, or the first multiparty executive election. In countries holding separate legislative and executive elections, both the first multiparty executive and the first multiparty legislative elections are coded as first multiparty elections, resulting in these countries having two first multiparty elections. Multiparty elections in newly independent countries are also coded as first multiparty elections.	0/1
Monitors	Whether international election monitors were present in a given election	0/1
Number of monitoring organizations	Number of monitoring organizations present for a given election	0–7
Post-conflict	The first election after a conflict	0/1
Post-coup	The first election after a military coup	0/1
Previous monitors	Whether the previous election was monitored by international observers	0/1
Single-party elections	Elections in states not allowing multiparty elections	0/1
Transition	The monitoring organization described the election as transitional	0/1
Turnover	The incumbent party retained power after the election	0/1
Years since last election	Number of years elapsed since the last election	1–16

Sources: Election monitoring reports, U.S. State Department Reports, SIPRI's conflict data (http://www.pcr.uu.se/research/UCDP/index.htm., last accessed May 13, 2009), the Archigos dataset on the survival of leaders (thanks to Hein Goemans for providing early access to this data; see http://mail.rochester.edu/~hgoemans/data.htm, last accessed February 1, 2010), the Database on African Elections (African Elections Database undated), and comprehensive election information sources, most notably the Parline data base of the International Parliamentary Union (http://www.ipu.org/parline/parlinesearch.asp, last accessed May 13, 2009), Electionworld, which now resides on Wikipedia (http://en.wikipedia.org/wiki/User:Electionworld/Electionworld, last accessed March 1, 2010), the Lijphart Elections Archive (Lijphart undated), and extensive searches in LexisNexis.

TABLE A.5

Mission attributes

Name	Content	Values
Ballot count	Does the mission observe ballot counting?	0/1
Days	Number of days the longest delegation of a given organization is present in a country	2–333
Final report	Whether the election monitoring organization issues a final report	0/1
High-quality monitors	Organizations in Figure 3.2 that rise above the 50 percent threshold, meaning that these organizations are more than 50 percent likely to criticize a highly problematic election (where a highly problematic election is defined as an election where the overall assessment of election quality is coded as unacceptable by either DIEM or QED).	0/1
IGO	The monitoring organization is an intergovernmental organization	0/1
IGO democracy score	The average polity2 score of the member states of an IGO in a given year.	-10 to 10
Low-quality monitors	Organizations in Figure 3.2 that fall below the 50 percent threshold, meaning that these organizations are less than 50 percent likely to criticize a highly problematic election (where a highly problematic election is defined as an election where the overall assessment of election quality is coded as unacceptable by either DIEM or QED).	0/1
Media	Level of media analysis by an observer group. Formal analysis is systematic and scientific, breaking down coverage to percentages for various candidates or parties. Informal analysis is anything else.	0 = None 1 = Informal 2 = Formal
Number of observers	The number of observers a given organization has present on the day of the election	1–2,000
Pages	Number of pages of final report issued by a given organization	1–216
Post press releases	Number of press releases after the election by the observer organization	0–7
Pre press releases	Number of press releases before the election by the observer organization	0–10
Pre-election visits	Number of pre-election visits by the observer organization	0–6
Quick count	Does the observer group participate in a quick count or parallel vote tabulation?	0/1
Rallies	Does the observer observe election rallies?	0/1
Western NGO	The monitoring organization is a Western nongovernmental organization	0/1

Sources: Individual election monitoring reports.

TABLE A.6

Country variables

Name	Content	Values
Corruption	Measures behaviors such as patronage, nepotism, job reservations, "favor-for-favors," secret party funding, and suspicious politics-business ties. Lagged by one year in the analysis. *Source*: Political Risk Group*	0–6, continuous Higher values equal less corruption
Democracy score	A measure of democracy in a country in a given year. *Source*: PolityIV	-10 to 10, ordered Higher values equal more democracy
Freedom House status	The Freedom House measure of the democracy in a country in a given year. *Source*: Freedom House	0–2, ordered 2 = Free 1 = Partly Free 0 = Not Free
Government stability	The stability of the government based on popular support, government unity, and legislative strength. Lagged by one year in the analysis. *Source*: Political Risk Group*	0–12, continuous Higher values equal higher stability.
Ln foreign aid lag	The natural log of total foreign aid. Lagged by one year in the analysis. *Source*: World Development Indicators, Official development assistance and official aid in current US$	Continuous
Ln GDP lag	The natural log of GPD. Lagged by one year in the analysis. *Source*: United Nations Measure for GDP per capita at current prices in U.S. dollars	Continuous
Ln Population lag	The natural log of the population size. Source: U.S. Census Bureau Total Midyear Population Data	Continuous
Organizational member	Indicator for whether the country was a member of an organization that was currently conducting monitoring in its member. *Source*: Organizational records from the OAS, COE, OSCE, AU/OAU CS, and CIS. The UN was not included since all states are members. The EU was not included because it monitors nonmember states only	0/1
Political rights	The level of political rights in a country in a given year. *Source*: Freedom House	1–7, ordered Lower values equal greater political rights
Sanctions	The presence of democracy-related sanctions in the year of the election. *Source*: Marinov 2005.	0/1

*http://www.prsgroup.com/. Last accessed May 13, 2009.

based on the maximum level of each type of irregularity reported in the body of the report by any organization present. For example, if three missions visited a given election and coded the level of election day cheating as 2, 2, and 3, respectively, then the election day cheating (MAX) would equal 3. This produces a more comprehensive measure of what the election was actually like and what the monitoring organizations may reasonably have seen or have heard other organizations report.

The Presence of Monitors

This measure is used in the analysis in Chapter 7. To establish the presence of monitors in a given election, it was often necessary to communicate directly with each organization to verify their records because final reports were often unavailable or websites provided incomplete information. Organizations sometimes posted documents that were unclear about whether organizations actually sent a delegation or made an assessment based on secondary information. Sometimes they sent only pre-election delegations but listed this as having monitored the election. Getting the record straight going back ten to fifteen years often required extensive research by the organizations in response to a request, and sometimes they corrected their websites after further research. In addition, every election in the dataset was searched in the *LexisNexis* database for news stories about international observers or international monitors, or the names of international monitoring organizations specifically. These stories were then read to establish whether they indicated that international observers were present. Based on this information it was possible to create a more complete record and to add a category for cases that were monitored by organizations other than those included in the study. For example, although none of the twenty-one formal organizations acted alone, monitors were coded as present in Kenya's 1997 election because foreign donors formed an ad hoc umbrella group of observers. Although it is possible that some missions are omitted because the records have been lost, the data are as accurate as possible after extensive consultation with representatives at the respective organizations.

Turnover

This measure is used in the analysis in Chapter 7. The coding of "Turnover" follows these rules:

In a parliamentary system, it is coded 0 if the incumbent prime minister or someone from the same party keeps the post of prime minister after the election.

In a presidential system it is coded 0 if there is a presidential election only and the incumbent party retains the office of the president. If there is a legislative election only, it is coded 0 if the party with the most seats before the election retains the most seats after the election. If there is a general election, it is coded 0 if the incumbent leading party in the legislature maintains its leading role and the incumbent party of the president retains its incumbency. However, because it is a presidential system, it is also coded 0 if there is a general election and the incumbent party of the president retains its incumbency, even if the legislative lead party loses its plurality.

In single-party or no-party states it is generally coded as 0. This is also true if there has been a coup since the last election and the leaders of the coup or the party of the coup leaders retain power, if someone is installed as acting president prior to the election and then wins the election, if a president's chosen successor is elected to replace the president, or if the elected offices do not represent the true power of state, that is, Iran.

In newly independent countries it is coded as missing if the election is the first and no power-holding party was established by the time of the elections.

If an election had to be rerun, it is coded missing.

It is coded 1 otherwise, although there are some unique cases, explained further in the documentation for the variable.[8]

The variable is coded missing in forty-one cases, or about 3 percent of the data.

Appendix B: Statistical Supplement to Chapter 3

The probability of being criticized can be analyzed more systematically with an ordered logistic model using as a dependent variable the most critical summary assessment by any organization present. Such analysis need only include monitored elections, so the potentially endogenous relationship between monitoring and criticism is eliminated. Because it is concerned with criticism of the election, however, this analysis needs to control for the quality of the election. To avoid bias from the monitoring organizations themselves, the two overall measures from the U.S. State Department dataset ("overall assessment" and "level of problems") are used as a third-party evaluation of the acceptability of the election and the level of problems in the election.[1]

Table B.1 shows that solitary monitoring organizations are less likely to be critical. Indeed, simulations[2] based on the model in Table B.1 suggest that when an organization is present alone, then the likelihood that an election is criticized drops from about 13.2 to about 4.1 percent, or about a two-thirds drop.[3] The overall percentages differ from Table 3.2 in Chapter 3 because the other quality variables are included in the analysis, but the relative decrease in the likelihood is remarkably similar.

TABLE B.1

Determinants of most critical overall assessment by monitors

Only one organization	0.276***
	(0.095)
Election quality#	8.200***
	(3.143)
Level of problems#	2.504***
	(0.618)
Observations	328
Log likelihood	-230.3
Pseudo r-squared	0.270
Number of clusters	114

Notes: Ordered logit, robust standard errors clustered on countries (in parentheses). For simplicity of presentation, the two cut-values are not reported. For discussion of variables, see the Appendix A.

#These are the overall assessments variables from Table A.1 in Appendix A.

*** $p < 0.01$, ** $p < 0.05$, * $p < 0.1$.

Appendix C: Statistical Supplement to Chapter 4

Dependent Variable

Because the monitors' summary assessment is an ordered three-level variable, the models are standard ordered logistic regressions, which estimate the probability of observing the different levels of assessments. In this analysis the dependent variable, acceptability, is inversed so that it is coded 1 if the organization states that the election represents the will of the voters, is free and fair, or in other ways frankly endorses the outcome; 0.5 if the organization is entirely ambiguous, outright states that it has no opinion, or is simply silent; and 0 if the organization explicitly states that the election does not represent the will of the voters, is not free or fair, or otherwise delegitimizes the outcome of the election.

Analysis

The models are clustered on countries to address the issue of lack of independence between observations. Table C.1 shows odds ratios, which means that coefficients larger than 1 denote an increase in the odds of endorsement, while coefficients smaller than 1 denote a decrease in the odds of endorsement.

TABLE C.1

Ordered logit of monitors' overall election assessment

	Model 1	Model 2	Model 3	Model 4
IGO		4.947***	4.818***	5.570***
		(2.604)	(2.539)	(2.274)
IGO democracy score		0.867***	0.857***	0.860***
		(0.043)	(0.042)	(0.0415)
Western NGO		0.894	0.830	
		(0.432)	(0.379)	
Pre-election violence (MAX)		1.328**	1.271**	1.271*
		(0.184)	(0.157)	(0.158)
Election day violence (MAX)		1.140	1.123	1.119
		(0.150)	(0.157)	(0.159)
Legal problems (MAX)	0.707**	0.728**	0.740**	0.741**
	(0.101)	(0.118)	(0.112)	(0.113)
Pre-election cheating (MAX)	0.670***	0.538***	0.563***	0.566***
	(0.098)	(0.091)	(0.096)	(0.0991)
Pre-election administration (MAX)	0.840	0.788	0.836	0.840
	(0.131)	(0.130)	(0.141)	(0.141)
Election day cheating (MAX)	0.468***	0.458***	0.462**	0.461***
	(0.081)	(0.082)	(0.081)	(0.0799)
Election day administration (MAX)	0.849	0.707*	0.648**	0.649**
	(0.152)	(0.146)	(0.132)	(0.133)
Log foreign aid (lagged one year)		1.186	1.231**	1.234**
		(0.130)	(0.130)	(0.130)
First multiparty election		1.024	1.146	1.135
		(0.320)	(0.365)	(0.358)
Transition		2.594*		
		(1.344)		
Turnover			2.391***	2.390***
			(0.758)	(0.761)
N	559	531	530	530
Wald chi2	58.48	131.09	115.85	100.97
Probability > chi2	0	0	0	0
Pseudo r-squared	0.176	0.204	0.214	0.214
Log likelihood	-400.89	-372.53	-367.59	-367.7

Notes: Coefficients reported are odds ratio. Robust standard errors, clustered on countries, are in parenthesis.

Source: Model 1 is reproduced with permission from Kelley 2009a.

* $p \leq 0.1$; ** $p \leq .05$; *** $p \leq 0.01$.

Appendix D: Statistical Supplement to Chapter 7

with Mark Buntaine

ADDITIONAL DESCRIPTION OF MATCHING PROCESS

Matching has long been discussed as a strategy for making causal inference in an observational setting.[1] The basic intuition behind the matching strategy is to modify observational data so that they more closely approximate experimental data, which has several advantages. The most important of these advantages in this study is the random assignment of observed units to treatment and control groups.[2] In experimental settings, when a sample is drawn from the population of interest and assigned randomly to treatment and control groups, the probability that the value of any (omitted or observed) control variable is correlated with treatment assignment in the observed sample goes asymptotically to zero with increased sample size. This means that the random assignment of a representative and sufficiently large sample to treatment ensures unbiased causal inference about the effect of the treatment in experimental settings.

Matching modifies observational data so that it more closely approximates experimental data by improving the "balance" in the "treated" and "control" groups. While there are several ways to examine whether an observation sample is balanced, matching attempts to produce a dataset where the values of control variables do not predict selection into the treatment, or more formally:

$$p(X|T=0) = p(X|T=1)$$

where p is the *observed* probability, X is a matrix of control variables, and T is the treatment state. Several methods and rules can be employed to conduct matching (discussed briefly in the following section), but they all attempt to select certain observations and remove others from the observational dataset such that in a modified, observed dataset the different treatment states are drawn from the same population as identified by sample statistics. These sample statistics are used to show that post-matching balance has improved, which decreases concerns about selection bias.[3]

Several limitations and assumptions are built into matching procedures generally.[4] Most important, matching is subject to the same concerns about omitted variables as is typical in regression analysis. Matching procedures optimize balance on the variables that are used in matching, which does not necessarily lead to balance on control variables that are either not included or not observed. To the extent that the different treatment states remain unbalanced on theoretically important control variables, matching does not ameliorate concerns over selection bias and incorrect inference. (Chapter 7 returns to this point later.)

Matching is not used to estimate variables' effects, but rather to process data so that it gains some of the advantages of experimental data. If exact matching is employed (usually when only a few discrete variables are used as predictors), a simple difference of means test or other simple statistical tool is needed to estimate the causal effect of the treatment. When exact matching is not possible, perfect balance between the set of observations in each treatment state will not be achieved. In cases where balance is substantially improved, there is decreased association between the levels of the control variables and the treatment state. In such cases where perfect balance is not attained, completing standard regression analysis on the matched dataset can decrease bias by making estimation of the treatment effect conditional on the values of control variables.[5] While standard parametric regression models can be used to estimate variable effects, the treatment effect estimate is not as dependent on model specification because many of the strong regression assumptions are substantially met in the matched dataset.

The matching for this chapter was done using a genetic matching search algorithm developed for the statistical computing language *R* in the package Matching.[6] This software package was integrated and called through the *R* package MatchIt, which integrates the functionality of several available *R*-language matching packages.[7] The primary difficulty with matching techniques based on a propensity score is that the analyst never knows whether their propensity model is specified *correctly enough* that they should stop searching and proceed with post-matching analysis. As Daniel Ho et al. argue, no scientific integrity issues arise if the analyst explores many different matching possibilities and chooses the technique that produces the best balance. The difficulty is that the analyst never know "how good is good enough."[8]

Genetic matching provides a way to automatically search through high numbers of matched samples using an evolutionary algorithm to find the matching solution that produces the best balance in accordance with the rules specified by the analyst.[9] Genetic matching uses a weighted Mahalanobis distance to determine the optimal weight that each variable should have in determining the distance between any two observations. Unlike standard Mahalanobis distance, where each variable is weighted equally in determining the distance between two vectors, a weighted Mahalanobis distance allows the importance of each variable for the distance measure to vary so long as it improves balance in the matched sample. The algorithm iteratively searches through a population of different matching solutions using evolutionary heuristics to minimize the maximum balance discrepancy between the treatment and control groups on any included matching variable. With genetic matching, a weight matrix with non-zero values on the diagonal is the object on which the evolutionary heuristics operate. A population of matched samples is created using different weight matrices and the loss function is the smallest p-value between the treatment and control groups on a single included matching variable as computed by Kolmogorov-Smirnov tests and paired t-tests for difference of means. Matching solutions that decrease the maximum discrepancy between the treatment and control groups are passed on to the following generation. Other crossover and mutation observations are also passed along to ensure that the algorithm searches the full space of possible matched samples.

Each treatment observation was matched to one control observation, with replacement, in each population based on the weighted Mahalanobis distance between the observations. Matching with replacement was completed because the number of treatment units often exceeded the number of control units.[10] Interaction terms were also added and the algorithm rerun for any second-order interaction where the standardized balance statistic exceeded 0.2. It can be difficult or impossible to assess sample balance at higher dimensions (interaction/multiplication of two or more variables). Thus, it is possible that even if the sample is balanced for a single dimension, it may not be balanced on higher dimensions because certain model variables co-vary (are not independently distributed) from one another. By adding interaction terms where necessary, balance on at least the second dimension of the sample is ensured.

Before genetic matching was completed, observations that did not have common support using the convex hull test built into the MatchIt program were discarded. As Gary King and Langche Zeng argue, model dependence and the opportunity for biased estimation is higher with extrapolation than with interpolation.[11] Thus, in a matching context, the treatment and control groups should have *common support*. As King and Zeng describe, an intuitive explanation of common support in two dimensions would be to stretch a rubber band around the tacks on the thumb-board.[12] If this process were completed for the two-dimensional values of any treatment group, then control observations that do not fall within this area would be discarded, and vice versa. This concept generalizes to multiple dimensions. In essence, the convex hull test discards treatment or control observations that would require extrapolation to match with

Table D.1

Determinants of the three different measures of election quality

	Model 1	Model 2	Model 3
Dependent variable	Election quality	Problems	Turnover
Monitors	1.0392***	-0.7897***	1.3231***
	(0.3400)	(0.2708)	(0.4247)
Previous election acceptable	2.0893****		
	(0.3365)		
	[0.0143]		
Level of problems in previous election		0.4503****	
		(0.0916)	
		[-0.0234]	
Turnover in previous election			0.8556**
			(0.3341)
			[-0.0346]
Democracy (Freedom House status), lagged one year	0.7387**	-0.8575***	1.6533****
	(0.3586)	(0.3225)	(0.4816)
	[-0.0311]	[0.0324]	[0.0341]
Log of foreign aid, lagged one year	0.0162	0.0185	-0.0700*
	(0.0320)	(0.0358)	(0.0410)
	[-0.0143]	[-0.0144]	[-0.0342]
Democracy-related sanctions	-0.4141	0.2835	-0.3300
	(0.4775)	(0.4148)	(0.5842)
	[0.0148]	[0.0315]	[0.0167]
First multiparty election	0.8412*	-0.7592**	-0.2138
	(0.4398)	(0.3513)	(0.5184)
	[0.0238]	[0.0124]	[0.0000]
Post-coup election	0.0326	0.1135	1.2761**
	(0.5717)	(0.5094)	(0.6325)
	[0.0000]	[0.0000]	[-0.0203]
Corruption, lagged one year	02890**	-0.1652	0.1288
	(0.1454)	(0.1163)	(0.1593)
	[-0.0268]	[-0.0388]	[-0.0601]
Government stability, lagged one year			-0.1053
			(0.0777)
			[0.0171]
Year (centered)	-0.0419	0.0138	-0.0012
	(0.0299)	(0.0238)	(0.0381)
Model	Ordered logit	Ordered logit	Logit
unmatched n	321	308	293
matched n	287	277	263

Notes: All models exclude single-party elections and elections in countries rated free by Freedom House the year before the election. Reporting is as follows: coefficient estimate; (standard error); [standardized balance: (mean$_t$ - mean$_c$)/sd$_t$]. Cut-points of ordered models are not reported for simplicity.

****$p < 0.001$, ***$p < 0.01$, **$p < 0.05$, *$p < 0.1$.

TABLE D.2
Predicted values for Table D.1, Model 2

		Acceptable election			Ambiguous	Unacceptable	
		no problems	*minor problems*	*moderate problems*	*moderate problems*	*moderate problems*	*major problems*
Not free	No monitors	1%	3%	17%	7%	23%	48%
	Monitors	1%	7%	28%	9%	23%	30%
Partly free	No monitors	1%	8%	29%	9%	23%	29%
	Monitors	3%	16%	38%	9%	17%	15%

Value scenario for predicted probabilities in Table D.1.

Variable	Value
Problems in last election	Unacceptable with moderate problems
Democracy-related sanctions	No
First multiparty election	No
Post-coup election	No
Foreign aid	Mean
Corruption	Mean
Year	Center value

the other group. This is a further conservative check to ensure that matched pairs are not based on strong distributional assumptions.

Statistical Results

Tables D.1 and D.3 display the results of the statistical models. Table D.2 along with Figures 7.5 and 7.6 in Chapter 7, display the predicted values based on the models in Table D.1.

Robustness Checks

To test the robustness of the findings, the analysis was tested on several different subsets using different measures for democracy (note, as in Chapter 7, all models exclude single-party states). The subset used in Chapter 7 excludes all the elections in countries that are rated free by Freedom House in the year before the election. For overview and simplicity, the tables below each focus on one of the Models 1–9 and show the coefficient on the monitoring variable for different subsets. The first line in each table is the actual model from Table D.1

TABLE D.3
The effect of quality monitoring on election outcomes

	Model 4	Model 5	Model 6	Model 7	Model 8	Model 9
Dependent variable	Election quality	Election quality	Problems	Problems	Turnover	Turnover
Low-quality monitors	0.6069 (0.4988)		-0.6235 (0.4015)		0.9986 (0.7406)	
High-quality monitors		1.3311*** (0.3957)		-0.9162*** (0.3047)		1.2774*** (0.4536)
Previous election acceptable	2.1352*** (0.6494) [0.0000]	2.4119*** (0.4060) [0.0069]				
Level of problems in previous election			0.3849** (0.1630) [-0.0777]	0.5133*** (0.1079) [0.0251]		
Turnover in previous election					0.9427 (0.7848) [-0.0893]	1.1111*** (0.3756) [-0.0160]
Democracy (Freedom House status), lagged one year	1.1538* (0.5919) [-0.0941]	0.4748 (0.4480) [0.0158]	-1.3922*** (0.5186) [0.0000]	-0.4035 (0.4002) [0.0000]	1.2999* (0.8483) [0.0338]	2.1555*** (0.6974) [-0.0717]
Log of foreign aid, lagged one year	0.1582 (0.1023) [-0.0268]	0.0007 (0.0366) [-0.0032]	-0.0993* (0.0537) [-0.0290]	0.0661 (0.0416) [-0.0096]	-0.0587 (0.1558) [-0.0187]	-0.0926** (0.0464) [-0.0172]
Democracy-related sanctions	-1.5499* (0.8389) [0.0000]	-0.4775 (0.5492) [0.0000]	0.6332 (0.6977) [0.0921]	0.2101 (0.4992) [0.0240]	-2.3520 (1.6702) [0.0466]	0.3472 (0.6947) [0.0270]

First multiparty election	1.1782*	0.6283	-1.1860**	-0.3456	-0.1500	-0.5052
	(0.6273)	(0.5752)	(0.5096)	(0.4606)	(1.0056)	(0.6624)
	[0.0000]	[0.0189]	[0.0344]	[0.0199]	[0.0000]	[0.0207]
Post-coup election	0.9306	-0.4476	-0.9927	0.8713	2.2036*	0.9628
	(0.9177)	(0.7444)	(0.8144)	(0.6649)	(1.2092)	(0.8861)
	[0.0527]	[0.0000]	[0.1569]	[0.0000]	[-0.0000]	[-0.0665]
Corruption, lagged one year	0.1035	0.3195*	-0.3198	-0.177	0.4232	0.0613
	(0.3006)	(0.1664)	(0.2295)	(0.1323)	(0.3887)	(0.1758)
	[-0.0360]	[0.0164]	[-0.0810]	[-0.0341]	[-0.1022]	[-0.0559]
Government stability, lagged one year					-0.1537	-0.0607
					(0.1728)	(0.0898)
					[-0.0516]	[0.1105]
Year (centered)	-0.0384	-0.0623	-0.0211	0.0199	0.0892	-0.0623
	(0.0490)	(0.0361)	(0.0403)	(0.0277)	(0.0793)	(0.0460)
unmatched n	168	254	162	242	156	232
matched n	110	212	106	203	95	199

Notes: All models are ordered logits, and exclude single-party elections and elections in countries rated free by Freedom House the year before the election. Furthermore, Models 1, 3, and 5 compare low-quality monitors to no monitors and therefore exclude elections that were monitored by quality monitors. Similarly, Models 2, 4, and 6 compare quality monitors to no monitors and therefore exclude elections that were monitored by low-quality monitors. Reporting is as follows: coefficient estimate; (standard error); [standardized balance: (mean$_t$ − mean$_c$)/sd$_t$]. Cut-points of ordered models are not reported for simplicity.

$^{***}p < 0.001$, $^{**}p < 0.01$, $^{**}p < 0.05$, $^{*}p < 0.1$.

or D.3, which is discussed in Chapter 7. Additional lines add different subset specifications.

The alternative subsets are as follows:

TABLE D.4
Alternative Subsets

Subset	Description
Freedom	Excludes elections in countries that are rated free by Freedom House in the year before the election
Polity6	Excludes elections in countries that are coded below -6 or over 6 on the polity2 democracy scale in the year before the election
Polity7	Excludes elections in countries that are coded below -7 or over 7 on the polity2 democracy scale in the year before the election
Political rights 2–6	Excludes elections in countries that are coded below 2 or over 6 on the Freedom House political rights scale in the year before the election
Political rights 3–5	Excludes elections in countries that are coded below 3 or over 5 on the Freedom House political rights scale in the year before the election
Prior election	Excludes elections in countries where the previous election was considered either ambiguous or acceptable

Aside from the democracy variable, the other control variables included in the alternate specifications are all the same as in the models in the chapter, so the only things that change are the subset and the type of democracy measure used for matching and control. Models use the same democracy measure for matching and as a control as is used to subset. Thus, models using the polity2 measure to subset also use polity2 for matching and as a control. Models using the political rights measure to subset also use political rights for matching and as a control. The models using the prior election quality to subset also uses polity2 for matching and as a control. The reporting of significance is as follows: **** $p \leq 0.001$, *** $p \leq 0.01$, ** $p \leq 0.05$, * $p \leq 0.1$.

TABLE D.5

Model 1 specifications: Election quality

Subset	Coefficient on monitors	Standard error
Freedom [1,2]	1.0392***	0.3400
Polity6[2]	1.4308***	0.4658
Polity7	1.1735***	0.3894
Political rights 2–6[2]	0.8830***	0.3435
Political rights 3–5[1]	1.7062***	0.5296
Prior election[3]	2.4492***	0.7895

[1] No observed problems with proportional-odds assumption.

[2] If all variables are dropped except monitors, it remains a significant predictor of election quality in the expected direction. This verifies that matching is making the variable monitors conditionally independent from the other variables.

[3] Results do not change if non-significant variables are removed by AIC search and matching is performed on restricted set of variables.

TABLE D.6

Model 2 specifications: Problems

Subset	Coefficient on monitors	Standard error
Freedom[1]	-0.7897***	0.2708
Polity6[1]	-0.8797**	0.3409
Polity7	-0.3100	0.2991
Political rights 2–6	-0.4284*	0.2297
Political rights 3–5[1]	-0.6146	0.3853
Prior election[2]	-0.9109**	0.4219

[1] There are problems with the proportional odds assumption, as the estimate coefficients are not within the standard errors of the other estimates.

[2] Results do not change if non-significant variables are removed by AIC search and matching is performed on restricted set of variables

TABLE D.7

Model 3 specifications: Turnover

Subset	Coefficient on monitors	Standard error
Freedom[1]	1.3231***	0.4247
Polity6	0.6129	0.5753
Polity7	1.0084*	0.5233
Political rights 2–6	0.5935*	0.3299
Political rights 3–5	1.0159**	0.4889
Prior election[2]	1.7958**	0.8804

[1] If all variables are dropped except monitors, it remains a significant predictor of election quality in the expected direction. This verifies that matching is making the variable monitors conditionally independent from the other variables.

[2] Imbalance remains problematic when matching on a restricted set of variables that does not include first multiparty elections and sanctions.

Table D.8
Model 4 specifications: Election quality

Subset	Coefficient on monitors	Standard error
Freedom	0.6069	0.4988
Political rights 2–6	0.7039	0.5438

Table D.9
Model 5 specifications: Election quality

Subset	Coefficient on monitors	Standard error
Freedom	1.3311****	0.3957
Political rights 2–6	0.9743**	0.3878

Table D.10
Model 6 specifications: Problems

Subset	Coefficient on monitors	Standard error
Freedom	-0.6235	0.4015
Political rights 2–6	-0.2612	0.3594

Table D.11
Model 7 specifications: Problems

Subset	Coefficient on monitors	Standard error
Freedom	-0.9162***	0.3047
Political rights 2–6	-0.4763*	0.2670

Table D.12
Model 8 specifications: Turnover

Subset	Coefficient on monitors	Standard error
Freedom	0.9986	0.7406
Political rights 2–6	-0.1005	0.5726

TABLE D.13
Model 9 specifications: Turnover

Subset	Coefficient on monitors	Standard error
Freedom	1.2774***	0.4536
Political rights 2–6	1.375****	0.4035

The robustness checks show that the findings reported in the chapter are fairly robust in most other subset specifications. All the coefficients remain negative. Tables D.5 to D.7 show that for Models 1–3, twelve of the fifteen alternate subsets return statistically significant results for the presence of monitors. Tables D.8–D.18 show that for Models 4–9 the results are the same, except the significance for low-quality monitors in Model 6 disappears, which is still consistent with the expectation that low-quality monitors have no effect or are less effective.

The alternative models show that the findings are sensitive to subset specification, however. This reinforces the argument that relationships only operate under certain conditions, and it appears that different subsets vary in capturing these conditions. The variance in results may also partly be because subsetting and matching reduces the sample sizes significantly.

Appendix E: Case Summaries

with Kiril Kolev

This appendix contains the summaries of the case studies discussed in Chapter 8.[1] They appear in alphabetical order. A brief abstract opens each case study. The objective of the cases is to assess the progress achieved over time, trace the responsiveness to the recommendations of monitors, and identify conditions that modify this responsiveness.

ALBANIA: THE IMPORTANCE OF LEVERAGE

The persistent and consistent engagement of international monitors has been quite successful in promoting several legal reforms in Albania, often having a strong and visible hand in the formulation of reforms. However, chronic underdevelopment and a weak state[2] have undermined their efforts as politicians continue to find new ways to manipulate elections. The turnover in power in 1997 followed a year of near chaos and a United Nations (UN) resolution authorizing humanitarian assistance and enforcement for the Organization for Security and Co-operation in Europe (OSCE) monitoring of the June parliamentary election.[3] The presence of monitors may have improved that election and contributed to the turnover in power, yet the election was still very poorly conducted. Whatever progress has been made more recently has come only when international actors with leverage backed the efforts of monitors, such as the European Union (EU) has done in connection with Albania's membership application. Even this pressure, however, was slow to motivate changes.

International election monitors' involvement in drafting and reforming electoral laws in Albania has been exceptionally durable, starting in 1991 and continuing with election law reform in 2008. The Council of Europe (COE) and OSCE both pushed for reforms of the electoral laws as they participated in direct consultations with the country's governments and often headed meetings to assist in the reform efforts. A new electoral law prior to the 1996 election brought several changes related to previously raised concerns: division of media time, the composition and operation of the electoral commissions at the national and sub-national levels, and the division of the voter districts.[4] The OSCE praised several aspects of the electoral law.[5] However, the electoral commission reforms did not increase the independence of the commission as hoped. The composition of the central election commission (CEC) was to be decided by the president and the prefectures; administrative bodies appointed by the government appointed the nonparty members of the zonal commissions. On both counts, the government maintained control over the CEC personnel.

Crises and war or civil unrest have contributed to poor elections. As a result, the country made significant improvements in the early 1990s, but the situation worsened in the mid-1990s when economic conditions and the Kosovo War destabilized the country. The deterioration of the overall political environment culminated in a complete breakdown of the electoral process in 1996 and an election in 1997 that produced a turnover in power from the Democratic Party of Albania (PDS) to the Socialist Party of Albania (PSS). This followed near anarchy in Albania after the collapse of a Ponzi scheme and a UN Security Council Chapter VII humanitarian operation.

Before the 1997 election, the OSCE initiated a technical advisory group (TAG). The CEC rejected some specific recommendations regarding the work of the electoral commissions.[6] However, the OSCE reported that some of the reforms were in line with monitor recommendations. Notably, appointment procedures for the CEC and local electoral commissions were changed.[7] The 1997 election was thus in some regards an improvement over the 1996 election. Despite the continuing instability in the country, international monitors, further reinforced by the UN Security Council resolution, considered it "acceptable."[8]

Monitoring organizations were also heavily involved in 2000 when Parliament adopted a new Electoral Code, which was further amended in 2001.[9] The OSCE hosted a working group consisting of representatives from the coalition parties, the opposition parties, the OSCE, the COE, and the International Foundation for Electoral Systems (IFES).[10] The group produced a draft that was passed without major changes,[11] and the subsequent 2001 election was deemed poor "due more to insufficient political will than technical deficiencies in the Electoral Code."[12] After the election, the OSCE made further legal recommendations, and "by April 2003 [Albania] had successfully addressed most of the recommendations contained in the ODIHR [Office for Democratic Institutions and Human Rights] Final Report on the 2001 election."[13] Further rounds of consultations and reforms followed between 2004 and 2008. In 2004, OSCE/ODIHR issued the report "Joint Recommendations on the Electoral Law and the Electoral Administration in Albania." The main criticisms concerned the influence of major parties on the appointment of officials, compilation and updating of voter registers, party finance legislation, and control of the government over the CEC. Under the OSCE leadership, the political parties once again set out on a process of electoral reform. Albania then reformed its electoral code again twice in 2005. Yet another round of reforms produced a new election law in late 2008, once again under significant guidance by the international institutions. The changes concerned, among other things, the electoral system and voter registration. The OSCE/ODIHR and the Venice Commission assessed these positively in a joint legal opinion.[14] After the 2009 parliamentary election, the COE remarked specifically on the "considerable progress thanks to the introduction of new voter registration and identification procedures and the adoption of an improved legal framework."[15] Still, there was room for improvement. Thus, in several cases, Albania continued to make improvements in line with monitors' recommendations.

Although Albania has followed many of the international monitors' recommendations on the electoral law, it has still struggled to follow other recommendations and conduct elections that meet international election standards. In each election politicians undermined progress by continuing to find new ways to manipulate the system, thus prompting yet more recommendations to refine the law. Still, although Albania has clearly not "graduated" from the class of countries that hold substandard elections, its efforts to provide access and listen to international organizations have been noticeable. The opportunity that monitors have had to freely criticize and recommend changes has prompted reforms of the electoral laws as well as of electoral institutions. Slowly, but not very surely, administrative improvements have occurred.

Improvements in Albanian elections have coincided with an increased realization that the quality of elections had consequences for EU relations. The OSCE warned before local elections in 2003 that "significant improvement in the conduct and contest of the local government elections will have a major impact on the European Union Stabilization and Association process, which began on 31 January 2003."[16]

However, the 2003 local elections proved disappointing and the OSCE reported that "despite some improvements, Albania has not yet been able to move beyond elections being a main focus of attention and source for political tension, particularly when there has been noticeable progress in institutional development elsewhere in the country. Moreover, this is an issue that continues to set Albania apart from the other countries of the region, which have largely left election disputes behind. The political system in Albania is still predominantly characterized by polarization."[17] The OSCE lamented "the lack of credibility in the political system, where the citizens have come to view corruption, criminality, and rule of law problems as ever-present and unchanging constants in their lives, leading to widespread apathy and overall cynicism."[18]

Before the 2005 election, the OSCE warned once again of repercussions for Albania's integration into Euro-Atlantic structures. The EU added to the pressure by explicitly stressing the need for Albania to implement the recommendations it received regarding the electoral process.[19] The international monitors were disappointed once again, however. While they continued to note that the elections "marked some progress," they also complained that they only met international standards in part, and that the major political parties showed lack of political will and responsibility.[20] No matter how hard the monitoring organizations urged reforms and worked with the authorities to amend the legal framework, each new election presented new ways that the political parties sought to manipulate the system, and the electoral law had to be continually amended to prevent each and every conceivable misuse of the law.

The election in 2009 was the first to be described as presenting "tangible" progress and meeting "most" international standards. The OSCE praised the fact that the new electoral code had implemented several past OSCE recommendations. The increased effort to improve the quality of the election was tied to Albania's application to the EU, which clearly stated that the election would be seen as a "litmus test" for Albania's democracy.[21] Monitors praised the CEC's administration of the election as professional. But, as in elections past, these accomplishments were still marked by politicization and serious violations of the election process,[22] leading the OSCE to say Albania still fell short of the highest international standards. Most notably, the vote counting was assessed as bad or very bad in a third of the ballot counting centers. The authorities have followed many of the recommendations of monitors and allowed them to play a visible role in the legal reforms. As a result, some progress has been made, facilitated by monitors and EU leverage, but in the polarized and volatile political environment, it has not been sufficient. Indeed, instability has followed the 2009 election as the Socialists' eventual refusal to recognize the results led to political stalemate and violent protests in the streets.

ARMENIA: PAPER COMPLIANCE

Armenia was extensively monitored between 1995 and 2008 and monitors were actively involved in the revision of election laws, thus providing a concrete example of how international monitors directly influence the domestic process. However, although Armenia adopted the recommended legal reforms, the operational qual-

ity of elections improved little, primarily because of the delicate security situation and the military and economic dependence on Russia combined with the lack of any serious conditionality from the West. Instead, deficiencies shifted from a complicated and cumbersome electoral process with outdated voter registers and incompetent electoral commissions in the 1990s to unregulated campaign practices, unfair use of state resources, vote buying, business influences over the media, and an unfair and nontransparent appeals process after 2000. Armenia demonstrates most poignantly the adage, "You can lead a horse to water, but you cannot make it drink."

Armenia has invited advice from international monitors and followed several of their legal recommendations, but poor implementation has deprived the reforms of any real effects. The conflict in Nagorno-Karabakh overshadowed reforms by crippling the Armenian economy in the mid-1990s[23] and increasing Armenia's dependency on Russian military assistance and trade.[24]

Monitoring started out haltingly. The international groups provided considerable technical assistance for the 1995 election and constitutional referendum, but authorities did not cooperate and the election was highly problematic. The OSCE voiced many serious concerns, but also praised the progress. President Levon Ter-Petrossian, who had been president since 1991, manipulated the voting and was re-elected in 1996. His former colleagues eventually forced him to resign in February 1998.[25] The subsequent 1998 election improved slightly, but was still characterized by fraud, intimidation, and some violence. Observers were highly critical. In a landslide victory, the May 1999 election brought to power two charismatic leaders, Karen Demirchian and Vazgen Sarkisian, who co-headed the Unity bloc. But in October 1999, armed gunmen stormed Parliament and killed the prime minister and seven others. In retrospect, Radio Free Europe argued that the event was a real turning point for Armenia, marking the end of democratization efforts and enabling President Robert Kocharian to quickly consolidate power.[26] In 1999 and 2003, all the international monitors except the Commonwealth of Independent States (CIS) once again deemed the elections fraudulent. International monitors may have reduced the incumbent's vote share in the 2003 presidential election,[27] but he nonetheless engaged in sufficient fraud to maintain a firm grip on power. Domestic protest never mobilized sufficiently.

Meanwhile, Western conditionality was weak. The COE did not explicitly use Armenia's membership application to gain concessions on the electoral law. Instead, the COE hoped that admitting both Armenia and Azerbaijan would promote peace between them. The list of changes that the COE considered as a matter of urgency prior to admission in the organization in 2000 focused primarily on legislation to improve human rights violations.[28] Furthermore, despite the flawed 2005 constitutional referendum, Armenia received aid from the U.S. Millennium Challenge Account and Armenia's foreign minister promised Congress that the democracy shortfalls would be addressed.[29] In this environment, the international monitors were unable to bring much leverage to bear on the government. Some institutional reform did improve the 2007 parliamentary election.[30] However, Armenian parties continued to rely on their leaders' charisma rather than on ideology or policy,[31] and the ruling Armenian Republican Party (HKK) nearly doubled its seats, thereby solidifying its grip on power. After the election, the OSCE made no less than forty-four recommendations, many of them repetitions from previous elections.[32] The 2008 election was again problematic, characterized as yet another "failed test,"[33] and observers criticized the weak party institutionalization and pervasive clientelism. Violence and unrest broke out after the 2008 presidential election and the situation only stabilized after the government imposed a state of emergency and resorted to heavy-handed suppression.

Over the years, the biggest success for the international monitoring organizations, led by the OSCE and the COE, was the extensive reform of the electoral law over several rounds of amendments. In 1996, the OSCE indicated that election law improvements increased the transparency of the election process. This included setting deadlines for the publication of preliminary and final results, the right for candidates' proxies to receive copies of the precinct results, and the ability to validate ballot papers at the precinct.[34] A modification of the election law in February 1999 also included many recommendations from the 1998 final election report. For example, one of the tiers of election administration—the community election commissions—was abolished and domestic nonpartisan observers were recognized.[35] In 2002 and 2005, the law was again amended in a way that reflected the recommendations made by experts on behalf of OSCE/ODIHR and the Venice Commission.[36] First, the electoral system was made more proportional. In addition, partially addressing a recommendation made in 1998, the 11 regional electoral committees were replaced by 56 territorial and 1,877 polling station committees. The new rules also removed the rule allowing political parties to withdraw their nominees to electoral commissions. The OSCE argued that this should enhance the independence of the electoral administration by protecting the members during their terms of office.[37] However, Armenian authorities failed to make the composition of those commissions representative of the balance of power within Parliament. In addition, the lack of provisions for publishing detailed electoral results by the electoral commission and the transparency of the vote-counting procedures remained major concerns in the 2003 elections.[38] Nevertheless, the OSCE was mostly satisfied with the electoral law and berated its implementation more than its content.[39]

The electoral code was amended once again in 2005 to require training of electoral commissioners, and the Washington-based Institute for Democracy and Electoral Assistance (IDEA) was hired to implement the training.[40] The OSCE reported that the amendments improved the "formation of election commissions, voting procedures and tabulation and publication of voting results."[41] In 2005, the OSCE was also instrumental in a large and relatively successful effort to update the voter registries. For both the 2005 and 2006 round of amendments, Armenia asked the OSCE to comment on the texts and adopted several of the recommendations.[42] The report on the subsequent amendments articulated at least twelve areas of improvements, "particularly concerning issues such as distribution of tasks within election commissions, electoral deposits for candidacy, voting and counting procedures, and recall of election commission members."[43] After the code was amended again in 2007, the OSCE again noted that amendments took into account a number of the recommendations from its final report on the May 12, 2007, parliamentary election.[44] In sum, between 1995 and 2008 Armenia reformed its electoral code significantly, and most of the changes followed the intense involvement and specific recommendations by international organizations. This is thus a clear case where the influence of monitors can be traced and documented.

However, multiple legal reforms meant little in an environment of corruption and vote buying. In the conclusion of its 1999 report, the National Democratic Institute (NDI) stated: "It is unfortunate that the improvements in the Election Code were undermined by administrative irregularities and manipulations of the system by those at the national and local levels who ignored these advances and lacked respect for the will of the electorate."[45] And although Armenia decentralized the electoral commission somewhat, the government kept control by not making it representative of the distribution of power between the political parties and by keeping its work nontransparent. The 2003 elections contained a very high level of obvious fraud and the reports of the observers were very specific in recording all the violations. In response, Armenia's president created a working group to study the reported violations. The working group dismissed all criticisms, but the OSCE stood by its claims.[46] In 2007 the European Parliament (EP) complained that lack of punishment for previous election-related violations created an "atmosphere of impunity" on behalf of politicians and disillusionment among voters.[47] In 2008, the OSCE stated that the electoral process as a whole suffered from lack of accountability and transparency, which was the result of poor counting procedures and a slow and nontransparent appeals process.[48] It praised the organization of the CEC and the improvement in the voter lists, but lamented that widespread vote buying dwarfed these improvements and that Armenia was not seriously attempting to run clean elections.[49]

It expressed its frustration with the lack of progress in Armenia in its final report, when it listed a whole new set of recommendations, stressing that "these do not repeat all recommendations made in previous OSCE/ODIHR Reports or Assessments, *a number of which have not yet been implemented and remain valid*. Overall, the conduct of democratic elections requires genuine political will to implement the respective OSCE commitments and other standards that the Republic of Armenia has freely entered into, at all levels of the process" (emphasis added).

Bangladesh: Slowly but Surely?

Bangladesh demonstrates that highly contentious winner-take-all politics in poor and violent societies are not particularly susceptible to influence by international monitors. The unelected military-backed caretaker government in 2008 was able to implement more reforms than had occurred previously, and although the reforms followed many of the recommendations of the international monitoring organizations over the years, the impetus for these reforms was quite domestic. Some commentators argue that international donors and international election monitors have contributed to better elections in Bangladesh, persuading parties to accept defeat gracefully and helping to institutionalize the caretaker model to improve elections.[50] Others have considered Bangladesh a model for other Muslim countries in transition, and seen involvement by the international community as essential for countering extremist trends and ensuring free and fair elections.[51] However, this same incentive to keep the situation calm and display a successful Muslim democracy may also have contributed to overly gentle assessments of the quality of elections, which continue to have many shortfalls.

Since its independence from Pakistan in 1971, Bangladesh has had a history of political turmoil and military rule. Its first two prominent leaders, Sheikh Mujibur Rahman and Ziaur Rahman, were both assassinated in military coups. Their regimes were followed by military dictatorships.[52] The two major political parties, the Awami League (AL) and the Bangladesh Nationalist Party (BNP), were formed by these two leaders and later led by their daughter and widow, respectively.

After a bloodless coup in 1982, General Hussain Muhammad Ershad became president and ruled the country under Islamism and autocracy. After both the AL and the BNP boycotted the 1988 election, the international community began to scrutinize Ershad's Jatiya Party and his military regime, which eventually collapsed in 1990.[53] The ensuing 1991 election was the first democratic election ever held, and the NDI and the Commonwealth Secretariat (CS) monitored the election. Seventy-three parties participated, but the AL and the BNP dominated.[54] This marked the beginning of a persistent two-party system.

Despite significant differences in political ideology, early contests between the AL and the BNP were fueled mainly by the personal rivalry between their leaders. International monitors have urged election candidates to become more issue-oriented,[55] and have encouraged political debates and party involvement with voter education.[56] However, the politics have remained focused on political families, party history, and vague promises of economic growth and social stability. Voters are often uneducated and "profound cultural and structural obstacles to democratization"[57] persist.

Bangladesh's winner-take-all politics has produced a recurring pattern where the ruling party refuses a meaningful role for the opposition, the opposition walks out, and society is paralyzed by strikes and boycotts.[58] Often, the losing party refuses to participate in government and threatens to withdraw all its MPs. The AL did this in 1996 and 2001, the BNP in 2008. This constant rivalry has paralyzed the ability of Bangladesh to improve the electoral process. To address this core problem, international observers have urged Bangladesh to amend the constitution to allow opposition parties a fairer opportunity to participate in the government,[59] but so far the bitter rivalry between the two leading parties has prevented progress.

Monitors have observed elections in Bangladesh since 1991 and made a host of recommendations. However, the preoccupation with interparty conflict left government with little commitment or effort to follow the monitors' recommendations between the 1991 and 1996 elections. One big change did occur by 1996, however, namely, the institutionalization of the caretaker government. This was something monitors had recommended, but it was clearly also born out of domestic necessity due to the intense distrust between parties. Training for officials had also improved by 1996, and the problem of indelible ink that monitors had criticized earlier appeared fixed. The 1996 election also saw the emergence of the domestic monitoring organization, Fair Election Monitoring Alliance.[60] Another election in 2001 saw further improvements, but elections remained highly problematic and many recommendations were unmet.

Had this study been written before 2008, the overall assessment would have been that very few recommendations were ever followed. The events of 2007 and 2008 improved the picture, however. A major confrontation between the BNP and the AL in 2006–7 about the leadership of the caretaker government led to extreme political chaos and to the postponement of the election scheduled for January 2007. Actually, following acute disagreement between the two factions over the impartiality of the electoral commission and other political arrangements, on January 11, 2007, the international monitors suspended their activities, arguing that the conditions for credible elections did not exist. On the same day the military forced President Iajuddin Ahmed to cancel the election and implement a state of emergency.[61] Originally intended to last only ninety days, the state of emergency continued until December 2008 and a military-based caretaker government ruled the country during this nearly two-year period. Amnesty International reported ongoing political violence, arbitrary arrests, and excessive use of force against protesters. Although the caretaker government violated many areas of human rights, together with a newly appointed electoral commission it implemented very comprehensive reforms.

Some of the notable improvements concerned the issue of electoral commission independence, the implementation of anti-corruption programs, and redistricting. Already in 1991, the NDI had noted that some districts had double the voting power of neighboring districts and recommended redistricting. This recommendation was one of the longest-standing unaddressed criticisms, and was taken into consideration prior to the 2008 election, when Bangladesh completely overhauled the constituency boundaries for the first time since independence.[62] Some of the other reforms followed monitor recommendations, while others did not. Thus, the 2008 election addressed the longstanding concern about voter lists and ID cards. Better tabulation procedures were adopted, security improved, and other practices that monitors had criticized, such as suspending mobile phone service on election day, were curtailed. After repeated criticism, Bangladesh also addressed campaign finance issues. Another major recommendation from the early years concerned the independence of the election commission.[63] For the 2008 election, the caretaker government appointed a more balanced and highly regarded electoral commission, which—although the president retained the power to appoint the chief election commissioner and other election commissioners—the NDI described as depoliticized and professional.[64] The international election monitors also experienced smaller victories. For example, the NDI sent a pre-election mission that recommended that the electoral commission review and preferably cease the practice of shutting down mobile phone networks as a security measure. The government had planned to shut down mobile networks on polling day, but at the last minute it cancelled this.[65]

The 2008 election produced a record turnout of 87 percent and international monitors considered it successful and a substantial improvement over prior polls. The NDI noted only "minor" administrative problems, mostly related to voter confusion or waits.[66] Thus, Bangladesh has seen considerable improvements, many of which followed the recommendations of international monitors. The caretaker government played a large role in driving the reforms, but was acting partly in response to international recommendations. That said, elections in Bangladesh still leave much to be desired and the monitors made many recommendations after the 2008 election; the Asian Network for Free Elections (ANFREL) alone made seventy-nine recommendations.

Bulgaria: Motivated but Slow

The situation in Bulgaria was ideal for international monitors: Both domestic and international factors motivated the country to change and it had much to learn. Its performance is similar to that of other highly monitored countries in Eastern Europe that have sought to join European institutions. However, Bulgaria also demonstrates that changes may take a very long time, and that when the incentive structures change backsliding may occur. Nevertheless, Bulgaria did adopt international election standards very quickly and benefited considerably from the socialization efforts by the COE, the OSCE, and other monitoring groups. The NDI and the International Republican Institute (IRI) were intensely involved in democracy assistance programs of various kinds, in addition to election monitoring in the early years. Progress has been great, but with the disappearance of the EU membership incentives, some backsliding has occurred.

Bulgaria's commitment to EU membership and the reorientation of the economy toward the West facilitated the necessary reforms of the electoral process and a fairly high level of responsiveness to international monitors. The transition was characterized by a relative lack of significant economic or military influence from nondemocratic countries. This allowed Bulgaria to engage in both extensive legal reforms and effective implementation of the adopted changes. In addition, Bulgaria enjoyed a peaceful transition process with no significant security threats, despite a serious economic downturn in 1997. As early as 1997, the head of the OSCE Parliamentary Assembly stated that Bulgaria "has gained excellent experience in organizing elections and that elections were normal and free."[67] However, following EU accession, concerns regarding the integrity of the electoral process resurfaced and the OSCE was present in 2006 and in a "limited" capacity in 2009.

Early problems associated with elections in Bulgaria were primarily the result of lack of experience with democratic procedures and restructuring of the balance of power between the competing parties. Allegations of fraud, including fear and intimidation, while present in the early elections and primarily in rural areas, were of a limited nature. After the 1990 election, international monitors recommended changes to the electoral law. The Bulgarian Association for Fair Elections and Civil Rights circulated these recommendations to public officials. The draft electoral law included many of the recommendations by international monitors and civil rights groups: precise time tables for preparing the voter registries, time tables for holding elections, voter eligibility provisions, provisions about the handling of complaints, prohibition of distribution of ballots before the election, and procedures for publication of individual polling station results.[68] Starting in 1991, the elections were deemed to have been completely free and fair, or with only minor problems. The IRI and the NDI noted Bulgaria had made great efforts to follow the recommendations of monitors from 1990 and stated, "Indeed, the election incorporated many of the specific recommendations made by the international delegation in 1990."[69] Media and media regulations had improved, and Bulgaria had reformed the electoral system and followed recommendations to redraw district boundaries that had dated to the 1940s. In both 1990 and 1991, competent parallel vote tabulations encouraged by international monitors eased tensions while the nation awaited final results.[70] The authorities followed the advice on counting and releasing of results by 1994. The OSCE and IRI observation of the 1996 election was cursory, although the IRI had engaged in a two-year program to build up the opposition parties. The 1997 pre-election campaign was so calm that the COE even called it "dull."[71]

Thus, in the early years Bulgaria adopted many of the recommendations of international monitors. Furthermore, although it took more than fourteen years for the recommendation to be adopted, Bulgaria eventually improved the ballot design as recommended. Another recommendation first brought up by international monitors in 1994 and repeated many times since concerned campaign finance regulation. This, too, was finally accomplished in 2009.[72]

In addition to making recommendations about the electoral process, international election monitors also played a major role in ensuring that the young opposition parties were organized and prepared to participate in the political process. The advice given by monitors was targeted not so much at reducing fraud, which was not systematic and rampant, but rather at leveling the playing field and overcoming the significant institutional and organizational advantages of the Socialist Party, which inherited the grassroots network of its predecessor—the Bulgarian Communist Party. The most notable recommendation that was followed in this area concerned the introduction of primary elections for the presidency.[73] In a similar vein, international monitors pushed strongly for ensuring that smaller parties had equal access to public media outlets.

Nevertheless, Bulgaria has not addressed all the issues monitors have raised. The accuracy of voter lists remains a concern despite repeated, strong criticisms by multiple organizations. By 2009, the CEC had still not been made a permanent body. Furthermore, on several occasions international monitors criticized the practice of adopting electoral reforms just a few months before elections.

After Bulgaria joined the EU, new criticisms have emerged. Monitors have criticized the introduction of clear ballot boxes. In 2005, 2006, and 2009, problems of vote buying grew, and public confidence in the electoral process declined. Bulgaria did adopt a law to prohibit vote buying, as recommended by monitors, but this did not lessen the problems in the 2009 election. Absentee voting was also a problem in 2006, and the OSCE claimed that the existing regulations lacked safeguards against multiple voting.[74] In 2007 the OSCE repeated the criticism, yet in 2009 enough safeguards had still not been implemented to prevent out-of-country voters from voting multiple times.

The strong early efforts combined with the more recent backsliding suggest that EU conditionality played an important role in Bulgaria. This has been true in Bulgaria in general, not only regarding elections. The EU used election assistance to get governments to adhere to institutional reform commitments that were negotiated immediately after transition in 1990.[75] The slow pace of reforms in the mid-1990s led the incumbents to lose power in 1997, as opposition parties used progress reports issued by organizations like the European Commission to discredit the government. Thus, in Bulgaria, EU and North Atlantic Treaty Organization (NATO) conditionality was a "benign yet effective tool of democracy promotion."[76] The activities of organizations like OSCE and COE were important mechanisms through which the EU sought to influence the political processes in Bulgaria. More problems resurfaced, however, when Bulgaria no longer faced the conditionality incentives derived from the pre-accession criteria that the EU put forward. It remains to be seen whether the robust backlash by Bulgarian media, which extensively covered vote-buying practices, will manage to resolve the problems that surfaced in 2009.

El Salvador: International Meddling for Both Good and Bad

El Salvador has been labeled one of the most successful transformations from conflict to democracy.[77] The international community played a considerable role in the transition,[78] but it was mostly the United States and the UN that drove the changes toward peace, not international election monitors. The Organization of American States (OAS) engagement prior to 1990 was mostly symbolic. Since then, change has been slow, and fear of conflict has softened pressure by international monitors. Indeed, throughout the 1990s the international community focused more on the success of the peace agreements and the continued holding of passable elections, than on pushing hard for improvements. Thus, the incumbent Alianza Republicana Nacionalista (ARENA) was able to shrug off most of the monitors' criticisms and even stop hosting monitors altogether for several elections. Throughout, poverty and lack of capacity have made it difficult to address administrative problems although improvements began with the presidential election in 2004. These changes and the changes in 2009 were brought about by the gradual erosion of support for ARENA domestically as well as by traditional supporters such as the United States. With 2009 bringing both parliamentary and presidential elections, the international community refocused its attention and efforts on addressing longstanding criticisms by the international monitors increased and began to show results. The opposition Farabundo Marti National Liberation Front (FMLN)-backed candidate won for the first time and El Salvador witnessed its first post-conflict transfer of powers. The case clearly demonstrates, however, that international monitors play second fiddle to other major actors.

During the civil war from 1982 to 1992, Salvadorian elections were heavily criticized as being little more than an attempt to provide a façade of competitiveness and legitimacy for the benefit of the United States, which had its own agenda.[79] The elections were problematic and the voter registries highly flawed.[80] Subsequently, voter turnout declined significantly,[81] as voters became disillusioned with the inability of political parties to provide a nonviolent way to settle differences. The OAS monitored these elections (with an additional observer, the International Human Rights Law Group, also present in 1985), but at that time the OAS monitoring operations were mostly symbolic. The organization had not yet developed a systematic framework for its operations, nor did the unit for the promotion of democracy, in which subsequent OAS monitoring capacities were housed, yet exist.[82] Furthermore, despite "Orwellian doubletalk," these were U.S.-sponsored elections.[83]

However, positive trends in El Salvador's electoral environment started with changed global conditions and peace negotiations. The opposition united before the 1988 election,[84] and the 1988 and 1989 elections produced a change in power, launching the era of the ARENA.

Following the end of the civil war, El Salvador conducted acceptable but poorly administered elections throughout the 1990s. The United States, Canada, and other developed nations sought to sustain and improve the security situation and were pleased that elections remained peaceful, even if they still suffered from several flaws. The 1991 election was overseen by the Central Electoral Council, were quite calm, and, despite confusion, ran smoothly. The IRI called the election a success, but far from perfect, and stressed that the presence of hundreds of international observers had contributed to the verification of the results and endorsement of the process.[85] However, some argue that the leniency of the OAS report made the government complacent about addressing reforms.[86]

After the 1991 election, the UN, the United States Agency for International Development (USAID), and several other international actors were heavily involved in resolving issues to facilitate elections to consolidate the peace. A Supreme Electoral Tribunal (TSE) replaced the Central Electoral Council, but for the 1994 elections this body was heavily criticized for its partisanship and ineffectiveness, although it did manage to follow some monitor recommendations for the second round of voting in the presidential election. Despite problems, the historic nature of the 1994 election nevertheless led it to be dubbed as the "elections of the century."[87]

For the 1997 election the Salvadoran government had initially decided it no longer needed international monitors. Its reversal just a few weeks before the election permitted the IRI and the OAS to send only small delegations. In 1999, the OAS sent a mission but issued no public report.[88] For the next two elections none of the international observer groups returned. Thus, in the decade following the end of the civil war, international actors did not push very hard for further reforms. The IRI and OAS made brief appearances in 2004, but international monitors did not return in full force until 2009, when legislative and presidential elections coincided and the ARENA was losing support.

The main contribution of the international monitors in the 1991 and 1994 elections was to add legitimacy to the process.[89] Following the 1991, 1994, 1997, and 2004 elections, international monitors made many recommendations to improve the quality of elections both through administrative and legislative actions. However, over these eighteen years, El Salvador made little progress on the legislative issues that the international monitors identified. A committee came up with a set of recommended reforms after the 1994 election to address the monitors' criticisms, but these were not implemented.[90] Although the institutionalization of the peace agreement and the integration of the FMLN were indeed major legislative and political achievements, election monitors did not drive these.

Indeed, in election after election, El Salvador ignored the recommendations by international monitors to depoliticize the electoral commission, and to regulate the voter registry. Campaign finance regulation, an area focused on more recently, was not adopted either. During every election monitors criticized the voter registry and the system of ID cards, tabulation delays, later opening of polling stations, and other logistical issues, but to no avail. Indeed, conditions persisted or even got worse over the 1990s. Some argue that El

Salvador actually regressed and came to exemplify electoral authoritarianism, because the ARENA maintained power by preserving the institutional status quo.[91] Thus, the ARENA effectively blocked reforms in the 1990s.[92] International monitors had a difficult time pushing for reforms because the peace was still young and the ARENA incumbency suited the political preferences of the international community. The elections were also marked by low voter turnout.

However, by 2004 El Salvador improved the voter registry and use of ID cards. Indeed, the OAS and the IRI were quite positive about the progress, the IRI even saying, "Salvadorans should be proud of holding elections that in many ways could serve as a model for other nations."[93] In 2009, other areas that had been criticized by international monitors also improved: For the presidential election, most polling stations opened on time,[94] the tabulation was not excessively delayed, intimidation decreased, and poll workers were better trained. After the January legislative election the electoral code was amended to allow more Salvadorans living abroad to vote, as monitors had recommended.

The improvements between the January legislative and municipal elections and the March presidential election were notable. The EU had been very frustrated after the January election, criticizing the TSE as highly partisan and pointing to serious legislative gaps.[95] The EU wrote, "Despite 47 amendments in the past 16 years, the Electoral Code is an incomplete framework since several fundamental areas still lack legislation or adequate regulations. . . . The persisting shortcomings of the electoral legislation after so many elections is a reminder of poor political will of the Legislative Assembly to approve significant changes to the Constitution and the Electoral Code as generally agreed by all political interlocutors and has, as a consequence, originated among the public a certain degree of lack of credibility in the TSE as an institution."[96]

The observers were significantly more pleased with the March 2009 presidential election, which led to a peaceful turnover of power after a record 63 percent turnout and a 2 percent margin of victory.[97] The EU noted that 97 percent of voting stations opened on time, a vast improvement from January, when three-quarters of stations opened late. With the assistance of the OAS, the election also successfully tested "residential voting" (voting in local neighborhoods, something that monitors had long recommended) in some areas. While access to resources and media was still skewed in the government's favor, there were no major irregularities. The EU reported great improvement from the January election: "In-between the Legislative and Presidential elections, the TSE introduced a number of measures aimed at improving the election process. . . . All of these initiatives had a positive impact on the process and demonstrated the

TSE's openness to recommendations for improvements and its commitment to ensuring a transparent and efficient election process."[98] The chief of the OAS mission said, "The Salvadorian authorities applied 'in great part' the recommendations made by the OAS observers."[99] However, like the EU, he also highlighted that "some things must be corrected" to further improve the Salvadoran electoral system.

Both in 2004 and 2009 reports of international meddling persisted, however. Prior to the 2004 election, the ARENA connected an FMLN victory to potential sanctions by the United States, suggesting that the country would deport the numerous migrant workers from El Salvador working there. Since remittances from the United States by immigrants comprised about 14 percent of the El Salvador GDP, this quickly became a top campaign issue. Two domestic monitoring groups reported the rumor was also fueled by comments made by U.S. officials. During a visit to El Salvador in February 2004, Assistant Secretary of State Roger Noriega commented to the media that he thought it was "fair to note that the FMLN campaign has emphasized its differences with [the United States] concerning CAFTA [the U.S.-Central American Free Trade Agreement] and other subjects." He continued, "and we know the history of this political movement, and for this reason it is fair that the Salvadoran people consider what type of relations a new government could have with us."[100] Similarly, White House Special Assistant Otto Reich noted in a March 13 telephone interview with the Salvadoran press that "we are concerned about the impact that an FMLN victory would have on the commercial, economic, and migration-related relations that the United States has with El Salvador."[101] The U.S. government did not refute these statements, and although a few U.S. politicians criticized them, the Salvadoran press did not pick up on this.

U.S. meddling continued in 2009.[102] In a letter, thirty-three congressional Republicans denounced the FMLN and warned of repercussion should they gain power.[103] From the U.S. House Floor, Republican Representatives Trent Franks, Dan Burton, and Dana Rohrabacher made similar explicit threats of economic repercussions of electing the FMLN, and received front-page press in El Salvador.[104] However, in contrast to the administration of George W. Bush, the administration of Barack Obama took a more neutral line. Both the U.S. State Department and the embassy in San Salvador formally declared U.S. neutrality and promised to work with whichever party won the presidency.[105]

It remains to be seen whether the new FMLN government will work to implement the many new recommendations following the 2009 election. After the election, the EU mission was hopeful that El Salvador finally might have reached a turning point.

Georgia: Not So Rosy

Georgia has been marked by two leaders who gained power through extra-constitutional means, and consolidated their mandates through elections that were (sometimes) reasonably free and fair, but not very competitive. The continuing tensions in its two separatist regions of South Ossetia and Abkhazia distracted from reform efforts.[106] The state crumpled under poverty and corruption.[107] Meanwhile Eduard Shevardnadze's adeptness at balancing between Moscow and the West ensured continued aid from the West, and the serious criticisms by international monitors gained little attention. As the regime weakened and international pressure for reform grew, international monitors helped the domestic opposition call attention to the abuses in the 2003 election that prompted the historic Rose Revolution. However, the so-called revolution disappointed. Its leader, Mikheil Saakashvili, forced the ill-reputed President Shevardnadze to resign prematurely and he was elected president in 2004 with a huge mandate. He used his mandate, however, to increase the power of the presidency. The government failed to address many of the concerns of the international monitors. In 2007, corruption and discontent prompted new street protests and calls for the resignation of the president, early parliamentary election, and revisions to the election law.[108] A snap election of questionable quality followed in January 2008. The war with Russia later that year further hampered Georgia's efforts to democratize. The divisive politics in Georgia and the executive branch dominance over the other state agencies has kept elections highly contentious. International monitors accepted the two elections in 2008, but not without long lists of criticisms and recommendations. The government has initiated a "new wave of democratic reforms," but several opposition parties are boycotting the process and the results are not yet visible.

With well more than twenty missions from the major organizations between 1992 and 2008, Georgia has been more heavily monitored than most other countries. However, Georgian domestic politics has not been particularly conducive to monitors. Poverty, corruption, and the volatile security situation in the separatist regions of South Ossetia and Abkhazia hampered the influence of monitors from the very beginning.[109] Following a political crisis and a vacuum in the presidential office as a result of the departure and then death of Georgia's first post-independence president, Zviad Gamsakhurdia, Shevardnadze grained power through extra-constitutional means. He consolidated his mandate through elections that were reasonably free and fair, but not very competitive. The 1992 and 1995 elections were judged reasonably good given the lack of experience. The OSCE said the 1992 election met international standards. The COE said about the 1995 election that "despite the irregularities directly observed by the committee, which were regarded as minor, the election had proceeded calmly and apparently in acceptably normal and lawful conditions."[110] Shevardnadze balanced adeptly between Moscow and the West, and led a regime that mixed crime and corruption with a powerful presidency and a 1995 liberal constitution, as well as "democratic decorations, such as competitive elections and relatively open media, that had the dual effects of dividing the democratic opposition while appeasing the West."[111] When his power began to weaken after the 1998 economic crisis in Russia, he sacked the government and held a new parliamentary election in 1999 and himself won re-election in 2000 in a fraudulent election. The West began to pressure for greater democratic reforms,[112] and several elites defected from the ruling party, including Saakashvili.

International monitoring organizations became very active in the years leading up to the 2003 election. The COE criticized Georgia for failing to meet the commitments it made upon accession to the council in 1999 and threatened to review Georgia's membership. By being present, outspoken, and explicit about their dissatisfactions with the reforms in the country, the international organizations provided additional support for the popular uprising.[113] Other international nongovernmental organizations (NGOs), especially the Open Society Institute of the Soros Foundation, played crucial roles,[114] as did the parallel vote tabulation and the exit polls, which showed a lead for the opposition in contradiction to the official results. Civil society actors, inspired by Serbian groups, also became active domestic monitors leading up to the 2003 election. The fraudulent election led to massive popular protests and the so-called Rose Revolution. This set the stage for the second leadership change through extra-constitutional means. Saakashvili used the large protests after the election to force Shevardnadze to resign. He then won the extraordinary presidential election early the following year by a massive margin, 96 percent of the vote, and, to the concern of the West, effectively consolidated his power through reforms after the election.

Although it was an obvious improvement on the 2003 election, observers still criticized the 2004 election on many accounts such as the composition of the CEC, the election administration, and the voter lists. The 2004 partial re-run of the 2003 parliamentary election was also fraught with problems. Many polling stations reported 95 to 100 percent turnout. Anomalies were abundant. For example, in twenty-eight polling stations with high voter turnout the National Movement–Democrats received 95 to 100 percent of the vote.[115] Still, the international monitors noted that "in marked contrast to previous elections, the CEC implemented a number of recommendations made by the OSCE/

ODIHR in previous reports."[116] These included enhanced voter education, a centralized computerized voter database, and improved secrecy of the vote, among other things.

Progress after the 2004 elections has been limited. The reforms to concentrate power in the presidency were presented as efforts to secure swift implementation of pro-democratic initiatives, but instead they slowed them.[117] The lack of true political dialogue between the incumbent and the opposition sidelined the preferences of the opposition.[118] This concern was most recently voiced following the 2008 constitutional reform plebiscite, when the opposition's demands for granting more power to Parliament were not considered.[119] Furthermore, although the Rose Revolution was taken as evidence of the presence of strong domestic civil society mobilization, later analysis has argued that the revolution failed, because the civil society was not actually that strong, but instead driven by protégés of the old regime and too reliant on external funding and training.[120]

Thus, following some troublesome years, the fall of 2007 again brought protesters into the streets and forced the president to call an early election for January 2008. In preparation, several legal amendments passed. The OSCE criticized the practice of last-minute revisions to the law, but noted in the needs assessment mission report that the amendments "seem to take into consideration the result of consultations held between the OSCE/ODIHR, the Venice Commission of the Council of Europe (VC/CoE) and the Georgian authorities in 2007. They also appear to address a number of recommendations offered in the 2006 Joint Opinion on the Electoral Code and in the reports of earlier election observation missions."[121]

The election campaign was highly problematic. To boost votes in the first round and prevent opposition voters from uniting against him in a runoff, Saakashvili combined the implementation of social welfare programs with campaigning, stacked the CEC with partisan members, and occasionally used intimidation and pressure.[122] The international community feared further instability.[123] The West was pulling for Saakashvili, Russia for the opposition. Despite the problems in the pre-election period, polling day was fairly organized and peaceful, although some precincts were chaotic and had problems with the ink used to safeguard against multiple voting. The counting was slow and had many "procedural shortcomings."[124] When exit polls showed Saakashvili with around 53 percent, just enough to avoid a second round, the opposition cried foul, leaving the election observers in a difficult and prominent position.[125]

In its report on Georgia's commitments to the COE, the COE praised the 2008 presidential election, saying that notwithstanding all its problems, "this was for the first time a genuinely competitive election enabling the Georgian people to express their political choices."[126] However, the list of recommendations was very long, criticizing the biased electoral administration and media, the forceful crackdown on protestors, the voter list, training of electoral officials, lack of transparency in party funding, and the use of intimidation—criticisms that are difficult to reconcile with the phrase "genuinely competitive." The IRI also said the election met international standards, but had technical problems, but then likewise cited problems with the voter lists, unfair access to government resources, poor administration and checking of the invisible ink to prevent multiple voting, instances of intimidation, and the like.[127] The NDI added concerns about abuse of government resources to buy votes, such as the distribution of vouchers for fuel and medicine labeled as a "gift from the president."[128]

Before the parliamentary election, the authorities passed several legal amendments and took a number of actions that responded to prior monitoring recommendations. For example, the authorities lowered the threshold for parliamentary representation and extended the time for public scrutiny of the voter list. They also implemented voter education on the process of inking, improved the training of officials and data transparency, and addressed several other issues.[129] However, the changes also introduced features that favored the incumbent party, particularly concerning the use of incumbent resources. After the parliamentary election, the COE, EP, and OSCE[130] were still positive, but noted that despite a revision to the CEC structure to increase party representation, the CEC once again failed to act independently. The election campaign was highly polarized, the incumbent party abused state resources, and the media lacked balance. Voter registries still were messy, the vote count and tabulation was highly problematic in many instances, and complaints were poorly handled. The districts were still hugely imbalanced, with only 4,000 votes needed in one district to elect one MP, but 140,000 votes in another—a problem that the OSCE first criticized in 1999. In short, the parliamentary election were not much of an improvement on the 2008 presidential election, which had been plagued by similar problems. With strong caveats, however, international monitors endorsed both the presidential and the parliamentary election.

Overall, between 1992 and 2008, the record on following the international monitors' specific recommendations was very mixed. Some areas were addressed. This included a reduction in the precinct size, which, after continual criticisms since 1995, was finally reduced to 1500 for the 2008 elections. The 2008 election was also the first since 1995 that monitors did not criticize officials for failing to check identity documents. Several partial improvements have also occurred. The voter lists, while still problematic, have gone from handwritten disasters to computerized databases. Voter education is better, and the threshold for representation in Parliament has been lowered to 5 percent, as recommended. The composition of the CEC has been revised, although it is still criticized as biased. After years of criticism that police were present in polling stations, monitors did not complain about this in 2008. However, there were problems with other unauthorized personnel who asked to check documents. Importantly, several areas of recommendations have never improved despite continual criticisms since 1995 or 1999. Thus, the district sizes are still hugely uneven, abuse of government resources persists, the inking of hands to prevent multiple voting continues to be poorly implemented, and—most glaringly— tabulation of ballots continues to be highly problematic.

Thus, Georgia's progress in holding free and fair elections is not impressive, but improvements have occurred. After the 2008 elections, the NDI has taken on a role as mediator. In April before the election the NDI published a code of conduct for political parties and nine parties signed the code. After the election the NDI has continued to moderate a "special cross-party working group to reform the electoral system and to draft a new Electoral Code,"[131] but several opposition parties that refused to take their seats after the 2008 parliamentary election are also refusing to join the process, because they still consider the election fraudulent and are demanding new elections. Some reforms to strengthen the Parliament have proceeded, but results so far have been lacking.

Guyana: Uphill Battle

The international engagement in Guyana's elections since 1992 has been extraordinary, and has included mediation, logistical assistance, and advice and monitoring. Monitors, particularly the Carter Center (CC), were influential in concrete and visible ways in mediating solutions that facilitated the historic 1992 election. Nevertheless, elections have remained disputed and violent. Some recommendations by monitors have been followed, but many have been ignored and the contested voter lists and tallying systems have triggered repeated protest. Despite their consistent and sizable efforts, the influence of monitors was hampered by violent, winner-take-all politics in an ethnically polarized and poor society. The 2006 election was more peaceful than anticipated given the prevailing level of fear. It provided hope of progress as continued international assistance and domestic efforts boosted confidence in the election and voters tired of continued violence. However, since then, the government has not attempted to address the remaining concerns expressed by monitors.

After Forbes Burnham, Guyana's leader since 1964, died in 1985, five opposition parties formed the Patriotic Coalition for Democracy (PCD) and began to press for electoral reforms, including the presence of international observers of the political process.[132] Burnham's successor, Desmond Hoyte, could not repress the opposition as Guyana's economy was shrinking and foreign investment and assistance from the International Monetary Fund (IMF) was essential.[133] Due to these combined internal and external forces, Guyana became the object of intense foreign pressure for instituting free and fair elections. Election monitoring organizations, such as the CC, the OAS, and the CS had a very high level of access to the Guyanese political process and worked closely to achieve progress,[134] while the IFES and the United Nations Development Programme (UNDP) provided extensive logistical support.

However, democratic transition has been hampered by the country's history of deep ethnic divisions that solidified into the main cleavage of political competition, accompanied by violence as the primary tool for resolving differences. The country is comprised of ethnic Indians (43 percent) and Africans (30 percent). The People's Progressive Party (PPP) and the People's National Congress (PNC) represent these two major groups, respectively. The former party, which represents the more sizable portion of the population, has unsurprisingly won all four elections in Guyana since the fall of authoritarianism in 1992. Because the constitution gives the winning party the presidency and with it almost unlimited political power, the deeply divided ethnic groups are always ready to challenge elections because the losers fear exclusion from decision making.[135] This has led to a series of disputed elections. As a result, Guyana has been stuck in a recurrent pattern of voting along ethnic lines, poor administration of elections, and violent electoral aftermath from 1992 to 2001. Nonetheless, the elections throughout the period managed to stay competitive and relatively free and fair. Some commentators argue that the monitors' biggest achievement was preventing ethnic conflict from completely jeopardizing the democratization process.[136]

Although the amount of progress achieved over the fourteen-year period of substantial foreign involvement is modest, the 2006 election indicated the country may have reversed its prior tendencies and is now more open to civilized political dialogue and democratic elections, despite numerous outstanding issues. Still, much work remains to reform the electoral institutions. A 2006 survey found the electoral commission to be the social institution with the least trust among citizens, gaining the confidence of only 45.7 percent.[137]

The CC (then under the aegis of the Council of Freely Elected Heads of Government) sent its first mission to Guyana only a month after the adoption of the Elections Law Act of 1990. The organization pointed out two main areas for improvement of the recently adopted legislation, including a provision for compiling new voter lists by performing house-to-house visits and reshuffling the composition of the CEC by replacing its chairman.[138] A visit by President Jimmy Carter in October 1990 was heralded as a breakthrough by the newspapers in Guyana when Carter persuaded Hoyte to give in to opposition demands for electoral reforms, including the counting of votes at polling station levels and compilation of a new voter list.[139] However, when the voter list was finally published it was found to contain an error rate of nearly 35 percent. President Carter refused to monitor the election unless a revised list was submitted to the CC three weeks before the election, to allow sufficient time to assess the list. The election was subsequently postponed until the list could be improved. The CC sent a mission to audit the list and was satisfied with its accuracy. Hoyte also gave in to demands to reconstitute the electoral commission, again under CC pressure. Initially, the chairman was directly appointed by the government, as were all the members of this body, giving it little independence. This law was partially amended in 1992, transferring the appointment powers of commissioners to the chairman of the CEC, although the chairman remained entirely dependent on the party in power.[140] With the crucial support of broad international pressure, the CC thus played a very constructive role leading up to the 1992 election.[141]

The IFES and the UNDP provided extensive logistical support for the 1992 election. Nevertheless, violence on election day nearly toppled the election. According to the CC, this near disaster was averted partly due to its presence and direct intervention by President Carter himself, who remained at the elections commission with the chairman to assist and ensure police protection, as well as by a CC quick count that helped instill confidence in the process.[142] After the 1992 election, the CS and the CC made several recommendations for reforms such as increasing the number of polling stations, improving training for officials, issuing ID cards, improving electoral commission communication with the media and public, and completely overhauling the voter list.

In 1997, the president died of a heart attack. An election was held in late 1997, but the tabulation process was marred by serious irregularities. Aside from slightly increasing the number of polling stations, few of the recommendations from the 1992 election were followed. The CS produced extensive reports on the difficulties associated with implementation of then-existing requirements for voter identification cards and procedures for vote tabulation.[143] The PNC rejected the apparent PPP victory and violent protest followed. The Caribbean Community (CARICOM) mediated the Herdmanston Accord, in which the parties agreed to constitutional reform and a new election within three years. Among the most notable changes the accord introduced was a recommendation first voiced by the OAS in its report from 1997 to make the CEC a permanent standing body. Further improvements included splitting the number of members between the government and the opposition, giving three seats to each rival party. One remaining concern, however, was that the power to appoint the chairman of the CEC still rested with the president.[144] Meanwhile, in 2001, a high court decision voided the 1997 election results due to the problems with voter ID cards. A new election was scheduled for March 2001, and the government signed a memorandum of understanding (MOU)[145] with the donor community and invited international observers.[146]

Unfortunately, given Guyana's poor social and political development, the tight schedule led to a repeat of the problems with the voter lists, voting cards, training, voter education, and so forth. In response to the problems in 1997, for the 2001 election a national ID card was introduced, as cited in the CS report from that year,[147] but issuing those cards in a timely manner turned out to be difficult as well and led to a delay in the polling date. The media was also partial and unprofessional, despite a new media code of conduct.[148] For instance, the national TV channel devoted more than 75 percent of its coverage to the governing PPP and the coverage was overwhelmingly positive.

However, the polling day itself went quite smoothly, although some constituents voted without IDs and other were turned away despite being on the voting list.[149] Confusion broke out toward the end of the day as some polling stations extended their hours to accommodate complaints. Contrary to 1997, the counting and tabulation was honest but inefficient, the computer system had to be abandoned, and tensions rose over the slow release of preliminary results.[150] The final results were further confirmed by the CC quick count and a later audit confirmed that the voter lists had been highly accurate. However, after the election, unrest broke out once again as voters claimed they had been left off the list. Once again the opposition petitioned the high court for an injunction. Tensions rose, posing danger in the streets. After a court-ordered recertification process, the president was sworn in, but the opposition still refused to accept the results. In the end, the international observers declared their satisfaction that that poll had met international standards, but the CC bemoaned the "'winner-take-all' political system with its recurring patterns of ethnic voting and political polarization."[151] The EU echoed this sentiment: "Elections in deeply divided societies will always be prone to dispute unless there is a broader political determination to reach accommodation across the ethnic and political divide. Guyana, sadly, is no exception to this rule."[152] The CS mediated the efforts to restart negotiations between the government and opposition.[153]

After the 1997 and 2001 disputed elections, the 2006 elections, which once again had to be delayed in order for adequate preparations to be made, took place in an environment of fear and allegations of anticipated fraud.[154] Despite monitor recommendations for a comprehensive review of electoral legislation and processes, the 2006 election proceeded under the same framework as the 2001 election.[155] The electoral commission had not been revised nor had term limits been imposed. After 2001 the monitors had also pointed out the need for improved campaign finance and media regulations, and the creation of a body to enforce election-related codes of conduct for political parties and the media.[156]However, this did not occur, although the media did act considerably more professionally. Still, the state radio was allowed a monopoly. However, Guyana did introduce a continuous registration system, in line with monitor recommendations. Local polling stations' results were also posted, as monitors had recommended in 2001, and other administrative aspects also improved slightly. Once again, Guyana signed an MOU about technical and financial assistance for the election with the governments of the United States, Canada, the United Kingdom, and the EU.[157] USAID funded significant technical assistance. However, the voter lists were once again the central contentious issue in the election, and monitors recommended once again that they be entirely revised,[158] and that the electoral commission be made more independent. Voter education programs also were still lagging. The count was thorough and transparent, but again slow. However, the 2006 poll was surprisingly peaceful, as the front page of the *Guyana Chronicle* of August 29 declared.[159] The CC, the CS, and the OAS were satisfied with the vote, although the OAS was generally much more positive. The OAS conducted a quick count and met with political leaders during the transmission of results. Contrary to past years, the political leaders accepted the results and committed to promoting peace.[160]

Several factors likely contributed to the lack of post-election violence. In early 2006, the IFES launched a program to reduce violence through monitoring, called EVER (Election Violence Education and Reduction).[161] The final project report explores several reasons that the election was more peaceful than in past. The report gives some credit to international observers, greater election transparency, and fewer irregularities, but it also stresses domestic factors: The political rhetoric by leaders was more peaceful, appealing for acceptance of election outcomes, and civil organizations also urged calm[162] and arranged events to promote peace.[163] The IFES noted, "The quality of the election and the attitude of the parties both made it easier for supporters to accept the results and these are all factors contributing to the post-election peace."[164] Voters also indicated that they were tired of election violence.[165]

Over the years, international election monitors thus have had some modest, but identifiable, successes.[166] Still, ethnicity remains the most substantial predictor of electoral success. Guyana risks being stuck in a pattern of violent crime that impedes social progress, and civil groups have been calling for a broader consensus-based system of governance to allow democratic progress.[167] Electoral engineering and basing the election of Parliament on proportional representation have not succeeded in ending the dominance of ethnic politics that has permeated the country's most recent history. This has proven to be the biggest challenge for foreign monitors.

INDONESIA: A SLUGGISH BEHEMOTH

The Western press likes to hold Indonesia up as an example that democracy can work in large, poor countries, does not need decades to take hold, and will not be hijacked by Islamic parties.[168] Despite huge administrative problems, the 1999 election drew quick praise from the international monitors. Certainly elections in Indonesia are a massive exercise that is far more representative today than under the dictatorship of Suharto and the year 2004 saw the first direct election of a president. International actors, including monitoring organizations, have supported the domestic demands for democracy. Still, the devil is in the details: At least in terms of election quality, progress has not been as solid as enthusiasts proclaim.[169] Indeed, an examination of all the election monitoring reports from 1999, 2004, and 2009 shows that Indonesia has repeatedly ignored most of the recommendations by the international monitors. The influence of international monitoring organizations has been reduced by political power struggles, endemic corruption, terrorism, poverty, the impeachment of the president in 2001, the insurgency in Aceh, and the tsunami in December 2004 that claimed 169,000 lives. In nations having little experience with democracy, like Indonesia, such challenges impede speedy progress and modify the influence of international monitoring organizations. Amid excitement about democratization of the largest Muslim-majority country in the world, international election monitoring organizations have been too quick to assume progress and ease their pressure on the authorities to reform.

Indonesia is often held up as an illustration that democratic transitions can take place quickly, even under challenging circumstances.[170] The 1999 election drew quick praise from the international monitors despite huge administrative problems and appeals from domestic groups to wait until the tabulation process was complete.[171] It is true that elections in Indonesia are more representative today than under Suharto: the year 2004 saw the first direct presidential election, defeat of the incumbent, and the withdrawal of the military from politics. Still, at least in terms of election quality, progress has not been as rapid or as dramatic as enthusiasts proclaim.[172] With a voting age population of nearly 150 million, the Indonesian elections are one of the largest procedural undertakings in the world.

Already by 1996 several international democracy promotion NGOs such as the NDI had become involved in Indonesia, and after Suharto's resignation they stepped up their involvement, helping domestic monitoring organization to organize. The NDI and later the IFES were also involved in commenting on the draft electoral legislation.[173] For the 1999 election, the UNDP authorized U.S.$90 million for voter education, monitoring, and election administration, as the Indonesian government officially asked the UNDP to organize all international activity for the election.[174] However, the funding for domestic monitoring was a mixed blessing, leading to a fragmented group of organizations focused on competing for funding and dealing with disbursements.[175] The reports of the international monitoring organizations pointed out many flaws in the administration of the 1999 election, and the majority of these were still present ten years later in the 2009 election.

Indeed, an examination of all the election monitoring reports from 1999, 2004, and 2009 shows that most of the recommendations by the international monitors have been repeatedly ignored. In some aspects, in the eyes of the observers and other commentators, election quality actually decreased after 2004.[176] Ironically, in 2009 only the ANFREL sent a regular monitoring mission, and it was quite small. The EU only sent observers to report internally to the commission, and the CC sent a "limited mission." It seems that the decrease in attention may have been partly the product of wishful thinking about Indonesia's ability to run elections. The 2009 elections had substantial problems with the voter list, the automated tabulation system broke down, and the seat allocation was so confusing that it was later corrected by the constitutional court. The ANFREL did judge that "people have been allowed to have their say."[177] However, the ANFREL also wrote, "The road to consolidation of democracy has not been even and the many problems that plague the political process, such as the prevalence of corruption at all levels of government, vote buying, and other forms of 'money politics' and highly personalized political parties with weak platforms, have all contributed to a sense of disillusionment among citizens which may be responsible for a lower voter turnout this year."[178]

Tabulation and release of results has been a problem throughout Indonesian elections. During the 1999 election, the NDI and the CC worked closely with domestic monitors and called attention to the quick count by the Rectors Forum, a monitoring organization the NDI had helped train to conduct the quick count.[179] However, other donors mistrusted the quick count and instead helped create a Joint Operations and Media Center, which was to release election results in parallel with the official process. As it turned out there was tremendous difficulty getting the results out, and the process was confusing because of the different sources of reporting.[180] Official results were not released until about two months after the election. Counting and tabulation remained a problem in 2004, and in the 2009 election the authorities had to abandon an attempt at automatic tabulation due to lack of sufficient testing and preparation. The ANFREL called the counting process "chaotic," and noted that it opened room for fraud.[181]

Another persistent problem has been voter lists. After the 1999 election a door-to-door canvassing exercise was undertaken to create a voter database, but the whole issue of voter registration remained problematic. Voter cards were issued too late and many voters were not properly informed about the voting process. After the 2004 legislative election, monitors recommended that registration be reopened in time for more people to register before the presidential election. However, despite some efforts, voter lists remained in poor shape, sometimes containing handwritten updates. Polling officials also often forgot to check hands for inking, a problem that persisted throughout the 2004 and 2009 elections. For the 2009 elections, the voter list was again one of the largest problems. It was so problematic, in fact, that a few days before the presidential election, the court ruled that the lists be abandoned altogether. Unfortunately, many voters never learned about the change. Furthermore, the lack of a voter list made multiple voting easier, especially since polling officials were still lax in checking for inking of fingers despite earlier monitor criticism.

Yet another persistent problem has been the convoluted election laws, which among other things do not provide clear guidelines on seat distribution or presidential election.[182] As a result, both the NDI and the IFES called for simplifications and clarifications of the electoral codes after the 1999 election. The 2004 elections occurred after four constitutional amendments to create a new political system and an extensive web of new laws to govern elections. The revisions resulted from public pressure, and most scholars considered them progress.[183] The NDI was involved in the legal revisions, working with politicians at all levels and providing advice on several draft laws.[184] For the 2004 election, the EU considered the new legal framework adequate and a remarkable achievement in the short time available, but wished for a further consolidation and simplification of the laws in the future. One of the main problems is that under the Indonesian system, a new electoral law precedes each election, and this makes it hard for officials to familiarize themselves with the changing content. For example, before the 2009 election, the election law was promulgated too late to allow time to create all the regulations needed to expand upon articles in the law. It also was very long and seen as creating more problems than it solved.[185] Combined with the lack of training for officials, which is common in many young democracies, this created several implementation problems. Still concerned about many weaknesses with the electoral system ranging from dispute resolution to campaign finance, the CC made numerous recommendations for how to improve the law, not least of which was to adopt a permanent election law so that there would be continuity, preparation time, and training time.

The official bodies administrating the elections have also created confusion. In 1999, five different bodies had overlapping authorities to oversee the election.[186] Throughout the years, the National Election Commission (KPU) has had predominant authority in overseeing elections.[187] The Elections Supervisory Committee (PANWAS) handles election-related complaints.[188] It existed in 1999, but lacked a clear mandate and the means to carry out sanctions.[189] Electoral law reform in 2003 partially clarified its mandate and helped improve its performance.[190] Administratively, the 2004 elections were considered major progress since the 1999 election, especially because of the organization of a KPU secretariat, the enactment of rules and procedures, the enactment of a code of conduct, and the KPU handling of the budget.[191] Still, the EU lamented many administrative inefficacies and lack of accountability and transparency. However, the PANWAS has continued to lack real independence from the KPU. After conflicts ensued over complaint resolution in the 2004 legislative election, the KPU curtailed the PANWAS's power for the subsequent presidential election. The EU thus recommended more sanctioning power and independence for the PANWAS in future elections.[192] By the 2009 elections, however, the CC continued to express concerns about dispute resolution and the independence of the dispute resolution bodies. In the 2009 elections, the CC also complained about the new process for constituting the KPU without regard for the need for appropriate skills and experience. Thus, the CC argued that the performance of the KPU deteriorated significantly and that the KPU lacked a sufficient mandate, resources, independence, and experience.[193] After several members of the KPU had been arrested on corruption charges in 2005, the commission acted cautiously and lacked the confidence of voters.[194] Thus, the criticisms and recommendations of monitors about the system for the bodies administrating elections have led to few improvements.

Throughout elections international monitors have complained of poorly trained poll station workers and of poorly educated voters.[195] Such problems are not surprising in such a populous and poor country, but the continually changing laws and procedures, electoral systems, and voting processes have exacerbated these problems. Materials arrived late at polling stations in all election years and delays in opening polling stations persist. Problems with unwieldy and insecure ballots have also persisted. However, after a disaster with double-punched ballots in 2004, the marking process was finally changed to the use of pens rather than nails as the ANFREL and others recommended.

Another persistent problem has been with the lack of oversight of the use of money politics. The KPU limited total party campaign spending to 110 billion rupiah (U.S.$15 million) in 1999. This was about one-tenth of what the Golkar party advocated—reflecting how affluent certain parties were.[196] Campaign finance reporting and regulation is particularly important because the prevalence of *politik uang* (money politics), which is the practice of providing money or goods in exchange for votes. For example, Golkar has been accused of using food or favorable terms on loans to buy votes. The World Bank was so concerned about the incumbent's use of social safety net funds for vote buying that it delayed disbursement of an approved $1.1 billion loan until after the election.[197] Despite criticisms by international monitors, money politics continued in the 2004 election. The EU received a number of reports that participants were receiving money for attending mass rallies. Some people even made it a profession to attend various rallies for payment.[198] This problem is particularly hard to correct because it is a widely accepted practice in Indonesia. The PANWAS's lack of sanctioning mechanisms worsened this problem. The new 2008 election law addressed many of these problems, requiring more stringent reporting. Nevertheless, after the 2009 legislative election the CC still reported many campaign finance problems, particularly with lack of oversight.[199] Individual candidates also were not required to file reports.[200] The law still did not provide for adequate sanctions for violations of the regulations.

Not all the recommendations by monitors have been ignored, however. In 2004, monitors criticized the processes for political party registration and nomination of candidates as discriminatory.[201] They also criticized the limit of the presidential second-round campaign to three days. None of these criticisms resurfaced in 2009, however. As noted, by 2009 ballots were also marked with pens rather than being punched by nails. After the 2004 election, an official with the KPU stated in an interview that foreign agencies not only "provided financial assistance to help us purchase equipment, but also their presence as observers has reduced possible fraud, especially in the vote counting process."[202]

Still, although elections are now competitive, progress in the administration and regulation of elections has been very modest. Democracy may be holding on in Indonesia, not because of improved election quality, but despite the lack of it.[203] The lackluster showing of monitoring groups for the 2009 elections suggests that international election monitoring organizations have been too quick to assume progress and ease their pressure on the authorities to reform.

Kenya: One Step Forward, Two Steps Back

Since 1992, international monitors encouraged some reforms and donors were successful at pushing for elections. However, improvements in Kenya's election conduct were weak and reversals were common. Thus, despite a decent election in 2002, the situation has not improved in the long run, illustrating that, even if monitors may improve a single election, the overall effect on a country may not be profound or lasting. International monitors largely failed in Kenya for several reasons. First, there never was a sustained period of pro-democratic governments. Second, violence has dominated Kenya's democratization process, and incumbent leaders benefited economically and politically from the continuing unrest and the dysfunctional institutional and political environment. Thus, violent, winner-take-all politics has prevented progress. Third, in this environment, international monitors and other organizations faced a dilemma: If they pushed for reforms, they would destabilize the political environment. Last, monitoring efforts have been blamed for actually undermining the democratization process by being too hesitant in their criticism, and for lack of objectivity and competence.

After gaining independence from Great Britain in 1956, Kenya was dominated by two main parties—the Kenya African National Union (KANU) and the Kenya African Democratic Union (KADU). The former represented the numerous Kikuyu and Luo ethnic groups, while the KADU represented a variety of smaller ethnic groups.[204] After a brief period under a federalist parliamentary system, in 1963 Kenya adopted a strong presidency and centralized system of governance. The subsequent unequal representation of the various ethnic groups led to continuous tension that culminated in a social movement in 1990 organized by a coalition of intellectuals, lawyers, and church leaders that all opposed the KANU's continued dominance of the Kenyan political landscape.[205]

The KANU cracked down on the fledging opposition movement, but after international donors froze planned aid, President Daniel arap Moi agreed to change the constitution to allow for multiparty elections and to organize the first multiparty election in the country since 1996 on December 29, 1992. However, a divided opposition, organizational advantages, electoral fraud, and majoritarian electoral laws gave Moi a sweeping victory. When ethnic clashes erupted during and after the election, international actors tried to calm the violence and urged the opposition to take the seats in Parliament and seek redress through legal channels. Eventually, Moi temporarily suspended the new Parliament and regained control. The international donor group soon resumed aid to Kenya, citing some economic and political progress. The beginning of multiparty elections in Kenya was thus rather dismal.

To gain legitimacy after significant international criticism in the years after the 1992 election, Moi agreed to negotiate with opposition leaders in 1997.[206] However, the concessions—a statement in the constitution that Kenya was a multiparty democracy, as well as the provision for an independent electoral commission, a project that never really came to fruition—were cosmetic. The electoral law was improved somewhat, addressing some prior monitor criticisms; it became easier to run for office, and the system for allowing political rallies was fairer. Media conduct even improved. However, these modest improvements, although in line with the recommendations of monitors,[207] were overshadowed by violence and other problems. The Donors Democratic Development Group, which had formed to monitor the 1997 election, concluded most ambiguously: "The Election Observation center considers that the outcome of the election can in the main be accepted as a credible expression of the political will of the Kenyan people. We consider, however, that in 5 percent of the Parliamentary contests, the irregularities, in the poll and count were so great as to invalidate the elections in these particular constituencies and, consequently, the legitimacy of the overall KANU majority in the National Assembly."[208]

The only decent election, in 2002, which was called after Moi announced his retirement, was also accompanied by the least amount of violence.[209] The opposition overcame significant personal and ethnic differences and formed the National Rainbow Coalition (NARC), which ultimately removed the KANU from power.[210] In the election, several monitor recommendations were followed: Indelible ink was used, ballots were no longer marked with numbers that made it possible to trace voters, voting materials were distributed in time, and registration and tabulation and other issues improved. Although they also had plenty of criticisms,[211] international monitors were generally pleased with the election. The hopes quickly vanished, however, as President Mwai Kibaki consolidated his presidential power and increased repression. By 2007, many of these gains were either lost or overwhelmed by other irregularities.[212] Furthermore, many recommendations were left unaddressed. In spite of repeated criticisms in 1992, 1997, and 2002, polling stations nearly always opened late, a proper dispute resolution system was absent, the vast imbalances in constituency size and structure were never addressed, campaign finance was not properly regulated, the publication of procedures and results continued to be problematic, and abuse of government resources persisted. Despite a relatively calm polling day, the 2007 election completely disintegrated during the tallying procedure, and deadly violence erupted for months.

Although international monitors were able to guide and encourage some re-forms and international donors were successful at pushing for elections and negotiations with the opposition, improvements in Kenya's election conduct were weak and reversals were common. Kenya thus is very much a "one step forward, two steps back" story.

International monitors were unable to improve elections in Kenya for several reasons. First, there never was a sustained period of pro-democratic govern-ments. The initial opening up of the regime, achieved through implementation of aid conditionality measures, did not lead to democratization,[213] despite nu-merous domestically initiated reform movements and a relatively robust civil society. Second, violence has dominated the Kenya democratization process. Politically motivated killings started with the 1992 election, continued in 1997,[214] when around 2,000 people were killed, and then subsided in 2002, before in-creasing again in 2007, when between 700 and 1,200 people were estimated to have died in clashes following the election.[215] The incidences of violence were not only motivated by the significant ethnic diversity of the country, but were also bolstered by incumbent leaders, who benefited economically and politi-cally from the continuing unrest in the country.[216] Politicians who benefited from the dysfunctional institutional and political environment in the country thus ignored most of the international monitors' recommendations for reforms. Third, in this environment, international monitors and other organizations faced a dilemma. On the one hand, real reforms required a cessation of vio-lence; yet pushing for reforms further destabilized the political environment and risked continued violence. Finally, the same organizations have not con-sistently monitored the polls. No organization monitored more than two of the four elections between 1992 and 2007 polls. More consistency and follow-up might be achieved if the same organizations returned.

Several criticisms have been aimed at monitors in Kenya. Kenyan opposi-tion party Forum for the Restoration of Democracy (FORD) famously called them "tourists."[217] Some criticize the IRI's ambiguous assessment in 1992 that although the election was not completely clean the result was not "altogether invalid."[218] In 1997, the monitors concluded that the presidential election was acceptable, but questioned the legitimacy of the parliamentary vote, where win-ning margins were tighter. Thus, some argued that monitors impeded further democratization by being too generous in their assessment of unfair elections in 1992 and 1997, and that the donor countries—concerned with stability over democratization—interfered with the process.[219] Politicians exploited this con-cern by simply trying to appease foreign donors to not cut off aid. This has led critics of election observers to state that monitors in fact undermined, rather than supported, a process of democratization in this region of the world.[220] The assessments of the 2007 election were similarly confusing. For example, the IRI said that the parliamentary vote was considered fair, but the presidential vote was highly problematic.[221] As noted in Chapter 5, in spite of an atrocious pre-election campaign, the EU and other organizations initially released positive statements as election day was unfolding calmly, but then quickly revised their assessments as violence erupted. Furthermore, the international press accused the IRI of withholding the results of a poll on election day that favored the opposition. The IRI vehemently denied the charges.[222] Even more seriously, the Independent Review Commission that the UN, the Kenyan government, and the African Union (AU) organized after the 2007 election reported that monitors had at times based their claims on misunderstandings. The commission noted that monitors sometimes jumped to conclusions that discrepancies in figures were due to fraud. The reporting of partial results, combined with the unclear methods of communication, gave the appearance of unfounded increases in votes, when in reality, many of these increases were distributed evenly across parties and were merely the result of an update of the partial figures.[223]

Thus the record of international election monitoring in Kenya has been marked by some specific improvements overshadowed by backsliding in 2007 and by questions about the objectivity and competence of the monitoring organizations themselves. Post-2007 reforms remain to be tested in future elections.

LESOTHO: DEADLOCK

Lesotho remains poor and mired in struggles over its electoral system. The CS and the South African Development Community (SADC) have played a substantial role in the evolution of the electoral system and in providing mediation. The reforms of 2001 were quite remarkable and the SADC was credited greatly. Still, despite electoral reforms, political deadlock continues. The main contention is not about ethnicity or ideology, but about "competition for jobs,"[224] because of the "the high premium placed on being in government."[225] Thus distracted, Lesotho has followed some monitor recommendations to improve the administration of elections, but many other recommendations remain unaddressed. Lesotho shows that despite heavy external involvement by South Africa, the UN, and international monitors, in a poor country with little democratic experience domestic power struggles can derail progress.

Despite a homogeneous population, Lesotho was not predisposed to democratization: It had a history of conflict, a strong and politically active military, and a very weak economy that remains almost entirely dependent on South Africa. The population has not enthusiastically supported democracy.[226] Furthermore, previous experience with democracy lasted only from 1965 to 1970, when the Basotho National Party (BNP) ruled. Its leader, Chief Leabua Jonathan, resumed authoritarian methods following defeat in the 1970 election, which was most likely won by the Basutoland Congress Party (BCP). Over the next fifteen years, Jonathan led the country to economic collapse. His rule was divisive and alienated rural, anti-apartheid, and royalist subgroups within the otherwise ethnically homogeneous society.[227] His bad leadership resulted in a military coup in 1985.[228]

However, in 1988, Lesotho authorities invited the Commonwealth Secretariat, the Organisation of African Unity, and the South African government to assist the democratization of the country as the military stepped aside due to growing external pressure, violence, and continued factionalism within the political leadership.[229] In the late 1980s, foreign donors helped sponsor the rise of civil society organizations, which have played important roles in elections.[230] A National Constituent Assembly was appointed in 1990 to draft a new constitution.

The adoption of a majoritarian system in 1993 was inherited from the British colonial rule.[231] It allowed the BCP to sweep all sixty-five seats in a complete rejection of the past authoritarianism of the BNP. This election was seen as an important transition and its flaws were overlooked. A crisis soon followed, however, with the assassination of the deputy prime minister. Diplomacy from SADC, the UN, and the OAU helped restore the BCP government, but the prime minister broke away and formed the Lesotho Congress for Democracy (LCD).[232]

The electoral system prompted massive riots again after the 1998 election, when the recently formed LCD obtained seventy-nine out of eighty seats despite having won only around 60.5 percent of the vote, thus completely shutting out the two largest traditional parties. The international monitors said the election itself had been acceptable, but a judicial review by a South African judge found that the election documentation was so disarrayed that "legitimacy of the results could not be accurately judged."[233] The complete chaos that ensued was quelled by the South African army, but not without much criticism.[234] To appease the malcontents, the SADC pushed hard for the adoption of a mixed member electoral system that would have compensatory seats to prevent absolute losers from feeling sidelined and thereby reducing the probability of violence and unrest.[235] After heavy negotiations, this compromise was adopted in 2001.

According to most analysts, the reforms of 2001 were remarkable and the 2002 election contrasted sharply with the parody observed in Zimbabwe, for example.[236] The SADC was credited with not only promoting a better electoral law framework, but working closely with local authorities to prepare better voter lists, provide a sufficient number of polling stations, and establish a process for handling election complaints.[237] The introduction of the mixed electoral system increased popular support for the state.[238] In the 2007 election, however, the formula for allocating seats again created conflict, because the parties circumvented the allocation rules by forming alliances to manipulate the distribution of seats.[239] Despite SADC mediation attempts, the parties remain deadlocked.

Administratively, Lesotho has made some progress over the years. Voter lists and the registration process are not perfect, but they have improved considerably. Officials are better trained and logistical aspects of the election are smoother. Still, domestic battles over the fundamental questions of the electoral system have distracted from other essential reforms that monitors have suggested over the years. Abuse of government resources continues, the media still require some regulation, and Lesotho has repeatedly ignored monitors' recommendations regarding the regulation of campaign finance.

MEXICO: CONSTRUCTIVE ENGAGEMENT

Mexico has successfully transformed itself from authoritarianism to democracy. As with most such transformations, the main credit goes to domestic actors. Election monitors reinforced the pressures of opposition parties, but their role was not decisive. That said, international observers have played at least three roles in Mexico. They have facilitated domestic monitoring through interaction with and exposing domestic actors to election monitoring techniques. They have played an important verification role both domestically and internationally. Finally, echoing opposition demands, they have made recommendations for changes, many of which have been addressed. This constructive interaction was facilitated by the domestic political opening, international pressures, and sustained engagement by mostly U.S. observer groups. However, Mexico also illustrates that change is slow and the closely contested 2006 election revealed that continued involvement is needed.

For seven decades the Institutional Revolutionary Party (PRI) held a hegemonic grip on power in Mexico, making it the longest-reigning political party in the world.[240] However, as Mexico grew more urban and incomes rose, cycles of economic crises undermined the regime and pressures for reform increased.[241] The 1988 general election marked a turning point in Mexican politics, as massive fraud led to divisions within the political system. Mexico had staunchly denied international monitors access to the election, arguing they would interfere in internal affairs. Early election returns indicated a narrow victory for Cuauhtémoc Cárdenas, who had resigned from the PRI in protest over Carlos Salinas's nomination and was running as a candidate for the National Democratic Front. However, the computer system collapsed right before the count was completed. After days of delay, incumbent-dominated electoral authorities gave the victory to Salinas. The Congress later voted to burn the ballot papers.[242] Opposition parties and other countries widely viewed the election as fraudulent, although the opposition still managed to gather a significant number of seats in both houses.

After the mass protests that accompanied this disputed victory, the PRI government had to implement political reforms to regain public confidence.[243] Two opposition parties played important complementary roles in pushing for reforms. The right-wing National Action Party (PAN), which had played a weak but consistent opposition role throughout the PRI's authoritarianism, kept up protests and negotiations with the PRI for concessions. Meanwhile, claiming that the PRI had stolen his victory in the 1988 election, Cárdenas founded the Party of the Democratic Revolution (PRD) and insisted on thorough reforms. As both these parties gained strength over successive elections, winning enough in 1997 to end the PRI's two-thirds Senate majority and its absolute majority in the lower chamber, these parties facilitated a "'virtuous circle' of democratization."[244]

Several other factors also contributed to this political opening over successive elections throughout the 1990s. Preparations for Mexico's participation in the negotiations for the North American Free Trade Agreements (NAFTA) and the Organization for Economic Co-operation and Development (OECD) enabled greater international influence over Mexico's democratization process, as Mexico needed a reputation as stable to maintain vital international investment.[245] Internally, the Zapatista—an indigenous revolutionary group based in Chiapas—engaged in armed conflicts with the government and caused security threats. The PRI government's inability to pacify the Zapatista drained its popularity and offered opposition parties a chance to gain public support.[246] The 1995 economic crises also increased pressure on the government to reform. The international election monitors were thus operating in an environment with several strong pressures on the government.

Domestic observer groups and NGOs also deserve much of the credit for the transformation of Mexican elections during the next fifteen years, but international observers such as the CC were instrumental in building up this domestic capacity.[247] Not only did they help form these national groups and train them, but they also facilitated their visits to observe elections in the United States and elsewhere.[248] This involvement began before the 1994 election. The CC sent missions, offered advice, and exposed central Mexican civil society activities to experiences overseas to bolster their capacities to build domestic observation.[249] The details deserve attention for their discussion of micro-level processes of influence:

> The Center encouraged opening the door for international observation of elections and then sent monitoring missions to watch important races and recommend improvement in Mexico's electoral administration. These missions included the July 13, 1992, state elections in Michoacán and Chihuahua, two pre-election trips before the 1994 national elections. . . . The Center began by inviting leaders from Mexico's human rights community to participate in Carter Center election observation missions in other countries. In 1990, Sergio Aguayo, the president of Mexico's nongovernmental Academy of Human Rights, joined a delegation of The Carter Center's Council of Presidents and Prime Ministers of the Americas and the NDI in observing the Haiti elections. In Haiti, Aguayo was partnered with Gregorio Atienza, the former secretary-general of NAMFREL [National Citizens' Movement for Free Elections], the election monitoring group in the Philippines that detected and denounced the attempt by Ferdinand Marcos to commit electoral fraud in 1986. Aguayo returned to Mexico and completed his project of organizing eight different grassroots groups to become domestic election observers. Those domestic observers then invited The Carter Center and its Council of Presidents and Prime Ministers of the Americas to observe state elections in Michoacán and Chihuahua on July 13, 1992. Dr. Pastor, then-executive secretary of the Council, negotiated an arrangement with the Office of the President of Mexico, which permitted the group to be recognized by the government as the first international group to work with Mexicans in observing a Mexican election. . . . As a gesture of reciprocity, The Carter Center invited all the major political parties and civic organizations to observe the U.S. presidential election in November 1992. The group delivered a statement on its observation and recommended ways to improve the electoral process in the United States, which were published in a report. Also in 1992, two other Mexican leaders, Julio Faesler of the Council for Democracy and Miguel Basáñez of the National Accord for Democracy (ACUDE), joined the Center's observation of elections in Guyana. They used this experience to help build national election observer groups in Mexico.[250]

Over the years monitors have also made many recommendations that Mexico has followed. Before the 1994 election, the CC sent two missions to study the electoral reforms and make recommendations: "In September 1993, a small team representing three members of the Council visited Mexico to study the electoral reforms being discussed at that time in the Mexican Congress. That team's report to the Council, *Electoral Reform in Mexico*, was subsequently published and distributed widely in Mexico and the United States. It was also translated into Spanish and published in *Este Pais* in January 1994. The 1993 report was controversial, but we are gratified by the positive impact it seems to have had in Mexico. Many of the recommendations in that report were implemented, including the agreement to commission an external audit of the voter registration list, the increased autonomy of Federal Electoral Institute (IFE) from political party influence, greater access for national election observers, and the decision to accredit international visitors to observe the elections."[251]

During 1994 pre-election meetings with presidential candidates, the IFES also raised concerns about problems with the IFE's lack of independence, and after the election it recommended disentanglement of the IFE from the Interior Ministry and more citizen involvement in its board.[252]

Monitors also played an important verification role in the 1994 election. As the election approached, the government realized that, despite numerous reforms to the election law,[253] the election had little chance of being viewed as legitimate without international monitors. As one commentator said, "A fraudulent election could be deadly for the ruling party."[254] Thus, the government eventually decided to invite monitors for the first time in 1994. The late invitation meant that the CC, the IRI, and the NDI had to pool their resources to manage. Despite skepticism, the election, while not perfect, was much better than the 1988 election.[255] Together with domestic actors, international observers placed campaign and party finances on the political agenda and encouraged the government to permit a televised debate between the main presidential candidates.[256] The widely reported presence of international observers may also have also facilitated the unusually high voter turnout, reduced violence, and increased the acceptance of the election results, as demonstrated in pre- and post-election surveys.[257]

During the 1990s, international monitors, the CC in particular, continued to engage in the electoral reforms.[258] Another key issue in the 1994 election was the lack of regulations on parties' campaign expenditures.[259] In line with opposition demands, observers recommended reasonable expenditure ceilings, auditing party finances, providing public financing, and limiting parties' ability to purchase media spots independently, recommendations that opposition parties also advocated.[260] Subsequently, as part of the 1996 reforms the Mexican government drastically increased the level of public financing to political parties and implemented spending limits.

The independence of the IFE, which monitors had stressed in the 1994 election, became one of the central tenets of another round of electoral reforms in 1996. In November 1996, a constitutional amendment made the IFE fully autonomous and included independent citizen counselors on its board.[261] Reforms also established the Electoral Tribunal of the Federal Judiciary (TEPJF) as the highest jurisdictional authority in electoral matters and granted it more power.

In the 1997 midterm election, the PRI lost its legislative majority for the first time, setting the stage for further reforms. Observers were generally pleased with the election, praising the election bodies, although concerns about vote buying and fraud in rural areas remained. Observers were even more satisfied with the 2000 election, which saw the first change of presidential power in more than seventy years as the PRI lost. This moment was a culmination of a decade of domestic reform efforts that had ushered in a "veritable electoral revolution."[262] For the 2000 election, the CC applied a novel approach to election monitoring, stationing observers in party headquarters and other central locations.[263] Thanks to all the reforms, the electoral institutions functioned well. The election was professionally administered, and voter registration and turnout was high.

Thus, the Mexico electoral system improved tremendously over the years. Many monitor and opposition concerns have been met. A few concerns do remain. For example, in 2000, the EP noted that Mexicans living abroad could not vote and urged the government to introduce absentee voting.[264] Procedures were adopted for the 2006 election, but the EU has recommended further simplification.[265] Other problems have been relieved somewhat but not eliminated, such as late opening of polling stations and problems with the special polling stations for persons who are not able to vote in their home station. Both international and domestic organizations have also criticized the misuse of public resources.[266] A special congressional commission was established in 2000 to monitor the misuse of public funds, but the public remains skeptical.[267] Likewise, international monitors have repeatedly criticized the media.[268] Reforms in 1997[269] and 2000[270] helped, but problems persist.

The 2006 presidential election was very closely contested and there was confusion over the projections during the counting and release of results.[271] Because the margin of victory was 0.56 percent, the election was followed by a partial recount and a two-month-long dispute until the Electoral Tribunal finally validated the results. Despite the controversy monitors were largely satisfied,[272] and public confidence in the IFE remained as high as 64 percent even after the election.[273] Still, the closeness of the election revealed some remaining weaknesses in the election process.[274] After monitoring Mexican elections for a decade, the

CC did not go to the 2006 election. However, the EU sent a mission. Given the controversy, the mission recommended, among many other things, implementing a second-round runoff between candidates when no candidate receives the majority of vote.[275] In December 2009, Mexico's president proposed a runoff amendment,[276] and Mexico has undertaken further reform efforts.[277] Although there is room for monitors to continue to engage,[278] the cumulative progress in Mexico since 1988 has been impressive.[279] By far the most of the credit for this electoral revolution goes to domestic actors: opposition parties, voters, and election bodies such as the IFE and the Electoral Tribunal.

However, international monitors have played a supportive background role. In addition to helping domestic observers and recommending reforms, they have lent credibility to the elections to help Mexico improve its reputation, or, as the CC says, "lend international visibility to Mexico's changes."[280]

That said, concerns remain over Mexico due to the rising drug-related crime that can destabilize the system and thus has prompted Freedom House to downgrade Mexico's freedom ranking.

NICARAGUA: EXCESSIVE MEDDLING AND DEAL MAKING

International monitors have played an important role in Nicaragua, but their success has been mixed. Their sizable presence in the post-conflict election was notable because, as discussed in Chapter 2, it was the first UN observation in a sovereign state.[281] The election was a vital part of the peace negotiations and the crucial role of the monitors helped build their reputation. In general, however, the persistent mistrust and political bias in the Nicaraguan election apparatus has relegated international monitors to serve as validators of election outcomes, rather than as catalysts for reforms. International monitors compensated for the lack of democratic institutions by keeping the general public informed and the politicians in check.[282] Given chronic instability, they were crucial in getting Nicaraguans to accept the outcomes of elections in 1996 and 2001. However, monitors were hampered by both domestic conditions and extensive international meddling. They did not succeed in creating long-term electoral reforms to the fundamental political problems of the election system. Daniel Ortega's return to power in 2006 led to regression as he sought to consolidate his power through the courts.

In 1979, the Sandinistas overthrew four decades of Somoza dictatorship and went on to govern during wartime with a very strong executive, but weak legislature and judiciary. The opposition parties remained small, weak, and divided.[283]

In 1990, exhausted and divided after ten years of war and world record inflation, Nicaragua had an extra incentive for running a respectable election, since doing so was explicitly tied to peace and to ending the U.S. trade embargo.[284] The international monitors played a crucial role in facilitating the 1990 election and a peaceful transition. However, the election produced a dual power structure. Although they lost the presidency, the Sandinistas retained control over the military and police and gained thirty-nine of ninety-two National Assembly seats— enough to block reforms. The elections after 1990 were not successful in consolidating electoral quality. Despite proportional electoral laws, Nicaragua evolved into a two-party system after the two main rivals engaged in numerous constitutional reforms that hindered the emergence of other serious, contending parties.

Monitors first visited Nicaragua in 1984, and electoral law reforms preceded every single election since then. The international pressure leading up to the 1990 election helped opposition forces to unite and press for reforms to the composition of the electoral commission. Marked by sharp legislative-executive conflict and economic and institutional crises, the years following the 1990 election were contentious and difficult and gradually eroded the power of Violet Chamorro's government. The United States and other donors and international financial institutions pressed for resolution of the crisis.[285] Subsequently, the year 1994 brought civil-military reform and in 1995 further constitutional reforms reduced the quasi-absolute powers power of the president, who had enjoyed almost full authority over Nicaragua's political life until then. Most important, the provisions disqualified family members of the sitting president to run for the presidency.[286] The reforms also addressed some concerns of monitors, who had criticized the electoral commission by making the Consejo Supremo Electoral (CSE)—or Supreme Electoral Council—solely responsible for the central register, the citizen identification program, the voter registry, and political party registration. However, the reforms also brought new appointment procedures, and monitors expressed concern about the independence of the CSE. The CC and the OAS argued that the method of choosing Electoral Council members should be based on explicit qualifications and not party affiliation[287]—a concern that worsened in the 2001 and 2006 elections.

Throughout the years, Nicaragua has made some progress. For example, the administration of election materials improved greatly for the 2001 election, also aiding result transmission and vote tabulation—an area of earlier monitor criticism.

Yet, in general, foreign monitoring organizations have had little success with pushing for and institutionalizing lasting electoral reforms. In 1996, for example, the IFES recommended the introduction of a permanent voter registry to replace the compilation of temporary voter lists before the election—a practice that led to confusion, inefficiencies, and inaccuracies.[288] Despite efforts by the CSE, serious problems with registering voters and issuing identity cards have persisted, and remain one of the most contentious issues. Many monitoring organizations have also tirelessly recommended measures to depoliticize the CSE, but the council has only grown more political over time, prompting monitors to repeat their recommendations for reforms. Monitoring organizations have also repeatedly pressed for clarifying the appeal processes, for legislation on political parties, and for greater transparency, among many other things.

The impact of monitors was undercut when two main parties—notably their leaders Manuel Ortego and Arnoldo Alemán—colluded in a 2000 pact and pushed for reforms that decreased political pluralism and increased partisanship throughout the electoral apparatus.[289] Meanwhile, recommendations concerning voter registries, campaign finances, and many other areas of concern were ignored or poorly implemented despite heavy criticism by the CC.[290] The IRI also criticized a provision for the outgoing president and runner-up to be appointed directly as deputies, as well as reducing the minimal percentage for outright presidential victory to 35 percent, provided that there is at least a 5 percent advantage over the next runner-up.[291]

Thus, by 2001 the CC, the organization with the most sustained involvement, noted, "Nicaragua has successfully conducted a series of democratic national elections, making alterations in the election law and system before each vote. Unfortunately, the changes have not led to cumulative progress."[292] Surprisingly, the Constitutional Liberal Party (PLC) President Enrique Bolanos undertook a widespread effort to fight corruption and reform the political system of the country, even though he had benefited from the flawed electoral practices.[293] This marginalized politically and resulted in a ten-month-long political crisis, which the OAS, supported by the CC, eventually mediated. The compromise was that the legislature elected in the upcoming 2006 election would decide whether to implement constitutional reform.

Leading up to the 2006 election, the CSE was plagued by political fights. The CC helped mediate a dispute in the CSE about whether voters with ID cards whose names could not be found on the register would be able to vote as provided by law. Given the extensive efforts by the United States and Venezuela, the CC also had to take the unusual step of publicly urging all foreign governments to stay out of the Nicaraguan elections.[294]

The number of new or unfulfilled recommendations listed by both the CC and the EU in their 2006 reports illustrates the lack of progress in Nicaragua's elections despite twenty-two years of electoral observation by major groups, some of which have sustained their involvement over many elections. The CC clearly captured the disillusionment of international organizations regarding the electoral process and their role in it: "Election observers can play a vital role in ratifying the legitimacy of a particular election process and even help cement an election system over time. But repeated recourse to international election observation even after national organizations have developed a demonstrated capacity to fulfill their role should be a cause for concern."[295] The 2008 local elections led to an electoral crisis. The elections, won by the Sandinista National Liberation Front (FSLN), were criticized for violence. The national monitors were not taken seriously and Nicaragua did not host international monitors. Thus, although there have been numerous improvements throughout the years, overall progress has been very limited.

Some argue that the main reason for the ultimately failed Nicaraguan transition lies with United States and other international actors.[296] The United States, due to its past involvement of supporting the Contras, the counter-insurgency movement that opposed the Sandinistas, continued to be an active supporter of the liberal PLC party after 1990, while the FSLN drew support and funding primarily from Venezuela. In 1990, the two main parties received large foreign donations, leaving third parties much poorer.[297] Foreign involvement in Nicaraguan elections persisted and reached a new high in 2006 with the United States and Venezuelan President Hugo Chávez battling for influence.[298] The EU report criticized the United States for "blunt intervention . . . discrediting the FSLN candidate in any possible manner."[299] Thus, the ability of monitors to promote meaningful reforms was reduced by other geopolitical processes and strategic interests at a much higher level.

However, the domestic environment likely played a larger role in hindering effective reforms. Plagued by violence, poverty, and inequality, Nicaragua has a historical and cultural legacy of looking to outsiders to solve disputes or support its side, and to produce authoritarian leaders and zero-sum politics. The two powerful parties have stripped state institutions of content.[300] The parties, dominated by strong leaders and clientelism, lack the political will for serious institutional reform, and instead rely on "deal making among a few players."[301]

Ortega's 2006 victory was assured by the 2000 pact that made it possible to win the presidency with as little as 35 percent of the vote.

Given the highly politicized election management and distrust thereof, one of the biggest contributions of the international monitors in Nicaragua has been to install confidence in the elections through their presence. Thus, voter turnout has remained high, but domestic political actors have continued to express a need for international observers to counter perceived biases.[302]

Panama: Both a Will and a Way

The Panama case highlights how the effectiveness of election observation depends on both domestic and international factors. The main contribution of international monitors in Panama was their role in the 1989 election in assisting the Catholic Church in setting up parallel vote counts, thus legitimizing the claims that the election had been stolen and forcefully bringing international attention to the fraud. The subsequent U.S. invasion in 1989 paved the way for the opposition to take power. Its dependence on the United States, combined with its economic growth, made it both willing and able to follow recommendations from monitors, whose role shifted toward simply verifying an already smooth process of voting and making a few recommendations. However, initially the monitors, led by former President Jimmy Carter, played an essential role in denouncing the fraud and thus bringing about the U.S. invasion that improved the political conditions.

Before 1989, international actors were not willing to pressure the dictatorship in Panama. Consequently, little came of the largely symbolic OAS mission in 1978, and in 1984 the only observers, which were from the United States, were too concerned about causing instability in Panama to be effective. This clearly illustrates the argument made in Chapter 4 about the conflict that monitors sometimes face between stability and truth. The election was close, but the delegation "questioned whether the flaws in the election were sufficiently egregious to merit US condemnation."[303] Thus, early observers were too weak to do much, even if the domestic conditions had been riper than they indeed were. However, by 1989 the capacity of the monitors, the interests of international actors, and the domestic environment had changed.

Following the 1984 election, the rampant corruption and human rights violations under the Noriega regime had spurred public dissent. In 1988, Manuel Noriega was indicted in the United States for drug trafficking and racketeering (after having been on the Central Intelligence Agency (CIA) payroll as an informant in previous years) and the United States imposed severe economic sanctions on Panama, leaving the economy in tatters leading up to the 1989 election.[304] The opposition requested the NDI and the IRI to monitor the election to provide moral support and with hopes that their assistance with a parallel vote tabulation would deter or publicize fraud to the international community. The NDI and the IRI formed a joint mission led by former Presidents Carter and Gerald Ford and other members of the CC's Council of Freely Elected Heads of Government. The mission knew the election would likely be rigged, but decided to monitor it regardless. The regime acquiesced to the presence of monitors partly because it underestimated the actual support for the opposition and partly because of the strong foreign and domestic pressure.

In the 1989 election, the incumbent Democratic Revolutionary Party (PRD) blatantly manipulated the vote-counting process with help from the military. Meanwhile, the parallel vote count conducted by the opposition and the Catholic Church in conjunction with the international observers indicated a clear victory for the opposition. This was central in identifying the extent to which the central government manipulated the electoral process and it provided key international officials, such as President Carter, who was working with the NDI/IRI joint mission, with enough support to publicly denounce the official voting results.[305] It was also at the core of official statements made by U.S. President George H. W. Bush and spurred the OAS to denounce the election, to no avail. Seven months after the Panama Defense Force (PDF) annulled the election results and Noriega declared himself "president for life," the United States invaded and installed the opposition in power in 1990.[306]

Later elections improved significantly and the role of monitors shifted toward simply verifying an already smooth process of voting and making a few recommendations. The NDI/IRI/Council mission's main recommendation in 1989 had been to reform the composition of the Electoral Tribunal. The Tribunal consisted of three magistrates appointed by pro-government groups and was the source of fraud and manipulation.[307] After the U.S. invasion brought the opposition to power in 1990, the new government changed the nomination process and allowed the magistrates to come from the three branches of the government.[308]

In 1994, CC observers conducted extensive pre-election meetings with incumbent President Guillermo Endara and his challengers.[309] After the election, the CC criticized the lack of media regulation, particularly the use of many anonymous TV advertisements. This problem was fully resolved in 1997, when a media law set prohibitions and sanctions against the publication and printing of materials from anonymous sources. The law also introduced regulations on censorship, taxes, and fees.[310]

The OAS observation mission of 1999 criticized the fact that people could register to vote in districts where they did not reside. The IFES recommended that the electoral tribunal review this policy. A 2002 reform required "change or update of electoral domicile to facilitate local suffrage,"[311] although complaints to the electoral tribunal regarding "fraudulent change of domicile" continued.[312]

Starting in 1999, Panama's electoral process was deemed to be of very good quality.[313] The country's fast economic recovery and large service-based industry have enabled the government to react to administrative recommendations and implement sophisticated computerized vote-counting systems. In 2004 and 2009, changes primarily concerned further procedural improvements in efficiency.

Thus, most of the serious problems observed by the monitors in Panama were related to the corrupt practices of the Noriega regime and its desperate attempt to maintain power. Once the opposition gained power, it was careful to avoid the previous regime's downfalls, and, owing much of its authority to assistance from the United States, it was receptive to the monitors and their recommendations.

Russia: Goliath Beats David

International monitors played a significant role in pushing through several legislative and administrative reforms in the 1990s. However, these efforts could not withstand the worsening political climate, which moved toward greater centralization and concentration of power in the Kremlin. As a result, monitors had little lasting or substantial impact on improving the real competitive nature of elections in Russia. Their effectiveness was further reduced by their timidity. They were useful and welcomed by Russian politicians in the first years after transition when they brought legitimacy and were still fairly hesitant to criticize Russia. Over time, Russia actively combated their efforts and undermined their influence. Russia demonstrates the ability of international monitors to socialize countries when domestic conditions are favorable. However, it also shows the dangers of regression when these conditions fail, suggesting that some socialization is not particularly deep, and that it is possible for countries to comply with many recommendations, yet still deprive voters of free and fair elections by manipulating the media and abusing incumbent resources. Furthermore, it shows just how difficult it is for monitors to influence great powers and that monitors are sometimes too cautious in their criticisms.

International monitors had significant influence on the electoral framework and administration of Russian elections during the 1990s, when the Russian authorities were favorably inclined toward reform. Thus, Russia reformed its institutional framework substantially after the 1993 election and followed many of the legal recommendations of the international monitoring organizations, most notably the IRI, the COE, and the OSCE. As the OSCE noted in 2003, "The legal framework for elections in the Russian Federation has generally improved with each successive election and has been found to be generally consistent with commonly recognized democratic principles and international commitments, including those in the Copenhagen Document."[314]

In the 1990s, many of the international monitoring reports recounted how Russia responded to their recommendations. In its 1995 report, the COE stated, "In our talks on this occasion with the Chairman of the Central Election Commission, Mr. Nikolai Ryabov, we were assured that our previous observations had been taken into account. The reports of our observer teams (and of other international observers) suggest that this indeed has been the case."[315] The IRI noted that after the 1993 referendum, "a number of IRI's suggested improvements were adopted by the time of the December 12, 1993 parliamentary elections,"[316] and that the vice chairman of Russia's Central Election Commission said IRI's report "served as the roadmap for the CEC in making improvements in the election law."[317] Eighteen of the twenty recommendations related directly to election law were partially or substantially adopted.[318] The COE also noted that the amendments passed before the 1999 election "respond to a certain degree to the recommendations of our report on the 1995 parliamentary elections (doc. 7430, Addendum V),"[319] and after further amendments in 2002, the OSCE noted that "several recommendations contained in the OSCE/ODIHR Final Report on the 1999 State Duma Elections have been implemented in the new laws."[320]

Thus, Russia responded to recommendations in several areas such as campaign finance reform, ballot counting procedures, publication of results, removal of the "against all" option, and the independence of the CEC. However, some areas deteriorated, such as the independence of the CEC, voter lists,[321] registration procedures, and the like. Recommendations regarding open and family voting, abuse of media, and incumbent resources were never addressed.

Initially, international monitors were willing to give Russia the benefit of the doubt and to encourage the transition despite difficulties. Furthermore, they were hesitant to criticize Russia too much. Russia's vast size and commensurate influence made it harder to exert leverage and develop issue linkage. The greatest opening was between 1994 and 1999, when Russia received substantial IMF loans, which peaked in 1998, when the country received more than $12 billion.[322] This period also saw the greatest improvements in the electoral framework and administration of elections in Russia. This period coincided with Russia's efforts to join the COE. Indeed, the "generally positive" evaluation of the 1995 election led to the recommendation for Russia's admission.[323] International monitors remained optimistic until and including the 2000 presidential election, arguing that "it marked the conclusion of a transitional period forged by President [Boris] Yeltsin since 1991."[324]

However, electoral conditions deteriorated further after the election of Vladimir Putin, who, despite numerous legal and procedural reforms, benefited from a weakly consolidated party system and a weak Parliament, which enabled him to control the media and oppress the opposition. At this stage, monitors became explicit about the lack of effort to follow their recommendations. For example, the OSCE 2004 report notes, "As voter lists were subsequently updated, the CEC did not periodically announce a revised total of registered voters, as it had been recommended to do by the OSCE/ODIHR following the 2003 State Duma elections."[325] Later the report notes: "The persistence of open voting and group voting, which are breaches of paragraph 7.4 of the Copenhagen Document, are particularly regrettable as, in response to an OSCE/ODIHR recommendation following the 2003 State Duma elections, the CEC had assured the EOM [Election Observation Mission] that revised instructions had been issued to all electoral commissions to prevent such practices."[326] By 2007 and 2008, the elections were widely criticized by Western monitors as procedurally correct, but flawed due to the incumbent party's extreme dominance of the media and government powers to shut out any real competition.[327]

Throughout, both Russian government officials and Western experts criticized the international monitors, albeit for different reasons. The government initially benefited from the added legitimacy that came with allowing foreign monitors to observe elections, but was later dissatisfied and claimed that monitors were meddling in the country's internal affairs. These criticisms became especially sharp toward the OSCE and eventually led to active attempts by Russia to curtail the power of the organization by seeking to push for reforms of the OSCE Office for Democratic Institutions and Human Rights.[328] In 2006, Putin signed a bill that restricted foreign NGOs' activities in the country following the "color revolutions" in Georgia, Ukraine, and Kyrgyzstan, where the NDI, the IRI, and others claimed to have played behind-the-scenes roles in stimulating those upheavals. For the 2007 parliamentary election, invitations to international monitors were issued late and restricted the number of observers. In 2007 and 2008, the OSCE decided, as a result of the obstacles put forward by the Russian government, to send no observers to monitor the presidential election.

Meanwhile, international experts were dissatisfied with the lack of firmness in monitoring evaluations and the overall lack of efficiency displayed by the observers.[329] For example, monitors were rather hesitant in their criticisms of the 1996 Russian election although Yeltsin abused state resources, manipulated the media, and repressed the opposition.[330] Even after the 2008 election, the COE, which was the only Western organization to observe the election, concluded that the election was "a reflection of the will of an electorate whose democratic potential was, unfortunately, not tapped."[331] The report then went on to explain why the election was neither really free nor fair.

SOUTH AFRICA: REMARKABLY UNREMARKABLE

Given the historical significance of the 1994 election in South Africa and the immense role the international community played in bringing this election about, it is remarkable how seemingly minor a role international election monitors have played in South Africa since then. International monitors from the EU, the IRI, the UN, and the CS pointed out numerous serious weaknesses in the 1994 election. Nearly all the weaknesses had been addressed by the 1999 election, however, and the presence of international observers remained mostly African for the next three elections. Although South Africa still struggles with many political and practical problems, the transition to proper elections occurred with remarkable ease, with the major concern being not the legitimacy of the elections, but—in the face of African National Congress (ANC) popularity—the tendency toward a dominant party system.[332] The credit due to international election monitors after 1994 is likely minor.[333]

South Africa's historic 1994 election was one of the most monitored elections ever. Observers from the EU, the CS, the UN, and the Organisation of African Unity (OAU) were sent to observe both the violence and the political processes in the year and half leading up to the election and they cooperated greatly.[334] For political reasons the time schedule of the election was extremely short and preparation time for such a vast undertaking was therefore strained to the maximum. The fact that many voters had destroyed their identity documents during the apartheid era greatly complicated the voting. Tensions led to much violence. The IRI talked about a "bloody campaign field strewn with sacrificial victims," and said that the campaign period was so dominated by fear that a free and fair campaign was impossible in many areas.[335] Computer hacking delayed the count, which in turn gave rise to rumors and suspicions in the media. Local media and international observer groups alleged that the results were eventually settled behind closed doors in political deal making to avoid a further post-election violence.[336] However, Jørgen Elklit, who served as an international member of the Independent Electoral Commission (IEC) and followed the entire centralized tallying process closely and was in charge of the seat allocation, says that although the results did end up satisfying the different parties, no such deal making occurred.[337] In the end, 86 percent of South Africans turned out to vote, and international monitors also acknowledged that despite various problems, the election was ultimately a historic success. For example, the IRI called the election "politically masterful and administratively calamitous; however, despite daunting challenges and crises the results finally reflected the will of a majority of voters."[338]

The international monitors had some concrete effects on the voting process. For example, after they issued a demarche in early March 1994, the IEC reorganized some of its operations to address the weaknesses.[339] In general, however, international monitors may have contributed to the peace, but they were not really able to fulfill their mandate of assessing the election. Thus, one commentator concluded "International observers are entitled to share in the reflected glory of the South Africa's success, but their share of the credit is less than many expected it to be."[340]

The activities of international monitors declined sharply after 1994; despite their heavy involvement in 1994 and an open invitation to return, the EU[341] and the IRI did not return, and only African organizations remained active. The CS and the Organisation of African Unity (OAU) monitored the 1999 election, joined by the Electoral Commission Forum of SADC (ECF). The AU, the SDAC, and the Electoral Institute of Southern Africa (EISA) monitored the 2004 and 2009 elections, but they had no long-term presence.

A new constitution and revisions to several electoral laws preceded the 1999 election. Most of the legal problems from the 1994 election were addressed and indeed the majority of the logistical issues were resolved as well. This involved specifying clearer divisions between the various electoral institutions, including a dispute-settling process, and making the IEC truly separate from the government by stopping direct funding by Parliament.[342] Remaining concerns in 1999 were the voter list, insufficient polling stations, and training of polling staff. The improvements in the 1999 election were enormous, but most likely not due to the presence of international monitors, but more likely due to the IEC. The problems of the 1994 election were very apparent and fixing them was a priority before the 1999 election. With the ANC holding a secure position in society, the government had every incentive to strive for proper and clean elections.

Few changes in the legal framework were made prior to the 2004 election, as indeed the issues had already been resolved by 1999.[343] The biggest concern in 1999, the voter list, was much improved by 2004, as was voter education. Compared to 1994, the level of violence in the election was again quite low, much as in 1999. The Independent Communications Authority of South Africa (ICASA) had published new regulations in 2003, to ensure equal coverage. However, there were complaints about the public broadcaster covering the ninety-minute launch of the ANC manifesto in Durban without covering similar launches by other parties. The complaint was dismissed, however, because the event occurred before the formal campaign started.[344] Following advice from monitors after the 1999 election, special voting was reduced to one day. The official voting day went smoothly with only minor problems. Further in line with comments by monitors after the 1999 election, the IEC increased the number of voting stations, and the staff was well trained. The staff was tired after the long polling and counting exercises, but the credibility of the counting was boosted by the introduction of independent auditing teams. After the election, EISA had only a few minor recommendations pertaining to the positioning of the voting booths and making ballots easier to tell apart. Finally, the mission urged the use of separate ballot boxes for the provincial and national elections to speed up counting. The mission also urged domestic monitoring organizations to become more active.[345] The SADC was equally positive.[346] The AU was concerned that polling agents sometimes helped voters to fold or mark their ballots, thus seeing their vote,[347] and that late at night some voting stations operated by candlelight. In general, however, the 2004 election went extremely well.[348] As one commentator noted, despite fears to the contrary, "South Africa's first decade of democracy will be remembered for the surprising ease with which seemingly intractable conflict was subjected to the routine functioning of democratic institutions."[349]

The 2009 election also went off very smoothly and was praised by the EISA, the SADC Parliamentary Forum. and the AU alike. Polling stations were still using the same ballot boxes for the national and provincial elections, and some officials were not properly trained in the counting procedures, which slowed up the count. The organizations did recommend a change in the electoral law to prohibit party activities near polling stations, and expressed concern that some stations had run out of voting materials.[350] These, however, were all minor issues. The main concern now is not with the quality of elections, but that a dominant-party regime has emerged.

Notes

CHAPTER ONE: INTRODUCTION

1. Ng 2008.

2. Zakaria 1997; Clark 2000; Carothers 2002; Carothers 2007; Lust-Okar 2009.

3. These organizations are commonly known interchangeably as *international election observers* or *monitors*. Although some organizations assign different meanings to these terms, no clear standard exists. This book therefore uses the terms interchangeably. However, *election supervision* usually does imply something unique, namely, that an organization, usually the United Nations (UN), is engaged in organizing and overseeing the elections.

4. Fairbanks 2004; Usupashivili 2004.

5. Office for Democratic Institutions and Human Rights 2008a.

6. Olearchyk 2008.

7. Puddington 2011, 2. For a definition of an "electoral democracy," see the 2010 Freedom House Report (Puddington 2010, 4.)

8. Dahl 1971. Levitsky and Way 2002; As Schedler argues, Robert Dahl's definition of democracy as civil and political rights plus fair, competitive, and inclusive elections remains widely accepted (2002a, 92).

9. Geisler 1993; Carothers 1997.

10. McIntire and Gettleman 2009.

11. Chand 1997, 559; Clark 2000, 30–31; Levitsky and Way 2005, 55; Calingaert 2006, 147.

12. Chivers 2004.

13. McCoy, Garber, et al. 1991; Anglin 1992; Kumar 1998; McCoy 1998; Pastor 1998; Mulikita 1999; Reilly 2002; Lyons 2004.

14. Beaulieu and Hyde 2009. See also work by Kelley (2012) that argues that monitors actually decrease boycotts.

15. According to the UN, "International election observation is: the systematic, comprehensive and accurate gathering of information concerning the laws, processes and institutions related to the conduct of elections and other factors concerning the overall electoral environment; the impartial and professional analysis of such information; and the drawing of conclusions about the character of electoral processes based on the highest standards for accuracy of information and impartiality of analysis. International election observation should, when possible, offer recommendations for improving the integrity and effectiveness of electoral and related processes, while not interfering in and thus hindering such processes. International election observation missions are: organized efforts of intergovernmental and international nongovernmental organizations and associations to conduct international election observation." United Nations 2005, 2.

16. Dai 2006. This exemplifies what Margaret Keck and Kathryn Sikkink labeled "information politics," whereby transnational actors seek to quickly generate politically usable information for the relevant actors. Keck and Sikkink 1998, 16.

17. Kriegler, Aboud, et al. 2008, 67.

18. Zakaria 1997; Schedler 2002a; Carothers 2007.

19. Freedom House, the U.S. State Department, and the European Commission, for example, all pay considerable attention to the information in the official reports from international monitoring organizations such as the Organization for Security and Cooperation in Europe (OSCE).

20. Levy 2010.

21. Office for Democratic Institutions and Human Rights 2008a.

22. In a joint statement the OSCE said the vote was "in essence consistent with most international standards for democratic elections, [though] significant challenges were revealed which need to be addressed urgently" (Office for Democratic Institutions and Human Rights 2008a). The head of the Council of Europe (COE) delegation said: "This election, although clearly not perfect, enabled the Georgian people to give a democratic response to the recent political crisis. . . . For the sake of the stability of the country I call upon all actors to conclude this election process in a manner that ensures the legitimacy in the eyes of Georgian people." The head of the European Parliament (EP) delegation said: "This election is another step forward in strengthening Georgia's young and still fragile democracy."

23. Russia's foreign ministry, weary of Georgia's pro-Western trajectory and fed up with the role of international observers in recent so-called colored revolutions, criticized the elections, while the deputy U.S. secretary of state said that the vote appeared democratic (Olearchyk, Belton, et al. 2008). The OSCE observer, Dieter Boden, later retracted his statements, claiming they had been misinterpreted.

24. Franck 1992, 50.

25. United Nations 2005, 2.

26. Bob 2002; Sell and Prakash 2004; Carpenter 2007; Stone 2008.

27. The European Union's (EU) Human Rights and Democratization Policy website, http://ec.europa.eu/external_relations/human_rights/eu_election_ass_observ/index.htm, last accessed on March 24, 2009.

28. The EP notes, "The scrutiny of elections is mainly aimed at strengthening the legitimacy of the electoral process, increasing public confidence in the elections, avoiding electoral fraud, better protecting human rights, and contributing to conflict solution." European Parliament 2001, 6, Section G. The Carter Center (CC) boldly claims that "experience around the world has shown that credible and impartial observers can strengthen an electoral process by reassuring voters that they can safely and secretly cast their ballots and that any electoral fraud will be detected." Carter Center 2010b. The Organization of American States (OAS) likewise stresses that "EOMs promote the ability to elect and be elected in an inclusive, free, and transparent fashion, and they help ensure that the popular will expressed by citizens at the ballot box is respected." General Committee 2008.

29. Asian Network for Free Elections 2001, 45.

30. Levitsky and Way 2002, 55.

31. Calingaert 2006, 147.

32. Chand 1997, 559.

33. For a small selection of the many available case studies, see Bjornlund, Bratton, et al. 1992; Anglin 1995; Schmeets and Exel 1997; McCoy 1998; Montgomory 1998; Kaiser 1999; Soremekun 1999; Brown 2000; Foeken and Dietz 2000; Baker 2002; Laakso 2002;

Balian 2003; Dorman 2005; Hart 2006; Hyde 2007; Obi 2008; Teshome-Bahiru 2008. For a sample of regional perspectives, see Anglin 1998; Middlebrook 1998; Abbink and Hesseling 2000; Sives 2001a; Sharon 2004; Gorovoi 2006.

34. Hyde 2007.

35. Bjornlund, Bratton, et al. 1992; Geisler 1993; Anglin 1995; Oquaye 1995; Carothers 1997; Riley 1997; Montgomory 1998; Kaiser 1999; Kew 1999; Foeken and Dietz 2000; Bjornlund 2004; McCoy 2004; Dorman 2005; Santa-Cruz 2005c; Hart 2006; Kriegler, Aboud, et al. 2008; Teshome-Bahiru 2008.

36. Some excellent general studies do exist (Asante 1994; Beigbeder 1994; Santa-Cruz 2005b), but they tend to raise more legal questions or focus on the origins of monitoring. Eric Bjornlund has written an excellent book that does take a global perspective but focuses its analysis exclusively through case studies (Bjornlund 2004).

37. Carter Center 2006b.

38. Johnston 2001; Checkel 2005.

39. Franklin 2008; Hafner-Burton 2008.

40. The common theoretical charge is that they are epiphenomenal, meaning that they merely appear causally related to behavior, but in reality they have no effects independent of the states' initial decisions to participate in them. Strange 1982; Mearsheimer 1994.

41. Crawford 1997; Killick 1997; Hathaway 2002; Knack 2004.

42. Huntington 1991; Whitehead 1996; Levitsky and Way 2005.

43. Lipset 1959; Carothers 1999; Diamond 2006.

44. Bueno de Mesquita and Downs 2006.

45. Hyde 2007, 38.

46. Green and Kohl 2007; Burnell 2008.

47. Lehoucq 2003.

48. European Commission 2007.

49. Davis-Robert and Carroll forthcoming.

50. General Secretariat of the Organization of American States 2007.

51. Elklit and Svensson 1997; Schedler 2002a; Lehoucq 2003; Elklit and Reynolds 2005; Calingaert 2006.

52. Friedrichs and Kratochwil 2009.

CHAPTER TWO: THE RISE OF A NEW NORM

1. This chapter draws partly on Judith Kelley (2008), "Assessing the complex evolution of norms: the rise of international election monitoring," International Organization 62(2): 221–255. Copyright © 2009 The IO Foundation. Reprinted with the permission of Cambridge University Press.

2. Bachman 1991.

3. Office for Democratic Institutions and Human Rights 2005a.

4. United Nations 1991; Elklit and Svensson 1997; Carter Center 2010b.

5. Wright 1964.

6. Garber 1984. For historical overviews, see Wright 1964; Jason 1991; Beigbeder 1994; Hyde 2006, chap. 2. 7. Conference on Security and Co-operation in Europe 1989.

8. Conference on Security and Co-operation in Europe 1990.

9. Organization of American States General Assembly 1990.

10. Conference on Security and Co-operation in Europe 1990.

11. Organization of American States General Assembly 1990.

12. Baker 1990.

13. Franck 1992.

14. Franck 1992, 87.

15. This change was made to appease criticisms by some member states that it unjustly singles out non-Western states for election observation. Thus the Organization for Security and Co-operation in Europe (OSCE) has recently begun to send lighter observation missions labeled "assessment missions" to its established democratic member states. In these "assessment missions," however, the OSCE typically stresses that no systematic election day observation of polling station procedures takes place. This trend, which began roughly with the mission to the 2004 U.S. presidential election, is not covered in this study.

16. Carter Center 2010b. Norms are "collective expectations for the proper behavior of actors with a given identity." Katzenstein 1996, 5. They can be thought of as "a relatively stable collection of practices and rules defining appropriate behavior for specific groups of actors in specific situations." March and Olsen 1998, 948. In that sense, inviting monitors has become an expected behavior for governments that lack strong democratic institutions and therefore domestic checks and balances on the election process.

17. Nadelmann 1990; Cortell and Davis 1996; Finnemore and Sikkink 1998; Checkel 2001; Johnston 2001; Simmons and Elkins 2004.

18. Finnemore and Sikkink 1998, 895.

19. Carter Center 2002.

20. Huntington 1991.

21. After the prolonged Florida election recount of 2000, the OSCE monitored the U.S. elections in 2002 and 2004.

22. Carter Center 1992, 16.

23. Santa-Cruz 2005a.

24. Carter Center undated.

25. This argument goes counter to that of Santa-Cruz. Santa-Cruz 2005a; Santa-Cruz 2005b, 686.

26. Franck 1992, 84; Beigbeder 1994, 104.

27. Franck 1992.

28. Klotz 1995; Prize 1997.

29. Franck 1992, 52.

30. Ebersole 1992–93, 94–95.

31. Dahl 1991.

32. Article 19(2).

33. Article 25.

34. Beigbeder 1994, 238.

35. Lyons and Mastanduno 1993; Barkin and Cronin 1994. Even during the earliest United Nations (UN) monitoring in colonial territories, France, Britain, and Portugal had claimed that the activity constituted interference in their internal affairs; see Asante 1994, 273.

36. Asante 1994, 262–63.

37. Luard 1988, 49.

38. Cutler 1985.

39. Kegley, Raymond, et al. 1998, 89.

40. See Asante 1994, 264; Crawford 1993, 14.

41. Military and Paramilitary Activities in and Against Nicaragua (Nicaragua v. U.S.) 1986 ICJ Rep. 14, 131 (judgment of June 27).

42. Mexican Election Decisions, Cases 9768, 9780, 9828; Inter-Am. C.H.R. 98, OEA/ser. L/V/II.77, doc. 7, rev. 1 (1989–1990), 119–20, cited in Asante 1994, 278.

43. Conference on Security and Co-operation in Europe 1991, Preamble.

44. Flynn and Farrell 1999, 511.

45. Fox 1995.

46. McFaul 2004, 153.

47. Even the UN secretary general noted: "The request for United Nations electoral verification in an independent country generated considerable discussion within the organization and one of the issues was whether the request could be reconciled with the provisions of Article 2, paragraph 7 of the charter. Opinions differed on the existence of an international dimension in the Haitian case." United Nations 1991, 14.

48. Boutros-Ghali 1996, 15–16.

49. United Nations 1988, point 2.

50. This article states that "nothing contained in the Charter shall authorize the United Nations to intervene in matters which are essentially within the domestic jurisdiction of any State."

51. United Nations 2001, point 2.

52. United Nations 2003.

53. Kelley 2008.

54. Franck 1992.

55. Powers and Goetz 2006.

56. Finnemore 1996, 160.

57. Odell 1982; Hall 1989.

58. Barkin and Cronin 1994, 114.

59. Franck 1992, 46–47; Powers and Goetz 2006.

60. Baker 1990.

61. Rich 2001, 22–23.

62. Flynn and Farrell 1999; Youngs 2001b, 2.

63. Bush 1990.

64. Huntington 1991.

65. Jason 1991, 1830–36.

66. Garber 1984, ii.

67. Huntington 1991, chap. 2; Franck 1992.

68. Linz and Stepan 1978; Schmitter and Karl 1991. A survey of eight African countries shows that individuals who perceive of election conduct as proper are more likely to consider the regime legitimate. Elklit and Reynolds 2002.

69. Quezada 1998, 16.

70. Chand 1997, 555. Seemingly it worked. In a pre-election poll 35 to 45 percent of those surveyed expected fraud and 65 percent expected violence. In post-election surveys, after international observers extolled the elections as the cleanest in Mexican history (International Foundation for Electoral Systems 1994, 29), only 24 percent thought that the elections were fraudulent while 61 percent thought they were clean. Council of Freely Elected Heads of State 1995, 10–11.

71. Lyons 2004.

72. United Nations 1991, Add. 2.

73. Bjornlund, Bratton, et al. 1992; Carter Center 1992, , 17.

74. Kingdon 1984.

75. Franck 1992, 87.

76. McCoy 1995, 18.

77. World Bank 1989, 60–61; EBRD 1990; Nelson and Eglinton 1992; Geisler 1993, 614; Kaiser 1999.

78. Geisler 1993, 614.

79. BBC 1992; Marinov 2005.

80. The difference in means in the log of foreign aid in the year before an election is significant at in a t-test at the 0.001 percent level.

81. Because foreign aid recipients are also likely to be poorer and less democratic—both variables associated strongly with the presence of monitors—the motivation for the monitoring is difficult to separate, but the relationship between foreign aid and monitoring is highly statistically significant and it holds even if established democracies are omitted from the analysis.

82. Marinov 2005; Hyde 2009.

83. See Kelley 2004a; Kelley 2004b; Vachudova 2005.

84. Pastor 1993.

85. Scherlen 1998.

86. See Zak 1987; Carothers 1997.

87. Kelley 2009.

88. Of the 442 monitored elections in this study, only 6 were coded as single-party states: 2 in Uganda in 1996 and 2 in Uganda in 2001 as well as elections in Swaziland in 1998 and 2003. These countries also claim that these elections were not under a single-party system, but a nonparty system.

89. Political Risk Group undated, 32.

90. The analysis uses the measure in the year before the election to avoid any change introduced by the election itself.

91. Political Risk Group undated, 29.

92. National Democratic Institute 2000b.

93. For an overview of the activities of different organizations up until the early 1990s, see Beigbeder 1994.

94. European Commission 2000.

95. European Commission 2007.

96. The Council of Europe (COE) and even the European Parliament (EP) occasionally sends delegations to nonmember states. For example, the COE sent a mission to the 2006 Mexican election.

97. Lean 2007a, 157.

98. These different functions are:

1. Organization and conduct of elections as in Cambodia in 1993.
2. Supervision of elections, as Namibia in 1988.
3. Verification of elections when the UN monitors and verifies its outcome as in South Africa 1994.
4. Coordination and support of international observers.
5. Training of domestic observers as in Mexico in 1994.

6. Technical assistance in preparing and organizing elections.

7. Follow and report, which is an internal procedure.

99. African Union 2009.

100. Anglin 1998; Bittiger 2008.

101. Carter Center 2009b.

102. The Electoral Commissions Forum of SADC (ECF) is an independent organization that facilitates cooperation between the electoral authorities of countries in the SADC.

103. United Nations 2005.

104. Garber and Cowen 1994.

CHAPTER THREE: THE SHADOW MARKET

1. Africa News 2002.

2. Fauriol 2006, 4.

3. Chivers 2007.

4. The letter first noted the importance of a successful election and then said: "Having been told that you are such a person who does care about the sustained economic and political growth of Kazakhstan, I decided to write to you to ask if you could kindly consider joining the OSCE [Organization for Security and Co-operation in Europe] observer team through the U.S. quota." The ambassador included email addresses and telephone extensions and asked recipients to "keep us posted" about the application process. Darby 2007.

5. Gershman and Allen 2006, 44.

6. Gorovoi 2006.

7. Potocki 2008, 1.

8. Potocki 2008, 1.

9. Potocki 2008, 3.

10. Munoz-Pogossian 2008.

11. Unit for the Promotion of Democracy 2004a.

12. Geisler 1993; Abbink 2000; Downie 2000, 44; Foeken and Dietz 2000; Brown 2001.

13. Buijtenhuis 2000.

14. United States State Department 2001, Section 3.

15. Laakso 2002, 457.

16. South African Development Community 2000, 18.

17. Commonwealth Observer Group 2000, 32.

18. European Union Election Observation Mission 2000.

19. Patten 2000.

20. "EU [European Union] behaviour (or at least local perceptions of it) allowed Mugabe to claim European arrogance and an infringement on its sovereignty, bolstering its case that Tsvangirai and the MDC [Movement for Democratic Change] are puppets of European interests. Zimbabwe had ruled out UK participants in the EU monitoring team and later added bans on officials from five other EU members, claiming they were all too pro-MDC. The EU insistence that it could name any monitors it wanted—although apparently accepting the ban on UK participation—was then used by Mugabe

and the local pro-government press as an example of neo-imperialism." Oxford Analytica 2002.

21. R. Mugabe, "Address to the nation marking the 2000 parliamentary election results," June 27, 2000.

22. Of the 442 monitored elections in the data, 242 were monitored by more than one of the organizations in the data. Of these, 209 have data on the assessment of more than one organization and can therefore be compared. In 76 of these elections, or 36 percent of the time, monitoring organizations disagreed on their overall assessment of the election.

23. Human Rights Watch 1998.

24. Downie 2000; Bjornlund 2004.

25. National Democratic Institute and International Republican Institute 1998, 2.

26. Downie 2000.

27. National Democratic Institute 1998.

28. International Republican Institute 1999, 4.

29. Joint International Observer Group 1998, 1–2.

30. Holmquist and Ford 1992, 97.

31. Holmquist and Ford 1992, 108.

32. Mutua 1994, 5. An Africa Watch report details the frequent and fatal incidents in 1993.

33. Mutua 1994, 5.

34. Barkan 1998; Ndegwa 1998; Foeken and Dietz 2000, 139; Howard and Roessler 2006.

35. International Republican Institute 1993.

36. Commonwealth Observer Group 1993b, 62.

37. Foeken and Dietz 2000, 145; Brown 2007.

38. European Commission 2007.

39. Davis-Robert and Carroll forthcoming.

40. McCoy 2004.

41. Lowenhardt 2005.

42. Kriegler, Aboud, et al. (2008), 130–32.

43. The following factors are important to interpreting Figure 3.3. Some highly controversial elections are omitted, such as the election in Bosnia and Herzegovina in 1996, when neither the U.S. State Department nor any monitoring organizations were willing to condemn an election. These omissions mean that the figure overestimates the rate of criticisms, in particular for organizations that tend to agree with the U.S. State Department. Second, assessment reports are disproportionately missing for the African Union (AU) and the Economic Community of West African States (ECOWAS), and as a result their rate of criticisms also may be overestimated. The same may be the case for the Organization of American States (OAS), because reports for the OAS before 1990 are not available, and this was a period when the organization tended to be much less critical. Lastly, it is important to note that some organizations have visited few highly problematic missions, either because the organizations are relatively new or because of their unique pattern of activity. For each organization the number of elections is therefore given in the parentheses. Thus, for example, the Carter Center's (CC) percentages are based on only three missions, Haiti in 1995, Mozambique in 1999, and Zambia in 2001. This is because the CC has largely focused on Latin America, and because the U.S.

State Department and other organizations in the area have been less critical of elections in the region.

44. Fawn 2006; Gorovoi 2006.

45. Anglin 1998, 485, 491.

46. Geisler 1993; Sives 2001b.

47. For both the 2007 parliamentary elections and the 2008 presidential elections, the Council of Europe (COE) sent observers to Russia, while the OSCE refrained due to lack of cooperation on the part of the government.

48. Laakso 2002, 445.

49. United States State Department 2001, Section 3.

50. Laakso 2002, 457. A separate mission sent by the Electoral Commission Forum of the SADC countries (ECF) also endorsed the elections.

51. South African Development Community 2000, 18.

52. Commonwealth Observer Group 2000, 32.

53. European Union Election Observation Mission 2000.

54. BBC Worldwide Monitoring, Zambia: OAU secretary-general endorses Mugabe's rejection of foreign observers, February 15, 2002.

55. Solovyov 2008.

56. Solovyov 2008.

57. Anglin 1998; Gorovoi 2006.

58. A Pearson chi2(6) test yields a probability of 0.003. This relationship is also robust in regression analysis. Statistical analysis of countries that invite monitors shows that less democratic countries are less likely to invite high-quality monitors. This is robust to controlling for other factors such as year trends, membership in organizations that conduct monitoring, and the type of the election held, such as whether it was first a multiparty, post-conflict, or post-coup election. For space reasons, the results are not shown. Of course, the absence of more credible monitors does not unequivocally prove that they were not invited—sometimes monitoring organizations simply refuse to go to highly autocratic regimes.

59. United Nations 2005.

Chapter Four: What Influences Monitors' Assessments?

1. Lenarčič 2008, 4.

2. This chapter draws partly on Judith Kelley (2009), "D minus Elections: The politics and norms of international election observation," *International Organization* 63(4): 765–87. Copyright © 2009 The IO Foundation. Reprinted with the permission of Cambridge University Press. The chapter also draws partly on Judith Kelley (2010), "Election Observers and Their Biases," *Journal of Democracy* 21(July): 158–72.

3. Several observers have been interviewed for this book, although most have preferred to remain anonymous. Several of the interviewees are thanked in the Preface. See also Mair 1997; Keohane, Macedo, et al. 2009.

4. Mair 1997.

5. Herman and Brodhead 1984. See especially Appendix 1 on bias in Freedom House missions to Zimbabwe 1979 and 1980, but also general comments of bias throughout the book.

6. Abrahamyan 2008.

7. Eorsi and de Pourbaix-Lundin 2008, 2.

8. European Parliament, Organization for Security and Co-operation in Europe, et al. 2008.

9. Sikkink 2002, 314. This analysis labels both nongovernmental organizations (NGOs) and intergovernmental organizations (IGOs) as transnational actors.

10. Kelley 2008.

11. Geisler 1993; Elklit and Svensson 1997.

12. Zakaria 1997.

13. Grant and Keohane 2005; Keohane, Macedo, et al. 2009.

14. Finnemore and Sikkink 1998; Keck and Sikkink 1998; Cooley and Ron 2002.

15. Bob 2002; Sell and Prakash 2004; Carpenter 2007; Stone 2008.

16. International Institute for Democracy and Electoral Assistance 2000, 11–12.

17. National Democratic Institute 1996a, 1.

18. National Democratic Institute 1996b, 3.

19. Commission of the European Union undated, Section G.

20. Kriegler, Aboud, et al. 2008, 67.

21. Fish 2005, 47.

22. Office for Democratic Institutions and Human Rights 2000b.

23. Office for Democratic Institutions and Human Rights 1999c.

24. Office for Democratic Institutions and Human Rights 2000b, 2.

25. Office for Democratic Institutions and Human Rights 2000b, 14.

26. Office for Democratic Institutions and Human Rights 2000b, 20, 29, 30, 31, 32.

27. Office for Democratic Institutions and Human Rights 2000b, 2.

28. Office for Democratic Institutions and Human Rights 2000b, 14.

29. Office for Democratic Institutions and Human Rights 2000b, 12, 15–20, 33–34.

30. Fish 2005, 47.

31. Fish 2005, 47–48.

32. Reported in Fish 2005, 47.

33. Office for Democratic Institutions and Human Rights 1996c, 1.

34. Office for Democratic Institutions and Human Rights 1996d, 1.

35. International Crisis Group 1996; Riley 1997; Downie 2000, 44.

36. Fawn 2006.

37. Stone 2004, 577.

38. Barnett and Finnemore 2001; Nielson and Tierney 2003.

39. Personal interview with Betilde Munuz-Pogossian, coordinator, Unit for Electoral Studies, Organization of American States (OAS), Washington, D.C., April 10, 2008. Commission of the European Union Undated, Section E.

40. Bob 2002; Carpenter 2007.

41. Brown and Moore 2001, 572.

42. A Democracy Score was created for each intergovernmental organization based on the polity2 variable from the Polity IV dataset. The score is the average level of democracy in all the member states of the organization in the year before the election. The score is 0 for NGOs, and an indicator variable is created for Western NGOs.

43. Carothers 1997; Elklit and Svensson 1997; McCoy 1998, 84.

44. International Institute for Democracy and Electoral Assistance 2000, 11–12.

45. Kew 1999, 30; Obi 2008, 75.

46. Kew 1999, 30.

47. Alesina and Dollar 2000.

48. As Robert Pastor argues, "foreign governments and funders with a stake in an election want the process approved quickly so that a new government can take hold." Pastor 1998, 159.

49. Bjornlund 2004.

50. As an aside, larger foreign aid recipients also were more likely to be monitored. For the source of the foreign aid variable, see the Appendix A, Table A.6.

51. Fish 2005, 50.

52. This dilemma is similar to that of other organizations that seek to promote various domestic reforms. Stone 2002; Kelley 2004a.

53. Joint International Observation Group 1998, 1–2.

54. International Republican Institute 1993, Appendix 11.

55. For a definition of first multiparty elections, see the Appendix A. First multiparty elections are defined as the first multiparty general election, the first multiparty legislative election, or the first multiparty executive election. In countries holding separate legislative and executive elections, both the first multiparty executive and the first multiparty legislative elections are coded as first multiparty elections, resulting in these countries having two first multiparty elections. Multiparty elections in newly independent countries are also coded as first multiparty elections. Thus, nearly 10 percent of all the elections in the data, or 127 elections, are first multiparty elections.

56. Bratton 1998.

57. Ward and Gleditsch 1998.

58. International Institute for Democracy and Electoral Assistance 2000, 12; van Kessel 2000.

59. Laakso 2002, 458.

60. Patten 2000.

61. Brown 2007.

62. Oxford Analytica April 2002, 1–2.

63. Reuters, "Kenya Votes in Close Polls," December 28, 2007.

64. European Union Election Observation Mission 2008, 27.

65. International Republican Institute 2007a.

66. Fish 2005, 49.

67. Galbraith 2009.

68. Donno 2010.

69. McCoy 1993.

70. United Nations 2005, 3.

71. Franck 1992, 51.

72. Franck 1992, 51.

CHAPTER FIVE: DO POLITICIANS CHANGE TACTICS TO EVADE CRITICISM?

1. For example, Thomas Carothers suggests that "the art of manipulating elections has developed just as rapidly as the art of aiding elections" (1999, 335)." And discussing "a panoply of alternative means of electoral containment" that politicians use, Andreas Schedler argues that "it appears, old dogs do learn new tricks" (Schedler 2002b, 105)." See also Emily Beulieu and Susan Hyde (2009), who suggest that boycotts are increasing because monitors are prompting a strategic shift in cheating.

2. Office for Democratic Institutions and Human Rights 2006, 3.

3. Schedler 2002b.

4. Schedler 2002b, 106.

5. Ottaway 2003.

6. Schedler 2002a, 40–41.

7. Case 1996, 437.

8. Rupnik 2007.

9. Santa-Cruz 2005c.

10. Huntington 1991; Valenzuela 2004.

11. Linz and Stepan 1996.

12. Geisler 1993; Carothers 1997.

13. Gandhi and Przeworski 2009.

14. For elections with more than one observer mission, the highest level of irregularities reported is used, on the assumption that monitoring organizations are much more likely to underreport irregularities than to manufacture or exaggerate them. Unsupported allegations of irregularities are not given as much weight as documented irregularities.

15. That is, one in three elections has the highest level of irregularities in either election day cheating, or the highest level of pre-election cheating, or the highest level of legal problems. Ninety-three out of 292 monitored elections with sufficient documentation to be coded on these variables contained the highest level of irregularities in at least one of these three categories.

16. They hide some of the detail of the data because they simply show the direction of a shift, not its magnitude. Thus, a decrease from the highest to the middle level appears as the same as a decrease from middle level to the lowest level, for example. However, having examined the more detailed data, this simplification actually represents the general trends well and is much clearer to read.

17. Note that some shift from overt cheating on election day to overt cheating before the election does not count as a decrease in overt cheating; there must be a net decrease in the combined categories (changes in timing are considered later).

18. There are twenty-four cases where the level of safer irregularities was moderate and the level of obvious cheating was low. These could be examined in greater detail too, but it is more compelling to look at the cases where the safer forms of irregularities were higher.

19. Fawn 2006.

20. Puddington 2011, 1.

CHAPTER SIX: INTERNATIONAL MONITORS AS REINFORCEMENT

1. United Nations 2005, 2.

2. Eorsi and de Pourbaix-Lundin 2008, 1.

3. Asian Network for Free Elections 2001, 45. The European Union (EU) argues, "Election observation can . . . help deter fraud (European Union's Human Rights and Democratization Policy website: http://ec.europa.eu/external_relations/human_rights/eu_election_ass_observ/index.htm, last accessed on March 24, 2009)." And the Carter Center (CC) claims that "experience around the world has shown that credible and impartial observers can strengthen an electoral process by reassuring voters that they can

safely and secretly cast their ballots and that any electoral fraud will be detected" (Carter Center 2010b)."

4. Diamond 1991, 7.
5. Bjornlund, Bratton, et al. 1992, 429.
6. Carothers 1997, 20.
7. For simplicity this chapter mainly discusses governments as the targets of international monitoring, but opposition parties may also cheat in elections.
8. Monga 1997, 165.
9. Stein 1982; Keohane 1984.
10. Hyde 2007.
11. Ichino and Schundeln 2010.
12. Levitsky and Way 2002, 55.
13. Herman and Brodhead 1984, 7–9; Scranton 1997.
14. National Democratic Institute and International Republican Institute 1989, 57.
15. Carter Center 2010a.
16. Carter Center 2010b.
17. United Nations 2005, 1.
18. Donno 2010.
19. Larson and Callahan 1990.
20. Stone 2002; Nielson and Tierney 2003.
21. Commission of the European Communities 2000, 16–17.
22. Brown and Moore 2001; Cooley and Ron 2002.
23. Keohane 1982, 346; Simmons 2000; Guzman 2002.
24. For more on the debate, see footnote 58.
25. World Bank 1989, 60–61.
26. Posner 1995, 138.
27. Donno 2010, 594.
28. Huntington 1991; Remmer 1995; Schimmelfennig, Engert, et al. 2003; Jacoby 2004; Schneider and Schmitter 2004; Vachudova 2005.
29. Franck 1992.
30. Schedler 2002b.
31. Kelley 2008.
32. Przeworski 1991; Weingast 1997; Hyde 2007; Tucker 2007.
33. McFaul 2005, 7.
34. Santa-Cruz 2005b, 82.
35. Stepan 1988.
36. Diamond 1991, 7.
37. International Republican Institute. 2004a.
38. European Union Election Observation Mission 2003.
39. Carter Center 1992, 12–13, 40–41.
40. See Figure 2.8 and accompanying discussion.
41. United Nations 2005, 2.
42. Checkel 1998; Johnston 2001; Risse 2003; Kelley 2004a; Checkel 2005.
43. Finnemore and Sikkink 1998.
44. Chand 1997, 547.
45. Simmons 2009.

46. The Organization for Security and Co-operation in Europe (OSCE) calls these missions "assessment missions."

47. For an overview, see Geddes 1999; Gleditsch and Ward 2006.

48. Carothers 1999, 304.

49. Johnston 2001.

50. Strohal undated.

51. Fox 1994, 110.

52. Monga 1997, 165.

53. Roessler 2005.

54. Rodrik 1997.

55. For example, Haas, Keohane, et al. 1993; Weiss and Jacobson 2000.

56. Checkel 2000; Kelley 2004a; Vachudova 2005; Kelley 2006; Levitsky and Way 2006.

57. Johnston 2001.

58. Research on conditionality is divided on its efficacy. Several scholars have found that linking political reforms to membership in international organizations like the EU has been effective (Schimmelfennig, Engert, et al. 2003; Jacoby 2004; Kelley 2004b; Vachudova 2005). However, scholars of economic conditionality are more divided about whether it can achieve positive economic policy changes (Mosley, Harrigan, et al. 1995; Collier 1997; Crawford 1997; Killick 1997). They point to numerous weaknesses in how the international financial institutions have implemented conditionality (Hermes and Lensink 2001). Direct sanctions have also long been criticized not only as impracticable and even harmful, but also as mostly unable to induce change (Hufbauer, Schott, et al. 2001). Some scholars disagree, however, pointing to effective cases such as South Africa. One study suggests that conditionality in preferential trade agreements has been effective at promoting human rights and democracy (Hafner-Burton and Tsutsui 2005). Scholars have also argued that we have underestimated the effects of sanctions by looking only at cases where they were implemented, and not at cases where the mere threats to use sanctions changed government behavior (Drezner 2003).

59. Levitsky and Way 2010, 40-50.

60. Donno 2010.

61. Hufbauer et al. 1990, 12; Levitsky and Way 2010, 41.

62. Epstein and Sedelmeier 2008; Sasse 2008; Sedelmeier 2008.

CHAPTER SEVEN: ARE MONITORED ELECTIONS BETTER?

1. The variable *Election Quality* is correlated at 0.75 with the Freedom House variable that codes countries that are "not free" = 0, "partly free" = 1, and "free" = 2. It is correlated at 0.81 with the polity2 variable. The "Problems" variable is correlated at -0.83 with the Freedom House variable and -0.85 with the polity2 variable.

2. Poe, Carey, et al. 2001.

3. Note that first elections in newly independent states, if multiparty, are considered as first multiparty elections as well and therefore also excluded.

4. Rubin and Thomas 1996; Clarke 2005.

5. Ho, Imai, et al. 2007.

6. Sartori 2003; Signorino 2003; Simmons and Hopkins 2005.

7. For an overview and technical aspects, see Mebane and Sekhon 1998; Diamond and Sekhon 2008; Sekhon and Grieve 2008.

8. If a candidate control variable has no observable or theoretical relationship with the outcome variable, its inclusion in a model decreases estimation efficiency and may lead to biased inference if it is correlated with one of the model variables. Achen 2005.

9. The variables 1–7 are all described under "Country variables" in Appendix A, Table A.6. The eighth variable, the quality of the previous election, is the lagged dependent variable.

10. I acknowledge with gratitude the highly professional contribution of Mark Buntaine to the matching analysis in this chapter.

11. The logistic regression techniques used to estimate variables' effects assumes that each variable has a constant effect on the linear predictor regardless of its level or that of another covariate. Not enough data are available to empirically confirm that monitoring does not influence election outcomes in single-party states, as only six elections were monitored in single-party states in this dataset. With so few observations, matching within the single-party only subset is not possible. Given the high risk of selection bias if single-party observations were to be included and the inability to balance on this variable, it is best excluded from analysis. Likewise, because highly democratic states have so little variation in election quality, modeling the effect of monitoring is not feasible. Furthermore, empirically and theoretically monitoring should not influence highly democratic elections. Thus, the analysis below excludes single-party states and established democracies.

12. For more on logistic regression, see Hilbe 2009.

13. Comparison of the coefficients is not definitive, because they are based on different samples, due to the matching process. Furthermore, the coefficient on monitors in Model 7 is higher than that in Model 6, but they do overlap within 1 standard deviation.

CHAPTER EIGHT: LONG-TERM EFFECTS

1. Kiljunen 2008.

2. Both elections in Serbia and in Montenegro were counted as national elections.

3. Office for Democratic Institutions and Human Rights 1997b.

4. International Republican Institute 1996c, 2.

5. For a detailed accounting of which recommendations were followed, see International Republican Institute 1996c, Appendix IX.

6. International Republican Institute 1996c, 2.

7. Carter Center 2006a, 39.

8. International Republican Institute 1992.

9. European Union Election Observation Mission 2001c, 5.

10. National Democratic Institute 2009, 5.

11. Maniruzzaman 1992, 59. See further the case summary in Appendix E.

12. Kabemba 2003, 17.

13. Interview with Denis Kadima, deputy leader of the observer mission sent to Lesotho by the Electoral Institute of Southern Africa (EISA). IRIN Humanitarian News and Analysis 2007.

14. Saari 2009.

15. Council of Europe Parliamentary Assembly 1996b, 4; Office for Democratic Institutions and Human Rights 2003c, 3.

16. Carothers 1997, 23.

17. Office for Democratic Institutions and Human Rights 2000a, 2.

18. Council of Europe Parliamentary Assembly 2008a, 5.

19. Mutua 1994, 5. An Africa Watch report details the frequent and fatal incidents 1993.

20. International Republican Institute 1993.

21. Commonwealth Observer Group 1993b, 62.

22. Foeken and Dietz 2000, 145; Brown 2007.

23. Carter Center 2009a.

24. Lopez-Pintor 1998.

25. Carter Center 2006a, 16.

26. Croissant 1998.

27. Gross 2009.

28. Gordon 1998.

29. Council of Europe Parliamentary Assembly 1996c, 1.

30. Dresser 1994, 58.

31. Likmeta 2009.

32. Youngs 2001a, 5.

33. McFaul 2004, 157.

34. Council of Europe Parliamentary Assembly 2000b.

35. Lipset 1959; Carothers 1999; Diamond 2006.

36. Henderson 2002.

37. In *Afrobarometor* Surveys Lesotho citizens consistently recorded the lowest support for democracy in the South African Development Community (SADC) region. Kabemba 2003, 13.

38. Office for Democratic Institutions and Human Rights 2008b, 28–29.

39. International Foundation for Electoral Systems 1999b, 29.

40. Quezada 1998, 178.

41. Carter Center 2000, 7.

42. Pastor 2000.

43. Chand 1997, 558.

44. International Foundation for Electoral Systems 2006.

45. Fairbanks 2004; Bunce and Wolchik 2009.

46. Peceny 1999; Bueno de Mesquita and Downs 2006.

47. National Democratic Institute and International Republican Institute 1989, 57.

48. The measure used here is the election monitors' overall assessment of the quality of the election as well as measures by Freedom House on the status of political rights in the country.

49. Commencement Address at American University in Washington, June 10, 1963.

50. A similar argument about the substance of reforms is found in work on the influence of European Institutions on ethnic monitory policies in Eastern European and Baltic countries. Kelley 2004a, conclusion.

CONCLUSION: THE GOOD, THE BAD, AND THE UGLY

1. Elklit 1999, 47.

2. Gettleman 2010.

3. Joint International Observation Group 1998, 1–2.

4. Patten 2000.

5. Commission of the European Communities 2000, 16–17.

6. United Nations 2005.

7. European Union Election Observation Mission 2001b, cover page. Such disclaimers remain routine.

8. United Nations 2005, 2, paragraph 4.

9. Office for Democratic Institutions and Human Rights 1999b, Chapter 14.

10. International Republican Institute 1994, 86–87.

11. See Chapter 4 for this example.

12. Compare, for example, statements in the pre-election delegation report to the 2008 Bangladesh election (National Democratic Institute 2008a, 1) with those in the final report (National Democratic Institute 2009, 1).

13. Kelley 2009, 62.

14. Office for Democratic Institutions and Human Rights, European Parliament, et al. 2008.

15. Kelley 2009. See also the opening quote to Chapter 3.

16. Council of Europe Parliamentary Assembly 2004, paragraph 30.

17. European Union Election Observation Mission 2002, 7.

18. For more discussion of this, see also Bjornlund 2004, 307.

19. Council of Europe Parliamentary Assembly 2000a, paragraphs 28–29.

20. United Nations Development Programme 2000, 24; Kelley 2009, 62.

21. Council of Europe Parliamentary Assembly 2007, appended memorandum, paragraph 10. Similarly, in 1994 in Mexico, the Carter Center (CC) recommended the limitation of private purchase of media spots. But in 2006 the European Union (EU) noted that Article 48.13 of the Election Law, which prohibits third persons to campaign through paid advertising in the broadcast media, appears to violate the citizen's right to freedom of expression as set out in Article 19 of the United Nations (UN) Universal Declaration of Human Rights. Such a restriction should therefore be removed from the Law." European Union Election Observation Mission 2006a, 53.

22. In the Cameroon in 1997, for example, the Commonwealth Secretariat (CS) thought it important to be present so that La Francophonie would not be the only organization rendering an assessment. Anglin 1998, 485.

23. General Committee 2008, 32; Davis-Robert and Carroll forthcoming.

24. Elklit 1999, 34.

25. International Institute for Democracy and Electoral Assistance 1995.

26. See, for example, Council of the European Union 2005.

27. Levy 2010.

28. Lipset 1959; Carothers 1999; Diamond 2006.

29. Elklit also notes the need for international experts to first address the many prerequisite legal and operational aspects of the electoral process before sending in international observers. Elklit 1999, 48.

30. Much has been written on this important topic. For a sample of useful studies on election and conflict, see Kumar 1998; Ottaway 1998; Sisk and Reynolds 1998; Mulikita 1999; Snyder 2000; Reilly 2002; Lyons 2004.

31. Schimpp and McKernan 2001.

32. Bratton 1998.

33. The declaration notes that "international election observation missions are expected to issue timely, accurate and impartial statements to the public. . . . presenting their findings, conclusions." United Nations 2005, 3, Article 7.

34. National Democratic Institute 2000a, 2.

35. Author's personal experience with attempting to obtain the report.

36. Møller and Skanning 2010; Levitsky and Way 2010.

37. Argersinger 1985.

38. Pastor 2004.

39. Kennedy 1963.

40. Carter Center 2000, 7–8.

41. Personal communication with Carter Center staff. Caroll 2010.

42. Lean 2007b.

43. Garber and Cowen 1994; Estok, Nevitte, et al. 2002; Bjornlund 2006.

44. For the 1987 Philippine elections, the National Democratic Institute (NDI) invited nationals of Bangladesh, Haiti, Chile, Korea, Panama, Pakistan, Paraguay, and Taiwan to participate in the delegation. Many of the individuals returned to their respective countries inspired by the Philippine experience in election reform and monitoring and, more important, with specific ideas that they sought to implement in their respective countries. For example: Jose Miguel Barros of Chile became a leader of the Committee for Free Elections (CEL), which played a critical role in ensuring the fairness of the October 5, 1988, plebiscite; Jean Claude Roi, in his role as technical advisor to the provisional election committee in Haiti, introduced a voter registration system based on the Philippine model; Aurelio Barria of Panama organized the National Civic Crusade, modeled on the National Citizens' Movement for Free Elections (NAMFREL). Barria became its first chairman, before being exiled; Father Fernando Guardi, also of Panama, stimulated church involvement in encouraging fair elections and played a critical role in establishing a church-sponsored quick count operation.

APPENDIX A: DATA DESCRIPTION

1. More information on the project, including coding books and manuals, can be found online at the website for the Project on International Election Monitoring: http://press.princeton.edu/titles/9748.html. Additional discussion of the data can also be found in Kelley and Kolev 2010.

2. For the criteria for what counted as a mission, see the discussion of the "Monitors" variables in the tables below.

3. See footnote 1.

4. Poe, Carey, et al. 2001.

5. Elklit and Svensson 1997; Elklit 1999; Elklit and Reynolds 2002; Schedler 2002a; Lehoucq 2003; Elklit and Reynolds 2005.

6. International Institute for Democracy and Electoral Assistance 1995; General Secretariat of the Organization of American States 2007; General Committee 2008; Commission of the European Union undated.

7. European Commission 2007.

8. The full coding rules are available online at http://press.princeton.edu/titles/9748.html.

APPENDIX B: STATISTICAL SUPPLEMENT TO CHAPTER 3

1. Using the level of democracy in the same year yields similar results.
2. Using the clarify method. Tomz, Wittenberg, et al. 2003.
3. The 95 percent confidence interval ranges from 45 to 2 percent. Results not shown.

APPENDIX D: STATISTICAL SUPPLEMENT TO CHAPTER 7

1. Rubin 1973; Donald 1979.
2. Ho, Imai, et al. 2007, 205.
3. Simmons and Hopkins 2005.
4. Ho, Imai, et al. 2007, 216–24.
5. Rubin and Thomas 1996.
6. For write-up of the software package, see Sekhon 2007.
7. Ho, Imai, et al. 2007.
8. Ho, Imai, et al. 2007, 18.
9. For an overview and technical aspects, see Mebane and Sekhon 1998; Diamond and Sekhon 2008; Sekhon and Grieve 2008.
10. Dehejia and Wahba 1999.
11. King and Zeng 2007.
12. King and Zeng 2007.

APPENDIX E: CASE SUMMARIES

1. We are grateful to Valerie Bunce, Jorgen Elklit, Devin Hagerty, Susan Hyde, Jennifer McCoy, and Andreas Schedler, who have offered their country expertise on several of these cases. Any remaining errors naturally remain our own.
2. Levitsky and Way 2005, 33.
3. Halperin and Lomasney 1998, 135.
4. International Republican Institute 1996a, 15.
5. Office for Democratic Institutions and Human Rights 1996b, 2.
6. Office for Democratic Institutions and Human Rights 1997a, 7.
7. Office for Democratic Institutions and Human Rights 1997a, 5.
8. Office for Democratic Institutions and Human Rights 1997a, 1.
9. Office for Democratic Institutions and Human Rights 2001, 1.
10. Organization for Security and Co-operation in Europe Presence in Albania 2000, 2.
11. Organization for Security and Co-operation in Europe Presence in Albania 2000, 3.
12. Office for Democratic Institutions and Human Rights 2001.
13. Office for Democratic Institutions and Human Rights 2003b, 2–3.
14. Office for Democratic Institutions and Human Rights 2009a, 5.
15. Council of Europe Parliamentary Assembly 2009b, paragraph 9.
16. Office for Democratic Institutions and Human Rights 2003b, 1.
17. Organization for Security and Co-operation in Europe Presence in Albania 2004, 1.
18. Organization for Security and Co-operation in Europe Presence in Albania 2004, 1.
19. Elbasani 2004, 40.
20. Office for Democratic Institutions and Human Rights 2005b, 1.
21. Likmeta 2009.

22. Office for Democratic Institutions and Human Rights 2009a, 1.

23. Croissant 1998.

24. Weitz 2008, 1.

25. Astourian 2000.

26. Coalson and Tamrazian 2009.

27. Hyde 2007, 39.

28. Council of Europe Parliamentary Assembly 2000b.

29. Nichol 2006, 12.

30. Ruiz-Rufino 2007, 1.

31. Ruiz-Rufino 2007, 2.

32. Office for Democratic Institutions and Human Rights 2007b, 28–31.

33. Transitions Online 2008.

34. Office for Democratic Institutions and Human Rights 1996a.

35. Office for Democratic Institutions and Human Rights 1999a, 3.

36. Office for Democratic Institutions and Human Rights 2002a, 4.

37. Office for Democratic Institutions and Human Rights 2002b, 4.

38. Office for Democratic Institutions and Human Rights 2003d.

39. Office for Democratic Institutions and Human Rights 2003a.

40. International Institute for Democracy and Electoral Assistance.

41. Office for Democratic Institutions and Human Rights 2005c, 5.

42. Office for Democratic Institutions and Human Rights 2007b.

43. European Commission for Democracy Through Law (Venice Commission) and Office for Democratic Institutions and Human Rights 2007, 3.

44. Office for Democratic Institutions and Human Rights 2007b, 2.

45. National Democratic Institute 1999a.

46. Office for Democratic Institutions and Human Rights 2003a, 23–24.

47. European Parliament 2007, 3.

48. Office for Democratic Institutions and Human Rights 2008b.

49. Office for Democratic Institutions and Human Rights 2008b, 28–29.

50. Ahmed 2003, 59. He notes, "As an example, reference can be made to the attempt by donors and international election observer teams to persuade the BNP [Bangladesh Nationalist Party] to accept the results of the seventh parliamentary elections held in 1996. The BNP initially refused to concede defeat, alleging that the BAL [Bangladesh Awami League], in connivance with the Election Commission, snatched away a victory that was due to it. The representatives of important diplomatic missions in Bangladesh met the BNP chief and requested her to accept the election results. Various international election observer teams, such as the National Democratic Institute (NDI) team, the EEC [European Economic Community] team, and the Japanese team also called upon the BNP to accept the defeat graciously and with dignity. Ultimately, the BNP agreed to join the seventh parliament. It is not argued that other factors were unimportant in influencing the decision of the BNP not to reject the election results outright. What is observed here is that the BNP was aware of the dangers associated with challenging the opinion of the international teams of observers and the opinion of the representatives of major donor agencies; hence it acquiesced."

51. Karim and Fair 2007, 1.

52. National Democratic Institute 1991, 7.

53. National Democratic Institute 1991, 7–8.

54. National Democratic Institute 1991, 10.
55. Carter Center and National Democratic Institute 2001; European Union Election Observation Mission 2001a.
56. National Democratic Institute 1991; Commonwealth Observer Group 1996; National Democratic Institute 1996b.
57. Asian Network for Free Elections 2001, 7.
58. National Democratic Institute 2009, 5.
59. National Democratic Institute 1996b.
60. Nevitte and Canton 1997, 55.
61. Commonwealth Observer Group 2008.
62. National Democratic Institute 2008b.
63. National Democratic Institute 1991, 23.
64. National Democratic Institute 2008b, 8.
65. National Democratic Institute 2009, 19.
66. National Democratic Institute 2009, 9.
67. Bulgarian Radio 1997, 9.
68. National Democratic Institute and International Republican Institute 1991, 33.
69. National Democratic Institute and International Republican Institute 1990, 2.
70. National Democratic Institute and International Republican Institute 1991.
71. Council of Europe Parliamentary Assembly 1997.
72. Office for Democratic Institutions and Human Rights 2009b, 12.
73. International Republican Institute 1996b.
74. Office for Democratic Institutions and Human Rights 2005d, 6.
75. Youngs 2001a, 29.
76. McFaul 2004, 157.
77. Forsythe and Rieffer 2000, 1003.
78. Call 2002.
79. Herman and Brodhead 1984; Munck 1993.
80. Baloyra 1993.
81. Baloyra-Herp 1995, 52.
82. Kelley 2008. See also Chapter 2.
83. Herman and Bello 1984; Stahler-Sholk 1994.
84. Munck 1993.
85. International Republican Institute 1991, 28.
86. Montgomery 1998.
87. Stahler-Sholk 1994, 9.
88. Unit for the Promotion of Democracy 2000.
89. International Republican Institute 1991, 28; Hartlyn, McCoy, et al. 2008, 90.
90. Call 2002, 582–83.
91. Wolf 2009.
92. Barnes 1998, 69.
93. International Republican Institute 2004b. Curiously, the International Republican Institute (IRI) never publicly issued anything beyond a two-page preliminary statement.
94. This was a big improvement over the January local and legislative elections when three-quarters of all polling stations opened at least half an hour late.
95. European Union Election Observation Mission 2009a.
96. European Union Election Observation Mission 2009a, 4.

97. Department of Electoral Cooperation and Observation 2009.

98. European Union Election Observation Mission 2009b, 2.

99. Department of Electoral Cooperation and Observation 2009.

100. CommonBorders 2004, 15; Committee in Solidarity with the People of El Salvador 2009. CommonBorders states that "Many people believed that the U.S. government could and would prohibit the over two billion U.S. dollars in family remittances (equaling 14 percent of El Salvador's GDP) from even entering the country. Many people, especially in the poorest and most rural regions, told us that fear of losing family remittances was their major rationale for supporting the ARENA [Alianza Republicana Nacionalista] candidate. Fear surrounding the impact of an FMLN [Farabundo Marti National Liberation Front] victory on U.S.-El Salvador relations was further incited by the public statements made by prominent U.S.-government representatives in the months and weeks leading up to the election.... Many in El Salvador and abroad felt these comments were not respectful of the autonomy of the Salvadoran people or their rights to a free and fair democratic process." CommonBorders 2004, 15.

101. CommonBorders 2004, 15; Committee in Solidarity with the People of El Salvador 2009.

102. Committee in Solidarity with the People of El Salvador 2009, 6.

103. Committee in Solidarity with the People of El Salvador 2009, 5.

104. For the front page of the newspaper *Diario de Hoy*, see http://www.borev.net/assets_c/2009/03/DiarioDeHoy1.html. Last accessed on April 10. 2010.

105. Committee in Solidarity with the People of El Salvador 2009, 6.

106. Council of Europe Parliamentary Assembly 1996a.

107. Tudoroiu 2007.

108. Freedom House 2008.

109. Office for Democratic Institutions and Human Rights 1992.

110. Council of Europe Parliamentary Assembly 1996a, paragraph 61.

111. Bunce and Wolchik 2011, chapter 6 (pages not yet known).

112. Mitchell 2009.

113. Fairbanks 2004; Bunce and Wolchik 2009.

114. On Soros funding, some Liberty Institute associates from Georgia traveled to Serbia to study how Slobodan Milosevic had been ousted. Commission on Security and Cooperation in Europe 2004, 4.

115. Office for Democratic Institutions and Human Rights 2004b, 21.

116. Office for Democratic Institutions and Human Rights 2004b, 9.

117. Lanskoy and Areshidze 2008, 155.

118. Mitchell and Sidamon-Eristoff 2009.

119. Office for Democratic Institutions and Human Rights 2008a.

120. Jones 2006; Tudoroiu 2007.

121. Office for Democratic Institutions and Human Rights 2007a, 3.

122. Office for Democratic Institutions and Human Rights 2008a.

123. Olearchyk 2008.

124. Office for Democratic Institutions and Human Rights 2008a.

125. Olearchyk 2008.

126. Council of Europe Parliamentary Assembly 2008b, paragraph 1.

127. International Republican Institute 2008a.

128. National Democratic Institute 2008c, 3.

129. Office for Democratic Institutions and Human Rights 2004b, 9.
130. Now also cooperating with the North Atlantic Treaty Organization (NATO) Parliamentary Assembly.
131. Council of Europe Parliamentary Assembly 2009a, 5.
132. Carter Center 1992, 17.
133. Carter Center 1992, 18.
134. Carroll and Pastor 1993, 10.
135. European Union Election Observation Mission 2001c, 5.
136. Carroll and Pastor 1993.
137. Bynoe, Thomas, et al. 2007, 102.
138. Carter Center 1992, 19.
139. Kahn 1990.
140. Carter Center 1992, 25.
141. Carroll and Pastor 1993, 10.
142. Carter Center 1992, 12–13.
143. Commonwealth Observer Group 1998.
144. Commonwealth Observer Group 2001, 11.
145. Under the memorandum of understanding (MOU), funding was secured from the European Union (EU), Inter-American Development Bank (IDB), United States Agency for International Development (USAID), United Kingdom Department for International Development (UKDFID), Canadian International Development Agency (CIDA) and United Nations Development Programme (UNDP). See http://www.gecom.org.gy/pdf/elections_MOU.pdf.
146. Carter Center 2001a, 9.
147. Commonwealth Observer Group 2001.
148. Carter Center 2001a, 7.
149. Carter Center 2001a, 37.
150. Carter Center 2001a.
151. Carter Center 2001a, 13.
152. European Union Election Observation Mission 2001c, 3.
153. BBC 2002.
154. Commonwealth Observer Group 2006, 42.
155. Commonwealth Observer Group 2006, 16.
156. Carter Center 2001a, 49.
157. Government of Guyana 2005.
158. Commonwealth Observer Group 2006, 25.
159. Commonwealth Observer Group 2006, 55.
160. Unit for the Promotion of Democracy 2006, iv.
161. International Foundation for Electoral Systems 2009.
162. International Foundation for Electoral Systems 2009, 9–10.
163. International Foundation for Electoral Systems 2009, 20–21.
164. International Foundation for Electoral Systems 2009, 10.
165. International Foundation for Electoral Systems 2009, 21.
166. Chand 1997, 547.
167. Commonwealth Observer Group 2006, 14.
168. Beech 2009; Mujani and Liddle 2009; Sukma 2009; The Economist 2009.
169. Diamond 2009.

170. Beech 2009; Mujani and Liddle 2009; Sukma 2009; The Economist 2009.

171. Bjornlund 2004, 277.

172. Diamond 2009.

173. Ellis 1998; National Democratic Institute 1999b.

174. Bjornlund 2004, 256–57.

175. Bjornlund 2004, 257. Eric Bjornlund further details the unintended consequences of the foreign support for domestic monitoring groups. Bjornlund 2004, chap. 12.

176. Sukma 2009.

177. Asian Network for Free Elections 2009, 6.

178. Asian Network for Free Elections 2009, 22.

179. Bjornlund 2004, 274–76.

180. Bjornlund 2004, 290–93.

181. Asian Network for Free Elections 2009, 46.

182. National Democratic Institute and Carter Center 1999, 3.

183. Dagg 2007.

184. National Democratic Institute 2005, 18.

185. Carter Center 2009a, 14.

186. International Foundation for Electoral Systems 1999a, 2.

187. European Parliament 2004, 6.

188. European Union Election Observation Mission 2004, 24.

189. European Union Election Observation Mission 1999, Sec 8.

190. European Union Election Observation Mission 2004, 25.

191. European Union Election Observation Mission 2004, 23–24.

192. European Union Election Observation Mission 2004, 25.

193. Carter Center 2009a, 15.

194. Carter Center 2009a, 18–19.

195. European Union Election Observation Mission 1999, Sec 5.2.

196. National Democratic Institute and Carter Center 1999, 22.

197. National Democratic Institute and Carter Center 1999, 15.

198. European Union Election Observation Mission 2004, 40.

199. Carter Center 2009a, 5.

200. Carter Center 2009a, 30.

201. European Union Election Observation Mission 2004, 33.

202. Quoted in Croissant and Martin 2006, 138.

203. Sukma 2009.

204. International Republican Institute 1992.

205. International Republican Institute 1992, 6.

206. Barkan and Ng'ethe 1998.

207. Ajulu 1998.

208. Election Observation Centre 1998, Executive summary.

209. Commonwealth Observer Group 2002.

210. Howard and Roessler 2006.

211. European Union Election Observation Mission 2002.

212. Gibson and Long 2009.

213. Holmquist and Ford 1992.

214. Carter Center 2003.

215. Bosire 2008.

216. Africa Watch 1993.
217. Geisler 1993.
218. Holmquist and Ford 1994, 8.
219. Brown 2001, 95; Nasong'o 2007.
220. Geisler 1993.
221. International Republican Institute 2008b, 30.
222. International Republican Institute 2007b.
223. Kriegler, Aboud, et al. 2008, 70–71. "The various domestic and international observer groups experienced problems in general with understanding the counting, tallying and transmission processes and the possibilities for them not being conducted strictly according to the various sets of instructions and guidelines issued. This might have led to assessments based on insufficient understanding of these processes, their regulatory foundation and the actual impact of problematic recruitment procedures, unclear rules and insufficient training. The main consequence of this incomplete comprehension of the entire counting, tallying, reporting and announcement process has been a tendency to deliver verdicts on the process which do not give a fully reliable picture of what actually happened after the original counting of votes at the polling station level. . . . These problems and the lack of proper understanding of the process reduce the usefulness of the observer reports The problems at KICC [the Kenyatta International Conference Center] and in the transmission of election results from constituency tallying centres to the national tallying centre must, however, be seen within the context of the other key factors in the entire electoral process: only this will allow a reliable and comprehensive assessment of the quality of the entire electoral process." Kriegler, Aboud, et al. 2008, 130–32.
224. Kabemba 2003, 17.
225. Interview with Denis Kadima, deputy leader of the observer mission sent to Lesotho by the Electoral Institute of Southern Africa (EISA). IRIN Humanitarian News and Analysis 2007.
226. In *Afrobarometer* Surveys Lesotho citizens consistently recorded the lowest support for democracy in the SADC region. Kabemba 2003, 13.
227. Gumbi 1995.
228. Commonwealth Observer Group 1993a.
229. Kabemba 2003, 6.
230. Kabemba 2003, 37–40.
231. Cho and Bratton 2006.
232. Kabemba 2003, 6.
233. Kabemba 2003, 6–7.
234. Fox and Southall 2004.
235. Southall 2003, 271.
236. Venter 2003.
237. Venter 2003, 28.
238. Cho and Bratton 2006.
239. Elklit 2008.
240. The Industrial Revolutionary Party (PRI) was the successor party to the National Revolutionary Party.
241. Schedler 2010.
242. International Foundation for Electoral Systems 1994, 5.

243. International Foundation for Electoral Systems 1994, 6.
244. Schedler 2000, 7.
245. Dresser 1994, 58.
246. International Foundation for Electoral Systems 1994, 3.
247. Quezada 1998, 178.
248. Carter Center 2000, 7.
249. Pastor 2000.
250. Carter Center 2000, 9–10.
251. Carter Center 1994b, 5.
252. International Foundation for Electoral Systems 1994, 29.
253. Scherlen 1998, 23.
254. Dresser 1994, 68.
255. Cornelius 1994, 70.
256. Chand 1997, 558.
257. "According to post-election surveys, about 61 percent of those asked thought that the elections were clean while 24 percent did not and 15 percent did not know. In addition, 64 percent felt that the Federal Electoral Institute (IFE) had performed very well. This contrasted sharply with pre-election polls taken in June 1994 when 35 ± 45 percent of those surveyed expected fraud while 65 percent expected violence." Chand 1997, 557.
258. Carter Center 2000, 7.
259. International Foundation for Electoral Systems 1994, 29.
260. Carter Center 1994a, 15; International Foundation for Electoral Systems 1994, 30.
261. Carter Center 1997, 4.
262. Schedler 2000, 8.
263. Pastor 2000, 23.
264. European Parliament 2000, 3.
265. European Union Election Observation Mission 2006a, 19.
266. Carter Center 1994a, 9; International Foundation for Electoral Systems 1994, 9.
267. European Union Election Observation Mission 2006a, 24.
268. European Union Election Observation Mission 2006a, 30.
269. International Foundation for Electoral Systems 1997, 8.
270. Carter Center 2000, 18.
271. European Union Election Observation Mission 2006a, 14.
272. The Council of Europe (COE) even declared that the federal elections in Mexico on July 2, 2006, were about "the best organised and conducted elections the Assembly has ever observed." Council of Europe Parliamentary Assembly 2006 5.
273. European Union Election Observation Mission 2006a, 12.
274. For a thorough discussion of the 2006 election, see Schedler 2007.
275. European Union Election Observation Mission 2006a, 52.
276. Rodriguez 2009.
277. Carrillo and Navarro undated.
278. National Democratic Institute 2006, 1.
279. Pastor 2006.
280. Carter Center 2000, 9.
281. Lopez-Pintor 1998.
282. Anderson and Dodd 2002, 93.
283. Dye, Butler, et al. 1995.

284. Carter Center 1990, 12.

285. Dye, Butler, et al. 1995.

286. International Republican Institute 1997.

287. Carter Center 1996, 38; Unit for the Promotion of Democracy 2002.

288. International Foundation for Electoral Systems 1996.

289. The pact primarily served the interests of Manuel Ortego and Arnoldo Alemán in consolidating their power and acquiring immunity from prosecuting Dye. Spence et al. 2000, 7–10.

290. Carter Center 2001b.

291. International Republican Institute 2002.

292. Carter Center 2001b, 29.

293. European Union Election Observation Mission 2006b.

294. Carter Center 2006a, 20.

295. Carter Center 2006a, 39.

296. O'Shaughnessy and Dodson 1999.

297. Lopez-Pintor 1998.

298. Carter Center 2006a, 16.

299. European Union Election Observation Mission 2006b, 14.

300. McConnell 2007, 88.

301. Dye, Spence, et al. 2000, 2.

302. Carter Center 2006a, 39.

303. Scranton 1998, 217.

304. National Democratic Institute and International Republican Institute 1989, 19–20.

305. National Democratic Institute and International Republican Institute 1989, 57. National Democratic Institute and International Republican Institute 1989, 61.

306. Carter Center 1994c, 2.

307. National Democratic Institute and International Republican Institute 1989, 2.

308. Carter Center 1994c, 3.

309. Carter Center 1994c, 8.

310. International Foundation for Electoral Systems 1999b, 8.

311. Unit for the Promotion of Democracy 2004b, 4.

312. Unit for the Promotion of Democracy 2004b, 18.

313. International Foundation for Electoral Systems 1999b, 29.

314. Office for Democratic Institutions and Human Rights 2003c, 3.

315. Council of Europe Parliamentary Assembly 1996b, 4.

316. International Republican Institute 1996c, 2.

317. International Republican Institute 1996c, 2.

318. For a detailed accounting of which recommendations were followed, see International Republican Institute 1996c, Appendix IX.

319. Council of Europe Parliamentary Assembly 2000a, paragraph 8.

320. Office for Democratic Institutions and Human Rights 2004a, 4.

321. Association of European Election Officials, 13.

322. Gordon 1998.

323. Council of Europe Parliamentary Assembly 1996b, 1.

324. Office for Democratic Institutions and Human Rights 2000a, 2.

325. Office for Democratic Institutions and Human Rights 2004c, 7.

326. Office for Democratic Institutions and Human Rights 2004c, 21–22.

327. The fact that the president ran as for the parliamentary elections as head of the United Russia list without stepping down from his office as president was unprecedented within the member states of the COE.

328. Fawn 2006.

329. Saari 2009.

330. Carothers 1997, 23.

331. Council of Europe Parliamentary Assembly 2008a, 5.

332. Alence 2004, 79.

333. Anglin 1995, 541.

334. Anglin 1995, 521.

335. International Republican Institute 1994, 85.

336. European Union Election Unit 1994, 6; International Republican Institute 1994, 120.

337. Personal interview, May 20, 2010, Aarhus University, Denmark.

338. International Republican Institute 1994, 1.

339. Anglin 1995, 539.

340. Anglin 1995, 541.

341. For the 1999 election, there was a small delegation of European Parliamentarians for Africa, but they did not issue a formal report.

342. Commonwealth Observer Group 1999.

343. Electoral Institute of Southern Africa 2004, 6.

344. Electoral Institute of Southern Africa 2004, 17.

345. Electoral Institute of Southern Africa 2004, 28–29.

346. South African Development Community Parliamentary Observer Mission 2004.

347. African Union 2004, paragraph 92.

348. Lemon 2005.

349. Alence 2004, 79.

350. Electoral Institute of Southern Africa 2009.

References

Abbink, Jon (2000). "Introduction: Rethinking Democratization and Election Observation." In *Election Observation and Democratization in Africa*, edited by J. Abbink and G. Hesseling, 1–17. New York, St. Martin's Press.

Abbink, Jon and Gerti Hesseling, eds. (2000). *Election Observation and Democratization in Africa*. New York, St. Martin's Press.

Abrahamyan, Gayane (2008). "Armenia: Dueling Protests Occur in Yerevan, as President Calls on Opponents to Sober-Up." *Eurasia Insight*.

Achen, Christopher (2005). "Let's Put Garbage-can Regressions and Garbage-can Probits Where They Belong." *Conflict Management and Peace Science* **22**(4): 327–39.

Africa News (2002). "Zimbabwe; Group's Poll Report Biased, Racist." Government of Zimbabwe, April 30, 2002.

Africa Watch (1993). Divide and Rule: State-Sponsored Ethnic Violence in Kenya. Washington, D.C., Human Rights Watch.

African Union (2004). Report of the African Union Observer Team on the National and Provincial Elections held in the Republic of South Africa on 14 April 2004. African Union, Addis Ababa, Ethiopia. (Reprinted in Election Update South Africa 10, June 7, 2004, at http://www.eisa.org.za.)

African Union. (2009). "The African Union Democracy and Elections Assistance Union (DEAU)." Retrieved August 24, 2009, from http://www.africa-union.org/root/AU/AUC/Departments/PA/ELECTION_UNIT/AU_Election_Unit.htm.

Ahmed, Nizam (2003). "From Monopoly to Competition: Party Politics in the Bangladesh Parliament (1973–2001)." *Pacific Affairs* **76**(1): 55–77.

Ajulu, Rok (1998). "Kenya's Democracy Experiment: The 1997 Elections." *Review of African Political Economy* **25**(76): 275–85.

Alence, Rod (2004). "South Africa after Apartheid." *Journal of Democracy* **15**: 78–92.

Alesina, Alberto and David Dollar (2000). "Who Gives Foreign Aid to Whom and Why?" *Journal of Economic Growth* **5**(1): 33–63.

Anderson, Leslie and Lawrence Dodd (2002). "Nicaragua Votes: The Elections of 2001." *Journal of Democracy* **13**(3): 80–95.

Anglin, Douglas (1992). "International Monitoring as a Mechanism for Conflict Resolution in Southern Africa." In *The Centre for Foreign Relations 7th International Conference on Peace and Security in Southern Africa*. Arusha, Tanzania.

Anglin, Douglas (1995). "International Monitoring of the Transition to Democracy in South Africa, 1992–1994." *African Affairs* **94**(377): 519.

Anglin, Douglas (1998). "International Election Monitoring: The African Experience." *African Affairs* **97**(389): 471.

Argersinger, Peter (1985). "New Perspectives on Election Fraud in the Gilded Age." *Political Science Quarterly* **100**(4): 669–87.

Asante, Kofi (1994). "Election Monitoring's Impact on the Law: Can It Be Reconciled with Sovereignty and Nonintervention?" *New York University Journal of International Law and Politics* **26**(2): 235–84.

Asian Network for Free Elections (2001). Bangladesh 8th Parliamentary Election. Bangkok, Thailand.

Asian Network for Free Elections (2009). A Decade of Democracy in Indonesia: The 2009 Legislative Election.

Association of European Election Officials (2010). Developing Accurate Voters' List in Transitional Democracies.

Astourian, Stephan (2000). "From Ter-Petrosian to Kocharian: Leadership Change in Armenia." *Berkeley Program in Soviet and Post-Soviet Studies Working Paper Series.* Berkeley, University of California, Berkeley.

Bachman, Ronald (1991). *Romania: A Country Study.* Washington, D.C., Federal Research Division, Library of Congress, U.S. G.P.O.

Baker, Bruce (2002). "When to Call Black White: Zimbabwe's Electoral Reports." *Third World Quarterly* 23(6): 1145–58.

Baker, James (1990). Remarks Before the CSCE Conference on the Human Dimension, Copenhagen, June 6. *U.S. Department of State Dispatch* 1(1), September 3.

Balian, Hrair (2003). "Building on Imperfection: Reflections on the Chechen Referendum." *Helsinki Monitor* 14(2): 85–88.

Baloyra, Enrique (1993). "The Salvadoran Elections of 1982–1991." *Studies in Comparative International Development (SCID)* 28(3): 3–30.

Baloyra-Herp, Anrique (1995). "Elections, Civil War, and Transition in El Salvador, 1982–1994." In *Elections and Democracy in Central America, Revisited,* edited by M. Seligson and J. Booth. Chapel Hill, University of North Carolina Press.

Barkan, Joel (1998). "Toward a New Constitutional Framework in Kenya." *Africa Today* 45(2): 213.

Barkan, Joel and Njuguna Ng'ethe (1998). "Kenya Tries Again." *Journal of Democracy* 9(2): 32–48.

Barkin, Samuel and Bruce Cronin (1994). "The State and the Nation: Changing Norms and Rules of Sovereignty in International Relations." *International Organization* 48(1): 107–30.

Barnes, William (1998). "Incomplete Democracy in Central America: Polarization and Voter Turnout in Nicaragua and El Salvador." *Journal of Interamerican Studies and World Affairs* 40(3): 63–101.

Barnett, Michael and Martha Finnemore (2001). "The Politics, Power, and Pathologies of International Organizations." *International Organization* 53(4): 699–732.

BBC (1992). "Kenya Moi Promises 'Free and Fair Elections'; Invites Foreign Observers (Excerpt from relay of President Moi's 30-minute address to the nation to mark Kenyatta Day, 20 October 1992)." *BBC Summary of World Broadcasts.*

BBC (2002). "Guyana: Commonwealth Envoy to Try to Get Government-Opposition Talks Restarted." *BBC Monitoring Latin America.*

Beaulieu, Emily and Susan D. Hyde (2009). "In the Shadow of Democracy Promotion: Strategic Manipulation, International Observers, and Election Boycotts." *Comparative Political Studies* 42(3): 392–415.

Beech, Hannah (2009). "Indonesia Elections: A Win For Democracy." *Time.*

Beigbeder, Yves (1994). *International Monitoring of Plebiscites, Referenda and National Elections: Self-determination and Transition to Democracy.* Dordrecht; Boston, M. Nijhoff.

Bittiger, Tim (2008). Ghana: Election Observation in West Africa—the Ecowas Experience, Ace Electoral Network.

Bjornlund, Eric (2004). *Beyond Free and Fair: Monitoring Elections and Building Democracy*. Washington, D.C., Woodrow Wilson Center Press; Johns Hopkins University Press.

Bjornlund, Eric (2006). "Improving Vote Count Verification in Transitional Elections." *Electoral Insights* (March).

Bjornlund, Eric, Michael Bratton, et al. (1992). "Observing Multiparty Elections in Africa: Lessons from Zambia." *African Affairs* **91**(364): 405–31.

Bob, Clifford (2002). "Merchants of Morality." *Foreign Policy* **129**(March/April): 36–45.

Bosire, Bogonko (2008). Kenya Death Toll Hits 693: Report. January 13, 2008. Retrieved on May 4, 2011, from http://www.iol.co.za/news/africa/kenya-death-toll-hits-693-report-1.385591?ot=inmsa.ArticlePrintPageLayout.ot.

Boutros-Ghali, Boutros (1996). An Agenda for Democratization. U. N. D. o. P. Information. New York, United Nations, Department of Public Information.

Bratton, Michael (1998). "Second Elections in Africa." *Journal of Democracy* **9**(3): 51.

Brown, L. David and Mark Moore (2001). "Accountability, Strategy, and International Nongovernmental Organizations." *Nonprofit and Voluntary Sector Quarterly* **30**(3): 569–87.

Brown, MacAlister (2000). "Election Observers in Cambodia, 1998: What Can We Learn?" *Government and Opposition* **35**(1): 77–89.

Brown, Stephen (2001). "Authoritarian Leaders and Multiparty Elections in Africa: How Foreign Donors Help to Keep Kenya's Daniel arap Moi in Power." *Third World Quarterly* **22**(5): 725–39.

Brown, Stephen (2007). "From Demiurge to Midwife: Changing Donor Roles in Kenya's Democratization Process" In *Kenya: The Struggle for Democracy*, edited by G. M. a. S. Nasong'o, 303–31. London; Dakar, Zed Books and Council for the Development of Social Science Research in Africa.

Bueno de Mesquita, Bruce and George Downs (2006). "Intervention and Democracy." *International Organization* **60**(3): 627–49.

Buijtenhuis, Robert (2000). "The 1996–7 Elections in Chad: The Role of the International Observers." In *Election Observation and Democratization in Africa*, edited by J. Abbink and G. Hesseling, 211–27. New York, St. Martin's Press.

Bulgarian Radio (1997). "Elections Were Fair, Say Foreign Observers." *BBC Summary of World Broadcasts*, April 22, 1997.

Bunce, Valerie and Sharon Wolchik (2009). "Democratization by Elections? Postcommunist Ambiguities." *Journal of Democracy* **20**(3): 93–108.

Bunce, Valerie and Sharon Wolchik (2011). *Defeating Authoritarian Leaders in Postcommunist Countries*. Cambridge, Cambridge University Press.

Burnell, Peter (2008). "From Evaluating Democracy Assistance to Appraising Democracy Promotion." *Political Studies* **56**(2): 414–34.

Bush, George H. W. (1990). "The UN: World Parliament of Peace. Address before the United Nations General Assembly." *U.S. Department of State Dispatch* **1**(6).

Bynoe, Mark, Clive Thomas, et al. (2007). *The Political Culture of Democracy in Guyana: 2006*. Nashville, Tennessee, Vanderbilt University.

Calingaert, Daniel (2006). "Election Rigging and How to Fight It." *Journal of Democracy* **17**(3): 138–51.

Call, Charles (2002). "Assessing El Salvador's Transition from Civil War to Peace." In *Ending Civil Wars: The Implementation of Peace Agreements*, edited by S. Stedman, D. Rothchild, and E. Cousens, 383–420. Boulder, Colorado, Lynne Rienner.

Carrillo, Manuel and Carlos Navarro. Undated. Mexico's New Electoral Reform and the Contribution of the Federal Electoral Institute. ACE Electoral Knowledge Network. Retrieved on May 5, 2011, from http://aceproject.org/today/feature-articles/mexico-s -new-electoral-reform-and-the-contribution-of-the-federal-electoral-institute.

Caroll, David (2010). Personal email correspondance, January 14, 2010.

Carothers, Thomas (1997). "The Observers Observed." *Journal of Democracy* **8**(3): 17–31.

Carothers, Thomas (1999). *Aiding Democracy Abroad: The Learning Curve*. Carnegie Endowment for International Peace.

Carothers, Thomas (2002). "The End of the Transition Paradigm." *Journal of Democracy* **13**(1): 5.

Carothers, Thomas (2007). "The 'Sequencing' Fallacy." *Journal of Democracy* **18**(1): 12–27.

Carpenter, Charli (2007). "Studying Issue (Non)-Adoption in Transnational Advocacy Networks." *International Organization* **61**(3): 643–67.

Carroll, David and Robert Pastor (1993). Moderating Ethnic Tensions by Electoral Mediation. Atlanta, Georgia, Carter Center.

Carter Center (1990). Observing Nicaragua's Elections, 1989–1990. Atlanta, Georgia.

Carter Center (1992). Observing Guyana's Electoral Process, 1990–1992. Atlanta, Georgia.

Carter Center (1994a). The August 21, 1994 Mexican National Elections, Fourth Report. Atlanta, Georgia.

Carter Center (1994b). Elections in Mexico: Third Report. Atlanta, Georgia.

Carter Center (1994c). The May 8, 1994 Elections in Panama. Atlanta, Georgia.

Carter Center (1996). The Observation of the 1996 Nicaraguan Elections. Atlanta, Georgia.

Carter Center (1997). The Carter Center Delegation to Observe the July 6, 1997 Elections in Mexico. Atlanta, Georgia.

Carter Center (2000). Observing the 2000 Mexico Elections. Atlanta, Georgia.

Carter Center (2001a). Observing the 2001 Guyana Elections. Atlanta, Georgia.

Carter Center (2001b). Observing the 2001 Nicaraguan Elections. Atlanta, Georgia.

Carter Center (2002). Final Report: Observing the 2002 Mali Presidential Elections. Atlanta, Georgia.

Carter Center (2003). Observing the 2002 Kenya Elections, Final Report. Atlanta, Georgia.

Carter Center (2006a). Observing the 2006 Nicaragua Elections. Atlanta, Georgia.

Carter Center (2006b). A Vote for Democracy. Online video, viewed May 4, 2011, at http://www.cartercenter.org/news/multimedia/PeacePrograms/ElectionObservation AVoteforDemocracy.html.

Carter Center (2009a). Final Report of the Carter Center Limited Observation Mission to the April 9, 2009, Legislative Elections in Indonesia. Atlanta, Georgia.

Carter Center. (2009b). "Timeline and History of The Carter Center." Retrieved August 21, 2009, from http://www.cartercenter.org/about/history/chronology_1980.html.

Carter Center. (2010a). "What Is Election Observation?" Retrieved January 8, 2010, from http://www.cartercenter.org/peace/democracy/nav_question1.html.

Carter Center. (2010b). "Why Is International Election Observation Important?" Retrieved January 7, 2010, from http://www.cartercenter.org/peace/democracy/nav_question2.html.

Carter Center (undated). The Journey to Democracy: 1986–1996, Columbia International Affairs Online.

Carter Center and National Democratic Institute (2001). Statement of the National Democratic Institute (NDI)/Carter Center Pre-election Delegation to Bangladesh's 2001 Parliamentary Elections. Dhaka, Bangladesh.

Case, William (1996). "Can the "Halfway House" Stand? Semidemocracy and Elite Theory in Three Southeast Asian Countries." *Comparative Politics* 28(4): 437–64.

Chand, Vikram (1997). "Democratisation From the Outside In: NGO and International Efforts to Promote Open Elections." *Third World Quarterly* 18(3): 543–61.

Checkel, Jeffrey (1998). "Review: The Constructivist Turn in International Relations Theory." *World Politics* 50(2): 324–48.

Checkel, Jeffrey (2000). Compliance and Conditionality. *ARENA Working Paper WP 00/18*, Oslo, ARENA.

Checkel, Jeffrey (2001). "Why Comply? Social Learning and European Identity Change." *International Organization* 55(3): 553–88.

Checkel, Jeffrey (2005). "International Institutions and Socialization in Europe: Introduction and Framework." *International Organization* 59(4): 801–26.

Chivers, Christopher (2004). "Yushchenko Wins 52% of Vote; Rival Vows a Challenge." *New York Times*, December 28, 2004.

Chivers, Christopher (2007). "Kazakh Letters Raise Questions on Election; Signs Hint State Tried to Sway Monitors." *International Herald Tribune*, 3.

Cho, Wonbin and Michael Bratton (2006). "Electoral Institutions, Partisan Status, and Political Support in Lesotho." *Electoral Studies* 25: 731–50.

Clark, Elizabeth (2000). "Why Elections Matter." *The Washington Quarterly* 23(3): 27–40.

Clarke, Kevin (2005). "The Phantom Menace: Omitted Variable Bias in Econometric Research." *Conflict Management and Peace Science* 22(4): 341–52.

Coalson, Robert and Harry Tamrazian (2009). "Ten Years Later, Deadly Shooting In Armenian Parliament Still Echoes." Radio Free Europe, Radio Liberty.

Collier, Paul (1997). "The Failure of Conditionality." *Perspectives on Aid and Development*: 51–77.

Commission of the European Communities (2000). COM(2000) 191 final. Communication from the Commission on EU Election Assistance and Observation. April 2, 2000.

Commission of the European Union (undated). "Reporting Guidelines." Retrieved March 13, 2008, from http://ec.europa.eu/external_relations/human_rights/election_observation/docs/2007_eu_eom_reporting_guidelines_en.pdf.

Commission on Security and Cooperation in Europe (2004). Georgia's Rose Revolution. Washington, D.C.

Committee in Solidarity with the People of El Salvador (2009). El Salvador Election Observation Report. Presidential Elections, March 15, 2009. Washington, D.C.

CommonBorders (2004). Final Report of the Electoral Observer Delegation: 2004 Presidential Election in El Salvador. Downloaded from http://www.commonborders.org/_pdf_/Salvdor_2004_report.pdf, May 3, 2011.

Commonwealth Observer Group (1993a). The General Election in Lesotho, 27 March 1993. London, Commonwealth Secretariat.

Commonwealth Observer Group (1993b). Presidential, Parliamentary and Civic Elections in Kenya: The Report of the Commonwealth Observer Group. London, Commonwealth Secretariat.

Commonwealth Observer Group (1996). Bangladesh Parliamentary Elections, 12 June 1996. London, Commonwealth Secretariat.

Commonwealth Observer Group (1998). Report of the Commonwealth Observer Group to the General and Regional Elections in Guyana. London, Commonwealth Secretariat.

Commonwealth Observer Group (1999). The National and Provincial Elections in South Africa. London, Commonwealth Secretariat.

Commonwealth Observer Group (2000). The Report of the Commonwealth Observer Group, The Parliamentary Elections in Zimbabwe, June 2000. London, Commonwealth Secretariat.

Commonwealth Observer Group (2001). The Report of the Commonwealth Observer Group: Guyana, 2001. London, Commonwealth Secretariat.

Commonwealth Observer Group (2002). Kenya General Election, 27 December 2002. London, Commonwealth Secretariat.

Commonwealth Observer Group (2006). Guyana General and Regional Elections, 28 August 2006. London, Commonwealth Secretariat.

Commonwealth Observer Group (2008). Bangladesh Parliamentary Elections, 29 December 2008. London, Commonwealth Secretariat.

Conference on Security and Co-operation in Europe (1989). Conference on the Human Dimension of the Conference on Security and Co-operation in Europe. Paris, France.

Conference on Security and Co-operation in Europe (1990). Conference on the Human Dimension of the Conference on Security and Co-operation in Europe. Copenhagen, Denmark, Conference on Security and Co-operation in Europe.

Conference on Security and Co-operation in Europe (1991). Document of the Moscow Meeting of the Conference on the Human Dimension of the CSCE, 3 October. Moscow.

Cooley, Alexander and James Ron (2002). "The NGO Scramble: Organizational Insecurity and the Political Economy of Transnational Action." International Security 27(1): 5–39.

Cornelius, Wayne (1994). "Mexico's Delayed Democratization." Foreign Policy 95: 53–71.

Cortell, Andrew and James Davis (1996). "How Do International Institutions Matter? The Domestic Impact of International Rules and Norms." International Studies Quarterly 40(4): 451–78.

Council of Europe Parliamentary Assembly (1996a). Addendum II to the Progress Report of the Bureau of the Assembly and the Standing Comittee: Information Report on the Parliamentary Elections in Georgia (5 November 1995). Strasbourg, France.

Council of Europe Parliamentary Assembly (1996b). Information Report on Parliamentary Elections in Russia (17 December 1995). Strasbourg, France.

Council of Europe Parliamentary Assembly (1996c). Russia's application for membership of the Council of Europe. Strasbourg, France.

Council of Europe Parliamentary Assembly (1997). Bureau of the Assembly and the Standing Committee(1): Information report on the general election in Bulgaria (19 April 1997). Strasbourg, France.

Council of Europe Parliamentary Assembly (2000a). Ad hoc Committee to Observe the Parliamentary Elections in Russia (19 December 1999). Strasbourg, France.

Council of Europe Parliamentary Assembly (2000b). Opinion No. 221 (2000): Armenia's Application for Membership of the Council of Europe. Strasbourg, France.

Council of Europe Parliamentary Assembly (2004). Ad Hoc Committee to Observe the Parliamentary Elections in the Russian Federation (7 December 2003). Strasbourg, France.

Council of Europe Parliamentary Assembly (2006). Observation of the Parliamentary and Presidential Elections in Mexico (2 July 2006). Strasbourg, France.

Council of Europe Parliamentary Assembly (2007). Observation of the Parliamentary Elections in the Russian Federation (2 December 2007). Strasbourg, France.

Council of Europe Parliamentary Assembly (2008a). Observation of the Presidential Election in the Russian Federation (2 March 2008). Strasbourg, France.

Council of Europe Parliamentary Assembly (2008b). Resolution 1603 (2008): Honouring of Obligations and Commitments by Georgia. Strasbourg, France.

Council of Europe Parliamentary Assembly (2009a). Honouring of Obligations and Commitments by Georgia. Information note by the co-rapporteurs on their fact-finding visit to Tbilisi (24–27 March 2009). Strasbourg, France, Committee on the Honouring of Obligations and Commitments by Member States of the Council of Europe (Monitoring Committee).

Council of Europe Parliamentary Assembly (2009b). Observation of the Parliamentary Elections in Albania (28 June 2009). Strasbourg, France.

Council of the European Union (2005). Press Release: The European Union and the United States Working Together to Promote Democracy and Support Freedom, the Rule of Law and Human Rights Worldwide. Brussels, Belgium, European Union.

Council of Freely Elected Heads of State (1995). The August 21, 1994 Mexican National Election. Fourth Report. Atlanta, Georgia, Carter Center.

Crawford, Gordon (1997). "Foreign Aid and Political Conditionality: Issues of Effectiveness and Consistency." *Democratization* **4**(3): 69–108.

Crawford, James (1993). *Democracy in International Law*. Cambridge, Cambridge University Press.

Croissant, Aurel and Beate Martin (2006). *Between Consolidation and Crisis Elections and Democracy in Five Nations in Southeast Asia*. Berlin, Lit Verlag.

Croissant, Michael (1998). *The Armenia-Azerbaijan Conflict: Causes and Implications*. London, Praeger Publishers.

Cutler, Lloyd (1985). "The Right to Intervene." *Foreign Affairs* **64**(1): 96–112.

Dagg, Christopher J. (2007). "The 2004 Elections in Indonesia: Political Reform and Democratisation." *Asia Pacific Viewpoint* **48**(1): 47–59.

Dahl, Robert (1971). *Polyarchy: Participation and Opposition*. New Haven, Connecticut, Yale University Press.

Dahl, Robert (1991). *Democracy and its Critics*. New Haven, Connecticut, Yale University Press.

Dai, Xinyuan (2006). "The Conditional Nature of Democratic Compliance." *Journal of Conflict Resolution* **50**(5): 690–713.

Darby, Seyward (2007). "Will You Be My Friend?" *Transitions Online* (August 16).

Davis-Robert, Avery and David Carroll (forthcoming). "Using International Law to Assess Elections." *Democratization*.

Dehejia, Rajeev and Sadek Wahba (1999). "Causal Effects in Nonexperimental Studies: Re-evaluating the Evaluation of Training Programs." *Journal of the American Statistical Association* **94**: 1053–62.

Department of Electoral Cooperation and Observation, OAS (2009). OAS Electoral Observation Mission to El Salvador Reports on "Historical" Elections and Expressed Recommendations. Press Release. Washington, D.C., Organization of American States.

Diamond, Alexis and Jasjeet Sekhon (2008). Genetic Matching for Estimating Causal Effects: A General Multivariate Matching Method for Achieving Balance in Observational Studies. Berkeley, University of California, Berkeley.

Diamond, Larry (1991). An American Foreign Policy for Democracy. *Policy Report*, Progressive Policy Institute.

Diamond, Larry (2006). "Some Social Requisites of Democracy: Economic Development and Political Legitimacy." *American Political Science Review* **100**(4): 675–76.

Diamond, Larry (2009). "How Is Indonesia's Democracy Doing?" *East Asia Forum*.

Donald, Rubin (1979). "Using Multivariate Matched Sampling and Regression Adjustment to Control Bias in Observational Studies." *Journal of the American Statistical Association* **74**(366): 318–28.

Donno, Daniela (2010). "Who Is Punished? Regional Intergovernmental Organizations and the Enforcement of Democratic Norms." *International Organization* **64**(4): 593–625.

Dorman, Sara Rich (2005). "'Make Sure They Count Nicely This Time': The Politics of Elections and Election Observing in Zimbabwe." *Commonwealth & Comparative Politics* **43**(2): 155–77.

Downie, Sue (2000). "Cambodia's 1998 Election: Understanding Why it Was Not a 'Miracle on the Mekong.'" *Australian Journal of International Affairs* **54**(1): 43–61.

Dresser, Denise (1994). "Five Scenarios for Mexico." *Journal of Democracy* **5**(3).

Drezner, Daniel (2003). "The Hidden Hand of Economic Coercion." *International Organization* **57**(3): 643–59.

Dye, David, Judy Butler, et al. (1995). Contesting Everything, Winning Nothing: The Search for Consensus in Nicaragua, 1990–1995. *Hemisphere Initiative*.

Dye, David, Jack Spence, et al. (2000). Patchwork Democracy: Nicaraguan Politics Ten Years After the Fall. *Hemisphere Initiatives*.

Ebersole, Jon (1992–93). "The United Nations' Response to Requests for Assistance in Electoral Matters." *Virginia Journal of International Law* **33**: 91–122.

EBRD (1990). Agreement Establishing the European Bank for Reconstruction and Development. Paris.

Elbasani, Arolda (2004). "Albania in Transition: Manipulation or Appropriation of International Norms?" *Southeast European Politics* **5**(1): 22–44.

Election Observation Centre (1998). Kenya General Elections 1997, Final Report, Donors' Democratic Development Group.

Electoral Institute of Southern Africa (2004). Election Observer Mission Report, South Africa. Auckland Park, South Africa.

Electoral Institute of Southern Africa (2009). Interim Statement: EISA Observer Mission to the 2009 South African National and Provincial Elections. Johannesburg, South Africa.

Elklit, Jørgen (1999). "Electoral Institutional Change and Democratization: You Can Lead a Horse to Water, but You Can't Make It Drink." *Democratization* **6**(4): 28–51.

Elklit, Jørgen (2008). "The 2007 General Elections in Lesotho: Abuse of the MMP System?" *Journal of African Elections: Elections and Democracy in Lesotho: Special Issue* **7**(1): 10–19.

Elklit, Jørgen and Andrew Reynolds (2002). "The Impact of Election Administration on the Legitimacy of Emerging Democracies: A New Comparative Politics Research Agenda." *Commonwealth & Comparative Politics* **40**(2): 86.

Elklit, Jørgen and Andrew Reynolds (2005). "A Framework for the Systematic Study of Election Quality." *Democratization* **12**(2): 147–62.

Elklit, Jørgen and Palle Svensson (1997). "What Makes Elections Free and Fair?" *Journal of Democracy* **8**(3): 32.

Ellis, Andrew (1998). A Commentary on Selected Aspects of Indonesia's Draft Electoral Legislation. Washington, D.C., National Democratic Institute.

Eorsi, Matyas Eorsi and Marietta de Pourbaix-Lundin (2008). "Armenia: Election Secrets Revealed." *Transitions Online*(April 22): 1–3.

Epstein, Rachel and Ulrich Sedelmeier (2008). "Beyond Conditionality: International Institutions in Postcommunist Europe After Enlargement." *Journal of European Public Policy* **15**(6): 795–805.

Estok, Melissa, Neil Nevitte, et al. (2002). The Quick Count and Election Observation: An NDI Guide for Civic Organizations and Political Parties. Washington, D.C., National Democratic Institute.

European Commission (2000). COM(2000) 191 final. Communication from the Commission on EU Election Assistance and Observation. April 2, 2000.

European Commission (2007). *Compendium of International Standards for Elections.* Brussels, Belgium.

European Commission for Democracy Through Law (Venice Commission) and Office for Democratic Institutions and Human Rights (2007). Final Joint Opinion on Amendments to the Electoral Code of the Republic of Armenia. Strasbourg, France, Organization for Security and Co-operation in Europe, Council of Europe.

European Parliament (2000). Delegation of Observers to Mexico for the Federal Elections of 2 July 2000. Brussels, Belgium.

European Parliament (2001). European Parliament resolution on the Commission communication on EU Election Assistance and Observation (COM(2000) 191 - C5-0259/2000 - 2000/2137 (COS)). Strasbourg, France.

European Parliament (2004). Account of the Mission to Observe the Legislative, Provincial and Regional Elections in Indonesia. Brussels, Belgium.

European Parliament (2007). Delegation to Observe the Parliamentary Elections in Armenia (12 May). Brussels, Belgium.

European Parliament, Organization for Security and Co-operation in Europe, et al. (2008). Joint Press Statement, February 20. Armenian presidential election mostly in line with international commitments, but further improvements necessary. Yerevan, Armenia.

European Union Election Observation Mission (1999). Indonesian Election Observation Mission Final Report. Brussels, Belgium, European Commission.

European Union Election Observation Mission (2000). Elections in Zimbabwe, 24–25 June 2000, Interim statement, Pierre Schori—Head of EU Election Observation Mission European Commission.

European Union Election Observation Mission (2001a). Bangladesh Parliamentary Elections, 1 October 2001. Brussels, Belgium, European Commission.

European Union Election Observation Mission (2001b). Election Observation Mission to Nicaragua, Presidential and Parliamentary Elections, 4 November 2001, Final Report. Brussels, Belgium, European Commission.

European Union Election Observation Mission (2001c). Guyana Long Term Observation Group & European Union Election Observation Mission, Guyana Elections, 19 March 2001. Brussels, Belgium, European Commission.

European Union Election Observation Mission (2002). Kenya General Elections, 27 December 2002, European Union Election Observation Mission, Final Report. Brussels, Belgium, European Commission.

European Union Election Observation Mission (2003). Guatemala General Elections 2003: European Union Electoral Observation Mission. Brussels, Belgium, European Commission.

European Union Election Observation Mission (2004). European Union Election Observation Mission to Indonesia 2004. Brussels, Belgium, European Commission.

European Union Election Observation Mission (2006a). European Union Election Observation Mission: Mexico 2006 Final Report. Brussels, Belgium, European Commission.

European Union Election Observation Mission (2006b). Final Report: Presidential and Parliamentary Elections, Nicaragua 2006. Brussels, Belgium, European Commission.

European Union Election Observation Mission (2008). Kenya Final Report: General Elections, 27 December. Brussels, Belgium, European Commission.

European Union Election Observation Mission (2009a). Preliminary Statement, Legislative, Municipal and PARLACEN Elections 2009. San Salvador, El Salvador, European Commission.

European Union Election Observation Mission (2009b). Preliminary Statement: Presidential Elections El Salvador 2009. San Salvador, El Salvador, European Commission.

European Union Election Unit (1994). Observing South Africa's 1994 National and Provincial elections. Johannesburg, European Commission.

Fairbanks, Charles (2004). "Georgia's Rose Revolution." Journal of Democracy 15(2): 110–24.

Fauriol, Georges (2006). The Role of Elections in Expanding Freedom and Building Democracy World Wide. Remarks by Georges Fauriol, International Republican Institute, at the World Affairs Council, Minneapolis, Minnesota, April 18.

Fawn, Rick (2006). "Battle Over the Box: International Election Observation Missions, Political Competition and Retrenchment in the Post-Soviet Space." International Affairs 82(6): 1133–53.

Finnemore, Martha (1996). "Constructing Norms of Humanitarian Intervention." In The Culture of National Security: Norms and Identity in World Politics, edited by P. Katzenstein, 153–85. New York, Columbia University Press.

Finnemore, Martha and Kathryn Sikkink (1998). "International Norm Dynamics and Political Change." *International Organization* **52**(4): 887–917.

Fish, Steven (2005). *Democracy Derailed in Russia: The Failure of Open Politics*. New York, Cambridge University Press.

Flynn, Gregory and Henry Farrell (1999). "Piecing Together the Democratic Peace: The CSCE, Norms and the 'Construction' of Security in Post–Cold War Europe." *International Organization* **53**(3): 505–35.

Foeken, Dick and Ton Dietz (2000). "Of Ethnicity, Manipulation and Observation: The 1992 and 1997 Elections in Kenya." In *Election Observation and Democratization in Africa*, edited by J. Abbink and G. Hesseling, 122–49. New York, St. Martin's Press.

Forsythe, David and Barbar Rieffer (2000). "US Foreign Policy and Enlarging the Democratic Community." *Human Rights Quarterly* **22**: 988–1010.

Fox, Gregory (1995). "The Role of International Law in the Twenty-First Century: Multinational Election Monitoring: Advancing International Law on the High Wire." *Fordham International Law Journal* **18**(5): 1658–67.

Fox, Jonathan (1994). "Latin America's Emerging Local Politics." *Journal of Democracy* **5**: 105–16.

Fox, Roddy and Roger Southall (2004). "The General Election in Lesotho, May 2002: Adapting to MMP." *Electoral Studies* **23**: 545–71.

Franck, Thomas (1992). "The Emerging Right to Democratic Governance." *American Journal of International Law* **86**(1): 46–91.

Franklin, James (2008). "Shame on You: The Impact of Human Rights Criticism on Political Repression in Latin America." *International Studies Quarterly* **52**(1): 187–211.

Freedom House. (2008). "Executive Summary, Georgia." Retrieved June 29, 2009, 2009, from http://www.freedomhouse.org/template.cfm?page=47&nit=452&year=2008.

Friedrichs, Jörg and Friedrich Kratochwil (2009). "On Acting and Knowing: How Pragmatism Can Advance International Relations Research and Methodology." *International Organization* **63**(4): 701–31.

Galbraith, Peter (2009). Excerpts: Galbraith's Letter to U.N. Secretary General. *New York Times*, September 30, 2009.

Gandhi, Jennifer and Adam Przeworski (2009). "Holding onto Power by Any Means? The Origins of Competitive Elections." In *Rationality and Conflict*. New Haven, Connecticut, Yale University Press.

Garber, Larry (1984). *Guidelines for International Election Observing*. Washington, D.C., International Human Rights Law Group.

Garber, Larry and Glenn Cowen (1994). "The Virtues of Parallel Vote Tabulations." *Journal of Democracy* **4**(2): 95–107.

Geddes, Barbara (1999). "What Do We Know About Democratization After Twenty Years?" *Annual Review of Political Science* **2**(1): 115.

Geisler, Gisela (1993). "Fair? What Has Fairness Got to Do with It? Vagaries of Election Observations and Democratic." *Journal of Modern African Studies* **31**(4): 613.

General Committee (2008). Report: "Best Practices in OAS Electoral Observation, 2004–2007." Washington, D.C., Permanent Council of the Organization of American States, Secretariat for Political Affairs, Department of Electoral Cooperation and Observation.

General Secretariat of the Organization of American States (2007). *Methods for Electoral Observation: A Manual for OAS Electoral Observation Missions. Prepared by Gerardo Munck.* Washington, D.C., Organization of American States.

Gershman, Carl and Michael Allen (2006). "The Assault on Democracy Assistance." *Journal of Democracy* 17(2): 36–51.

Gettleman, Jeffrey (2010). "With Outcome Foretold, Sudanese Elections Begin." *New York Times*, April 11, 2010.

Gibson, Clark and James Long (2009). "The Presidential and Parliamentary Elections in Kenya, December 2007." *Electoral Studies* 28(3): 497–502.

Gleditsch, Kristian Skrede and Michael Ward (2006). "Diffusion and the International Context of Democratization." *International Organization* 60(4): 911–33.

Gordon, Michael (1998). "Yielding to West, I.M.F. Will Double Russia Loan Offer." *New York Times*, July 12, 1998.

Gorovoi, Vladimir (2006). "CIS Election Observer Missions in Commonwealth States." *International Affairs: A Russian Journal of World Politics, Diplomacy & International Relations* 52(2): 79–87.

Government of Guyana (2005). Memorandum of Understanding. For the support of the next General Elections in Guyana Between Government of Guyana, Guyana Elections Commission & Donors, 20 July.

Grant, Ruth and Robert Keohane (2005). "Accountability and Abuses of Power in World Politics." *American Political Science Review* 99(1): 29–43.

Green, Andrew and Richard Kohl (2007). "Challenges of Evaluating Democracy Assistance: Perspectives from the Donor Side." *Democratization* 14(1): 151–65.

Gross, Jeremy (2009). Indonesia's 2009 Legislative Elections: Don't Step Backwards. *In Asia*, The Asia Foundation.

Gumbi, Leslie (1995). "Instability in Lesotho: A Search for Alternatives." *African Security Review* 4(4): 1–8.

Guzman, Andrew (2002). "A Compliance-Based Theory of International Law." *California Law Review* 90(6): 1823.

Haas, Peter, Robert Keohane, et al. (1993). *Institutions for the Earth: Sources of Effective International Environmental Protection.* Cambridge, Massachussetts, MIT Press.

Hafner-Burton, Emilie (2008). "Sticks and Stones: Naming and Shaming the Human Rights Enforcement Problem." *International Organization* 62(4): 689–716.

Hafner-Burton, Emilie and Kiyoteru Tsutsui (2005). "Human Rights in a Globalizing World: The Paradox of Empty Promises." *American Journal of Sociology* 110(5): 1373–1411.

Hall, Peter (1989). "Conclusion: The Politics of Keynesian Ideas." In *The Political Power of Economic Ideas: Keynesianism Across Nations.* Princeton, New Jersey, Princeton University Press.

Halperin, Morten and Kristin Lomasney (1998). "Guaranteeing Democracy: A Review of the Record." *Journal of Democracy* 9(2): 134–47.

Hart, Julie (2006). "Peacebuilding Through Election Assistance in Unstable Democracies: Observations from the Venezuelan Process." *Peace & Change* 31(1): 75–79.

Hartlyn, Jonathan, Jennifer McCoy, et al. (2008). "Electoral Governance Matters: Explaining the Quality of Elections in Contemporary Latin America." *Comparative Political Studies* 41(1): 73–98.

Hathaway, Oona (2002). "Do Human Rights Treaties Make a Difference?" *Yale Law Journal* **111**(8): 1935–2042.

Henderson, Sarah (2002). "Selling Civil Society: Western Aid and the Nongovernmental Organization Sector in Russia." *Comparative Political Studies* **35**(2): 139–67.

Herman, Edward and Walden Bello (1984). "US-Sponsored Elections in El Salvador and the Philippines." *World Policy Journal* **1**(4): 851–70.

Herman, Edward S. and Frank Brodhead (1984). *Demonstration Elections : U.S.-staged Elections in the Dominican Republic, Vietnam, and El Salvador.* Boston, South End Press.

Hermes, Niels and Robert Lensink (2001). "Changing the Conditions for Development Aid: A New Paradigm?" *Journal of Development Studies* **37**(6): 1.

Hilbe, Joseph (2009). *Logistic Regression Models.* Boca Raton, Florida, Chapman & Hall/CRC.

Ho, Daniel, Kosuke Imai, et al. (2007). "Matching as Nonparametric Preprocessing for Reducing Model Dependence in Parametric Causal Inference." *Political Analysis* **15**(3): 199–236.

Holmquist, Frank and Michael Ford (1992). "Kenya: Slouching toward Democracy." *Africa Today* **39**(3): 97–111.

Holmquist, Frank and Michael Ford (1994). "Kenya: State and Civil Society the First Year after the Election." *Africa Today* **41**(4): 5.

Howard, Marc and Philip Roessler (2006). "Liberalizing Electoral Outcomes in Competitive Authoritarian Regimes." *American Journal of Political Science* **50**: 365–81.

Hufbauer, Gary, Jeffrey Schott, et al. (1990). *Economic Sanctions Reconsidered.* Washington, D.C., Institute for International Economics.

Human Rights Watch. (July 26, 1998). "Cambodia: Threats, Intimidation Mar Campaign. Unequal Media Access Hampers Opposition Parties." Retrieved from http://www.hrw.org/en/news/2008/07/24/cambodia-threats-intimidation-mar-campaign.

Huntington, Samuel (1991). *The Third Wave: Democratization in the Late Twentieth Century.* Norman, University of Oklahoma Press.

Hyde, Susan (2006). Observing Norms: Explaining the Causes and Consequences of Internationally Monitored Elections. San Diego, University of California, San Diego.

Hyde, Susan (2007). "The Observer Effect in International Politics: Evidence from a Natural Experiment." *World Politics* **60**(1): 37–63.

Hyde, Susan (2009). "Catch Me if You Can: Why Leaders Invite International Election Monitors and Cheat in Front of Them." Presented at the 2009 Annual Meeting of the American Political Science Association.

Ichino, Nahomi and Matthias Schundeln (2010). Deterring or Displacing Electoral Irregularities? Spillover Effects of Observers in a Randomized Field Experiment in Ghana. *Working Paper,* Harvard University.

International Crisis Group (1996). Elections in Bosnia & Herzegovina. *ICG Bosnia Report.*

International Foundation for Electoral Systems (1994). Election Observation Final Report, Mexico, August 21, 1994. Washington, D.C.

International Foundation for Electoral Systems (1996). Electoral Observation: Nicaragua, 1996. Washington, D.C.

International Foundation for Electoral Systems (1997). Mexico's Mid-Term Elections, July 6, 1997. Washington, D.C.

International Foundation for Electoral Systems (1999a). Observation Mission Report Indonesia, General Elections, June 1999. Washington, D.C.

International Foundation for Electoral Systems (1999b). Panama, General Elections, May 2, 1999; IFES Election Observation Final Report. Washington, D.C.

International Foundation for Electoral Systems (2006). Guyana EVER Final Report. Washington, D.C.

International Foundation for Electoral Systems (2009). Guyana EVER Final Report. Washington, D.C.

International Institute for Democracy and Electoral Assistance (1995). Lessons learnt: international election observation: seventeen organizations share experiences on electoral observation: a roundtable jointly organized by the United Nations Electoral Assistance Division and International IDEA. Stockholm, Sweden, International Institute for Democracy and Electoral Assistance.

International Institute for Democracy and Electoral Assistance (2000). Determining Involvement in International Election Observation. Stockholm, Sweden.

International Institute for Democracy and Electoral Assistance. (May 17, 2006). "Building Electoral Capacity in Armenia." Retrieved November 11, 2009, from http://www .idea.int/europe_cis/armenia/mou_armenia.cfm.

International Republican Institute (1991). The March 1991 Elections in El Salvador. Washington, D.C.

International Republican Institute (1992). Kenya: Election Observation Report. Washington, D.C.

International Republican Institute (1993). Follow up statement IRI observer mission, Kenya General election 29-12-1992. Washington, D.C.

International Republican Institute (1994). Election Observation Report: South Africa's 1994 Presidential and Parliamentary Elections. Washington, D.C.

International Republican Institute (1996a). IRI Observation Report on the Albanian Parliamentary elections of May 26, 1996. Washington, D.C.

International Republican Institute (1996b). IRI Report on Bulgarian Primary Election, June 1, 1996. Washington, D.C.

International Republican Institute (1996c). Russia Presidential Election Observation Report. Washington, D.C.

International Republican Institute (1997). Nicaragua: Election Observation Report, October 20, 1996. Washington, D.C.

International Republican Institute (1999). Kingdom of Cambodia Parliamentary Elections July 26, 1998: Observation Report. Washington, D.C.

International Republican Institute (2002). Nicaragua: Election Observation Report, November 4, 2001. Washington, D.C.

International Republican Institute. 2004a. IRI Monitors Macedonia's Presidential Election. May 24, Washington, D.C.

International Republican Institute (2004b). Preliminary Statement, International Republican Institute, El Salvador, March 22, 2004. Washington, D.C.

International Republican Institute (2007a). IRI Delegation Praises Kenyan People for Successful Election, Urges Continued Acceptance of the Democratic Process. Preliminary Findings of IRI's International Election Observation Mission. Washington, D.C.

International Republican Institute (2007b). IRI Statement on Kenya Exit Poll. Washington, D.C.

International Republican Institute (2008a). Georgia Presidential Election, January 5, 2008. Election Observation Mission Final Report. Washington, D.C.

International Republican Institute (2008b). Kenya Presidential, Parliamentary and Local Elections, December 2007, Election Observation Final Report. Washington, D.C.

IRIN Humanitarian News and Analysis (2007). Lesotho: A small country whose volatile elections have caused big problems, 13 February 2007, UN Office for the Coordination of Humanitarian Affairs.

Jacoby, Wade (2004). *The Enlargement of the European Union and NATO: Ordering from the Menu in Central Europe*. Cambridge, Cambridge University Press.

Jason, Karen (1991). "The Role of Non-governmental Organizations in International Election Observing." *NYU Journal of International Law and Politics* **24**(4): 1795–1843.

Johnston, Alastair Iain (2001). "Treating International Institutions as Social Environments." *International Studies Quarterly* **45**(4): 487–515.

Joint International Observation Group (1998). Press Release. Phnom Pehn, Cambodia.

Jones, Stephen (2006). "The Rose Revolution: A Revolution without Revolutionaries?" *Cambridge Review of International Affairs* **19**(1): 33–48.

Kabemba, Claude (2003). From Military Rule to Multiparty Democracy: Political Reforms and Challenges in Lesotho, Electoral Institute of Southern Africa.

Kahn, Sharief (1990). "Hoyte Grants Key Opposition Demands." *Stabroek News* **5**(95): 1.

Kaiser, Paul (1999). "Power, Sovereignty, and International Election Observers: The Case of Zanzibar." *Africa Today* **46**(1): 28.

Karim, Tariq and Christine Fair (2007). Bangladesh at the Crossroads. Washington, D.C., United States Institute of Peace.

Katzenstein, Peter (1996). "Introduction: Alternative Perspective on International Security." In *The Culture of National Security: Norms and Identity in World Politics*, 1–32. New York, Columbia University Press.

Keck, Margaret and Kathryn Sikkink (1998). *Activists beyond Borders Advocacy Networks in International Politics*. Ithaca, New York, Cornell University Press.

Kegley, Charles, Gregory Raymond, et al. (1998). "The Rise and Fall of the Nonintervention Norm: Some Correlates and Potential Consequences." *Fletcher Forum of World Affairs* **22**(1): 81–97.

Kelley, Judith (2004a). *Ethnic Politics in Europe: The Power of Norms and Incentives*. Princeton, New Jersey, Princeton University Press.

Kelley, Judith (2004b). "International Actors on the Domestic Scene: Membership Conditionality and Socialization by International Institutions." *International Organization* **58**(3): 425.

Kelley, Judith (2006). "New Wine in Old Wineskins: Promoting Political Reforms through the New European Neighbourhood Policy." *Journal of Common Market Studies* **44**(1): 29–55.

Kelley, Judith (2008). "Assessing the Complex Evolution of Norms: The Rise of International Election Monitoring." *International Organization* **62**(2): 221–55.

Kelley, Judith (2009). "The More the Merrier? The Effects of Having Multiple International Election Monitoring Organizations." *Perspectives on Politics* **7**: 59–64.

Kelley, Judith (2011). "Do International Election Monitors Increase or Decrease Opposition Boycotts?" *Comparative Political Studies* **44**(11): 1527–56.

Kelley, Judith and Kiril Kolev (2010). Election Quality and International Observation: Two New Datasets. *Working paper*. Durham, North Carolina, Duke University.

Kennedy, John F. (1963). Towards a Strategy of Peace. Address by President Kennedy at The American University, Washington, D.C., June 10, 1963.

Keohane, Robert (1982). "The Demand for International Regimes." *International Organization* **36**(2): 325–55.

Keohane, Robert (1984). *After Hegemony: Cooperation and Discord in the World Political Economy*. Princeton, New Jersey, Princeton University Press.

Keohane, Robert, Stephen Macedo, et al. (2009). "Democracy-Enhancing Multilateralism." *International Organization* **63**(1): 1–31.

Kew, Darren (1999). "'Democrazy: Dem Go Craze, O': Monitoring the 1999 Nigerian Elections." *Issue: A Journal of Opinion* **27**(1): 29–33.

Kiljunen, Kimmo (2008). Keynote speech by Dr. Kimmo Kiljunen, Special Envoy of the Chairman-in-Office on Election-Related Issues. Chairmanship Seminar on Election-Related Issues, Vienna, 21–22 July 2008. Vienna, Austria, OSCE.

Killick, Tony (1997). "Principals, Agents and the Failings of Conditionality." *Journal of International Development* **9**(4): 483–95.

King, Gary and Langche Zeng (2007). "When Can History Be Our Guide? The Pitfalls of Counterfactual Inference." *International Studies Quarterly* **51**(1): 183–210.

Kingdon, John (1984). *Agendas, Alternatives, and Public Policies*. Boston, Little, Brown.

Klotz, Audie (1995). "Norms Reconstituting Interests: Global Racial Equality and U.S. Sanctions Against South Africa." *International Organization* **49**(3): 451–78.

Knack, Stephen (2004). "Does Foreign Aid Promote Democracy?" *International Studies Quarterly* **48**(1): 251–66.

Kriegler, Johann, Imani Aboud, et al. (2008). Report of the Independent Review Commission on the General Elections held in Kenya on 27th December 2007. Naroibi, Kenya.

Kumar, Krishna (1998). *Postconflict Elections, Democratization, and International Assistance*. Boulder, Colorado, Lynne Rienner.

Laakso, Liisa (2002). "The Politics of International Election Observation: The Case of Zimbabwe in 2000." *Journal of Modern African Studies* **40**(3): 437.

Lanskoy, Miriam and Giorgi Areshidze (2008). "Georgia's Year of Turmoil." *Journal of Democracy* **19**(4): 155–71.

Larson, James and Christine Callahan (1990). "Performance Monitoring: How It Affects Work Productivity." *Journal of Applied Psychology* **75**(5): 530–38.

Lean, Sharon (2007a). "External Validation and Democratic Accountability." In *Promoting Democracy in the Americas*, edited by S. Lean, T. Legler, and B. Dexter, 152–77. Baltimore, Johns Hopkins University Press.

Lean, Sharon F. (2007b). "Democracy Assistance to Domestic Election Monitoring Organizations: Conditions for Success." *Democratization* **14**(2): 289–312.

Lehoucq, Fabrice (2003). "Electoral Fraud: Causes, Types, and Consequences." *Annual Review of Political Science* **6**(1): 233–56.

Lemon, Anthony (2005). "South Africa's Third Post-apartheid Election, April 2004." *Electoral Studies* **24**(2): 319–26.

Lenarčič, Janez (2008). Closing remarks, Ambassador Janez Lenarčič, Director of the Office for Democratic Institutions and Human Rights, Chairmanship Election Seminar, Vienna, 21–22 July 2008.

Levitsky, Steven and Lucan Way (2002). "The Rise of Competitive Authoritarianism." *Journal of Democracy* **13**(2): 51–65.

Levitsky, Steven and Lucan Way (2005). "International Linkage and Democratization." *Journal of Democracy* **16**(3): 20–34.

Levitsky, Steven and Lucan Way (2006). "Linkage versus Leverage: Rethinking the International Dimension of Regime Change." *Comparative Politics* **38**(4): 379.

Levitsky, Steven and Lucan Way (2010). *Competitive Authoritarianism: Hybrid Regimes After the Cold War.* New York, Cambridge University Press.

Levy, Clifford (2010). "Ukraine Leader Drops Vote Challenge." *New York Times*, February 20, 2010.

Likmeta, Besar (2009). Albania Election "A Test for EU Bid." *AlbanianEconomy.com*, January 22, 2009.

Linz, Juan and Alfred Stepan (1978). *The Breakdown of Democratic Regimes.* Baltimore, Johns Hopkins University Press.

Linz, Juan and Alfred Stepan (1996). *Problems of Democratic Transition and Consolidation: Southern Europe, South America, and Post-communist Europe.* Baltimore, Johns Hopkins University Press.

Lipset, Seymour (1959). "Some Social Requisites of Democracy: Economic Development and Political Legitimacy." *American Political Science Review* **53**(1): 69–105.

Lopez-Pintor, Rafael (1998). "Nicaragua's Measured Move to Democracy." In *Postconflict Elections, Democratization, and International Assistance*, edited by K. Kumar. Boulder, Colorado, Lynne Rienner Publishers.

Lowenhardt, John (2005). "A Clash of Observations." *Helsinki Monitor* **16**(1): 1–3.

Luard, Evan (1988). *Conflict and Peace in the Modern International System: A Study of the Principles of International Order.* Albany, State University of New York Press.

Lust-Okar, Ellen (2009). "Legislative Elections in Hegomonic Authoritarian Regimes." In *Democratization by Elections: A New Mode of Transition*, edited by S. Lindberg, 226–45. Baltimore, Johns Hopkins University Press.

Lyons, Gene and Michael Mastanduno (1993). "International Intervention, State Sovereignty and the Future of International Society." *International Social Science Journal* **45**(4): 519–32.

Lyons, Terrence (2004). "Post-conflict Elections and the Process of Demilitarizing Politics: The Role of Electoral Administration." *Democratization* **11**(3): 36–62.

Mair, Stefan (1997). "Election Observation: Roles and Responsibilities of Long-term Election Observers." *ECDPM Working Paper* (22).

Maniruzzaman, Talukder (1992). "The Fall of the Military Dictator: 1991 Elections and the Prospect of Civilian Rule in Bangladesh." *Pacific Affairs* **65**(2): 203–24.

March, James and Johan Olsen (1998). "The Institutional Dynamics of International Political Orders." *International Organization* **49**(3): 451–78.

Marinov, Nikolay (2005). *Economic Pressure for Democratization and the Spread of Limited Government.* New Haven, Connecticut, Yale University Press.

McConnell, Shelley (2007). "Nicaragua's Turning Point." *Current History* **106**(697): 83–88.

McCoy, Jennifer (1993). "Mediating Democracy: A New Role for International Actors." In *New World Order: Social and Economic Implications*, edited by D. Bruce, 129–40. Atlanta, Georgia State University Business Press.

McCoy, Jennifer (1995). Invited Intrusion: International Election Monitoring and the Evolving Concept of Sovereignty. *Working Paper 95-1.* Atlanta, Georgia, Department of Political Science and Policy Research Center and the Carter Center, Georgia State University.

McCoy, Jennifer (1998). "Monitoring and Mediating Elections During Latin American Democratization." In *Electoral Observation and Democratic Transitions in Latin America*, edited by K. Middlebrook, 53–92. Center for U.S.-Mexican Studies, University of California, San Diego .

McCoy, Jennifer (2004). "What Really Happened in Venezuela?" *The Economist* 372(8391): 38–40.

McCoy, Jennifer, Larry Garber, et al. (1991). "Making Peace by Observing and Mediating Elections." *Journal of Democracy* 2(4): 102.

McFaul, Michael (2004). "Democracy Promotion as a World Value." *Washington Quarterly* 28(1): 147–63.

McFaul, Michael (2005). "Transitions From Postcommunism." *Journal of Democracy* 16(3): 5–19.

McIntire, Mike and Jeffrey Gettleman (2009). "A Chaotic Kenya Vote and a Secret U.S. Exit Poll." *New York Times*, January 30, 2009.

Mearsheimer, John (1994). "The False Promise of International Institutions." *International Security* 19(3): 5–49.

Mebane, Walter and Jasjeet Sekhon (1998). GENetic optimization using derivatives (GENOUD). Computer program available at http://sekhon.berkeley.edu/rgenoud/. Last accessed February 1, 2011.

Middlebrook, Kevin (1998). *Electoral Observation and Democratic Transitions in Latin America*. La Jolla, Center for U.S.-Mexican Studies, University of California, San Diego.

Mitchell, Lincoln (2009). *Uncertain Democracy: U.S. Foreign Policy and Georgia's Rose Revolution*. Philadelphia, University of Pennsylvania Press.

Mitchell, Lincoln and Andrew Sidamon-Eristoff (2009). "Georgia Needs a Different Path to Democracy." *Radio Free Europe Online*.

Møller, Jørgen and Svend-Erik Skanning (2010). "Beyond the Radial Delusion: Conceptualizing and Measuring Democracy and Non-democracy." *International Political Science Review* 3(2).

Monga, Celestin (1997). "Eight Problems with African Politics." *Journal of Democracy* 8: 156–70.

Montgomory, Tommie (1998). "International Missions, Observing Elections, and the Democratic Transition in El Salvador." In *Electoral Observation and Democratic Transitions in Latin America*, edited by K. Middlebrook, 115–40. La Jolla, Center for U.S.-Mexican Studies, University of California, San Diego.

Mosley, Paul, Jane Harrigan, et al. (1995). *Aid and Power: The World Bank and Policy-based Lending*. London; New York, Routledge.

Mujani, Saiful and R. William Liddle (2009). "Muslim Indonesia's Secular Democracy." *Asian Survey* 49(4): 575–90.

Mulikita, Njunga M. (1999). "Democratization and Conflict Resolution in Africa: The Role of International/Regional Election Observers." *Peacekeeping & International Relations* 28(3): 1.

Munck, Gerardo (1993). "Beyond Electoralism in El Salvador: Conflict Resolution through Negotiated Compromise." *Third World Quarterly* 14(1): 75–93.

Munoz-Pogossian, Betilde (2008). Coordinator, Unit for Electoral Studies, Organization of American States. Interview, April 10, Washington, D.C.

Mutua, Makau wa (1994). "Human Rights and State Despotism in Kenya: Institutional Problems." *Africa Today* **41**(4): 50.

Nadelmann, Ethan (1990). "Global Prohibition Regimes: The Evolution of Norms in International Society." *International Organization* **44**(4): 479–526.

Nasong'o, Shadrack (2007). "Political Transition without Transformation: The Dialectic of Liberalization without Democratization in Kenya and Zambia." *African Studies Review* **50**(1): 83–107.

National Democratic Institute (1991). Bangladesh Parliamentary Elections February 27, 1991, A Post Election Report. Washington, D.C.

National Democratic Institute (1996a). Preliminary Statement of the NDI Observer Delegation to the June 12, 1996 Parliamentary Election in Bangladesh. Washington, D.C.

National Democratic Institute (1996b). Second NDI Preliminary Statement: June 1996 Parliamentary Elections in Bangladesh. Washington, D.C.

National Democratic Institute (1998). Second Post-Election Statement on the Cambodian Election Process. Washington, D.C.

National Democratic Institute (1999a). Final Report on the May 30, 1999 Parliamentary Elections in Armenia. Washginton, D.C.

National Democratic Institute (1999b). The New Legal Framework for Elections in Indonesia, A Report of an NDI Assessment Team. Washington, D.C.

National Democratic Institute (2000a). Statement of the NDI International Delegation to Mexico's July 2, 2000 Elections. Mexico City, Mexico.

National Democratic Institute (2000b). Statement on the Refusal by the Government of Zimbabwe to Accredit NDI and Others to Observe the June 24–25 Elections. Washington, D.C.

National Democratic Institute (2005). Advancing Democracy In Indonesia: The Second Democratic Legislative Elections Since The Transition. Washington, D.C.

National Democratic Institute (2006). Statement of the NDI Pre-Election Delegation to Mexico's 2006 Presidential Elections. Mexico City, Mexico.

National Democratic Institute (2008a). Bangladesh: Statement of the National Democratic Institute Pre-election Delegation on the 2008 Parliamentary Elections. Washington, D.C.

National Democratic Institute (2008b). Statement of the NDI Election Observer Delegation to Bangladesh's 2008 Parliamentary Elections. Washington, D.C.

National Democratic Institute (2008c). Statement of the NDI Election Observer Delegation to Georgia's 2008 Presidential Election Tbilisi, Georgia.

National Democratic Institute (2009). Final Report on the Bangladesh 2008/2009 Elections. Washington, D.C.

National Democratic Institute and Carter Center (1999). International Election Observation Delegation to Indonesia's June 7, 1999, Legislative Elections. Washington, D.C.

National Democratic Institute and International Republican Institute (1989). The May 7, 1989 Panamanian Elections. Washington, D.C.

National Democratic Institute and International Republican Institute (1990). Post-Election Statement. International Delegation to Bulgarian National Elections. Appendix X to the Final Report. Sofia, Bulgaria.

National Democratic Institute and International Republican Institute (1991). The October 13, 1991 Legislative and Municipal Elections in Bulgaria. Washington, D.C.

National Democratic Institute and International Republican Institute (1998). Terms of Reference for Cambodia Assessment Mission. Washington, D.C.

Ndegwa, Stephen (1998). "The Incomplete Transition: The Constitutional and Electoral Context in Kenya." *Africa Today* **45**(2): 193.

Nelson, Joan and Stephanie Eglinton (1992). *Encouraging Democracy: What Role for Conditioned Aid?* Washington, D.C., Overseas Development Council.

Nevitte, Neil and Santiago Canton (1997). "The Role of Domestic Observers."*Journal of Democracy* **8**(3): 47–61.

Ng, Sheere (2008). "Lazy Eye. Election Observation Was on the Relaxed Side in Lalitpur." *Nepali Times*, 395

Nichol, Jim (2006). Armenia, Azerbaijan, and Georgia: Political developments and implications for US interests. *Issue Brief for Congress*, Congressional Research Service.

Nielson, Dan and Michael Tierney (2003). "Delegation to International Organizations: Agency Theory and World Bank Environmental Reform." *International Organization* **57**(2): 241–76.

Obi, Cyril (2008). "International Election Observer Missions and the Promotion of Democracy: Some Lessons from Nigeria's 2007 Elections." *Politikon: South African Journal of Political Studies* **35**(1): 69–86.

Odell, John (1982). *U.S. Monetary Policy: Markets, Power, and Ideas as Sources of Changes.* Princeton, New Jersey, Princeton University Press.

Office for Democratic Institutions and Human Rights (1992). Elections in Georgia. Prague, Czech Republic, Conference on Security and Co-operation in Europe.

Office for Democratic Institutions and Human Rights (1996a). Armenian Presidential Elections: September 24, 1996 Final Report. Warsaw, Poland, Organization for Security and Co-operation in Europe.

Office for Democratic Institutions and Human Rights (1996b). Observations of the Parliamentary Election in Albania, 26 May and 2 June 1996. Warsaw, Poland, Organization for Security and Co-operation in Europe.

Office for Democratic Institutions and Human Rights (1996c). Preliminary statement on the elections in Bosnia and Herzegovina on 14 September 1996. Warsaw, Poland, Organization for Security and Co-operation in Europe.

Office for Democratic Institutions and Human Rights (1996d). Second statement on the elections in Bosnia and Herzegovina on 14 September 1996. Warsaw, Poland, Organization for Security and Co-operation in Europe.

Office for Democratic Institutions and Human Rights (1997a). Albania: Parliamentary Elections, June 29, 1997. Warsaw, Poland, Organization for Security and Co-operation in Europe.

Office for Democratic Institutions and Human Rights (1997b). Report on the implementation of recommendations contained in the final report on the presidential election in Armenia, 22 September 1996. Warsaw, Poland, Organization for Security and Co-operation in Europe.

Office for Democratic Institutions and Human Rights (1999a). Final report on the parliamentary elections in Armenia, 30 May 1999. Warsaw, Poland, Organization for Security and Co-operation in Europe.

Office for Democratic Institutions and Human Rights (1999b). The ODIHR Election Observation Handbook, Fourth Edition. Warsaw, Poland, Organization for Security and Co-operation in Europe.

Office for Democratic Institutions and Human Rights (1999c). Preliminary statement on the parliamentary elections in the Russian Federation, 19 December 1999. Warsaw, Poland, Organization for Security and Co-operation in Europe.

Office for Democratic Institutions and Human Rights (2000a). Russian Federation Presidential Elections: 26 March, 2000. Warsaw, Poland, Organization for Security and Co-operation in Europe.

Office for Democratic Institutions and Human Rights (2000b). Russian Federation, Elections to the State Duma, 19 December 1999, Final Report. Warsaw, Poland, Organization for Security and Co-operation in Europe.

Office for Democratic Institutions and Human Rights (2001). Republic of Albania Parliamentary Elections—24 June–19 August 2001. Warsaw, Poland, Organization for Security and Co-operation in Europe.

Office for Democratic Institutions and Human Rights (2002a). Needs assessment report on the 19 February 2003 presidential election in Armenia, 11–15 December 2002. Warsaw, Poland, Organization for Security and Co-operation in Europe.

Office for Democratic Institutions and Human Rights (2002b). OSCE/ODIHR Needs Assessment Mission Report, 11–15 December 2002, Republic of Armenia, Presidential Election, 19 February 2003 Warsaw, Poland, Organization for Security and Co-operation in Europe.

Office for Democratic Institutions and Human Rights (2003a). Final report on the presidential election in Armenia, 19 February and 5 March 2003. Warsaw, Poland, Organization for Security and Co-operation in Europe.

Office for Democratic Institutions and Human Rights (2003b). Needs assessment mission report 11–16 July 2003, on 12 October local government elections in Albania. Warsaw, Poland, Organization for Security and Co-operation in Europe.

Office for Democratic Institutions and Human Rights (2003c). Needs assessment report on the 7 December 2003 parliamentary elections in the Russian Federation. Warsaw, Poland, Organization for Security and Co-operation in Europe.

Office for Democratic Institutions and Human Rights (2003d). Republic of Armenia: Parliamentary Elections, 25 May 2003. Warsaw, Poland, Organization for Security and Co-operation in Europe.

Office for Democratic Institutions and Human Rights (2004a). Final report on the elections to the State Duma of the Russian Federation, 7 December 2003. Warsaw, Poland, Organization for Security and Co-operation in Europe.

Office for Democratic Institutions and Human Rights (2004b). Georgia Partial Repeat Parliamentary Elections, 28 March, 2004. Warsaw, Poland, Organization for Security and Co-operation in Europe.

Office for Democratic Institutions and Human Rights (2004c). Russian Federation Presidential Election, 14 March 2004. Warsaw, Poland, Organization for Security and Co-operation in Europe.

Office for Democratic Institutions and Human Rights (2005a). Election Observation. A decade of monitoring elections: the people and the practice. Warsaw, Poland, Organization for Security and Co-operation in Europe.

Office for Democratic Institutions and Human Rights (2005b). Final report on the parliamentary elections in Albania, 3 July 2005. Warsaw, Poland, Organization for Security and Co-operation in Europe.

Office for Democratic Institutions and Human Rights (2005c). Needs assessment mission report on the constitutional referendum in Armenia, 27 November 2005. Warsaw, Poland, Organization for Security and Co-operation in Europe.

Office for Democratic Institutions and Human Rights (2005d). Republic of Bulgaria Parliamentary Elections, 25 June 2005. Warsaw, Poland, Organization for Security and Co-operation in Europe.

Office for Democratic Institutions and Human Rights (2006). Republic of Kazakhstan Presidential Election 4 December 2005, Final report. Warsaw, Poland, Organization for Security and Co-operation in Europe.

Office for Democratic Institutions and Human Rights (2007a). Needs Assessment Mission Report on the Extraordinary Presidential Election in Georgia Scheduled for 5 January 2008. Warsaw, Poland, Organization for Security and Co-operation in Europe.

Office for Democratic Institutions and Human Rights (2007b). Republic of Armenia Presidential Election 19 February 2008 OSCE/ODIHR Needs Assessment Mission Report, 4–5 December 2007. Warsaw, Poland, Organization for Security and Co-operation in Europe.

Office for Democratic Institutions and Human Rights (2008a). Georgian election in essence consistent with most commitments but challenges must be addressed urgently. Press Release. Tbilisi, Georgia, Organization for Security and Co-operation in Europe.

Office for Democratic Institutions and Human Rights (2008b). Republic of Armenia Presidential Election, 19 February 2008. Warsaw, Poland, Organization for Security and Co-operation in Europe.

Office for Democratic Institutions and Human Rights (2009a). Republic of Albania Parliamentary Elections, 28 June 2009. Final Report. Warsaw, Poland, Organization for Security and Co-operation in Europe.

Office for Democratic Institutions and Human Rights (2009b). Republic of Bulgaria: Parliamentary Elections, 5 July 2009. Warsaw, Poland, Organization for Security and Co-operation in Europe.

Office for Democratic Institutions and Human Rights, European Parliament, et al. (2008). Georgia: Parliamentary Elections, 21 May 2008. Warsaw, Poland, Organization for Security and Co-operation in Europe.

Olearchyk, Roman (2008). "Georgia Election Process Labeled as 'Rigged.'" *Financial Times*, January 4, 2008.

Olearchyk, Roman, Catherine Belton, et al. (2008). "Georgia's Saakashvili Scores Poll Victory." *Financial Times*, January 6, 2008.

Oquaye, Mike (1995). "The Ghanaian Elections of 1992—a Dissenting View." *African Affairs* **94**(375): 259.

Organization for Security and Co-operation in Europe Presence in Albania (2000). Summary Report, International mediation in preparation for the 2000 local elections. Tirana, Albania, Organization for Security and Co-operation.

Organization for Security and Co-operation in Europe Presence in Albania (2004). Semi-annual OSCE report on activities in Albania. Tirana, Albania, Organization for Security and Co-operation.

Organization of American States General Assembly (1990). Unit for the Promotion of Democracy, Organization of American States.

O'Shaughnessy, Laura Nuzzi and Michael Dodson (1999). "Political Bargaining and Democratic Transitions: A Comparison of Nicaragua and El Salvador." *Journal of Latin American Studies* **31**: 99–127.

Ottaway, Marina (1998). "Angola's Failed Elections." In *Postconflict Elections, Democratization, and International Assistance*, edited by K. Kumar, 133–51. Boulder, Colorado, Lynne Rienner.

Ottaway, Marina (2003). *Democracy Challenged: The Rise of Semi-authoritarianism*. Washington, D.C., Carnegie Endowment for International Peace.

Oxford Analytica (2002). Zimbabwe: EU moves unlikely to harm Mugabe campaign. *OxResearch* **1**.

Oxford Analytica (April 2002). EU/AFRICA: Doubts grow over election observers, OxResearch **1**.

Pastor, Robert (1993). *Integration with Mexico: Options for US Policy*. New York, Twentieth Century Fund.

Pastor, Robert (1998). "Mediating Elections." *Journal of Democracy* **9**(1): 154.

Pastor, Robert (2000). "Exiting the Labyrinth." *Journal of Democracy* **11**(4): 20–24.

Pastor, Robert (2004). America Observed. Why foreign election observers would rate the United States near the bottom. *American Prospect*.

Pastor, Robert (2006). "What the U.S. Could Learn from Mexico." *LA Times*.

Patten, Chris (2000). Speaking Points of Chris Patten, Speech/00/225—European Parliament—Strasbourg, 4 July.

Peceny, Mark (1999). "Forcing Them To Be Free." *Political Research Quarterly* **52**(3): 549–82.

Poe, Steven, Sabine Carey, et al. (2001). "How Are These Pictures Different—A Quantitative Comparison of the US State Department and Amnesty International Human Rights Reports, 1976–1995." *Human Rights Quarterly* **23**: 650–77.

Political Risk Group (undated). A Business Guide to Political Risk for International Decisions. Part II: International Country Risk Guide.

Posner, Daniel (1995). "Malawi's New Dawn." *Journal of Democracy* **6**: 131–45.

Potocki, Rodger (2008). "Belarus: Shhh! Elections in Progress." *Transitions Online*(September 30).

Powers, Kathy and Gary Goetz (2006). The Evolution of Regional Economic Insitutions (REI) into Security Institutions or the Demise of Realist Military Alliances? *Duke University Seminar on Global Governance and Democracy*. Durham, North Carolina, Duke University.

Prize, Richard (1997). *The Chemical Weapons Taboo*. Ithaca, New York, Cornell University Press.

Przeworski, Adam (1991). *Democracy and the Market: Political and Economic Reforms in Eastern Europe and Latin America*. Cambridge: Cambridge University Press.

Puddington, Arch (2010). *Freedom in the World 2010: Erosion of Freedom Intensifies*. Washington, D.C., Freedom House.

Puddington, Arch (2011). *Freedom in the World 2011: The Authoritarian Challenge to Democracy*. Washington, D.C., Freedom House.

Quezada, Sergio (1998). "Electoral Observation and Democracy in Mexico." In *Electoral Observation and Democratic Transitions in Latin America*, edited by K. Middlebrook, 167–85. San Diego, University of California Press.

Reilly, Benjamin (2002). "Post-Conflict Elections: Constraints and Dangers." *International Peacekeeping* **9**(2): 118.

Remmer, Karen (1995). "Review: New Theoretical Perspectives on Democratization." *Comparative Politics* **28**(1): 103–22.

Rich, Roland (2001). "Bringing Democracy into International Law." *Journal of Democracy* **12**(3): 20–34.

Riley, Christopher (1997). "Neither Free Nor Fair: The 1996 Bosnian Elections and the Failure of the U.N. Election Monitoring Mission." *Vanderbilt Journal of Transnational Law* **30**(5): 1173–1214.

Risse, Thomas (2003). "'Let's Argue!': Communicative Action in World Politics." *International Organization* **54**(1): 1–39.

Rodriguez, Olga (2009). "Mexico's Calderon Proposes Major Political Reform." *Associated Press*. Mexico City.

Rodrik, Daniel (1997). TFPG Controversies, Institutions, and Economic Performance in East Asia (February 1997). *NBER Working Paper No. W5914*. Cambridge, Massachussetts.

Roessler, Philip (2005). "Donor-Induced Democratization and the Privatization of State Violence in Kenya and Rwanda." *Comparative Politics* **37**(2): 207–27.

Rubin, Donald B. (1973). "The Use of Matched Sampling and Regression Adjustment to Remove Bias in Observational Studies." *Biometrics* **29**(1): 185–203.

Rubin, Donald and Neal Thomas (1996). "Matching Using Estimated Propensity Scores: Relating Theory to Practice." *Biometrics* **52**(1): 249–64.

Ruiz-Rufino, Ruben (2007). "The Parliamentary Election in Armenia, May 2007." *Electoral Studies* **27**: 356–90.

Rupnik, Jacques (2007). "From Democracy Fatigue to Populist Backlash." *Journal of Democracy* **18**(4): 17–25.

Saari, Sinikukka (2009). "European Democracy Promotion in Russia before and after the 'Colour' Revolutions." *Democratization* **16**(4): 732–55.

Santa-Cruz, Arturo (2005a). "Constitutional Structures, Sovereignty, and the Emergence of Norms: The Case of International Election Monitoring." *International Organization* **59**(3): 663–93.

Santa-Cruz, Arturo (2005b). *International Election Monitoring, Sovereignty, and the Western Hemisphere Idea: The Emergence of an International Norm.* New York, Routledge.

Santa-Cruz, Arturo (2005c). "Monitoring Elections, Redefining Sovereignty: The 2000 Peruvian Electoral Process as an International Event." *Journal of Latin American Studies* **37**(4): 739–67.

Sartori, Anne (2003). "An Estimator for Some Binary-outcome Selection Models without Exclusion Restrictions." *Political Analysis* **11**(2): 111–38.

Sasse, Gwendolyn (2008). "The Politics of EU Conditionality: The Norm of Minority Protection during and beyond EU Accession." *Journal of European Public Policy* **15**(6): 842–60.

Schedler, Andreas (2000). "Mexico's Victory: The Democratic Revelation." *Journal of Democracy* **11**(4): 5–19.

Schedler, Andreas (2002a). "The Menu of Manipulation." *Journal of Democracy* **13**(2): 36–50.

Schedler, Andreas (2002b). "The Nested Game of Democratization by Elections." *International Political Science Review* **23**(1): 103–22.

Schedler, Andreas (2007). "The Mexican Standoff: The Mobilization of Distrust." *Journal of Democracy* **18**(1): 88–102.

Schedler, Andreas (2010). "Mexico: Democratic Transition and Beyond." In *Politics in the Developing World*, edited by P. Burnell, V. Randall, and L. Rakner, 439–51. Oxford, Oxford University Press.

Scherlen, Renee (1998). "Lessons to Build On: The 1994 Mexican Presidential Election." *Journal of Interamerican Studies & World Affairs* **40**(1): 19.

Schimmelfennig, Frank , Stefan Engert, et al. (2003). "Costs, Commitment and Compliance: The Impact of EU Democratic Conditionality on Latvia, Slovakia and Turkey." *Journal of Common Market Studies* **41**(3): 495–518.

Schimpp, Michele and Aud McKernan (2001). Elections and Conflict: An Issues Paper. Washington,D.C., USAID, Elections & Political Processes Division, DCHA/DG.

Schmeets, Hans and Jeanet Exel (1997). *The 1996 Bosnia-Herzegovina Elections: An Analysis of the Observations*. Dordrecht, The Netherlands; Boston, Kluwer Academic.

Schmitter, Philippe and Terry Karl (1991). "What Democracy Is . . . and Is Not." *Journal of Democracy* **2**(3): 75–88.

Schneider, Carsten and Philippe Schmitter (2004). "Liberalization, Transition and Consolidation: Measuring the Components of Democratization." *Democratization* **11**(5): 59–90.

Scranton, Margaret (1997). "The Impact of Election Observers in Central America." In *Elections and Democracy in Central America, Revisited*, edited by J. Booth and M. Seligson, 183–201. Chapel Hill, University of North Carolina Press.

Scranton, Margaret (1998). "Electoral Observation and Panama's Democratic Transition." In *Electoral Observation and Democratic Transitions in Latin America*, edited by K. Middlebrook, 53–90. La Jolla, Center for U.S.-Mexican Studies, University of California, San Diego.

Sedelmeier, Ulrich (2008). "After Conditionality: Post-accession Compliance with EU Law in East Central Europe." *Journal of European Public Policy* **15**(6): 806–25.

Sekhon, Jasjeet (2007). "Multivariate and Propensity Score Matching Software with Automated Balance Optimization: The Matching package for R." *Journal of Statistical Software* **VV**(II): 1–52.

Sekhon, Jasjeet and Richard Grieve (2008). A new non-parametric matching method for bias adjustment with applications to economic evaluations, University of California, Berkeley.

Sell, Susan and Aseem Prakash (2004). "Using Ideas Strategically: The Contest Between Business and NGO Networks in Intellectual Property Rights." *International Studies Quarterly* **48**(1): 143–75.

Sharon, Lean (2004). *Evaluating Election Monitoring in the Americas*. Conference Papers—Midwestern Political Science Association.

Signorino, Curt (2003). "Structure and Uncertainty in Discrete Choice Models." *Political Analysis* **11**(4): 316–44.

Sikkink, Kathryn (2002). "Restructuring World Politics : The Limits and Assymmetries of Soft Power." In *Restructuring World Politics: Transnational Social Movements,*

Networks, and Norms, edited by S. Khagram, James Riker, and Kathryn Sikkink, 301–19. Minneapolis, University of Minnesota Press.

Simmons, Beth (2000). "International Law and State Behavior: Commitment and Compliance in International Monetary Affairs." *American Political Science Review* **94**(4): 819–35.

Simmons, Beth (2009). *Mobilizing for Human Rights: International Law in Domestic Politics*. New York, Cambridge University Press.

Simmons, Beth and Zachary Elkins (2004). "The Globalization of Liberalization: Policy Diffusion in the International Political Economy." *American Political Science Review* **98**(1): 171–89.

Simmons, Beth and Daniel Hopkins (2005). "The Constraining Power of International Treaties: Theory and Methods." *American Political Science Review* **99**(4): 623–31.

Sisk, Timothy and Andrew Reynolds, eds. (1998). *Elections and Conflict Management in Africa*. Washington, D.C, United States Institute of Peace Press.

Sives, Amanda (2001a). "Election Observation and Deepening Democracy in the Commonwealth." *Round Table* **90**(361): 507–28.

Sives, Amanda (2001b). "A Review of Commonwealth Election Observation." *Commonwealth & Comparative Politics* **39**(3): 132.

Snyder, Jack (2000). *From Voting to Violence: Democratization and Nationalist Conflict*. New York, Norton.

Solovyov, Dmitry (2008). "Russia Cuts Foreign Observers to Presidential Poll." *Reuters*.

Soremekun, Kayode (1999). "Disguised Tourism and the Electoral Process in Africa: A Study of International Observers and the 1998 Local Government Elections in Nigeria." *Issue: A Journal of Opinion* **27**(1): 26–28.

South African Development Community, Parliamentary Forum (2000). Election Observation Mission, Observers' Report on National Assembly Elections in Zimbabwe, 24–25 June 2000. Windhoek, Namibia.

South African Development Community Parliamentary Observer Mission (2004). Report of the SADC Parliamentary Observer Mission to South Africa: 1st–18th April 2004. (Reprinted in Election Update South Africa 10, 7 June 2004, at http://www.eisa.org.za). South African Development Community.

Southall, Roger (2003). "An Unlikely Success: South Africa and Lesotho's Election of 2002." *Journal of Modern African Studies* **41**(2): 269–96.

Stahler-Sholk, Richard (1994). "El Salvador's Negotiated Transition: From Low-intensity Conflict to Low-intensity Democracy." *Journal of Interamerican Studies and World Affairs* **36**(4): 1–59.

Stein, Arthur (1982). "Coordination and Collaboration: Regimes in an Anarchic World." *International Organization* **36**(2): 299–324.

Stepan, Alfred (1988). "The Last Days of Pinochet?" *New York Review of Books* **2**.

Stone, Randall (2002). *Lending Credibility: The International Monetary Fund and the Post-Communist Transition*. Princeton, New Jersey, Princeton University Press.

Stone, Randall (2004). "The Political Economy of IMF Lending in Africa." *American Political Science Review* **98**(4): 577–91.

Stone, Randall (2008). "The Scope of IMF Conditionality." *International Organization* **62**(4): 553–736.

Strange, Susan (1982). "Cave! Hic Dragones: A Critique of Regime Analysis." *International Organization* **36**(2): 479–96.

Strohal, Christian (undated). "Interview by Meike Scholz." Retrieved January 11, 2010, from http://www.inwent.org/ez/articles/074379/index.en.shtml.

Sukma, Rizal (2009). "Indonesian Politics in 2009: Defective Elections, Resilient Democracy." *Bulletin of Indonesian Economic Studies* **45**(3): 317–36.

Teshome-Bahiru, Wondwosen (2008). "International Election Observers in Africa: The Case of Ethiopia." *Alternatives: Turkish Journal of International Relations* **7**(1): 119–37.

The Economist (2009). "The Indonesian Surprise." April 2, 2009.

Tomz, Michael, Jason Wittenberg, et al. (2003). CLARIFY: Software for Interpreting and Presenting Statistical Results. Version 2.1. Available at http://gking.harvard .edu/.

Transitions Online (2008). "Our Take: Soviet Armenia." *Transitions Online*, March 7, 2008.

Tucker, Joshua (2007). "Enough! Electoral Fraud, Collective Action Problems, and Post-Communist Colored Revolutions." Perspectives on Politics 5(3): 535–51.

Tudoroiu, Theodor (2007). "Rose, Orange, and Tulip: The Failed Post-Soviet Revolutions." *Communist and Post-Communist Studies* **40**(3): 315–42.

Unit for the Promotion of Democracy (2000). Progress Report of the General Secretariat of the Organization of American States on the Activities of the Organization to Implement the Mandates of the Santiago Summit. XVIII Meeting of the Summit Implementation Review Group. Washington, D.C., Organization of American States.

Unit for the Promotion of Democracy (2002). Report of the Electoral Observation Mission, National General Elections, Regional Elections in Costa Atlantica, Nicaragua, 2001–2002. Washington, D.C., Organization of American States.

Unit for the Promotion of Democracy (2004a). OAS will not observe Venezuelan elections. Press Release. Washington, D.C., Organization of American States.

Unit for the Promotion of Democracy (2004b). Report of the OAS Electoral Observation Mission in the Republic of Panama General Elections 2004, Organization of American States.

Unit for the Promotion of Democracy (2006). Report of the Electoral Observation Mission General and Regional Elections in Guyana August 28, 2006. Washington, D.C., Organization of American States.

United Nations (1988). UN General Assembly Resolution A/res/43/157. Enhancing the Effectiveness of the Principle of Periodic and Genuine Elections. 8 December. New York.

United Nations (1991). Reports of the Secretary General to the General Assembly. Enhancing the Effectiveness of the Principle of Periodic and Genuine Election.

United Nations (2001). Respect for the Principles of National Sovereignty and Non-Interference in the Internal Affairs of States in Electoral Processes as an Important Elment for the Promotion and Protection of Human Rights.

United Nations (2003). Respect for the Principles of National Sovereignty and Diversity of Democratic Systems in Electoral Processes as an Important Element for the Promotion and Protection of Human Rights.

United Nations (2005). Declaration of Principles for International Election Observation and Code of Conduct for International Election Observers. Commemorated October 27, 2005, at the United Nations, New York.

United Nations Development Programme (2000). UNDP and Electoral Assistance: Ten Years of Experience. New York.

United States State Department (2001). Country Reports on Human Rights Practices 2000. Washington, D.C.

Usupashivili, David (2004). An analysis of the presidential and parliamentary elections in Georgia—a case study. *Election Assessment in the South Caucasus, 2003–2004*, 75–100. Washington D.C., International Institute for Democracy and Electoral Assistance.

Vachudova, Milada (2005). *Europe Undivided Democracy, Leverage, and Integration after Communism*. Oxford; New York, Oxford University Press.

Valenzuela, Arturo (2004). "Latin American Precidencies Interrupted." *Journal of Democracy* 15(4): 5–19.

van Kessel, Ineke (2000). "Stability or Democracy: On the Role of Monitors, Media and Miracles." In *Election Observation and Democratization in Africa*, edited by J. Abbink and G. Hesseling, 50–75. New York, St. Martin's Press.

Venter, Denis (2003). "Democracy and Multipary Politics in Africa: Recent Elections in Zambia, Zimbabwe, and Lesotho." *EASSRR* 19(1): 1–39.

Ward, Michael and Kristian Gleditsch (1998). "Democratizing for Peace." *American Political Science Review* 92(1): 51–61.

Weingast, Barry (1997). "The Political Foundations of Democracy and the Rule of Law." The American Political Science Review 91(2): 245–63.

Weiss, Edith and Harold Jacobson, eds. (2000). *Engaging Countries: Strengthening Compliance with International Environmental Accords*. Cambridge, Massachusetts, MIT Press.

Weitz, Richard (2008). "International Challenges Arise From Armenia's Problematic Elections." *Central Asia-Caucasus Analyst* 5.

Whitehead, Lawrence (1996). *The International Dimensions of Democratization: Europe and the Americas*. Oxford, Oxford University Press.

Wolf, Sonja (2009). "Subverting Democracy: Elite Rule and the Limits to Political Participation in Post-War El Salvador." *Journal of Latin American Studies* 41(3): 429–65.

World Bank. (1989). "Sub-Saharan Africa: From Crisis to Sustainable Growth." International Bank for Reconstruction and Development.

Wright, Theodore (1964). *American Support for Free Elections Abroad*. Washington, D.C., Public Affairs Press.

Youngs, Richard (2001a). Democracy Promotion: The Case of European Union Strategy, Center for European Policy Studies.

Youngs, Richard (2001b). *The European Union and the Promotion of Democracy*, Oxford, Oxford University Press.

Zak, Marilyn (1987). "Assisting Elections in the Third World." *Washington Quarterly* 10(4): 175–93.

Zakaria, Fareed (1997). "The Rise of Illiberal Democracy." *Foreign Affairs* 76(6): 22–43.

Index

Liberal Party (PLC), 254, 255; continued elections problems in, 136, 139; and Contras, 145, 255; and corruption, 254; and democracy, 252, 254; and democratic transition, 253, 255; and domestic capacity, 255; and domestic pressures, 149; and donors, 253; and economy, 253; election of 1984 in, 151, 253; election of 1989 in, 52; election of 1990 in, 33, 75, 98, 151, 253; election of 1996 in, 151, 252; election of 2001 in, 151, 252; election of 2006 in, 151, 254, 255; election of 2008 in, 255; and electoral commissions, 253; and electoral system, 252; and European Union, 163, 254, 255; and government, 252–53, 254, 255; and International Foundation for Electoral Systems, 253–54; and International Republican Institute, 151, 254; and legal framework/electoral laws, 253, 255; and opposition, 252–53; and Organization of American States, 253, 254; and political parties, 253, 254, 255; and poverty, 255; and recommendations, 253–54; Sandinista National Liberation Front (FSLN), 145, 255; and Sandinistas, 145, 252, 253, 255; stagnation in, 176; and United Nations, 23, 252; and United States, 145, 253, 254, 255; and Venezuela, 254, 255; and violence, 255; and voter identification, 253, 254; and voter registers, 253–54; and voters, 255; and vote tabulation, 253
Niger, 4
Nigeria, 69, 72, 159
nongovernmental organizations (NGOs), 3, 34, 38, 45, 60; and autonomy dilemma, 176; and bias, 65–66; consistency and follow-up by, 151; and donors, 102; funding of, 65; and Georgia, 229; global operations of, 19; and Indonesia, 238; and Mexico, 149, 248; as more critical, 158; multiple and diverse stakeholders in, 65; and Russia, 260; size and length of stay of, 38–39; and United States, 16, 26; Western, 65–66
noninterference, 22–23, 24
nonintervention, 22, 24
nonprofit institutes, 34
Noriega, Manuel, 256, 257, 258
Noriega, Roger, 227
normative environment, 27
norm entrepreneurs, 21
norms, 60; and biases, 63; changing environment of, 21–23; demonstration and institu-

tionalization of, 106; differences in, 76; evolution of, 18; and socialization, 11, 106; teaching new, 110. *See also* international standard(s)
North American Free Trade Agreements (NAFTA), 30, 148, 248
North Atlantic Treaty Organization (NATO), 47, 223
Norwegian Helsinki Council (NHC), 38

Obama, Barack, 227
objectivity, 6–9, 15, 60, 155, 156–66, 242
observation. *See* monitoring/observation
observers. *See* monitors/observers
Office for Democratic Institutions and Human Rights (ODIHR), 34, 108, 212–13, 216, 230, 259, 260
one-party system, 144
opposition, 5, 103; and Bangladesh, 219; boycotting by, 6; and Bulgaria, 222; effect of endorsements on, 75; and Georgia, 230, 232; and Guyana, 27, 233, 234, 235; and invitations to monitors, 44; and Kenya, 242, 243, 244; and likelihood of endorsement, 71; and Mexico, 247, 248, 251; and monitors' verification role, 10; and Nicaragua, 252–53; and Panama, 256, 257, 258; and pre-election violence, 72; and Russia, 144, 260; stifling of, 59; and Western progress reports, 148
Organisation Internationale de la Francophonie (OIF), 37–38, 50, 53
Organization for Economic Cooperation and Development (OECD), 148, 248
Organization for Security and Co-operation in Europe (OSCE), 17–18, 35–36, 44–45; and Albania, 136, 211, 212–14; and Armenia, 59, 133, 146, 148, 149, 215, 216, 217; assessment missions of, 173, 268n15, 278n46; as biased, 50; and Bosnia, 48, 173; and Bosnia and Herzegovina, 62–63, 69, 74, 165; and Bulgaria, 134, 221, 222, 223; changing reporting practices of, 80; and Commonwealth of Independent States, 38, 52; consistency and follow-up by, 174; democracy and membership in, 29; and established democracies, 178; and European Union membership, 148; and Georgia, 7–8, 65, 143, 228–30, 231; and Kazakhstan, 77; and manuals, 57; member states of, 22; and monitoring standards, 162; quality of, 120; records of, 182;

247; limited and predictable coverage of, 98; and Mexico, 251; percentage covered, 40; proper procedures at, 106; and South Africa, 262, 263

poverty: and El Salvador, 224; and Georgia, 228; and Guyana, 232; and Indonesia, 237; and Lesotho, 245; and Nicaragua, 255. *See also* economy

pre-election period, 39, 68, 82; assessment of, 17; cheating in, 66, 67, 83, 84, 87, 90; evaluation of, 66; and Georgia, 7; and Guyana, 89; incidence of problems in, 85, 86; and Kenya, 72, 245; and legal problems, 83; manipulation in, 80–82; monitoring visits in, 131; monitor-recommended changes in, 105; monitors' neglect of, 80–81; and shift from election day problems, 80–81, 83–86, 87, 90–92; violence in, 72, 73, 76, 81, 82, 84, 86, 87, 91, 92–93, 160

progress bias, 63, 70–73

Project on International Election Monitoring, 14

proliferation dilemma, 177

Putin, Vladimir, 100, 144, 171, 259–60

Quality of Elections Data (QED), 182, 183, 185, 186

Rahman, Mujibur, 218

Rahman, Ziaur, 218

rationalism/rationalist logic, 10–11, 99, 109, 168, 170

recommendations, 168; about administration, 105, 131–32; and Bangladesh, 218, 219, 220–21; and Bulgaria, 222; and El Salvador, 225; follow-up on, 179; and Georgia, 230–31; and Guyana, 232, 234; implementation of, 136–41, 173; inattention to, 177; and Indonesia, 237, 238, 241; and Kenya, 243, 244; and Lesotho, 245, 247; and Mexico, 247, 249–50; and Nicaragua, 253–54; and Panama, 257; as reinforcing international expectations, 10; as repeatedly ignored, 174; and Russia, 258, 259, 260; and South Africa, 261, 262. *See also* assessments; backsliding/regression; endorsement, likelihood of; reports

Rectors Forum, 238

regression. *See* backsliding/regression

Reich, Otto, 227

reports, 40, 82; contradictions in, 62–63, 163–64; difficulties in obtaining, 181–82; failure

to issue final, 175; and Indonesia, 238; moratorium on statement of, 179; recommendations in, 105, 131–32; structure of, 50. *See also* assessments; endorsement, likelihood of; recommendations

Resistência Nacional Moçambicana (RENAMO), 27

resource dilemma, 177

Rhodesia, 19, 37. *See also* Zimbabwe

Rohrabacher, Dana, 227

Romania, 102

Russia, 258–60; and administration of elections, 147, 162, 258; and "against all" voting option, 165, 259; antidemocratic pressures of, 170; and Armenia, 146, 215; backsliding by, 148, 258, 259; and Belarus, 172; and biases of monitors, 50, 62; and campaign finances, 259; Central Election Commission, 259, 260; and civil society, 149, 170; consistency and follow-up in, 151; continued election problems in, 136, 139, 141; and Council of Europe, 53–54, 100, 144, 147, 151, 165, 258, 259, 260; and democratic transition, 258, 259; and domestic actors/conditions, 258; and domestic pressures, 149; election of 1993 in, 136, 258, 259; election of 1995 in, 147; election of 1996 in, 144, 260; election of 1999 in, 62, 66, 90, 92, 165, 259; election of 2000 in, 62, 78, 144, 259; election of 2003 in, 260; election of 2007 in, 46, 260; election of 2008 in, 46, 54, 100, 144, 260; elections of 1990s in, 171; and electoral commissions, 259, 260; and electoral framework, 147; and European Union, 69; as following recommendations, 144; and Georgia, 7, 228, 229, 230, 260; and government, 258, 259–60; and incumbents, 258, 259, 260; and International Republican Institute, 133, 136, 258, 259, 260; and legal framework/electoral laws, 258; and legitimacy, 258, 260; and lenient monitors, 54–55, 164; and media, 144, 258, 259, 260; in mid-1990s, 170; and National Democratic Institute, 260; and nongovernmental organizations, 260; and opposition, 144, 260; and Organization for Security and Co-operation in Europe, 46, 50, 54, 62, 65, 69, 92, 100, 144, 151, 161–62, 165, 258, 259, 260; and political parties, 259; and recommendations, 258, 259, 260; referendum of 1993 in, 133, 136; and Saakashvili, 3; and

of, 167, 168; and measure of election quality, 114–115; and monitored vs. nonmonitored elections, 115, 117, 124, 126, 127, 129,
130; as positive sign, 159. *See also* politicians, incumbent
Tymoshenko, Yulia, 7, 167

Uganda, 24, 29, 37, 90, 98, 270n89
Ukraine: backsliding in, 4; election of 2004 in,
7, 75, 98, 167; election of 2010 in, 7, 167;
Orange Revolution in, 7; and Organization
for Security and Co-operation in Europe,
65; regime change in, 5, 103; and Russia,
260
United Kingdom, 16, 37–38, 236, 242
United Nations (UN), 157; and Afghanistan,
74, 166, 173; and Albania, 147, 211; and Bosnia, 48; and Bosnia and Herzegovina, 63,
74, 165; and Cambodian election of 1998,
49; Charter of, 22, 24; Commission on the
Racial Situation in the Union of South
Africa, 22; Covenant on Civil, Political,
and Social Rights, 19; critical assessments
by, 52, 53; Declaration of Principles for
International Election Observation and
Code of Conduct for International Election Observers, 40, 57, 75–76, 97, 101, 105,
156, 162, 163, 175, 265n15; and decolonization, 21; and electoral assistance, 21; electoral commission for, 26; and El Salvador,
145, 146, 223, 225; General Assembly, 22,
23; and Haiti, 23; and high-security settings, 33; and Kenya, 245; and Latin America, 19; length of missions of, 39; and Lesotho, 245, 246; and Mexico, 178; missions
of, 37; and Nicaragua, 23, 252; and peacekeeping missions, 37; records of, 182; Resolution 688, 22; resolution on "Sovereignty
and Non-interference," 23–25; resolution
on "The Principle of Periodic and Genuine
Elections," 23–25; restricted mandate of,
57; and security and logistics, 37; Security Council, 22, 147, 212; security role
of, 39; size of missions of, 39; and South
Africa, 261; special coordinator for electoral assistance for, 26; and Trust and Non-
Self-Governing Territories, 16; Trusteeship
Council, 21; Universal Declaration of
Human Rights, 21, 22, 23
United Nations Development Programme
(UNDP), 37; assessment missions of, 173;

and Guyana, 233, 234; and Indonesia, 238;
and Lesotho, 143
United States, 16, 26, 38; and Afghanistan, 47,
172; and Armenia, 216; and Belarus, 46;
black voters in, 79; and Bosnia and Herzegovina, 69; desire for cooperation with,
147–48; election of 2000 in, 17, 154, 176;
and El Salvador, 88–89, 172, 175, 223, 224,
227; and foreign aid, 29, 70; and Georgia,
7; and Guyana, 236; and Mexico, 247, 249;
and Nicaragua, 145, 253, 254, 255; and
nongovernmental organizations, 102; and
Organization for Security and Co-operation in Europe, 176; and Panama, 43, 149,
150, 256, 257; redistricting in, 79; State
Department, Human Rights Practices
reports, 14, 82, 86, 113, 182, 183, 184, 186;
and Zimbabwe, 48, 54
United States Agency for International Development (USAID), 26–27; assessment missions of, 173; and El Salvador, 145, 225; and
Guyana, 236; and NGO funding, 65
U.S. Millennium Challenge Account, 216
Uzbekistan, 31, 98

Venezuela, 46–47, 50, 145, 254, 255
Venice Commission, 213, 216, 230
violence, 86, 152; and Armenia, 215, 216; and
Bangladesh, 218, 220; and conducive conditions for monitors, 172, 173; and democracy promotion, 15; and effectiveness of
monitors, 170, 171; effect of monitors on,
179; election day, 89; elections held amid,
173–74; and Guyana, 89, 104, 150, 232, 233,
234, 236; and Kenya, 72, 144, 242, 243, 244,
245; and Lesotho, 246; and Mexico, 250;
and Moi, 49; and Nicaragua, 255; as obsta-
cle to progress, 142–43; pre-election, 72, 73,
76, 81, 82, 84, 86, 87, 91, 92–93, 160; reduction of, 6; and South Africa, 81, 261; and
stability bias, 72–73; and subdued vs. high-
profile assistance, 179; and Zimbabwe, 54.
See also irregularities
vote buying, 81, 82; and Armenia, 215, 217; and
Bulgaria, 223; and Indonesia, 238, 241; and
Mexico, 251
vote counts, 40; and Albania, 214; and Georgia,
231; and Guyana, 232, 234, 235; improvements in, 140; and Indonesia, 239; and
Mexico, 251; monitor-recommended
changes in, 105; and Panama, 149, 150, 170,

vote counts (*continued*)
256, 257; parallel, 40, 41, 100, 149, 150, 170,
179, 222, 229, 256; and quick count, 41, 179,
234, 235, 236, 238; and Russia, 259; and
South Africa, 261. *See also* vote tabulation
voter education: and Bangladesh, 219; and
Georgia, 230, 231; and Guyana, 235, 236;
and Indonesia, 238, 240
vote results reporting: and Indonesia, 238–39;
and Mexico, 251; and Russia, 259
voter identification: and Bangladesh, 220; and
El Salvador, 225, 226; and Guyana, 234,
235; monitor-recommended changes in,
105; and Nicaragua, 253, 254
voter lists/voter registers, 78; and Albania, 213;
and Armenia, 215, 217; and Bangladesh,
220; and Bulgaria, 222–23; compilation of,
69; and El Salvador, 224, 225, 226; errors
in, 81; and Georgia, 230, 231; and Guyana,
232, 234, 235, 236; improvements in, 140;
and Indonesia, 238, 239; intentional vs.
unintentional problems with, 82–83; and
Lesotho, 247; manipulation of, 81; and
Nicaragua, 253–54; and South Africa, 262;
visibility of problems with, 82
voter registration: and Albania, 213; and Indonesia, 239; and Kenya, 243; and Lesotho,
247
voters: and Bulgaria, 222; education of, 106;
and El Salvador, 224, 226; and Indonesia,
238; ink for, 7, 219, 230, 231, 232, 239, 243;
intentional vs. unintentional problems
with, 83; intimidation of, 54, 82; and Mexico, 250; and Nicaragua, 255; omission of,
72; prevention of disenfranchisement of,
105; restrictions on, 81; rights of, 83; and
Russia, 258; socialization of, 99; and South
Africa, 261
vote tabulation, 40, 41, 77, 81; and Bangladesh,
220; and Bulgaria, 222; and El Salvador,
225, 226; fraud in, 40; and Georgia, 229,
231; and Guyana, 234, 235; improvements
in, 140; and Indonesia, 237, 238, 239; and
Kenya, 243; monitor-recommended

changes in, 105; and Nicaragua, 253; oversight of, 74; and Panama, 100, 256, 257;
parallel, 256, 257. *See also* vote counts
voting: and ballot design in Bulgaria, 222; family, 50, 259; and handling of ballot boxes,
40, 74, 77, 81, 82; and Indonesia, 239; and
Kenya, 243; logistical issues during, 81; and
recommended changes in ballots, 105; and
Russia, 259, 260; and South Africa, 263;
violation of secrecy of, 81

Wallachia, 16
West: and Afghanistan, 159; and Armenia, 215;
and Bosnia and Herzegovina, 69; and Bulgaria, 221; and Cambodia, 70; desire for
cooperation with, 147, 169–70; and end of
Cold War, 26; and Georgia, 3, 228, 229,
230; and Indonesia, 237; and need for legitimacy of allies, 47; and Russia, 147–48, 260;
and sovereignty and noninterference, 24
Wilson, Woodrow, 21
winner-take-all politics, 108, 110, 142–43, 152,
170–71; and Bangladesh, 218, 219; and conducive conditions for monitors, 172, 173;
and democracy promotion, 15; and Guyana,
232, 235; and Kenya, 242
World Bank, 29, 102, 241
World Trade Organization, 30
World War I, 21
World War II, 21

Yanukovych, Viktor, 7, 167
Yeltsin, Boris, 144, 259, 260
Yushchenko, 5

Zambia, 27, 98
Zimbabwe, 246–47; election of 1985 in, 19, 90,
91; election of 2000 in, 48, 54, 66, 69, 91,
160, 164; election of 2002 in, 29, 43, 46, 48,
91, 164; election of 2008 in, 72; and lenient
monitors, 54–55, 164; and National Democratic Institute, 34; pre-election violence in,
72; and special relationship bias, 69; violence in, 160. *See also* Rhodesia